Justice and Equity in Climate Change Education

This volume looks at the ways in which climate change education relates to broader ideas of justice, equity, and social transformation, and ultimately calls for a rapid response to the need for climate education reform.

Highlighting the role of climate change in exacerbating existing societal injustices, this text explores the ethical and social dimensions of climate change education, including identity, agency, and societal structure, and in doing so problematizes climate change education as an equity concern. Chapters present empirical analysis, underpinned by a theoretical framework, and case studies which provide critical insights for the design of learning environments, curricula, and everyday climate-change-related learning in schools.

This text will benefit researchers, academics, educators, and policymakers with an interest in science education, social justice studies, and environmental sociology more broadly. Those specifically interested in climate education, curriculum studies, and climate adaption will also benefit from this book.

Elizabeth M. Walsh is Associate Professor in Science Education and Meteorology and Climate Science at San José State University, USA.

Routledge Research in Education, Society and the Anthropocene

This series offers a global platform to engage scholars in continuous academic debate on key challenges and the latest thinking on education and society and the role of education in the Anthropocene. It provides a forum for established and emerging scholars to discuss the latest debates, issues, research and theory across the field of education research relating to society and the Anthropocene.

Rethinking Education in Light of Global Challenges
Scandinavian Perspectives on Culture, Society and the Anthropocene
Edited by Karen Bjerg Petersen, Kerstin von Brömssen, Gro Hellesdatter Jacobsen, Jesper Garsdal, Michael Paulsen and Oleg Koefoed

Ecosophy and Educational Research for the Anthropocene
Rethinking Research through Relational Psychoanalytic Approaches
Alysha J. Farrell

Justice and Equity in Climate Change Education
Exploring Social and Ethical Dimensions of Environmental Education
Edited by Elizabeth M. Walsh

Justice and Equity in Climate Change Education

Exploring Social and Ethical Dimensions of Environmental Education

Edited by Elizabeth M. Walsh

NEW YORK AND LONDON

First published 2022
by Routledge
605 Third Avenue, New York, NY 10158

and by Routledge
2 Park Square, Milton Park, Abingdon, Oxon, OX14 4RN

Routledge is an imprint of the Taylor & Francis Group, an informa business

© 2022 selection and editorial matter, Elizabeth M. Walsh; individual chapters, the contributors

The right of Elizabeth M. Walsh to be identified as the author of the editorial material, and of the authors for their individual chapters, has been asserted in accordance with sections 77 and 78 of the Copyright, Designs and Patents Act 1988.

All rights reserved. No part of this book may be reprinted or reproduced or utilized in any form or by any electronic, mechanical, or other means, now known or hereafter invented, including photocopying and recording, or in any information storage or retrieval system, without permission in writing from the publishers.

Trademark notice: Product or corporate names may be trademarks or registered trademarks, and are used only for identification and explanation without intent to infringe.

Library of Congress Cataloging-in-Publication Data
A catalog record for this title has been requested

ISBN: 978-0-367-34470-2 (hbk)
ISBN: 978-1-032-16256-0 (pbk)
ISBN: 978-0-429-32601-1 (ebk)

DOI: 10.4324/9780429326011

Typeset in Baskerville
by SPi Technologies India Pvt Ltd (Straive)

Contents

List of Illustrations	vii
Preface	viii
List of Contributors	xi

Introduction: Climate Change Education Must
Be Education for Justice: Historical and Conceptual
Foundations for Centering Equity in Climate Change
Education   1
KATHERINE SOVER AND ELIZABETH M. WALSH

PART I
Theoretical Perspectives of Equity and Justice in
Climate Change Education   39

1   Bringing Climate Injustices to the Forefront:
Learning from the Youth Climate Justice Movement   41
RUPINDER KAUR GREWAL, ELLEN FIELD, AND PAUL BERGER

2   Psychological Perspectives of Climate Equity: Reducing
Abstraction and Distance through Engaged Empathy   71
ANANYA M. MATEWOS, BENJAMIN TORSNEY, AND DOUG LOMBARDI

3   Public Pedagogy, Climate Change Activism
and the Case for Ecosocialism   98
MIKE COLE

vi *Contents*

PART II
**Case Studies and Enactments of Climate Change
Education for Equity and Justice** 115

4 Equitable and Just by Design: Engaging Youth of
Color in Climate Change Education 117
NA'TAKI OSBORNE JELKS AND CRYSTAL JENNINGS

5 A Course on Natural Disasters Gets Real: Living the
Impacts of Climate Change in the US Virgin Islands 145
MICHELE L. GUANNEL, GREGORY GUANNEL, IMANI DANIEL, NAILAH
COPEMANN, ANGELISA FREEMAN, AND BETHANY GOOD

6 "A Different Kind of Middleman": Preservice Science
Teachers' Agency for Climate Change Education 174
ASLI SEZEN-BARRIE AND LUCY AVRAAMIDOU

7 Leadership in Eco-Justice Environmental Educational
Practice: A Case for Climate Change Curricula through
Poetic Inquiry that Involves Storytelling and Walking the
Land 198
KELLY YOUNG AND ANDREJS KULNIEKS

8 Land-Based Environmental Education as a
Climate Change Resilience: A Learning Experience
from a Cross-Cultural Community Garden 214
RANJAN DATTA, JEAN KAYIRA, AND PRARTHONA DATTA

9 Children's Environmental Identity Development in a
Changing Arctic Environment 234
CARIE GREEN

10 Contested Agency and Authorship in Middle
School Girls' Climate Science Digital Storytelling:
Disentangling Individual and Collective Agency 252
ELIZABETH SMULLEN AND ELIZABETH M. WALSH

Index 279

List of Illustrations

Figures

I.1	A conceptual diagram of the subdisciplines at the intersections of equity, climate change, and education	2
4.1	Environmental Citizenship Behavior Model	120
4.2	ET leaders engaging in an urban agriculture community action project during an ETSI	131
4.3	ET leaders clean up a polluted creek site after learning about water infrastructure challenges in Atlanta's communities of color	132
4.4	ET leader encouraging motorists in DeKalb County, Georgia, to vote	136
6.1	Primary and secondary data sources and related contexts	185
9.1	A model of Environmental Identity Development	238
10.1	The roles each student took on in relation to the construction of the story and film	260

Table

6.1	Sample representation from the data analysis process	186

Preface

In October of 2010, I attended the first National Research Council Roundtable on Climate Change Education in Washington, D.C. as a young graduate student in the learning sciences. With Al Gore's *An Inconvenient Truth* released just four years prior, the vast majority of the conversation at this round table focused on politics and conceptual understanding. I remember raising a question related to equity in a small group discussion only for it to be minimized and blankly dismissed. In the published summary of that event, *justice* is only mentioned in relation to one presentation (focused on eco-justice as a motivation for religious communities), and the only mention of *equity* is from the closing Q&A, in which a participant asked why there had been such a lack of attention to equity issues and a lack of diversity in the round table participants. Like the majority of climate change education and communication at that time and to date, the focus was on a loud group of white climate denialists, the politicization of the climate change movement, improving the communication practices of climate scientists, climate change framings in the media, and behavioral and conceptual change. Just over ten years later, the nascent field of climate change education is still struggling to shrug off these narrow early beginnings and transform into a holistic, multidimensional field that attends to more than just the most socially and historically privileged voices and concerns. For nearly a decade, climate change educators were seemingly stuck in a loop of defending climate change as a thing that needed to be addressed, generating hundreds of scholarly journal pages on understanding and persuading climate deniers, with little energy left for climate change education that addressed the human dimensions and consequences of a changing climate system. While this intellectual debate raged in the media and scholarly circles, climate impacts were already taking their toll on lives, communities, and cultural survival.

Looking back, it is unsurprising that the same racist, colonial, and neoliberal institutions that led to climate change in the first place similarly supported an initial education effort around climate change that continued to privilege the voices of a powerful few over the many who

Preface ix

were already experiencing disastrous impacts in their own lives, and whose risks due to climate change have only grown in the decade since. As climate change impacts become more and more undeniable in popular discourse, it has been harder to ignore the substantial justice and equity consequences of our greenhouse gas emissions, and thankfully as a field climate change education has begun to more often include considerations of racism, sexism, poverty, colonialism, agency, and social transformation. However, clearly the field still has much work to do, and with climate impacts harming individuals every day, we must act quickly as we are already behind.

To that end, this volume brings together the writings of researchers who have been working at the front lines of climate change education, and presents both conceptual frameworks for considering the equity, justice, and ethical dimensions of climate change, and case studies of research and educational programs that seek to foreground, theorize, and promote the voices of those who have been silenced and marginalized. While I have sought to include a diverse set of communities, voices, research styles, and educational environments, I am the first to acknowledge that this volume is by no means comprehensive or even particularly complete. There are many, many voices and communities who are not represented in this volume who should be elevated, and as editor I apologize deeply for all omissions. My goal with this work is for it to be a set of tools for those of us seeking to equitably respond to climate change and to provide ideas and frameworks, pedagogies and findings that we can all use to do better in our work. I hope that there are future volumes that include more voices and critique the work presented in this book, as we become more adept at both articulating theory related to education for climate justice and enacting those theories to support equitable and just social transformation.

I would like to acknowledge the vast sea of friends, colleagues, and participants without whom this work would not have been possible. Firstly, I am grateful to the students, teachers, scientists, and learners who have agreed to be a part of this research, and have given us the gift of their insights and their time. I also provide my utmost gratitude to my colleagues Dr. Gina Quan and Dr. Tammie Visintainer for their feedback, and my students Kate Sover and Liza Smullen, whose work has critically shaped the direction of this volume.

In climate change responses, the theme of choice is a recurring one. Who gets to choose the future we face? What choices will we make? In another ten years, our climate trajectory will only be clearer, and our available choices may diminish. The world we find ourselves in will be an axiological mirror, reflecting back to us what we valued as our choices, and who we privileged and valued enough to entrust with those choices. If our choices amplify injustices, those consequences will be real and devastating. Climate change education without justice is education for

x *Preface*

the destruction of many: of many lives, of many homes, and of many cultures. As Kate and I argue in the Introduction to this volume, without beginning from a place of justice, one cannot truly claim to be doing climate change education. My hope is that this volume can help move us to more fully just and equitable climate change education, and I look forward to seeing where the field takes us.

Elly Walsh

Contributors

Lucy Avraamidou, University of Groningen, Netherlands.
Lucy Avraamidou is Rosalind Franklin Fellow and Associate Professor of Science Education at the University of Groningen in the Netherlands. She received her Ph.D. in Science Education from Pennsylvania State University in the USA. Upon completion, she worked as Research Associate at the NSF-funded Center of Informal Learning and Schools (CILS) at King's College London. Her research is associated with theoretical and empirical explorations of what it means to widen and diversify STEM participation in school and out-of-school settings through the lens of intersectionality. At the heart of her work is an exploration of minoritized individuals' science identity trajectories and negotiations with the use of life- history and narrative inquiry methods. She currently serves as a member of the Executive Board of the European Science Education Research Association (ESERA), as associate editor of *Studies in Science Education*, as a lead editor for *Cultural Studies of Science Education*, and as associate editor for the *Journal of Research in Science Teaching*.

Paul Berger, Lakehead University, Canada.
Dr. Paul Berger is a white middle-aged male climate change activist in Thunder Bay. He teaches climate change education at the Faculty of Education at Lakehead University and conducts research on climate change education.

Mike Cole, Bishop Grosseteste University and University of East London, UK.
Mike Cole is Emeritus Research Professor in Education and Equality at Bishop Grosseteste University, Lincoln, UK and the University of East London. While personally engaging in public pedagogy for many years (though he did not use that term), he first became aware of public pedagogy literature when, on being appointed as Professor in Educational Studies at the University of East London in May 2013, he was assigned to the International Centre for Public Pedagogy. His latest books include

xii *Contributors*

Education, Equality and Human Rights: Issues of Gender, 'Race', Sexuality, Disability and Social Class (fourth edition, 2018); *Theresa May, the Hostile Environment and Public Pedagogies of Hate and Threat: The Case for a Future Without Borders* (2020); *Trump, the Alt-Right and Public Pedagogies of Hate and for Fascism: What Is to Be Done?* (2018); and *Climate Change, the Fourth Industrial Revolution and Public Pedagogies: The Case for Ecosocialism* (2021), all published by Routledge.

Nailah Copemann, Eulalie R. Rivera K-8 School, St. Croix, VI.
Ms. Nailah Copemann hails from St. Croix and is a 2019 graduate of the University of the Virgin Islands (UVI). At UVI, she majored in English and graduated *magna cum laude*. Due to her love of science, she taught other undergraduates in the Science 100 class for over three years as Peer Instructor, including serving as Lead Peer Instructor to manage and guide the other Peer Instructors. After graduating from the St. Thomas campus of UVI in 2019, she moved back home to St. Croix, where she supported a summer teacher education workshop and has been teaching seventh grade English. During the summer of 2020, she completed the typesetting of a book for local culture-bearer and author, Dr. Richard A. Schrader Sr., called Sonny Barnes from West End. She is currently working on the typesetting of another book for him.

Imani Daniel, St. Thomas Recovery Team, St. Thomas, VI.
Ms. Imani Daniel is a native Virgin Islander who is committed to community empowerment, sustainability, and creating a culture of preparedness in the Virgin Islands. After studying Political Science and Neuropsychology at the Johns Hopkins University in Baltimore, Maryland, she returned home to continue her professional career. Since her return in 2015, she has held several positions promoting Marine and Environmental Science educational outreach, local governance, and most recently disaster management, recovery, and preparedness. In her three years as Chair and Executive Director of the St. Thomas Recovery Team (STRT), a Voluntary Organization Active in Disaster (VOAD), Imani oversaw several community resilience programs including vulnerable homeowner home rebuilds, food security initiatives, mentoring UVI students on locally relevant disaster management career paths, and more. Imani envisions a stronger and more resilient territory and hopes that her efforts and network can help provide a more equitable future for all Virgin Islanders.

Prarthona Datta, Grade 8 student, Canada.
Prarthona Datta is 13 years old and a Grade 8 student in Canada. Her interests include children-led community garden and climate change solutions, and youth empowerment through antiracist and social justice activities.

Contributors xiii

Ranjan Datta, Mount Royal University, Canada.
Ranjan Datta, Ph.D. is Canada Research Chair-II in Community Disaster Research in Indigenous Studies at the Department of Humanities at Mount Royal University, Calgary, Alberta, Canada. His research interests include community disaster research, advocating for Indigenous environmental sustainability, community-led climate change solutions, Indigenous energy management, decolonization, Indigenous reconciliation, research, and cross-cultural research methodology.

Ellen Field, Lakehead University, Canada.
Dr. Ellen Field is a white-settler female, a mom, and Assistant Professor in the Faculty of Education at Lakehead University. She teaches environmental education in the B.Ed program and climate change education in the M.Ed program and conducts research on climate change education. Ellen is Associate Editor of the *Canadian Journal of Environmental Education* and Co-Chair of the Canadian Regional Hub of Monitoring and Evaluation of Climate Change Education (MECCE).

Angelisa Freeman, University of the Virgin Islands Orville E. Kean Campus, St. Thomas, VI.
Ms. Angelisa Freeman holds Associate's Degrees from both the Clarence F. Bryant College and the University of the West Indies, and she taught middle school for three years on her home island of St. Kitts. She is completing her Bachelor's of Science degree in Biology, with a minor in Environmental Science, at the University of the Virgin Islands. Her current research focuses on identifying common challenges of UVI students experienced during Hurricanes Irma and Maria, with the goal of informing the identification, evaluation, and development of hurricane preparedness in the UVI community. She believes that hurricane challenges over the years are likely to reoccur in the future. Thus, it is necessary to mitigate the effects and prevent unnecessary loss, trauma, and instability. Focusing on these challenges can help formulate effective strategies to recognize and implement hurricane preparedness in the community. Her future goals include gaining a graduate or master's degree while continuing to pursue research in the fields of education and biology.

Bethany Good, Grand Canyon University, USA.
Ms. Bethany Good started working with Dr. Michele Guannel in UVI's Summer Undergraduate Research Program, during the summer of 2020. She completed her freshman year at the University of the Virgin Islands. She transferred to Grand Canyon University in Phoenix, Arizona, as a sophomore to pursue a degree in Biology with a focus on Secondary Education. Her work focuses on how well UVI students are prepared for hurricanes based on sources they use to learn about an

xiv *Contributors*

incoming hurricane, along with qualitatively analyzing essays where students shared their experiences during Hurricanes Irma and Maria. After she graduates with her Bachelor's degree, Ms. Good plans to teach high school level biology abroad and possibly pursue a Master's degree.

Carie Green, South Dakota State University, USA.
Carie J. Green earned her Ph.D. in Education from the University of Wyoming, and a dual Master's in Environment and Natural Resources and American Indian Studies. Her research evolves around young children's environmental identity development and participatory research with young children. She was the recipient of a National Science Foundation CAREER: A longitudinal study of the emotional and behavioral processes of Environmental Identity Development among rural and non-rural Alaskan children. She currently serves as the Profilet and Dejong Family Endowed Professor of Early Childhood Education and Outreach at South Dakota State University.

Rupinder Kaur Grewal, Lakehead University, Canada.
Rupinder Kaur Grewal is a Sikh, Canadian Punjabi female, and Master of Education Candidate at Lakehead University, Thunder Bay. Her thesis work is on amplifying the voices of black, Indigenous, and racialized youth in the Climate Justice Movement. She is an Ontario-certified high school teacher interested in social justice issues, intersectionality, social movements, climate change, and youth activism.

Gregory Guannel, University of the Virgin Islands Orville E. Kean Campus, St. Thomas, VI.
Dr. Gregory Guannel is Director of the Caribbean Green Technology Center at the University of the Virgin Islands, where he co-leads the update of the Hazard Mitigation Plan for the Territory. He is also developing a green infrastructure database to create a series of options for climate adaptation of coastal areas. Prior to joining UVI, Dr. Guannel was The Nature Conservancy's (TNC) Director of the Florida Urban Program, where he worked with various under-represented community groups to implement coastal climate adaptation strategies. This position at TNC followed from his work as Postdoctoral Fellow, then Research Associate, with the Natural Capital Project, where he developed a series of decision support tools to investigate the potential for investment in green infrastructure to reduce coastal risk. Dr. Guannel started his career as a coastal engineer in a consulting firm. Born and raised on the island of Martinique, he has a Master's in Public Works from the Ecole Supérieure des Travaux Public (Paris, France), a Master's in Coastal and Ocean Engineering from Texas A&M University, and a Ph.D. in Civil Engineering from Oregon State University.

Contributors xv

Michele L. Guannel, University of the Virgin Islands Orville E. Kean Campus, St. Thomas, VI.
Dr. Michele Guannel is Assistant Professor of Biology at the St. Thomas campus of the University of the Virgin Islands. She grew up in New England, USA, where she pursued a B.A. in Biology from Smith College. Later, she researched the biogeography of toxigenic phytoplankton in pursuit of her M.S. and Ph.D. degrees in Oceanography from the University of Washington. At these institutions and through other positions she has worked with elementary students to postdoctoral scholars on studies of Earth, Atmospheric, and Ocean Sciences, Math, Writing, and Professional Skills, for over 20 years. Dr. Guannel's research explores the power of service learning and other high-impact practices, to increase recruitment, retention, and persistence of UVI students in STEM fields. She measures the impacts of project-based learning and real-world applications through quantitative assessments of student affinity for, and engagement in, STEM fields, as well as the phenomenological analysis of themes that emerge from students' lived experiences. She is working closely with social science colleagues to build transdisciplinary approaches to the "wicked problems" of disasters, especially within general education programs for entry-level university students.

Na'Taki Osborne Jelks, Spelman College, USA.
Dr. Na'Taki Osborne Jelks is Assistant Professor in the Environmental and Health Sciences Program at Spelman College. She investigates urban environmental health disparities; the role that place, race, and social factors play in influencing health; the impact of climate change on vulnerable populations; and the connection between urban watersheds, pollution, the built environment, and health. Jelks is particularly interested in approaches that engage environmentally overburdened communities in monitoring local environmental conditions, generating actionable data for community change, and developing effective community-based interventions that revitalize toxic, degraded spaces into healthy places. A nationally recognized leader in engaging urban communities and youth of color in environmental stewardship through hands-on land and watershed restoration initiatives, environmental education, and training, Jelks is Co-Founder of the West Atlanta Watershed Alliance, a community-based, environmental justice organization that works to grow a cleaner, greener, healthier, and more sustainable West Atlanta. Jelks also co-founded the National Wildlife Federation's Atlanta Earth Tomorrow Program in 2001 and served as the program director from 2005 until 2017.

Crystal Jennings, National Wildlife Federation, USA.
Crystal Jennings is Senior Manager of Youth Leadership Programs at the National Wildlife Federation. As a staff member of the Education and

xvi *Contributors*

Engagement team of the Federation, Crystal oversees the integration and expansion of existing and new national program models for youth leadership development. Specifically, she oversees the Atlanta Earth Tomorrow® Program, a leadership development and environmental justice education program, for youth of color. Under the tutelage of Dr. Na'Taki Osborne Jelks, Crystal first coordinated the Earth Tomorrow® Summer Institute, which provides students with in-depth opportunities to learn more about environmental justice issues, develop leadership skills, and engage in outdoor activities. After assuming full responsibility for administration of the program in 2017, Crystal worked directly with students, teachers, community partners, and funders to enhance program growth in Atlanta as well as to lead the addition of Earth Tomorrow® modeled programs in Niagara Falls, NY and Detroit, MI. Crystal is passionate about inspiring youth to take action on environmental justice issues impacting their day-to-day lives and seeing them take a life-long interest in ensuring justice for all. She began her career with NWF in 2009 as the Global Warming Intern at the National Advocacy Center, in DC. She also served as the Oil Spill Response Coordinator for the Eastern Gulf Coast Region upon returning to Atlanta, her hometown, which is also where she earned her BS in Environmental Science from Spelman College.

Jean Kayira, Antioch University New England, USA.
Jean Kayira is Associate Professor and Director of the Environmental Studies Ph.D. program at Antioch University New England in New Hampshire, USA. Jean's research interests focus on Indigenous knowledge and environmental education, decolonizing research methodologies, cross-cultural and community-based education and research, and youth participatory action research.

Andrejs Kulnieks, University of Saskatchewan, Canada.
Andrejs Kulnieks is Assistant Professor at the Curriculum Studies Department at the University of Saskatchewan. His research interests include literacies, (eco)poetic inquiry, curriculum theory, language arts, Indigenous environmental studies, eco-justice environmental education, and climate change. His co-edited book, *Contemporary Studies in Environmental and Indigenous Pedagogies: A Curricula of Stories and Place*, was published with Sense Publishers (now Springer).

Doug Lombardi, University of Maryland, College Park, USA.
Doug Lombardi holds a Ph.D. in Educational Psychology from the University of Nevada, Las Vegas, and is Associate Professor in the Department of Human Development and Quantitative Methodology, University of Maryland, College Park. As the head of the Science Learning Research Group (http://sciencelearning.net), he conducts

research examining scientific reasoning and thinking about knowledge claims. Much of this research is situated within the context of formal classroom settings and focuses on effective teaching tools and strategies to support deep learning and understanding, particularly about topics that pose local, regional, and global challenges (e.g., causes of current climate change, availability of freshwater resources, weaponized information). His research and theoretical positions have been published in journals such as *Educational Psychologist, Science Education, Contemporary Educational Psychology*, and *Learning & Instruction*. Doug has recently received early career research awards from NARST: A Global Organization for Improving Science Education through Research; the American Educational Research Association's Division C (Learning and Instruction); the American Psychological Association's Division 15 (Educational Psychology); and the Society for Text & Discourse. Doug is Associate Editor for two journals: *Contemporary Educational Psychology* and the *Journal of Research in Science Teaching*.

Ananya M. Matewos, St. Norbert College, USA.
Ananya Matewos, Ph.D., completed her doctoral education at the University of Southern California, Rossier School of Education. She is presently Assistant Professor of Education at St. Norbert College. She investigates learning and motivation around the instruction of socio-scientific and STEM disciplinary topics. Her research has been published in journals such as *Educational Psychology*, the *Journal of Teacher Education*, the *International Journal of STEM Education*, and the *Journal of Educational Research*, among others. Ananya serves as Co-Chair for the AERA Division C Youth Conference, the APA Division 15 Race and Diversity Committee, and the Graduate Student Affairs Committee.

Asli Sezen-Barrie, University of Maine, USA.
Asli Sezen-Barrie is Associate Professor in the School of Learning and Teaching and is affiliated with the RiSE (Research in STEM Education) Center at the University of Maine. She received her Ph.D. in Science Education from Pennsylvania State University. Upon completion, Dr. Sezen-Barrie worked as a faculty member at Towson University, where she led a middle school science major. Sezen-Barrie's research aims to provide theoretical and empirical contributions to designing meaningful and equitable science and engineering learning environments for all students, focusing on promoting teacher agency and student epistemic agency. While working on integrating climate change and engineering into science, Dr. Sezen-Barrie explores versatile aspects of science and engineering practices and ways for under-represented students to succeed in science classrooms. She serves on the editorial board of the *Journal of Research in Science Teaching* (JRST). She is Co-Chair of the Research Committee of the National Association of Research in Science

xviii *Contributors*

Teaching (NARST). She has worked with teachers on the Next Generation Science Standards—classroom implementations in the states of Maryland, Delaware, Virginia, and Maine. Her work was nominated for Early Career Research Awards at NARST and the International Society of Learning Sciences. She is a successful grant writer, securing funds as PI or co-PI from the National Science Foundation, the Department of Homeland Security, and the Maine Space Grant Consortium.

Elizabeth Smullen, San José State University and Horner Middle School, USA.
Elizabeth Smullen earned her Secondary Subject Science Credential and MA Science Education from San José State University in San José, CA. Her work focused on understanding the use of art, multimedia, and narrative to support youth agency and action in climate change science and community solutions. She is currently a middle school science teacher at Horner Middle School in Fremont, CA.

Katherine Sover, San José State University, USA.
Katherine Sover has a background in Applied Physics with a B.S. from the University of California, Davis. She completed her M.A. in Science Education at San José State University with an emphasis on informal learning environments. She is passionate about STEAM education and science outreach for people of all ages. She currently works with a science museum and a non-profit education group teaching, training, and learning more in the world of STEAM education.

Benjamin Torsney, Temple University, USA.
Ben Torsney holds a Ph.D. in Educational Psychology from Temple University and is Assistant Professor of Instruction in the Policy, Organization, and Leadership Studies Department. Ben's research is focused on: college students' engagement in schoolwork at various units of analysis; John Henryism, a form of high effort coping as a response to environmental stressors; college students' willingness to take environmental action; and the motivation of pre-service teachers to enter the teaching field.

Elizabeth M. Walsh, San José State University, USA.
Elizabeth ("Elly") Walsh is Associate Professor with a joint appointment in Science Education and Meteorology and Climate Science at San José State University. She received an M.S. in Oceanography and a Ph.D. in Learning Sciences from the University of Washington, and has experience both as an ocean scientist and science education researcher. Her work focuses on how youth participate in climate-change-related activities across the contexts of their lives, addressing issues of social justice and equity in science education, and exploring the role of politics and

social values in climate science learning. Recent work has included the use of art and narrative to support learner identity and agency in climate change, and participatory action research to foreground community voice and power in designing equitable climate change responses. Her work has been published in *Nature Climate Change*, the *Journal of the Learning Sciences*, and *Environmental Education Research*, amongst others, and has been funded by local governments and the National Science Foundation.

Kelly Young, Trent University, Canada.
Kelly Young is Professor at Trent University's School of Education and Professional Learning in Ontario, Canada. Her areas of research include language and literacy, curriculum theorizing, leadership in eco-justice environmental education, and arts-informed writing pedagogies. She is the founder of the Learning Garden Alternative program that engages pre-service teachers in a curriculum that inspires environmental leadership developed through a partnership between Trent University and GreenUP/Ecology Park in Peterborough, Ontario, Canada.

Introduction: Climate Change Education Must Be Education for Justice

Historical and Conceptual Foundations for Centering Equity in Climate Change Education

Katherine Sover and Elizabeth M. Walsh

Introduction

As we move forward through the 21st century, each year brings broken records and extreme events as climate change impacts gain intensity, and the year 2020 was no different. Around the world, environmental hazards raged as some of the most destructive fires burned in Australia, the Amazon Rainforest, and the Western United States, a record breaking 30 named storms moved across the Atlantic, and chart-topping heat occurred globally (Thompson, 2020). There were also large changes in political and social conversations around climate change as the USA poised itself to rejoin international agreements, following a change in political leadership, and the world saw a decline in global greenhouse gas emissions caused by possibly the most unprecedented event of 2020, a global health pandemic. Both climate and health crises have underscored the extreme social and equity disparities in exposure, risk, and access to care around the globe (Patterson, 2020). At the same time a civil rights crisis in the USA came to a head in the groundswell of activism and the Black Lives Matter movement following horrific acts of police violence and increasing racially motivated violence toward Asian American communities. Issues of equity were also exposed as schooling systems around the world shut down, creating food insecurity for those who relied on school meals, childcare complications for working families, and technological challenges for families without reliable devices and internet access. By the end of 2020, pandemic-related school closures resulted in an additional 72 million children pushed into learning poverty (World Bank, 2020). The same year has thrown climate and environmental inequities into stark relief and emphasized the complex entanglements between environmental, racial, social, and economic inequalities.

Environmental and climate change education must be recalibrated to align itself with racial justice and equity in an increasingly climate-volatile

DOI: 10.4324/9780429326011-1

world. Previous work in climate education and research has not directly addressed and aligned itself frequently enough with equity and justice and has yet to fully develop and unpack the multiple dimensions and issues within. Without consideration for the intersectoral linkages present in the most vulnerable and impacted regions, education cannot prevail as a climate and social-justice-oriented solution. Since the inception of global climate policies through the United Nations Framework Convention on Climate Change (UNFCCC) and the International Panel on Climate Change (IPCC), international equity has been a central touchpoint in policy discussions and organizations (IPCC, 2014a), but it has less frequently found its way into climate change education efforts. Here, we consider the intersections and importance of these related but too often isolated disciplinary conversations (Figure I.1).

This introductory chapter aims to ground the discussion of climate change education in the equity and justice issues inherent in the causes and impacts of climate change, connecting current education efforts to ongoing international conversations and agreements around climate adaptation and mitigation. Attention will first be paid to the causes of climate change, which grew out of inequitable historical practices. Given its unjust foundation, consideration is given to the issues of equity, justice, and fairness in adaptation to and mitigation of climate change. Many international organizations agree that education will play a part in any equitable solution to climate change. However, many of the

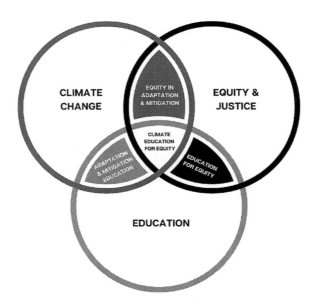

Figure I.1 A conceptual diagram of the subdisciplines at the intersections of equity, climate change, and education.

historical inequities at the root of climate change prevail through present-day teaching and research in climate change education. In addition to climate-specific injustices, education itself is rooted in historical practices of injustice that must be considered in their own right. Without attending to issues of equity and justice climate change education cannot reach an authentic, actionable, and just space. This chapter concludes with four principles to guide educational research, development, and teaching in climate and environmental education. In positing these principles, the hope is that the field can take up or contest these as needed and that they can serve as a stepping stone for further work for equity and justice in climate change education.

Equity and Justice Issues in Climate Change, Adaptation, and Impacts

Industrialization and Responsible Parties

Climate change is fundamentally an issue born of hundreds of years of inequitable and unjust practices and policies. Not everyone is equally responsible for climate change. Countries that industrialized first typically have larger and more robust economies today, and the countries that contributed and continue to contribute the most to global greenhouse gas emissions are those with larger GDPs and overall wealthier inhabitants (Cantore & Padilla, 2010; Füssel, 2010; Rabinowitz, 2012; Weir et al., 2017). Historically, the emissions from the first industrialized countries are not only higher in total volume but also higher on a per capita basis, indicating population is not an explanation for higher emissions (Cantore & Padilla, 2010). Within countries there also exists a more local inequity. The wealthier inhabitants of countries are often found to have higher carbon dioxide emissions compared to the average (Rabinowitz, 2012). There is also a strong correlation between measures of income inequality and emissions distributions (Cantore & Padilla, 2010). This inter- and intra-country disparity contributes to a widening socioeconomic gap within countries and between them.

The early economic supremacy of industrialized, high-emitting countries has privileged these countries with generally being viewed more favorably on a national stage. Ironically, nations are often recognized and rewarded for their role in creating large scale industrialization in the world. For example, Liverpool in the United Kingdom is marked by UNESCO as a World Heritage site for its role in the global mercantile trading system, a signifier of "progress" that masks a history of social inequality and greenhouse gas emissions (North et al., 2017). Industrialized nations are often praised for what is considered progress for humanity without acknowledging the environmental destruction and human consequences that occurred alongside. Being among the first to

4 *Katherine Sover and Elizabeth M. Walsh*

develop trading or manufacturing does not absolve nations of the responsibility to behave justly towards the environment or their citizens. The success and power come at the expense of contending with underlying systemic consequences of these nations' rise to power. It is clear an inequity exists between those who have and have not primarily caused climate change, but there is not as yet a unified and successful effort at combating this imbalance.

The unequal industrialization of the globe has led to modern inequities in the experience of impacts and adaptation needs. The burden of adaptation and climate impacts are placed on those who are least responsible for climate change (Adger et al., 2006; Mohai et al., 2009; Samson et al., 2011; Fiske et al., 2014; IPCC, 2014a; Weber et al., 2018; Kruger et al., 2020; Wilson, 2020). These most vulnerable groups include developing nations, minoritized groups, children, the elderly, individuals with a lower socioeconomic status, and historically marginalized groups (Miller Hesed & Ostergren, 2017; Mitchell & Chakraborty, 2018; Wilson, 2020). Climate hazards compound with social, economic, and political stressors most significantly for those in poverty (IPCC, 2014b). Low-income and marginalized groups are then at an additional disadvantage of having less capacity to both prepare for and cope with extreme climate events. The ability to prepare and cope is intimately tied to one's socioeconomic status and geographic area, both of which determine the most important asset: resources (Adger et al., 2003). This includes not only the existence of resources but the ability of any one group to be entitled and able to call upon those resources, whether they are consumable, physical, economic, or educational. The ability to call on available resources is not equitably distributed, with those of a lower socioeconomic status often facing additional systemic barriers to access. The ability to call on these resources is thus a resource itself. This leaves marginalized and poverty-stricken individuals and groups facing the highest impacts with the fewest resources to support or change their circumstances. The creation of this impact–adaptation divide, though partially driven by industrialist roots, cannot be fully understood without consideration of colonial and postcolonial structures.

Past and Present Impacts of Colonialism

The nations that first industrialized, developed manufacturing, and traveled the world in search of trade are often the same that sought to colonize others' lands and gain power. The hallmarks of colonialism persist in much of the world today. Poverty, loss of culture and language, and a lack of control of resources and development pathways are ever present in this time (Cameron, 2012). Colonialism can take many forms but always relies on a power dynamic between those who seek control and those who are subjugated. In exploitative colonialism, colonizers extract and harvest resources to spur on their own economic development

(Acemoglu et al., 2001; Tuck et al., 2014). The colonizers hold absolute power in their efforts to transfer as much potential capital as possible from the colonized land to the colonizers. Extractive states decimated local resources and terrorized local peoples in the mandatory cultivation of cash crops alongside extreme economic burdens within the colonies (Acemoglu et al., 2001). A prime example of this form of colonialism is the Belgian control in the Congo, where extreme and violent actions were perpetuated against the Congolese and their native lands for decades (Acemoglu et al., 2001). The lingering effects of this kind of system are present in many countries today where the local governments, economies, and natural resources have not been able to recover. Exploitative colonization robs precious resources, often in a way that causes extensive damage and destruction to the surrounding land and environment.

Another side of colonial efforts is that of settler colonialism, whereby the colonizers migrate to already occupied land to claim and use as their own (Acemoglu et al., 2001; Tuck et al., 2014). Primary examples of this form of colonialism can be found in the United States, Canada, Australia, and New Zealand. The central pursuit of settler colonialism is the land, as the colonizers seek to live in an already inhabited space. Settler colonialism relies on the tenet of land as property and an elimination of Indigenous and Native people (Wolfe, 2006; McGinty & Bang, 2016). Climate change has and continues to force Indigenous locals to change their entire way of living and being as they were once forcibly removed, had their land stolen, and were displaced or murdered by colonizers. At the same time, traditional methods of adaptation were often not upheld by the colonial powers, leading to destruction and degradation of the environment. Colonized peoples were forced into systems that perpetuated environmental destruction. Repercussions can be seen today in unsustainable dependencies on things like imported staple foods and tourism-based economies.

The compounding factor of colonialism is often left out of studies of vulnerability and adaptation in the modern day. When these issues are considered, it is as problems that need to be solved. Governments and organizations intervene in the problems in an effort to "improve" the lives of the people. This "will to improve" at its base is only a modification of colonial forms of power (Li, 2007). In Northern Canada, as an example, this "will to improve" can be seen in the way research has largely ignored the importance of resource extraction and shipping on human dimensions of climate change (Cameron, 2012). Colonial models of power such as this frame climate change as a technical, contemporary, and solvable problem. In doing so however, it limits discussion of equity, justice, and human dimensions at the core of climate change. Settler and exploitative colonial pasts are intertwined with many Indigenous communities and ignoring this founding ignores an important facet of a people's history and ways of being today.

6 *Katherine Sover and Elizabeth M. Walsh*

In the USA, colonial and post-colonial structures have distinctly impacted the ways in which individuals experience and adapt to climate change impacts. The geographic areas where minority and marginalized groups, often Black and Indigenous communities in the USA, live are often dictated by lingering colonial structures. Communities of newly freed Blacks in America in the 1880s were forced to settle on whatever land remained available (Miller Hesed & Ostergren, 2017). On the Eastern Shore of Maryland, they were denied full citizenship and faced racial segregation and violence (Andersen, 1998). Because of this treatment and lack of options, many were forced to settle on land along flood prone shorelines (Miller Hesed & Ostergren, 2017). This historical and institutional racism set these communities up for a lifetime of climate and weather-related issues as the areas they live in, once prone to some level of flooding, are now being severely impacted by climate-change-caused inundation during storms (Miller Hesed & Ostergren, 2017). These same areas have faced "sustained disinvestment" for decades as government and city planning efforts have not created meaningful advancements in the area's ability to prepare for or cope with climate change, leaving them increasingly vulnerable to climate impacts (Wilson, 2020). This phenomenon is both historical and contemporary as the systems that created this disparity were sanctioned by the US government (as discussed in a later section), and Black, Indigenous people, and people of color are continuously forced to live in environmentally degraded areas today. With city planning and government efforts often actively avoided in these communities, what is already a geographical disposition to greater climate impacts becomes an economically and, increasingly often, politically fueled inequality as well.

Neoliberal Economic and Political Structures

Modern climate change literature has converged on an understanding that neoliberal actions of political and economic systems have created increasing inequality around the globe (Fieldman, 2011). Neoliberal structures like deregulation, lower trade barriers, and price controls have contributed to increased socioeconomic pressures and increased vulnerability to climate changes (O'Brien & Leichenko, 2000; O'Brien et al., 2004). This two-fold impact, or "double exposure," exists in regions around the globe and serves to widen socioeconomic and development gaps between and within countries.

Neoliberal structures contribute to vulnerability by creating policies and incentives to alter economic contributions in an effort to grow individual assets. Wealthy corporations and individuals have the capital to engage in tax evading measures such as relocating to lower taxed or tax-exempt areas (Fieldman, 2011). With federal services and the flow of money often tied to wealthy and powerful corporations there can sometimes be conflict

Climate Change Education   7

between climate policies and economic growth and structures (North et al., 2017). Furthermore, there exists a potential incentive for wealthy, industrialized countries to continue their damaging environmental practices as they drive the profit and power they seek to maintain. For example, in developing policy in one UK city, arguments against neoliberal ideas that advocated for climate change mitigation were not actually advanced in economic policies. Instead, policies created to boost economic progress for the post-industrial city were favored over attempts to concretely remove long-term emission sources (North et al., 2017). This tension is frequently caused by a view that climate change policies are not economically feasible or do not spur on immediate economic gain.

Many world leaders contend with climate and sustainability not as a priority but as a hindrance to the primary directive of creating and maximizing economic growth (North et al., 2017). Thus, around the world, and in the USA specifically, climate change is often considered a political issue rather than an environmental, cultural, and societal issue. The very beginning of the global warming movement was met with a political anti-movement from conservative groups concerned by the 1992 Rio Summit and the potential threat to neoliberal economic policies (Jacques et al., 2008). This conservative movement continued to gain steam and attempted to gain legitimacy through use of scientific experts who were willing to align with the anti-movement cause (Oreskes & Conway, 2011).

While the fight has waged on in government, another challenge against climate change has risen in the form of political public opinion. Increasingly political and polarized messages of climate change are published in newspapers and other media sources (Chinn et al., 2020). The media's influence on public opinion is stronger than ever today and journalistic bias in the media has likely contributed to the public opinion (Boykoff & Boykoff, 2007; Nisbet, 2009). The influence of wealthy corporations and media representations created a clear divide by party line in the United States (McCright & Dunlap, 2011; Dunlap et al., 2016). This divide shows liberals/Democrats are more likely to have beliefs consistent with scientific climate consensus and show concern about environmental problems compared to conservatives/Republicans.

Within the USA, the combination of neoliberal economic and political influence is best illustrated by the role of wealthy corporations and politically conservative think tanks. Their actions have often worked directly against climate change as climate-friendly policy is often conceptualized as against their financial interests. Examples can be found in both oil and coal companies working alongside conservative foundations to debunk, refute, and erode the scientific foundation of climate change (McCright & Dunlap, 2000, 2003). A discussion of the psychological perspectives of conceptualizing climate change is included in this volume (see Chapter 2), as well as a critical look at capitalism and ecosocialism (see Chapter 3).

8 *Katherine Sover and Elizabeth M. Walsh*

One example of environmentally damaging, economically motivated behavior can be seen in the building of the Dakota Access Pipeline in the northern United States. The pipeline moves oil from fields in North Dakota to Illinois and in the process violates a prior treaty guaranteeing the "undisturbed use and occupation" of reservation land (Smithsonian Institution, 2018). There is extreme concern that an oil spill would threaten both water supply and cultural resources. An additional irony is that the route of the pipeline was adjusted from its original position due to potential threats to Bismarck, North Dakota's water source (Smithsonian Institute, 2018). There is an ongoing legal battle in which the Standing Rock Sioux Tribe hopes to find justice and protection from the politically minded and neoliberal policies that allowed the pipeline to begin construction in the first place. The problems facing the Standing Rock Sioux Tribe serve as an example of not only the neoliberal and political policies being enacted but of the historic injustices of settler colonialism that persist today. There is then an unignorable and unforgivable inequity between those who are responsible for climate change, at a historical and modern level, and those who shoulder the largest burden of impact and adaptation.

Intersections of Inequity

To best illustrate the intersections of these equity and justice issues, in both the causes of climate change and in current adaptation efforts, several examples can be discussed. There are multiple dimensions and intersections of inequities of climate change present around the globe. Here, we present two of the most well-studied contexts in which climate, socioeconomic, and educational inequities are clearly intertwined: (a) Pacific Island nations and small island developing states in Oceania, and (b) communities of Blacks, Indigenous peoples, and people of color in America. These two cases present the opportunity to explore and understand the relationships between and extent of inequitable and unjust structures. While not fully representative of all experiences, these two cases provide a gateway into contextualizing the issues of equity and justice into lived experiences to better understand pathways forward.

Case 1: Experiences of Pacific Island Countries and Small Island Developing Nations

Weir et al. (2017) provide an overview of climate change impacts and challenges from the perspective of those in the small island industrializing states in the Pacific, referred to as the Pacific Island countries. Traditional measures of adaptation in these island communities have been degraded overtime through colonial rule as colonial powers often forced adherence to Westernized understandings and use of the natural environment. At the same time, traditional climate adaptation and

Climate Change Education 9

understanding of the environment can no longer keep up with climate changes in these areas. There is no traditional way of mitigating or adapting to the severe impacts of sea level rise and ocean acidification in these Pacific Island communities, because these extreme conditions have not existed within recorded human history.

Coral reef ecosystems that provide coastal protection, food security, and tourism in these regions are already suffering major damages. Current climate models predict increasingly warmer oceans driving stronger storms. Increasing climate impacts could lead to inundation of coastal areas, salinization of the groundwater supply, and further destruction of reefs (Weir et al., 2017). In Pacific Island countries all fossil fuel is imported, and they account for less than 0.3% of global greenhouse gas emissions. Pacific Islanders are among the least responsible both for historical and contemporary causes of climate change. Many communities have an added challenge of having few chances to engage in education about anticipated climate changes or to learn about modern adaptation measures (Weir et al., 2017). With traditional measures no longer sufficient, limited access to modern adaptation technologies, and climate change threats on the rise, Pacific Islanders face increasing threats to health, safety, and livelihoods.

In the Marshall Islands, vulnerabilities arise stemming from colonial power dynamics that have had lasting effects despite the ending of direct colonial rule within the last century. Bordner et al. (2020) give an account of the treatment of the Marshall Islands by their colonial governing nation, the United States. When the USA chose the island of Bikini for weapons testing, the inhabitants were forced to relocate to the island of Kili. Kili is understood by the Marshallese to be uninhabitable for many of the same reasons that it is susceptible to climate change impacts. With limited fresh water and no lagoons or reefs, the island has always been vulnerable to storm surges and coastal inundation.

From 1946 to 1958 the USA set off 67 nuclear bombs around the island of Bikini, including the largest single detonation ever made (Bordner et al., 2020). The Marshallese as a result face dangerous side effects from fallout of the nuclear tests and radiation that still remain in the area. Communities living on Kili as well as other nearby islands such Enewetak are now as close as 12 nautical miles from a large nuclear waste repository the USA has left on Bikini (Bordner et al., 2020). Climate change impacts may also increase the danger of radiation as increasingly severe storms could cause leakages in the cement repository on the island. The USA continues to be the driving force maintaining the vulnerability of the Marshallese as they maintain military control over the area while doing little to ease their concerns.

Simple solutions to climate impacts in these vulnerable Pacific Island countries and small island developing states often rely on migration, immigration, and foreign aid, but issues of identity and of national

10 *Katherine Sover and Elizabeth M. Walsh*

sovereignty must be considered when asking nations to give up their lands, rights, and cultures while being subjected to the will of those who choose to aid them or once unjustly ruled over them.

Case 2: Geographic Government-Sanctioned Racism Against Black, Indigenous, and People of Color in the United States through Housing and Banking Policies

The United States has a longstanding relationship with discriminatory and intentionally racist practices that has persisted in full force following the federal abolishment of slavery. One clear example of this is in the racial segregation of every major metropolis. As Rothstein (2017) argues, this segregation is the result of explicit government policies and practices. Despite the common perception of racial segregation within cities as accidental or natural, Rothstein (2017) articulates a long history of intentional, government-implemented zoning, law enforcement, banking, and other practices that have inevitably led to the racist organization of housing and to perpetuating the financial subjugation of Black Americans and people of color even in supposed bastions of liberalism and equality like the San Francisco Bay Area. There is no such thing, argues Rothstein, as natural, accidental or "de facto segregation."

One demonstration of these explicitly racist housing practices is the purposeful, racially motivated housing discrimination during the 1930s. The Home Owners' Loan Corporation (HOLC) was established by the US government as part of the New Deal in 1933 (Hillier, 2003). Areas with older housing, poorer households, and predominantly African American and Black populations were most often given the lowest rating, Class D, leading to a lack of access to funding and higher interest rates (Hillier, 2003). The rating system was an intentional and legally accepted way to discriminate and deny Black and African families homes and loans. This practice became known as redlining, as the highest risk areas were colored red on physical maps of neighborhoods. Homeownership was and has been a primary mechanism for wealth building in the USA (Krivo & Kaufman, 2004). With policies such as redlining in place, areas that were already experiencing socioeconomic disadvantages continued to see the wealth gap increase. This process simultaneously devalued homes in primarily Black and African American neighborhoods while denying access to funding or competitive interest rates to move to other neighborhoods (Krivo & Kaufman, 2004). This process was specifically racist towards Black and African American families and became a government sanctioned method for lending, leading to significant financial damage spanning decades and generations.

These practices have further led to injustices in climate impacts. Using historical HOLC data (1935–1940 maps), US Census data, race and ethnicity percentages in census tracts, and surface temperature data Wilson (2020) investigated racially inequitable heat trends in the USA today. Heat is one of the leading threats to urban areas in the country and is projected to become more severe with increasing greenhouse gas emissions (Reidmiller et al., 2018). The occurrence of extreme heat in localized and often urban areas is known as an urban heat island (Mitchell & Chakraborty, 2015). Wilson (2020) found that areas marked with the two lowest HOLC ratings, HOLC Class C, "definitely declining" areas, and HOLC Class D, "hazardous" areas, had higher land surface temperatures than more highly rated areas. In the three cities examined, Baltimore, Maryland, Kansas City, Missouri, and Dallas, Texas, past redlined areas had higher proportions of residents who identified as Hispanic/Latinx, Black/African American, or both. People living with disabilities (Curriero et al., 2002) or chronic diseases (Kravchenko et al., 2013), children and the elderly (Kravchenko et al., 2013), minority groups (Whitman et al., 1997; O'Neill, 2003; Uejio et al., 2011), and those of lower socioeconomic status (Kravchenko et al., 2013; Mitchell & Chakraborty, 2018) are at a higher risk for experiencing a heat wave and are more vulnerable to heat impacts. In their study Mitchell and Chakraborty (2015) looked at heat risk through surveying variables such as land cover. When broken down by race the exposure related to land cover was found to be 52% higher for Black neighborhoods, 32% higher for Asian neighborhoods, and 21% higher for Hispanic neighborhoods compared to white neighborhoods nearby. The result is a climate impact that is far greater on the members of either the metropolitan center or non-white neighborhoods than their suburban and/or white counterparts.

The unevenly distributed heat exposure in cities today is caused by many factors including lack of green spaces and parks, more densely packed infrastructure, lack of foliage along city streets, and lack of vegetative cover (Mitchell & Chakraborty, 2015; Wilson, 2020), along with long standing racist lending and infrastructure decisions. Over time, planning decisions, such as those by the HOLC, shape the location and character of urban development and the distribution of subsequent ecological benefits. Former redlined areas have higher poverty rates, higher percentages of minority groups, and consequently are at greater risk of heat exposure (Wilson, 2020). Access to greenspace amenities often parallels an area's ability to access and fund adaptation technology such as air conditioning (Hayden et al., 2011; Haase et al., 2014; Rigolon & Nemeth, 2018; Sailor et al., 2019). Thus, disenfranchised and vulnerable communities face a policy-borne and systemically institutionalized increased threat and risk of climate change impacts.

Global Responses to Equity and Justice Issues

A History of Global Policy

In response to the increasing threats and impacts to the world many organizations have come into being to create frameworks for mitigation and

12 *Katherine Sover and Elizabeth M. Walsh*

adaptation to climate change. The United Nations Framework Convention on Climate Change (UNFCCC) was established in 1992 at the Rio Earth Summit (UNFCCC, 1992). The primary object of this convention was to stabilize greenhouse gas concentrations in the atmosphere and constrain them to a level that would prevent anthropogenic interference with the climate system at large. Clearly, for complex reasons, this goal was not realized. One important establishing principle of the Rio Summit was the pursuit of "common but differentiated responsibilities and respective capabilities" (UNFCC Original Convention, Article 3), establishing the desire to act equitably towards different countries' current positions and abilities. Additionally, the convention established at this time key financial commitments whereby industrialized and richer countries would provide the financial support for new and additional resources for developing countries (Original Convention, Article 4).

Five years later, the Kyoto Protocol was adopted in December 1997. The main feature of this agreement was a commitment by industrialized countries to limit and reduce their greenhouse gas emissions to an individual specified target while also participating in mitigation actions and reporting measures (Kyoto Protocol, 1997). A total of 37 countries, representing industrialized nations, economies in transition, and the European Union, were tasked with emission reduction targets (Annex B Kyoto Protocol). In line with the UNFCCC founding principle, this demonstrated an interest in differentiated responsibility based on those who were contributing the most to greenhouse gas emissions.

The most recent UNFCCC treaty, the Paris Agreement, was reached in December 2015. The central aim of this agreement was to limit global temperature increases to 2 degrees Celsius from pre-industrial levels and to pursue a tighter goal of limiting the rise to 1.5 degrees Celsius to reduce climate change risks and impacts (Paris Agreement, 2015, Article 2). The center of the agreement and the long-term temperature limitation is the nationally determined contributions (NDCs) that each nation must create and communicate. Several other key pieces of the Paris Agreement include mitigation efforts reaffirming the role of developed countries in making the largest emissions reductions (Article 4), as well as creating a framework for financial, technical, and capacity building assistance for those countries who need it most (Paris Agreement, 2015, Article 7, 8).

The mechanisms put in place through the UNFCCC for emissions targets and trading, development, finance, and reporting seek in general to create a fair space where all countries are working together for the greater good based on their responsibility and capability. The largest historical emissions contributors as well as the wealthiest nations are often expected to make the largest efforts. Conversations around financial contributions and reparations are frequently contentious. There is often a strong moral argument made that those who most contributed to climate change should be those who most fund our actions against it.

The driving principle of "common but differentiated responsibilities and respective capabilities" in general brings about ideas of equity or equitable actions and financing. However, conversations around financing climate change adaptation, mitigation, and reparations are rarely as straightforward.

Who's Paying?

Among some of the most contentious conversations around climate change policy is the role of finance. The UNFCCC recognizes that climate finance is important both for mitigation and adaptation to climate change (UNFCCC, Climate Finance). The IPCC also acknowledges the existence of a gap between the current adaptation needs and the adaptation funds available in the current world structures which highlights the importance of creating actionable and equitable financial mechanisms (IPCC, 2014b). The work at Rio, Kyoto, and Paris all made concentrated efforts to determine a scaled way to involve financial requirements and benefits. Many financial mechanisms and committees are in place to determine how to financially manage climate change. Among these, the Warsaw International Mechanism for Loss and Damage is designed to consider the associated impacts of climate change and to assess the extent of the loss and damage suffered (UNFCCC, Warsaw Mechanism). This mechanism aims to create a network of collaboration, understanding, and includes provisions on participating in the financial agreements. Additionally, the Paris Agreement reaffirmed the financial obligations of the most developed countries and invited voluntary contributions from other nations for the first time.

Beyond considering the perspective of the UNFCCC, many empirical studies have set out to determine where vulnerabilities lie and who should be held fiscally responsible. One way of considering all the factors is to look at metrics of responsibility for climate change, capability to assist, and vulnerability to climate change, and their correlations to one another (Füssel, 2010). The semi-quantitative analysis model of Füssel (2010) found a double inequity between responsibility and capability on one side and vulnerability to climate change impacts on the other. The most vulnerable are primarily poor nations, due to a lower adaptive capacity. For small and poorer nations, in practice, almost all adaptation-measure funding comes from industrialized countries (Weir et al., 2017). Even when the small countries prioritize funding to reach their own policies and actions, the majority of the funding comes from industrialized countries instead. In response to specific weather disasters there is a moral argument often broached for the most responsible party to make reparations. In the case of the devastating hurricanes Irma and Maria in 2017, reparations are argued to be morally justified from the stance that both Europe and America caused environmental degradation, expropriation of wealth, and enacted colonial slavery and genocide (Moulton & Machado, 2019). The intersecting complications implicate the United States as the party with the most responsibility to the Virgin Islands in a situation such as this (see Guannel et al., this volume, for a deeper discussion of colonialism in the US Virgin Islands and the impacts on education in the wake of the hurricanes). Considering the role of the USA in the foundations of climate change as well as its role in colonial rule over the area, financial reparations should be morally unavoidable. This strengthens the ethical position that the countries most responsible for climate change should be the most liable for both financial and technical assistance as those most impacted are least responsible.

IPCC Strategies for Equity in Adaptation

Another international organization working directly towards equitable climate policy and action is the IPCC. Equity is central to many of the reports and conclusions the IPCC generates, and these frequently emphasize the role of equity as critical to work around climate and the environment. Specifically, two IPCC subgroups, Working Groups II and III, concern themselves primarily with equitable adaptation to and mitigation of climate change (IPCC, 2014a).

The IPCC WGII recognizes that adaptation planning and implementation can be limited by financial resources, different perceptions of risk, competing values, and absence of leaders, among others (IPCC, 2014b, p. 28). These issues can be understood as stemming from prevailing inequities around the historical causes of climate change. The IPCC also refers to this semi-directly by acknowledging that differences in vulnerability and exposure are not from the impacts of climate change alone and arise from the multidimensional inequities that are created as products of different development processes and stages (IPCC, 2014b, p. 6). There are then differentiated risks of climate change, based on inequities already present. Because of this, the priority should be on finding adaptation actions for those most at risk, as they are least able to prepare for and cope with the impacts they face (IPCC, 2014a; Reidmiller et al., 2018, p. 25; Kruger et al., 2020). In order to respond equitably for all peoples, the constraints and binds that intersect them must be considered.

The IPCC WGII (2014b) recognized that the first step of adaptation is reducing vulnerability and exposure to present climate challenges. To this end, planning and implementation of adaptation measures can benefit from consideration of socio-cultural contexts and inclusion of diverse interests (p. 26). The report specifically notes that the inclusion of Indigenous, local, and traditional knowledge systems is a major resource that has not been used consistently. Decisions must be sensitive to the context and diversity of those that will be most affected in order to be most effective. Thus, all policy measures need to be considered not for their proposed pathways and outcomes alone, but also for the way in which they will affect the individuals impacted on a socio-cultural level. As such equity must be central to and at the base of all climate policies.

The same threads of equitable action are reflected in current social science literature and research. When science is the only focus of the climate change conversation it halts any discussion of the societal issues that may be present. Thus, equitable adaptation measures must consider the decision-making process and who does and does not have access to it (Grecksch & Klöck, 2020). As climate change conversations and adaptation measures are a political process, power is a key component, leading to the central question of who is involved and can fully participate in climate decision-making. The ability to participate in climate decision processes is not equally distributed across all people (Adger et al., 2003; Adger et al., 2006; Miller Hesed & Ostergren, 2017; Grecksch & Klöck, 2020). This means that adaptation resources will not always be utilized or distributed to those who need them most. Extending this idea of power further, there is then the possibility of inauthentic participation whereby participants can be manipulated by the more powerful group in the space (Morgan, 2012). In their access and allocation focused perspective, Grecksch and Klöck (2020) found that a focus on access to the decision-making process can help to better understand who, when, and how adaptation to impacts occurs. But, and arguably more importantly, this frame can also shed light on where there is a lack of adaptation measures taking place or being taken up by countries or citizens.

Equitable Climate Change Education: A Missing Piece

The idea of genuinely addressing inequity and injustice in climate change cannot be complete until the role of education is brought into the conversation. The work within the IPCC Working Groups II and III often touches on the idea of education as a way for equitable action going forward (IPCC, 2014a; IPCC, 2014b). All three past UNFCCC agreements also make a call for education, and in later agreements public awareness and training as well (UNFCCC, 1992; Kyoto Protocol, 1997; Paris Agreement, 2015). What the UNFCCC and IPCC fail to do, however, is acknowledge or unpack in a meaningful way the underlying equity dimensions present in environmental and climate change education.

Education is deeply rooted in its own set of historical injustices. Simply having learning spaces or educational opportunities in communities does not guarantee that community voices are represented or that all can participate. Climate impacts are felt around the globe, but not all those who experience climate impacts are equally able to participate in the discussions around it (Adger et al., 2006; Miller Hesed & Ostergren, 2017). This leads to both disruptions in knowledge construction around climate solutions and educational and adaptation resource flow to areas that need it most. And, as with broader climate decision-making, participation and inclusion in education can be inauthentic or co-opted by those more powerful and in control. Without unpacking the injustices and inequities in education there can be no assurance that it is providing for those it claims to be serving.

There are many critiques that can be made of environmental and climate change education literature and efforts to date. Many educators and researchers have critiqued the environmental education field for its approach and perspective, arguing that mainstream environmental and climate education has failed to adequately grapple with issues of race, power, and culture (Agyeman, 2002; Haluza-Delay, 2013) or has ignored social dimensions altogether (Walsh & Tsurusaki, 2014). The field of environmental and sustainability education policy research has a large geographic under-representation of Africa, South and Central America, Eastern Europe, and North and West Asia (Aikens et al., 2016). Not engaging with climate adaptation and prevention equally around the globe means missing vital narratives from diverse perspectives. Much of the current climate change and environmental education literature has had a narrow focus on issues of conceptual change or perception (e.g., Wolf & Moser, 2011; Dickinson et al., 2013), politics and communication (e.g., Leggett and Finlay, 2001; Nisbet, 2009), or behaviors and obstacles (e.g., Lorenzoni et al., 2007; Gonzalez-Gaudiano & Meira-Cartea, 2010; Monroe et al., 2019). Reviews of climate change communication and education repeatedly call for the field to expand from focusing on conceptual change and deficit-focused data transmission models, to expansively and holistically situating climate change in its emotional, ethical, social, and cultural context (Wibeck, 2013; Henderson et al., 2017). Notably, however, even the most recent of these reviews makes only passing references to issues of equity and justice, likely because there is simply a paucity of literature to review. Using a popular literature database when preparing for this work, a search for the topic "climate change education" yielded 6,420 results, yet only 96 results came up from a search of "climate change education" and "equity," and even fewer for "justice" or other similar terms. Clearly, the field needs to course-correct.

That said, the initial focus on conceptual and political concerns in climate change education, though troubling, is perhaps not surprising, given the field's need to respond to the ever-changing political landscape around climate change. As climate impacts continue to increase and social inequities serve to compound those impacts, however, the only solution forward is equitable and just education. To do so, educational research and efforts must focus on their own injustices while also foregrounding and dismantling the injustices surrounding climate change.

Theorizing Climate Change Education for Justice and Equity

The Climate Impact and Education Link

The same inequities at the foundation of climate change and adaptation challenges also exist in the realm of education. Areas experiencing chronic poverty and low-income households, often areas with higher percentages of non-white populations, are forced to face an intense bind that links their physical safety with societal disadvantages. Schools with larger non-white populations are often identified as low performing and have lower funding levels (Cass, 2010), higher rates of students in poverty (Darling-Hammond, 2015), significantly under-prepared teachers (Barton, 2003; Darling-Hammond, 2015), and face challenges such as slower reading progress as a result (Barton, 2003) compared to majority white districts. Marginalized students often experience an onslaught of stereotypes against them in schools as well. Black and Latinx students are particularly susceptible to targeting through racial stereotypes (Carter 2005; Horvat & O'Connor, 2006; Nasir et al., 2017) and school-related stereotypes grow stronger in middle school (Nasir et al., 2017).

These types of negative stereotypes and narratives can then influence how students identify with learning and their abilities. These stereotypes and biases can be taken up by educators and curriculum systems as well. This creates lessons focused around the dominant perspectives and leaves minority or marginalized students often unable to identify or participate in the same ways. In Indigenous communities in the USA there is often unequal treatment given to local understandings of science and environment compared to more dominant Westernized views (McGinty & Bang, 2016; Nxumalo & Cedillo, 2017). The space of early childhood environmental education predominantly features a colonialist perspective on the divide between the human and the non-human. This perspective is not present in many Indigenous ways of knowing and serves to further the dominant white perspective of science and the environment and the erasure of the minoritized voice and narrative (Nxumalo & Cedillo, 2017). This focus on Westernized understandings is compounded by the lack of Indigenous peoples in STEM and the climate change field specifically. There is a wide disparity in college attrition and graduation rates. In the USA, white and Asian American students enroll (Hussar et al., 2020) and graduate (de Brey et al., 2019) from university at significantly higher rates than Latinx and Black students. At all levels of higher education, Black, Latinx, and Indigenous students receive less than 20% of science degrees awarded (Bang et al., 2017). It is also worth foregrounding that though demographic statistics generally show high enrollment for Asian Americans, in part likely influenced by current immigration policies in the USA, individuals within this group are extremely diverse, have also experienced and continue to experience high levels of racism (including government-implemented policies of redlining, the unjust

18 *Katherine Sover and Elizabeth M. Walsh*

incarceration and internment of Japanese American citizens during World War II, and significant experiences of individual racist violence), and that the representation of Asian Americans within STEM is not reflective of this diverse community.

As the culture and content of many schools is centered on white middle-class values, students in poverty and students of color are more likely to be viewed through a deficit lens by their school systems (Milner et al., 2017). A racialized discourse of childhood innocence shows up through the use and positioning of nature for white versus Black or racial minority children. Nature for white children is allowed to be a space for play and discovery while for historically marginalized communities there is a restriction to the aspect of play, and nature is often used as a type of support for children who are considered "at risk" (Cairns, 2017). The same rescue and support focus can be seen in the examples of urban gardens that are positioned as ways to educate or fix children that are lacking in some way (e.g., relationship to nature, knowledge of healthy foods), or in the "damage-centered" focus that many Alaskan Native children are educated through, as opposed to legitimizing these young children's relationship with and knowledge of the land (Green, this volume). Black children are often positioned as uneducable and forced to face dehumanizing conditions and actions (Nxumalo & ross, 2019). In the USA, a child's educational experience is deeply tied to their geographic area and thus the climate impacts they must face as well.

There is then an undeniable link between the climate events students face and educational resources they have access to. An example of this is seen in the communities living on the Eastern Shore of the Chesapeake Bay in Maryland. Miller Hesed and Ostergren (2017) sought to understand this high climate impact area in relation to the communities' knowledge, participation, and resources. The communities felt that the area lacked both physical and fiscal resources to best prepare their homes for storms and flooding (Miller & Ostergren, 2017). They also felt they did not have adequate information and representation from their government on these same issues. Additionally, many individuals did not fully understand the serious nature of flooding and increasing likelihood of worsening storm surges and weather. Due to this lowered awareness of and education related to the issue, these community members were less likely to effectively prepare for potential disasters in the area. The authors concluded that both engagement with and education around these climate issues could potentially increase climate justice in these areas. The education efforts should not only come from policy makers but should also seek to leverage the knowledge within the community around traditional adaptation.

Climate Change Education Internationally

Internationally, environmental and climate education face many of the same intersecting justice issues. The dominant issue in many places is the

Westernization of the educational system. For example, Kayira (2015) argues that through colonization and Westernizing education, perceptions of African ways of knowing have been reduced to inferior ideas and concepts. Nations that held influence over African communities created practices in government, agriculture, and education that removed knowledge systems already in place. Despite most African nations gaining independence in the 1960s, the lingering effects of colonialism are ever present in the African education system. As an example of a devalued learning system, Kayira (2015) points to an Elder in rural Kenya. This Elder remarked in an interview that she did not feel knowledgeable as she had no formal education. Traditional understandings of knowledge would be that one would gain knowledge as they age, yet this Elder, who by all accounts would be considered knowledgeable, had replaced her educational value system with that of a Western viewpoint (Kayira, 2015). At the same time, the education systems in countries such as Malawi may not include Indigenous knowledge in many areas, including environment, forestry, and farming in the curriculum (Kayira, 2015).

The role of language as a form of injustice and inequity has been addressed often throughout the last two decades. This is discussed in a myriad of ways, two prominent ones being the root metaphors of dominant discourse (Bowers, 2002; Kruger et al., 2020) and the dominant language of education (Cloete, 2011; Kayira, 2015). Cloete (2011) questions the predominance and hegemony of English as the exclusive language for environmental education in many areas in Africa. In South Africa specifically, first language English speakers make up only 8.2% of the population, yet English remains the dominant medium for business, parliament, and more and more frequently the language of all levels of education (Cloete, 2011). Through privileging English there is a displacement of other languages and the cultural and historical understandings that they contain. The perspective of English leads to the suppression of traditional and cultural knowledge and resources about ownership, conservation, and animals, by creating its own discourses related to South Africa's natural environment (Cloete, 2011).

Centering Equity and Justice in Climate Change Education

Many peoples across the world in vulnerable positions from climate change threats are often at the additional disadvantage of facing educational inequities and injustices. These inequities and injustices have often been ignored when designing and implementing climate and environmental focused educational programs. However, many educators and researchers are now bringing into focus deeply problematic issues and discussions, as well as using critical and cultural frames to design education for equity. In addressing equity and justice there are many frames and perspectives that are being taken up. Given the ever-expanding

20 Katherine Sover and Elizabeth M. Walsh

educational inquiry and ever-changing world, we suggest that no one lens or framing can or should be utilized in every context. However, this introductory chapter aims to be not only informative but also practical for those who hope to move this field forward. While design principles are not a new concept for the field, many past attempts have not given thought or consideration to equity and justice in the manner which they deserve (e.g., Athman & Monroe, 2000; Monroe et al., 2008). Presented here is a set of guiding principles—for educators, researchers, and all those interested—to consider when developing, evaluating, and teaching climate change and environmental education programs which center equity and social justice. These principles draw on prominent frameworks, emergent ideas, and authors working in climate, environmental, emancipatory, and justice-centered education. The frameworks that were most influential in this development include ecojustice education, critical environmental education, critical theory, emancipatory education, and theories of individual and collective agency. While these frameworks may seem disparate, they converge on many of the key characteristics that belong in equity and justice focused climate and environmental education.

Ecojustice education is a framework that seeks to bring together the social and ecological sides of climate change to respond to ecological and social injustices within communities (Bowers, 2002; Lowenstein et al., 2010; Kruger et al., 2020). Critical environmental education has taken up the framing of critical theorists in respect to the climate change and environmental education movement and seeks to engage in a critical-conscious understanding of social-ecological issues (Stevenson et al., 2017; Stapleton 2019; Stapleton, 2020). Critical theory addresses equity and justice issues through the revealing, deconstructing, and challenging of power structures. As such it creates a space to consider the impacts, causes, and complications of climate change and how education can be part of the solution going forward (Tuck et al., 2014; McGinty & Bang, 2016; Nxumalo & Cedillo, 2017; Nxumalo & ross, 2019). Agency-centered frames focus on authentic participation and participant-generated action. Agency is still a rather understudied frame within climate and environmental science, but many psychological and sociological frames are now being theorized and researched in science contexts (McNeill & Vaughn, 2010; Morgan, 2012; Pierce, 2019; Engestrom et al., 2020).

The principles below are not an exhaustive list of necessary traits nor does a connection to a principle ensure the program in question is inherently equitable, or addresses the multitude of social justice and equity issues discussed in earlier sections. Instead, the hope is that these principles can serve as a place to start to evaluate the work being done, and as a foundation to consider when developing future research and programs. As the field continues to move forward and develop, so too will theoretical and practical frameworks, and we encourage adjustment of the guiding principles suggested here.

Guiding Design Principles

PRINCIPLE 1: EDUCATIONAL EFFORTS SHOULD USE MODERN, BEST PEDAGOGICAL
PRACTICES IN SCIENCE EDUCATION, AND MUST CONSIDER THE POSITIONALITY OF
DEVELOPERS, RESEARCHERS, EDUCATORS, AND LEARNERS

Any attempt at education for equity and justice must consider best pedagogical practices. Research and practical application of best practices
has evolved significantly over the last several decades. Educators and
researchers are in a position to create more equitable learning spaces
through their choice of pedagogy and practices. This principle, though
speaking generally to science education, is absolutely paramount for
educators and developers to start with in climate change education, thus
its inclusion here. There are far deeper discussions and considerations
of what constitutes best practices than will be provided here, yet this
chapter would be remiss without a high-level review.

Education must first contend with students as holistic beings, living
and existing within multiple overlapping epistemologies and identities.
Education is not for the express purpose of transferring knowledge from
one authoritative source. Students must be given the opportunity to
drive their own learning and authentically engage with curriculum and
programs (Chapman & Feldman, 2016; Koomen et al., 2018). One
prominent area of research and practice is in the space of culturing science education and in understanding knowledge funds and ways of
knowing, particularly for marginalized students (Ballenger & Rosebery,
2003; Gutiérrez & Rogoff, 2003; Hudicourt-Barnes, 2004; Rosebery &
Hudicourt-Barnes, 2006; Warren & Rosebery, 2007; Bang & Medin,
2010). To counter the privileged position of white/dominant Westernized
curricula, educators and researchers must consider their students from
a holistic perspective. Teaching and learning are cultural processes and,
because of this, certain ways of thinking and learning are often privileged above others (Bang et al., 2017). Creating opportunities for students to authentically engage with curricula, utilizing their own
experiences, gives space for a diversity of thought and action in the classroom or learning environment.

Beyond practices to engage with and leverage learners' skill sets there
also needs to be attention paid to the role of the educator or developer.
Educators and developers must consider their positionality, power differential, and potential biases as well as reflect on how they are interacting with their learners. We, the authors, acknowledge our own
positionality as white women. We have not personally experienced racism and are citizens of a colonizing power with ample resources to adapt
to climate change. Therefore, we will never truly understand most of the
injustices we have discussed in this chapter, and our contributions are
necessarily limited. Further, we recognize that there is a significant power
differential between us given our academic positions of tenured

22 *Katherine Sover and Elizabeth M. Walsh*

professor and graduate student. By examining our own biases, privileges, and limitations, and reflecting on these and seeking feedback throughout the writing process, we aimed to better limit the extent to which our contributions perpetuate and fail to challenge white supremacy.

When educators fail to acknowledge the assumptions they are operating under, learners can suffer as a result. One example of this failure can be found in a critical examination of a university environmental education class (Miller, 2018). An in-depth analysis of a particular student's experience revealed underlying racism present in the community and in the instructors themselves. The author found that instructors utilized a grit narrative as a suggestion to overcome the racist and limiting experiences the student faced. A grit mindset or narrative puts the onus on individuals to bear the brunt of racism, stereotypes, or other mitigating factors and to use grit, or determination, to succeed or persevere despite circumstances. Use of grit in educational models is often critiqued for ignoring underlying systemic injustices that directly impact students' abilities to succeed and achieve by centering failure on a student's individual perseverance. The author suggests that critical examinations of racial discourse must take place in environmental education in order to ensure students are being positioned for success (Miller, 2018). The educators themselves perpetuated an inequitable learning environment that set up a minority student to fail while forcing them to shoulder the burden of navigating racism and stereotyping. Without critically examining one's teaching and overarching biases, programs will underserve those who need them most (Miller, 2018). Educators and researchers must consider their role in students' education beyond the content they provide/create.

Reflection also provides pathways to examine present power differentials in teaching generally, and specifically in climate and environmental education. As mentioned, there is unequal opportunity to participate in conversations around climate change and participation can also be co-opted or made inauthentic (Adger et al., 2006; Miller Hesed & Ostergren, 2017). As learners and educators come together, critical conversations and attention must be paid to who is teaching and to whom. Throughout this chapter and throughout this volume, there are many educational program examples with a diversity of both learners and educators/ researchers. In some instances, marginalized and under-represented groups were being taught by those from the same space, in others learners were brought in to learn alongside locals in Indigenous spaces. In all cases, educators must carefully consider their role, critical understanding, and responsiveness to equity and justice issues of both their learners and the learning communities they are part of.

One way to develop best practices, cultural responsiveness, and reflectivity is to give educators support systems. Sezen-Barrie and Avraamidou (this volume) discuss the development of a pre-service teachers' agency in teaching and communicating science to students. In a similar vein, in

Climate Change Education 23

Morrison (2018), a critical friends group served as a source of professional development for a group of teachers. In both instances, as teachers grappled with their own understanding of climate challenges and their role as educators, they developed a better understanding of their capabilities and limitations, leading to a more critical view of how to approach climate and environmental science with diverse learners. By providing opportunities for educators to engage and grapple with their own understanding of equity and justice issues they can be better positioned to engage in best practices in their teaching.

PRINCIPLE 2: EDUCATIONAL EFFORTS SHOULD CENTER AND AMPLIFY THE VOICES, STORIES, HISTORIES, AND EPISTEMOLOGIES OF UNDER-REPRESENTED AND MARGINALIZED GROUPS INCLUDING THOSE MOST AFFECTED BY CLIMATE CHANGE AND ENVIRONMENTAL IMPACTS

Education around climate change has in the past focused on a myriad of things including issues of conceptual change or perception (e.g., Wolf & Moser, 2011; Dickinson et al., 2013), politics and communication (e.g., Leggett and Finlay, 2001; Nisbet, 2009), or behaviors and obstacles (e.g., Lorenzoni et al., 2007; Gonzalez-Gaudiano & Meira-Cartea, 2010; Monroe et al., 2019). What has been chronically missing from much of the educational canon is a focus and dedication to those most marginalized and silenced, both in educational and climate change discussions. As has been made clear in earlier sections, there are large disparities between the communities and countries that are most to blame for climate change and those who are most impacted by it, and those disparities are often mirrored in educational systems. Climate change education is poised to do more than simply correct an imbalance of voice. Through centering and amplifying those most impacted, a deeper understanding of climate change itself and the equity and justice issues inherent in it can be reached for all.

Many studies of climate change often center the physical climate system, and ignore human factors such as lived experience (Huntington et al., 2019). However, in education, many authors are already engaging in critical discussions around how to reexamine the current environmental education and research canon and who and what are included in it (see McLean, 2013; Tuck et al., 2014; McGinty & Bang, 2016; Nxumalo & Cedillo, 2017; Nxumalo & ross, 2019). One starting point for this work is to de-center the dominant climate narrative in places around the globe that are experiencing profound climate impacts (e.g., peoples in the Arctic; Huntington et al., 2019). Peoples in the Arctic have been using traditional adaptation methods for decades that are often ignored in favor of emissions-driven stories and decisions (Huntington et al., 2019). However, in climate science and climate adaptation, not only have Indigenous peoples' voices and narratives been missing, they have often been intentionally erased or ignored. Relegating perspectives of

Indigenous peoples as lesser than binds them to local landscapes and politics, thus effectively denying them participation on a global scale (Cameron, 2012). Thus, research and policy must consider climate change impacts and adaptation at the level of those who are most impacted (Huntington et al., 2019).

Nxumalo and Cedillo (2017) acknowledge that place-based environmental education often focuses on experiences with places without acknowledging the potential of the specific stories that go along with the places. The authors posit that Indigenous stories of place can serve to challenge colonial place-based narratives. This concept of restorying environmental education seeks to create critical engagement with what stories are made visible, remain invisible, and the whys and hows of those obscured. Restorying is critical for engaging with Indigenous communities and knowledge systems. This can look like educators, researchers, learners, and those who are local or Indigenous to the place experiencing and inquiring together in the environment (Nxumalo & Cedillo, 2017). Guannel et al. (this volume) utilized story as a means to provide students, who were directly impacted by severe hurricanes in the Virgin Islands, with an opportunity to voice their lived experiences and lessons learned. Ensuring the stories present in educational offerings are those of under-represented and marginalized groups works to combat a Western and predominately white understanding of the environment and the human position within it.

Education and research around multiple epistemologies for climate change education have been taken up more often in recent years. Science education and research in the past had given more weight to the epistemology provided by the curriculum than that which a student may have prior knowledge of (Bang & Medin, 2010). Giving space to multiple epistemologies works to remove the implicit values of the Westernized environmental canon. Recognizing the significance of Indigenous epistemologies can allow students to navigate overlapping identities and assist them in understanding different perspectives (Bang & Medin, 2010). Busch et al. (2019) comment on the current state of epistemologies and methodologies in climate change education research, and call for more research from sociocultural and critical perspectives.

One particular and problematic viewpoint of Westernized environmental curricula is the separation between humans and the natural world, an idea that is not present in many histories around the world (e.g. Kruger et al., 2020). An alternative system that is present in many traditional knowledge systems is to foreground relationships between people, the ecosystems in which they live, and the future human and non-human generations to come. In order to achieve this kind of education system, Kruger et al. (2020) put forward the idea of community-based learning. Place-based ecojustice education leverages the strengths of culture and environmental common ground as well as challenging entrenched assumptions at the base of ecological injustices. This allows for local community level response to address both historical and cultural experiences regarding the climate crisis. In another example of a community-based approach, Datta, Kayira, and Datta (this volume) analyzed the learning of children over a long-term community garden project. The authors include a child participant of the garden and give a unique perspective on the development and learning of participants of land-based cross-cultural learning.

PRINCIPLE 3: EDUCATIONAL EFFORTS SHOULD MAKE EXPLICIT THE CONNECTIONS BETWEEN INEQUITABLE SOCIAL SYSTEMS, CLIMATE CHANGE (PAST, CURRENT, AND FUTURE), AND MITIGATION AND ADAPTATION EFFORTS

Many have recognized the need for climate education to involve global justice (Kagawa & Selby, 2010) as well as the ability of this kind of education to address inter- and intra-generational climate injustices (Kanbur, 2015). To achieve this, environmental and climate change education should not stop at foregrounding local and Indigenous voices or centering the stories of the most impacted. Instead, it must take a step further to make an explicit connection between the existence of climate change, current mitigation and adaptation efforts, and the underlying social systems that have created the inequities and injustices present today. This principle seeks to bring education that aligns with the first two principles to an elevated level of understanding. Connecting past and present climate change to inequitable social systems is a crucial step to create education with a socio-critical focus. This socio-critical focus will become increasingly important as the students of today have to contend with ever worsening climate impacts and widening social and economic disparities. Equity and justice will be impossible to reach without education systems addressing the existence and perpetuation of climate change.

Many of the authors working to center marginalized voices and stories also seek to confront and dismantle the social and political systems at work (Nxumalo & Cedillo, 2017; Nxumalo & ross, 2019) (Principles 2 and 3). There are often inherent discussions of the connection between inequitable social systems and climate change when centering Indigenous voices and stories, such as in critical theory education and research (see Nxumalo & Cedillo, 2017; Nxumalo & ross, 2019). Educational programs and research that take up the approach of this principle are still rather under-theorized. In a 2017 review of climate education intervention papers, "very few" programs approached teaching climate change from both science and social science perspectives (Monroe et al., 2019, p. 807). Connecting the social and science worlds is the essential goal of the environmental justice movement. Environmental justice links injustice in the environment with social injustices such as racism (Stapleton, 2020). There is also an inherent understanding in the environmental

26 *Katherine Sover and Elizabeth M. Walsh*

justice movement that marginalized perspectives should not only be heard but centralized (Principles 2 and 3). Work in environmental justice is ongoing and many prominent scholars have theorized the space over the last few decades (see Allen, 2007; Pezzullo & Sandler, 2007; Pulido, 2017). One conceptualization that aligns well with much of the goals of Principle 3 is Stapleton's (2020) use of standpoint theory to analyze past attempts and theorize future work in climate and environmental curricula. In the past decade, youth has taken leadership of this environmental justice charge, driven largely by youth of color from around the globe (Grewal, Field, and Berger, this volume).

One study that situates climate change learning in both the science and social science spheres explores how an international education program centered around climate justice impacted American youth (Stapleton, 2019). In the study, high school participants engaged in a range of climate education activities including service learning, lectures, and action projects in Bangladesh (Principles 1 and 3). Nearly all participants came back with stories of the climate injustices they saw, grounded and contextualized in the reality of climate change and social consequences for the people of Bangladesh. These climate consequences were noticed by all participants as they remarked on the difference between the framing and teaching of climate change in America and the real lived experiences of those most impacted by it. The students also noticed the dynamics of power at play and felt a solidarity with the people of Bangladesh and implicated themselves as both part of the problem and solution.

These new critical-conscious understandings of climate change were developed through direct participation with those in these positions (Principles 2 and 3). The largest consequence of this study is that framing climate change education around not only the ecological impacts but the impacts of humans around the globe was deeply affecting (Stapleton, 2019). When climate education is based on the injustices that are felt by humans and non-humans alike there can be a richer connection and understanding between all. This understanding leads to engaging with the issue and appreciating their own culpability in the problems and impacts of climate change. This is also of importance for education in industrialized nations to help those who are the most impactful on the environment to understand the social and environmental consequences that are felt by others. Matewos, Torsney, and Lombardi (this volume) argue that fostering engaged empathy can prompt climate action by connecting knowledge to real world contexts or consequences.

Another example of a strong commitment to acknowledging the intersections of climate change can be found in the Portland, Oregon school district. In 2016, the district passed a resolution to develop an implementation plan for climate literacy. The policy document notes a need for "seeing a diversity of people around the world who are fighting the root causes of climate change," "investigat[ing] the unequal effects of climate change," "apply[ing] an equity lens" to responses, and the inclusion of

Climate Change Education 27

"people from 'frontline' communities, which have been hit the hardest by climate change" (Portland Public Schools, 2016) (Principles 2 and 3). This approach is among a very few currently taking a strong stance on climate and environmental education. Within this approach a critical element is the interest in exploring the unequal effects of climate change and finding the root causes of it. The connection of these two elements can create the critical lens necessary for justice and equity in education.

PRINCIPLE 4: EDUCATIONAL EFFORTS SHOULD DEVELOP AND ENCOURAGE LEARNERS AS AGENTS OF TRANSFORMATION AND EMPOWER THEM TO CREATE CRITICAL CHANGE IN BOTH LOCAL COMMUNITIES AND BROADER CONTEXTS

This fourth principle seeks to reflect the idealized goal of climate and environmental education, from the perspective of this introductory chapter. True expansive education should seek to not only address but also confront and dismantle inequities and injustices globally. To do so, learners must also be given the opportunity and tools to participate in the process, to have agency over their actions, and ultimately to develop into agents of change both locally and internationally. There are several prominent youth activists who can be seen as agents of change today (Grewal, Field, and Berger, this volume), but this level of action and agency must be brought into reach for all students.

Promoting change in terms of learner action, shifting attitudes, or supporting behavior change has been one of the most prominent models of climate education over the past decades. Of these, a popular focus has been behavior change models. However, theory and practice around the idea of behavior change at large does not address dimensions of equity and justice, and can in some cases exacerbate existing injustices (e.g., Walsh et al., 2016). In many reviews of the behavior change education frame, there is either no attention paid to underlying equity and justice issues, or they are only given brief lip service and are not prioritized (see Heimlich & Ardoin, 2008; Kollmuss & Agyeman, 2010). Payne (2020) examined the founding of the outdoor experiential programs that were developed to address attitude and behavior change in the late 1970s. Such programs sought to foster an attitude change in participants that would translate to behavior changes in their everyday lives. However, this goal often went unrealized. Still today many environmental programs place their content in a post-racial context and suggest sustainability actions as a cure for the environment (McLean, 2013). When environmental and climate programs focus solely on the environmental effects, they ignore the primary causes and their political and social structures (colonialism, industrialization, and economic and political structures) (McLean, 2013). Such programs instead focus on socially acceptable solutions for individuals to engage in such as biking, recycling, or buying local foods. When the values and calls to action are aligned with roles privileged by the middle class then there are inherent equity issues in taking up those behavior changes. Ignoring the social and geographic inequities around climate action contributes to the widening disparity already present. These surface solutions do not address the racialized systems that are underlying climate change and also do not provide any measures of action for those who are unable to engage in the middle-class situated options. Consequently, programs that focus on action or agency without critically intersecting equity and social justice cannot accurately develop participants as agents of change and transformation in their worlds (Principles 3 and 4).

In contrast to traditional behavior change models, creating agents of change or of transformation involves a deeper understanding of the science and social issues at the heart of climate change, the intersections with justice, and learner driven action. The result is that educational programs develop and encourage students as agents of change in their local communities and global contexts. There are many discussions around increasing participant agency and connection more broadly (e.g., Morgan, 2012). These agency design elements include being action-oriented, having direct impacts on learners, being rooted in the community, and involving social circles, thus giving rise to opportunities for authentic participation and involvement that is not traditionally found in much of formal education and research. This approach offers enhanced inclusion through acknowledging different ways of knowing or knowledge funds and promotes authentic learner connections through supporting capacity and empowerment (Principles 1 and 4). The use of agency-oriented learning supports the inclusion of all voices and perspectives, providing the opportunity for increased participation and development of one's own critical understanding (Principles 2 and 4).

From a theoretical perspective, the work on agency is often derived from psychology and sociology research, though these borrowed frames are still under-theorized in education (Engestrom et al., 2020). One prominent and growing frame is that of transformative agency. Engestrom et al. (2020) review the work that has thus far taken up transformative agency frames and utilizes a transformative agency by double stimulation frame specifically. The transformative agency by double stimulation (TADS) framework was proposed by Sannino (2015) and is based on double stimulation experiments from Vygotsky (1997). The idea of a double stimulus is that a person or group may face a conflict (first stimulus) which is overcome and turned into an artifact used as a sign (second stimulus). The sign then enables action from the conflicted scenario. The authors note specifically how this frame could be introduced to critical learning challenges today that have no obvious or correct solutions. Climate change and poverty are both specific and global, and often involve conflicted motives or paralyzing constructs. A pedagogy that assists learners in facing conflicts and constructing their own artifacts to break out of a paralysis of action would then give rise to transformation and action by the learners. While these frames are still gaining traction, some researchers and

Climate Change Education 29

educators around the world have been working to bring agency and transformative learning to climate and environmental programs already.

In their work on agency, identity, and science learning, Barton and Tan (2010) sought to develop critical science agency by positioning youth in a summer science program as community science experts (Principles 1, 3, and 4). They argue that this positioning gave students a platform to engage with ideas while also being involved in their community. Students created works around the concept of "urban heat islands" and reached out and worked with their communities to understand the knowledge already present and to further inform those around them. Another educational program that is striving to connect climate change education with equity and social justice is the National Wildlife Federation's Earth Tomorrow® Program. The program utilizes a lens of racial equity and social justice to engage youth of color in urban areas with ideas of climate change science and environmental justice for both the planet and populations that are disproportionately affected (Jelks and Jennings, this volume) (Principles 1–4).

One highly comprehensive climate change program that utilizes an agent of transformation frame specifically is a climate and environmental education certification in Vanuatu. Vanuatu is one of the most vulnerable countries to climate hazards and was the first country in the Pacific to pioneer technical and vocational programs on climate change across multiple levels (Pierce, 2019). The key philosophy of the program is that learners must be able to communicate their knowledge to others as a way to build community resilience and understanding of mitigation and adaptation measures, that is, the students would become agents of change in their communities and educate others. The depth of content as well as the combined fieldwork developed students' understanding in many areas including both scientific conceptual understandings of the basics of climate change, as well as higher societal implications such as gender equity and community needs. The result was learners who felt empowered to enact change in their communities and who were able to leverage their newly gained skills to support the broader community.

However, creating agents of change is not a straightforward exercise. Smullen and Walsh (this volume) found that agency and identity can be constrained when learners are simultaneously navigating relationships between one another as well as bidding for agency over their learning and artifact production. They also highlight the need for further study on both individual agency in climate and environmental science as well as further research into collective agency, as even the best intentions can lead to unexpected outcomes. More research is needed in this area to understand how learners can be supported as agents of change. Educational efforts such as those in Vanuatu and Earth Tomorrow can help push the field towards a more equitable and just education for all. They can serve as models for further program development and as a benchmark for where more research is needed.

Conclusion

The start of this chapter grounded the discussion of climate change education in the inequitable historical practices that led to those least responsible for climate change experiencing the most adverse effects (Adger et al., 2006; Mohai et al., 2009; Samson et al., 2011; Fiske et al., 2014; IPCC, 2014a; Weber et al., 2018; Kruger et al., 2020; Wilson, 2020). Climate hazards compound with social, economic, and political stressors most significantly for those in poverty (IPCC, 2014b, p. 6). Low-income and marginalized groups are then at an additional disadvantage of having a lower capacity to both prepare for and cope with extreme climate events. Thus, equitable adaptation measures must both ensure a just decision-making process that all can access and be a part of and will be substantially informed by whomever is in a position of power politically or otherwise (Grecksch & Klöck, 2020). The same inequities found in the historical causes of climate change and current adaptation challenges also exist in education systems around the globe. Areas experiencing chronic poverty, often areas with higher percentages of non-white populations, are forced to face injustices related both to climate and education simultaneously.

True climate change education must concern itself with the equity and justice dimensions present in education and the overlapping injustices in the lives of learners and their communities. To this end, we have presented four key principles to be taken into account when researching, developing, analyzing, or interacting with climate and environmental education. This first attempt is a way to help the field make a sharp turn and course-correct from previous focuses on individual behavior change, climate denial, politics, or other tangentially related ideas. Many ideas discussed here require much more attention and further research. As noted in Principle 3, science education programs and research with both social and science perspectives are still lacking in the field overall (Monroe et al., 2019). This is then a space where much focus can be applied as researchers and educators develop and implement new programs and interventions. More research must be done to better understand how climate and environmental programs can help learners understand the injustices present and connections between environmental changes, impacts, and social systems. Research is required to improve our conceptualizations of transformative agency, both individual and collective, and how it can be applied to educational spaces. The potential for transformative agency in climate education programs is too great to ignore.

By centering and highlighting the lived experiences and daily lives of those most impacted, all learners can understand the true reality of climate change and take on their calling as an agent of transformation. In the future, we hope to see our understandings of the issues raised here, and strategies for and successes in transforming our communities in just

Climate Change Education 31

and sustainable ways, grow far beyond the ideas presented in this chapter. We hope to see a proliferation of climate change education the centers equity and justice, that is, true climate change education.

References

Acemoglu, D., Johnson, S., & Robinson, J.A. (2001). The colonial origins of comparative development: An empirical investigation. *The American Economic Review, 91*(5), 247.

Adger, W.N., Huq, S., Brown, K., Conway, D, & Hume, M. (2003). Adaptation to climate change in the developing world. *Progress in Development Studies, 3*(3), 179–195.

Adger, W.N., Paavola, J., Huq, S., & Mace, M.J. (2006). *Fairness in adaptation to climate change.* MIT.

Agyeman, J. (2002). Culturing environmental education: From first nation to frustration. *Canadian Journal of Environmental Education, 7*(1), 5–12.

Aikens, K., McKenzie, M., & Vaughter, P. (2016). Environmental and sustainability education policy research: A systematic review of methodological and thematic trends. *Environmental Education Research, 22*(3), 333–359. https://doi.org/10.1080/13504622.2015.1135418

Allen, B.L. (2007). Environmental justice and expert knowledge in the wake of a disaster. *Social Studies of Science, 37*(1), 103–110. https://doi.org/10.1177/0306312706069431

Andersen, M.L. (1998). Discovering the past/considering the future: Lessons from the Eastern Shore. In C.C. Marks (Ed.), *A history of African Americans of Delaware and Maryland's Eastern Shore* (pp. 101–121). Wilmington: Delaware Heritage Commission.

Athman, J.A., & Monroe, M.C. (2000). Elements of effective environmental education programs.

Ballenger, C., & Rosebery, A.S. (2003). What counts as teacher research? Investigating the scientific and mathematical ideas of children from culturally diverse backgrounds. *Teachers College Record, 105*(2), 297–314.

Bang, M., & Medin, D. (2010). Cultural processes in science education: Supporting the navigation of multiple epistemologies. *Science Education, 94*(6), 1008–1026. https://doi.org/10.1002/sce.20392

Bang, M., Brown, B., Calabrese Barton, A., Rosebery, A., & Warren, B. (2017). Toward more equitable learning in science. In C.V. Schwarz, C. Passmore, & B.J. Reiser (Eds.), *Helping students make sense of the world using next generation science and engineering practices* (pp. 33–58). Essay, NSTA Press, National Science Teachers Association.

Barton, A.C., & Tan, E. (2010). We Be Burnin'! Agency, Identity, and Science Learning. *Journal of the Learning Sciences, 19*(2), 187–229. https://doi.org/10.1080/10508400903530044

Barton, L. (2003). *Inclusive education and teacher education: A basis for hope or a discourse of delusion.* London, England: Institute of Education, University of London.

Bordner, A.S., Ferguson, C.E., & Ortolano, L. (2020). Colonial dynamics limit climate adaptation in Oceania: Perspectives from the Marshall Islands. *Global Environmental Change, 61,* 102054. https://doi.org/10.1016/j.gloenvcha.2020.102054

32 *Katherine Sover and Elizabeth M. Walsh*

Bowers, C.A. (2002). Toward an eco-justice pedagogy. *Environmental Education Research, 8*(1), 21–34. https://doi.org/10.1080/13504620120109628

Boykoff, M.T., & Boykoff, J.M. (2007). Climate change and journalistic norms: A case-study of US mass-media coverage. *Geoforum, 38*(6), 1190–1204. http://dx.doi.org/10.1016/j.geoforum.2007.01.008

Busch, K.C., Henderson, J.A., & Stevenson, K.T. (2019). Broadening epistemologies and methodologies in climate change education research. *Environmental Education Research, 25*(6), 955–971. https://doi.org/10.1080/13504622.2018.1514588

Cairns, K. (2017). Connecting to food: Cultivating children in the school garden. *Children's Geographies, 15*(3), 304–318. https://doi.org/10.1080/14733285.2016.1221058

Cameron, E.S. (2012). Securing indigenous politics: A critique of the vulnerability and adaptation approach to the human dimensions of climate change in the Canadian Arctic. *Global Environmental Change, 22*(1), 103–114. https://doi.org/10.1016/j.gloenvcha.2011.11.004

Cantore, N., & Padilla, E. (2010). Equality and CO2 emissions distribution in climate change integrated assessment modelling. *Energy, 35*(1), 298–313. https://doi.org/10.1016/j.energy.2009.09.022

Carter, P.L. (2005). *Keepin' it real: School success beyond Black and White.* New York, NY: Oxford University Press.

Cass, J. (2010). Held captive: Child poverty in America. Retrieved from http://www.childrensdefense.org/library/data/heldcaptive-child-poverty.pdf

Chapman, A., & Feldman, A. (2016). Cultivation of science identity through authentic science in an urban high school classroom. *Cultural Studies of Science Education, 12,* 469–491.

Chinn, S., Hart, P.S., & Soroka, S. (2020). Politicization and polarization in climate change news content, 1985–2017. *Science Communication, 42*(1), 112–129. https://doi.org/10.1177/1075547019900290

Cloete, E.L. (2011). Going to the bush: Language, power and the conserved environment in southern Africa. *Environmental Education Research, 17*(1), 35–51. https://doi.org/10.1080/13504621003625248

Curriero, F.C., Heiner, K.S., Samet, J.M., Zeger, S.L., Strug, L., & Patz, J.A. (2002). Temperature and mortality in 11 cities of the eastern United States. *American Journal of Epidemiology, 155*(1), 80–87. https://doi.org/10.1093/aje/155.1.80

Darling-Hammond, L. (2015, June 29). Why is congress redlining our schools? *TheNation.* https://www.thenation.com/article/archive/why-congress-redlining-our-schools/

de Brey, C., Musu, L., McFarland, J., Wilkinson-Flicker, S., Diliberti, M., Zhang, A., ... Wang, X. (2019). *Status and trends in the education of racial and ethnic groups 2018 (NCES 2019-038). U.S. Department of Education.* Washington, DC: National Center for Education Statistics. https://nces.ed.gov/pubsearch/

Dickinson, J.L., Crain, R., Yalowitz, S., & Cherry, T. (2013). How framing climate change influences citizen scientists' intentions to do something about it. *Journal of Environmental Education, 44*(3), 145–158.

Dunlap, R.E., McCright, A.M., & Yarosh, J.H. (2016). The political divide on climate change: Partisan polarization widens in the U.S. environment. *Science and Policy for Sustainable Development, 58*(5), 4–23. https://doi.org/10.1080/00139157.2016.1208995

Climate Change Education   33

Engestrom, Y., Nuttall, J., & Hopwood, N. (2020). Transformative agency by double stimulation: Advances in theory and methodology. *Pedagogy, Culture & Society*, 1–7. https://doi.org/10.1080/14681366.2020.1805499

Fieldman, G. (2011). Neoliberalism, the production of vulnerability and the hobbled state: Systemic barriers to climate adaptation. *Climate and Development*, *3*(2), 159–174. https://doi.org/10.1080/17565529.2011.582278

Fiske, S.J., Crate, S.A., Crumley, C.L., Galvin, K., Lazrus, H., Lucero, L., ... Wilk, R. (2014, December). *Changing the atmosphere: Anthropology and climate change. Final report of the AAA global climate change task force* (137 pp). Arlington, VA: American Anthropological Association.

Füssel, H.-M. (2010). How inequitable is the global distribution of responsibility, capability, and vulnerability to climate change: A comprehensive indicator-based assessment. *Global Environmental Change*, *20*(4), 597–611. https://doi.org/10.1016/j.gloenvcha.2010.07.009

Gonzalez-Gaudiano, E., & Meira-Cartea, P. (2010). Climate change education and communication: A critical perspective on obstacles and resistances. In F. Kagawa and D. Selby (Eds.), *Education and climate change: Living and learning in interesting times* (pp. 241–244). Routledge.

Grecksch, K., & Klöck, C. (2020). Access and allocation in climate change adaptation. *International Environmental Agreements: Politics, Law and Economics*, *20*(2), 271–286. https://doi.org/10.1007/s10784-020-09477-5

Gutiérrez, K.D., & Rogoff, B. (2003). Cultural ways of learning: Individual traits or repertoires of practice cultural styles. *A Way of Talking About*, *32*(5), 19–25.

Haase, D., Larondelle, N., Andersson, E., Artmann, M., Borgstr€om, S., Breuste, J., ... Elmqvist, T. (2014). A quantitative review of urban ecosystem service assessments: Concepts, models, and implementation. *AMBIO*, *43*(4), 413–433. https://doi.org/10.1007/s13280-014-0504-0

Haluza-Delay, R. (2013). Educating for environmental justice. In R.B. Stevenson (Ed.), *International handbook of research on environmental education* (pp. 394–402). Essay, Routledge.

Hayden, M.H., Brenkert-Smith, H., & Wilhelmi, O.V. (2011). Differential adaptive capacity to extreme heat: A Phoenix. *Weather, Climate, and Society*, *3*(4), 269–280. https://doi.org/10.1175/WCAS-D-11-00010.1

Heimlich, J.E., & Ardoin, N.E. (2008). Understanding behavior to understand behavior change: A literature review. *Environmental Education Research*, *14*(3), 215–237.

Henderson, J., Long, D., Berger, P., Russell, C., & Drewes, A. (2017). Expanding the foundation: Climate change and opportunities for educational research. *Educational Studies*, *53*(4), p. 412–425.

Hillier, A.E. (2003). Redlining and the Home Owners' Loan Corporation. *Journal of Urban History*, *29*(4), 394–420. https://doi.org/10.1177/0096144203029004002

Horvat, E.M., & O'Connor, C. (Eds.). (2006). *Beyond acting White: Reframing the debate on Black student achievement*. Oxford, UK: Rowman & Littlefield.

Hudicourt-Barnes, J. (2004). Argumentation in Haitian Creole classrooms. *Harvard Educational Review*, *73*(1), 73–93.

Huntington, H.P., Carey, M., Apok, C., Forbes, B.C., Fox, S., Holm, L.K., ... Stammler, F. (2019). Climate change in context: Putting people first in the Arctic. *Regional Environmental Change*, *19*(4), 1217–1223. https://doi.org/10.1007/s10113-019-01478-8

34 *Katherine Sover and Elizabeth M. Walsh*

Hussar, B., Zhang, J., Hein, S., Wang, K., Roberts, A., Cui, J., ... Dilig, R. (2020). *The condition of education 2020 (NCES 2020-144). U.S. Department of Education.* Washington, DC: National Center for Education Statistics. Retrieved from https://nces.ed.gov/pubsearch/pubsinfo.asp?pubid=2020144

IPCC. (2014a). *Climate Change 2014: Synthesis Report. Contribution of Working Groups I, II and III to the Fifth Assessment Report of the Intergovernmental Panel on Climate Change* (Core Writing Team, R.K. Pachauri and L.A. Meyer, Eds.). (151 pp). Geneva, Switzerland: IPCC.

IPCC. (2014b). Summary for policymakers. In C.B. Field, V.R. Barros, D.J. Dokken, K.J. Mach, M.D. Mastrandrea, T.E. Bilir, ... L.L. White (Eds.), *Climate Change 2014: Impacts, Adaptation, and Vulnerability. Part A: Global and Sectoral Aspects.* Contribution of Working Group II to the Fifth Assessment Report of the Intergovernmental Panel on Climate Change (pp. 1–32). United Kingdom and New York, NY, USA: Cambridge University Press, Cambridge.

Jacques, P.J., Riley E.D., and Mark, F. (2008). The organization of denial: Conservative think tanks and environmental skepticism. *Environmental Politics, 17,* 349–385.

Kagawa, F., & Selby, D. (2010). Climate change education: A critical agenda for interesting times. In F. Kagawa and D. Selby (Eds.), *Education and climate change: Living and learning in interesting times* (pp. 241–244). New York: Routledge.

Kanbur, R. (2015). Education for climate justice. The many faces of climate justice: An essay series on the principles of climate justice. *Mary Robinson Foundation.* http://www.mrfcj.org/pdf/faces-of-climate-justice/Education-for-Climate-Justice.pdf

Kayira, J. (2015). (Re)creating spaces for uMunthu: Postcolonial theory and environmental education in southern Africa. *Environmental Education Research, 21*(1), 106–128. https://doi.org/10.1080/13504622.2013.860428

Kollmuss, A., & Agyeman, J. (2010). Mind the gap: Why do people act environmentally and what are the barriers to pro-environmental behavior? *Environmental Education Research, 3,* 239–260.

Koomen, M.H., Rodriguez, E., Hoffman, A., Petersen, C. & Oberhauser, K. (2018). Authentic science with citizen science and student-driven science fair projects. *Science Education.* https://doi.org/10.1002/sce.21335

Kravchenko, J., Abernethy, A.P., Fawzy, M., & Lyerly, H.K. (2013). Minimization of heatwave morbidity and mortality. *American Journal of Preventive Medicine, 44*(3), 274–282. https://doi.org/10.1016/j.amepre.2012.11.015

Krivo, L.J., & Kaufman, R.L. (2004). Housing and wealth inequality: Racial-ethnic differences in home equity in the United States. *Demography, 41*(3), 585–605. https://doi.org/10.1353/dem.2004.0023

Kruger, F., le Roux, A., & Teise, K. (2020). Ecojustice education and communitarianism: Exploring the possibility for African eco-communitarianism. *Educational Philosophy and Theory, 52*(2), 206–216. https://doi.org/10.1080/00131857.2019.1625769

Kyoto Protocol to the United Nations Framework Convention on Climate Change. (1997, December 11). https://unfccc.int/resource/docs/convkp/kpeng.pdf

Leggett, M., & Finlay, M. (2001). Science, story, and image: A new approach to crossing the communication barrier posed by scientific jargon. *Public Understanding Science, 10,* 157–171.

Li, T.M. (2007). *The will to improve: Governmentality, development and the practice of politics*. Durham, NC: Duke University Press.

Lorenzoni, I., Nicholson-Cole, S., & Whitmarsh, L. (2007). Barriers perceived to engaging with climate change among the UK public and their policy implications. *Global Environmental Change, 17,* 445–459.

Lowenstein, E., Martusewicz, R., & Voelker, L. (2010). Developing teachers' capacity for ecojustice education and community-based learning.

McCright, Aaron M. and Riley E. Dunlap. 2000. Challenging global warming as a social problem. *Social Problems, 47,* 499–522.

McCright, A.M., & Dunlap, R.E. (2011). The politicization of climate change and polarization in the American public's views of global warming, 2001–2010. *Sociological Quarterly, 52*(2), 155–194. https://doi.org/10.1111/j.1533-8525.2011.01198.x

McCright, A.M., & Dunlap, R.E. (2003). Defeating Kyoto: The conservative movement's impact on U.S. climate change policy. *Social Problems, 50*(3): 348–373

McGinty, M., & Bang, M. (2016). Narratives of dynamic lands: Science education, indigenous knowledge and possible futures. *Cultural Studies of Science Education, 11*(2), 471–475. https://doi.org/10.1007/s11422-015-9685-5

McLean, S. (2013). The whiteness of green: Racialization and environmental education. *The Canadian Geographer / Le Géographe Canadien, 57*(3), 354–362. https://doi.org/10.1111/cag.12025

McNeill, K.L., & Vaughn, M.H. (2010). Urban high school students' critical science agency: Conceptual understandings and environmental actions around climate change. *Research in Science Education, 42,* 373–399. http://doi.org/10.1007/s11165-010-9202-5

Miller, H.K. (2018). Developing a critical consciousness of race in place-based environmental education: Franco's story. *Environmental Education Research, 24*(6), 845–858. https://doi.org/10.1080/13504622.2017.1357802

Miller, C.D., & Ostergren, D.M. (2017). Promoting climate justice in high-income countries: Lessons from African American communities on the Chesapeake Bay. *Climatic Change, 143*(1–2), 185–200. https://doi.org/10.1007/s10584-017-1982-4

Milner, H.R., Cunningham, H.B., Murray, I.E., & Alvarez, A. (2017). Supporting students living below the poverty line. *National Youth-At-Risk Journal, 2*(2). https://doi.org/10.20429/nyarj.2017.020204

Mitchell, B.C., & Chakraborty, J. (2015). Landscapes of thermal inequity: Disproportionate exposure to urban heat in the three largest US cities. *Environmental Research Letters, 10*(11), 115005. https://doi.org/10.1088/1748-9326/10/11/115005

Mitchell, B.C., & Chakraborty, J. (2018). Exploring the relationship between residential segregation and thermal inequity in 20 U.S. cities. *Local Environment, 23*(8), 796–813. https://doi.org/10.1080/13549839.2018.1474861

Mohai, P., Pellow, D., & Roberts, J.T. (2009). Environmental justice. *The Annual Review of Environment and Resources, 34*:405–430. https://doi.org/10.1177/0020715209105147

Monroe, M.C., Andrews, E., & Biedenweg, K. (2008). A framework for environmental education strategies. *Applied Environmental Education & Communication, 6*(3–4), 205–216. https://doi.org/10.1080/15330150801944416

Monroe, M.C., Plate, R.R., Oxarart, A., Bowers, A., & Chaves, W.A. (2019). Identifying effective climate change education strategies: A systematic review of the research. *Environmental Education Research, 25*(6), 791–812. https://doi.org/10.1080/13504622.2017.1360842

Morgan, A. (2012). Inclusive place-based education for 'Just Sustainability.' *International Journal of Inclusive Education, 16*(5–6), 627–642. https://doi.org/10.1080/13603116.2012.655499

Morrison, S.A. (2018). Reframing Westernized culture: Insights from a Critical Friends Group on EcoJustice education. *Environmental Education Research, 24*(1), 111–128. https://doi.org/10.1080/13504622.2016.1223838

Moulton, A.A., & Machado, M.R. (2019). Bouncing forward after Irma and Maria: Acknowledging colonialism, problematizing resilience and thinking climate justice. *Journal of Extreme Events, 06*(01), 1940003. https://doi.org/10.1142/S2345737619400037

Nasir, N.S., McKinney de Royston, M., O'Connor, K., & Wischnia, S. (2017). Knowing about racial stereotypes versus believing them. *Urban Education, 52*(4), 491–524. https://doi.org/10.1177/0042085916672290

Nisbet, M. (2009). Communicating climate change: Why frames matter for public engagement. *Environment, 51*(2), 12–23.

North, P., Nurse, A., & Barker, T. (2017). The neoliberalisation of climate? Progressing climate policy under austerity urbanism. *Environment and Planning A: Economy and Space, 49*(8), 1797–1815. https://doi.org/10.1177/0308518X16686353

Nxumalo, F., & Cedillo, S. (2017). Decolonizing place in early childhood studies: Thinking with Indigenous onto-epistemologies and Black feminist geographies. *Global Studies of Childhood, 7*(2), 99–112. https://doi.org/10.1177/2043610617703831

Nxumalo, F., & ross, k. (2019). Envisioning Black space in environmental education for young children. *Race Ethnicity and Education, 22*(4), 502–524. https://doi.org/10.1080/13613324.2019.1592837

O'Brien, K., & Leichenko, R. (2000). Double exposure: Assessing the impacts of climate change within the context of economic globalization. *Global Environmental Change, 10*, 221–232.

O'Brien, K., Leichenko, R., Kelkar, U., Venema, H., Aandahl, G., Tompkins, H., … West, J. (2004). Mapping vulnerability to multiple stressors: Climate change and globalization in India. *Global Environmental Change, 14*, 303–313. https://doi.org/10.1016/j.gloenvcha. 2004.01.001.

O'Neill, Marie. (2003). Air conditioning and heat-related health effects. *Applied Environmental Science and Public Health, 1*, 9–12.

Oreskes, N., & Conway, E.M. (2011). *Merchants of doubt: How a handful of scientists obscured the truth on issues from tobacco smoke to global warming.* Bloomsbury.

Paris Agreement. (2015, December 12). https://unfccc.int/sites/default/files/english_paris_agreement.pdf

Patterson, J. (2020). Ten equity implications of the coronavirus COVID-19 outbreak in the United States. 16.

Payne, P.G. (2020). Amnesia of the moment in environmental education. *The Journal of Environmental Education, 51*(2), 113–143. https://doi.org/10.1080/00958964.2020.1726263

Pezzullo, P., & Sandler, R. (2007). Revisiting the environmental justice challenge to environmentalism. In P. Pezzullo and R. Sandler (Eds.), *Environmental justice and environmentalism* (pp. 1–24). Cambridge, MA: MIT Press.

Climate Change Education 37

Pierce, C. (2019). Realities of teaching climate change in a pacific island nation. In W. Leal Filho & S.L. Hemstock (Eds.), *Climate change and the role of education* (pp. 319–347). Springer International Publishing. https://doi.org/10.1007/978-3-030-32898-6_18

Portland Public Schools, RESOLUTION No. 5272. (2016). https://www.pps.net/cms/lib8/or01913224/centricity/domain/219/final%20climate%20change%20reso%205.11.16%20mr%20revised.pdf

Pulido, L. (2017). Historicizing the personal and the political: Evolving racial formations and the environmental justice movement. In R. Holifield, J. Chakraborty, and G. Walker (Eds.), *Routledge handbook of environmental justice* (pp. 15–24). Abingdon: Routledge.

Rabinowitz, D. (2012). Climate Injustice: CO2 from domestic electricity consumption and private car use by income decile. *Environmental Justice, 5*(1), 38–46. https://doi.org/10.1089/env.2011.0009

Reidmiller, D.R., Avery, C.W., Easterling, D.R., Kunkel, K.E., Lewis, K.L.M., Maycock, T.K., & Stewart, B.C. (Eds.). (2018). Impacts, risks, and adaptation in the United States: Fourth national climate assessment, Volume II. *Global Change Research Program.* https://doi.org/10.7930/nca4.2018

Rigolon, A., & Nemeth, J. (2018). What shapes uneven access to urban amenities? Thick injustice and the legacy of racial discrimination in Denver's parks. *Journal of Planning Education and Research.* Advance online publication. https://doi.org/10.1177/0739456X18789251

Rosebery, A., & Hudicourt-Barnes, J. (2006). Using diversity as a strength in the science classroom: The benefits of science talk. In R. Douglas (Ed.), *Linking science & literacy in the K-8 classroom* (pp. 305–320). Arlington VA: NSTA Press.

Rothstein, R. (2017). *The color of law: A forgotten history of how our government segregated America.* New York, NY: Liveright Publishling Corporation.

Sailor, D.J., Baniassadi, A., O'Lenick, C.R., & Wilhelmi, O.V. (2019). The growing threat of heat disasters. *Environmental Research Letters, 14*(5), 054006. https://doi.org/10.1088/1748-9326/ab0bb9

Samson, J., Berteaux, D., McGill, B.J., & Humphries, M.M. (2011). Geographic disparities and moral hazards in the predicted impacts of climate change on human populations: Spatially explicit impacts of climate change on human populations. *Global Ecology and Biogeography, 20*(4), 532–544. https://doi.org/10.1111/j.1466-8238.2010.00632.x

Sannino, A. (2015). The emergence of transformative agency and double stimulation: Activity-based studies in the Vygotskian tradition. *Learning, Culture and Social Interaction, 4,* 1–3.

Smithsonian Institution (Ed.). (2018). Standing rock sioux and Dakota access pipeline. https://americanindian.si.edu/nk360/plains-treaties/dapl

Stapleton, S.R. (2019). A case for climate justice education: American youth connecting to intragenerational climate injustice in Bangladesh. *Environmental Education Research, 25*(5), 732–750. https://doi.org/10.1080/13504622.2018.1472220

Stapleton, S.R. (2020). Toward critical environmental education: A standpoint analysis of race in the American environmental context. *Environmental Education Research, 26*(2), 155–170. https://doi.org/10.1080/13504622.2019.1648768

Stevenson, R.B., Wal, A.E.J., Heimlich, J.E., & Field, E. (2017). Critical environmental education. In A. Russ & M.E. Krasny (Eds.), *Urban Environmental Education Review* (pp. 64–71). Cornell University Press.

Thompson, A. (2020, December 22). The top five climate stories of 2020. *Scientific American.* https://www.scientificamerican.com/article/the-top-five-climate-stories-of-20201/.

Tuck, E., McKenzie, M., & McCoy, K. (2014). Land education: Indigenous, post-colonial, and decolonizing perspectives on place and environmental education research. *Environmental Education Research, 20*(1), 1–23. https://doi.org/10.1080/13504622.2013.877708

Uejio, C.K., Wilhelmi, O.V., Golden, J.S., Mills, D.M., Gulino, S.P., & Samenow, J.P. (2011). Intra-urban societal vulnerability to extreme heat: The role of heat exposure and the built environment, socioeconomics, and neighborhood stability. *Health & Place, 17*(2), 498–507. https://doi.org/10.1016/j.healthplace.2010.12.005

UNFCCC (United Nations Framework Convention on Climate Change). (1992, June 12). https://unfccc.int/resource/docs/convkp/conveng.pdf

Vygotsky, L.S. (1997). *Self-control. The collected works of L. S. Vygotsky: The History of the Development of Higher Mental Functions* (Vol. 4, pp. 207–219). New York: Plenum.

Walsh, E.M., & Tsurusaki, B. (2014). Social Controversy Belongs in the Climate Science Classroom. *Nature Climate Change, 4*(4), 259–263. https://doi.org/10.1038/NCLIMATE2143

Walsh, E.M., Jenkins, D., and Cordero, E. (2016). The promise of an energy tracker curriculum for promoting home-school connections and youth agency in climate action. *Journal of Sustainability Education, 11*, 1–15.

Warren, B., & Rosebery, A. (2007). *Teaching science to English language learners.* Arlington VA: NSTA Press.

Weber, T., Haensler, A., Rechid, D., Pfeifer, S., Eggert, B., & Jacob, D. (2018). Analyzing regional climate change in Africa in a 1.5, 2, and 3°C global warming world. *Earth's Future, 6*(4), 643–655. https://doi.org/10.1002/2017EF000714

Weir, T., Dovey, L., & Orcherton, D. (2017). Social and cultural issues raised by climate change in Pacific Island countries: An overview. *Regional Environmental Change, 17*(4), 1017–1028. https://doi.org/10.1007/s10113-016-1012-5

Whitman, S., Good, G., Donoghue, E.R., Benbow, N., Shou, W., & Mou, S. (1997). Mortality in Chicago attributed to the July 1995 heat wave. *American Journal of Public Health, 87*(9), 1515–1518. https://doi.org/10.2105/AJPH.87.9.1515

Wibeck, V. (2013). Enhancing learning, communication and public engagement about climate change - some lessons from recent literature. *Environmental Education Research, 20*(3), 386–411.

Wilson, B. (2020). Urban heat management and the legacy of redlining. *Journal of the American Planning Association,* 1–15. https://doi.org/10.1080/01944363.2020.1759127

Wolf, J., & Moser, S. (2011). Individual understandings, perceptions, and engagement with climate change: Insights from in-depth studies across the world. *WIREs Climate Change, 2*, 547–569.

Wolfe, P. (2006). Settler colonialism and the elimination of the native. *Journal of Genocide Research, 8*(4), 387–409. https://doi.org/10.1080/14623520601056240

World Bank. (2020, December 2). Pandemic threatens to push 72 million more children into learning poverty—World Bank outlines a new vision to ensure that every child learns, everywhere. Retrieved May 7, 2021, from https://www.worldbank.org/en/news/press-release/2020/12/02/pandemic-threatens-to-push-72-million-more-children-into-learning-poverty-world-bank-outlines-new-vision-to-ensure-that-every-child-learns-everywhere

Part I

Theoretical Perspectives of Equity and Justice in Climate Change Education

1 Bringing Climate Injustices to the Forefront

Learning from the Youth Climate Justice Movement

Rupinder Kaur Grewal, Ellen Field, and Paul Berger

April 22, 2021 was marked by an Earth Summit, organized by the Biden–Harris Administration, that brought 40 leaders from around the world together to pledge new greenhouse gas reduction targets. Xiye Bastida, a Mexican-born 19-year-old, was one of two youth activists invited to speak. Her speech to global leaders demanded holistic and inclusive solutions to climate change:

> You need to accept that the era of fossil fuels is over. We need a just transition to renewables worldwide so that we can stop emitting carbon and focus on drawing down carbon. But most importantly, all of these solutions must be implemented with the voices of frontline black, brown, and Indigenous communities as leaders and decision-makers. We demand comprehensive, non-Eurocentric climate education including literacy on climate justice, environmental, ancestral and Indigenous wisdom on historical movements … You are the naive ones, if you think we can survive this crisis in the current way of living. You are the pessimists if you don't believe we have what it takes to change the world. If you want to know why youth activists are rising up, it's because we're striving for joy. Joy for our communities and future generations. The climate crisis is so violent, and it has exacerbated so much injustice, it is time that you stop thanking us for being activists.
>
> (Leaders' Summit on Climate, 2021)

Bastida is advocating for system change that addresses multiple injustices, reaching far beyond generational injustices to include considerations of race, colonial histories, geopolitics, and Western economic power and privilege. Since Greta Thunberg's lone climate strike in 2018, the climate strike movement has continued to grow and evolve into a global network of youth climate activist groups focused on campaigns advocating for systemic change that center justice. Bastida's speech points to the disconnect between the dominant cultural perspective on

DOI: 10.4324/9780429326011-3

climate change as a technical problem and the current, often youth-driven, demand for climate justice-oriented discourses to generate responsive and inclusive actions to tackle climate change and its underlying causes.

There is finally now recognition by North American leaders of the urgent need to sharply reduce greenhouse gas emissions by 2030 to mitigate dangerous climate disruption (Davenport et al., 2021). With current climate change education responses inadequate (Field et al., 2019; Plutzer et al., 2016), and a window of opportunity for change opened by awareness of the need to act at every level, this chapter explores key ideas from the youth climate justice movement that formal education systems should embrace. We begin with the development of the movement, discuss some of its defining aspects, describe gaps in current climate change education, and conclude by proposing a framework for climate justice education for formal education systems. We believe that formal education structures, curricula, and practice must learn from the youth climate justice movement. Schooling should move beyond the current focus of knowledge and understanding of climate change science and climate impacts (Bhattacharya et al., 2020; Hargis & McKenzie, 2020; Wynes & Nicholas, 2019) and go through a pivotal reorientation of what schooling "is" and "does" in this current moment where, globally, we face an existential crisis (Kwauk & Casey, 2021). In this chapter, we argue that the youth climate justice movement provides a blueprint for transformative and transgressive pedagogies that formal education systems should learn from and integrate into their policies and practices.

Key Aspects of the Youth Climate Justice Movement

In this section, we provide context and outline defining aspects of the youth climate justice movement.

Emergence of the Youth Climate Justice Movement

The environmental justice movement preceded the climate justice movement in drawing attention to the disproportionate environmental degradation experienced by communities of color (McKenzie et al., 2017; Mitchell & D'Onofrio, 2016). Resistance to activities that harm the environment has, of course, been led by Black, Indigenous, and racialized communities (BIPoC) since long before the term *environmental justice* began to be used by Black people in the Civil Rights Movement in the USA in the 1960s (Stephens, 1996).

The climate justice movement is said to have begun by critiquing the carbon-driven economy as an indicator of larger inequities exploited by global capitalism (Schlosberg & Collins, 2014). The movement originated with a focus on eradicating the causes of climate change and

Bringing Climate Injustices to the Forefront   43

addressing the inequitable impacts of the oil industry (Bruno et al., 1999). CorpWatch, an NGO that helped organize the first-ever known Climate Justice Summit during COP 6 in 2000, became one of the major movement organizations, along with Climate Justice Now! at the Bali COP13 meetings in 2007 (Schlosberg & Collins, 2014). The climate justice movement focuses on how climate change disproportionately impacts marginalized groups and the world's poorest countries.

The movement recently gained tremendous traction, revitalized and invigorated by youth activists. In 2015, a group of students invited youth worldwide to miss school on the first day of the United Nations Climate Change Conference in Paris (Climate Strike, 2016). On November 30, 2015, supported by several organizations including 350.org, a *climate strike* took place in over 100 countries from Melbourne to Mexico City, with more than 50,000 people participating (Phipps et al., 2015). In addition to demanding 100% clean energy and to keep fossil fuels in the ground, protesters and activists were pushing for a bolder international agreement at the climate summit (Adam & Siddiqui, 2015). The international agreement was negotiated over the period of two weeks during the Paris United Nations Framework Convention on Climate Change's (UNFCCC) 21st Conference of the Parties (COP 21). The Paris Agreement was finally adopted on December 12, 2015, which was a "historic turning point for global climate action" as it was a point when "world leaders came to a consensus on an accord comprised of commitments by 195 nations to combat climate change and adapt to its impacts" (Denchak, 2021, para. 2).

The climate strike of November 2015 and the establishment of the Paris Agreement gave rise to a proliferation of new movements and organizations oriented towards climate justice, including: Zero Hour (2017), the Sunrise Movement (2017), and Fridays for Future (2018). However, this is not to say that there were none prior to 2015; other organizations include: Greenpeace (1971), the IPCC (1988), 350.org (2007), Guardians of the Forest, also known as Guardians of the Amazon (2013), and Project Drawdown (2014). Some have deep roots. For instance, Guardians of the Forest are a group of 120 Indigenous peoples in the Brazilian state of Maranhão who have been defending their land and the remaining Amazon rainforest for more than five centuries. When asked when they were founded, one of the leaders of the group, Olimpio Santos Guajajara, answered: "in 1500, the year the Portuguese landed in Brazil with an armada under the command of Pedro Álvares Cabral" (Libardi, 2020, para. 1).

Youth activism itself is also not new; youth aged 18–30 have participated in both local and international social movements across the world for decades. They have been instrumental in fighting for social justice, including in feminist, environmentalist, anti-war, immigrant rights, and the US Civil Rights movements. In relation to climate change activism,

44 *Rupinder Kaur Grewal et al.*

youth in Australia, for example, formed the Australian Youth Climate Coalition in November 2006 to organize and involve youth in demanding climate change actions from government leaders (Munro, 2009). What is relatively new and specific to the current youth climate justice movement is that youth activists are positioned as leaders, where they are asked to speak at international governmental meetings, have rallied millions, and are leading robust social movements aimed at stopping the existential crisis of our time (Bowman, 2020a; Han & Ahn, 2020). Canadian water warrior Autumn Peltier, Land Protector Quannah Chasinghorse, Little Miss Flint (Amariyanna "Mary" Copeny), the Guardians of the Forest, and Zeena Abdulkarim (from Zero Hour) are among many inspiring youths who are leading the climate justice movement today (Janfaza, 2020). The work achieved by such resilient Black, Indigenous, and racialized youth activists will be discussed in further sections.

Justice as Central for Youth Climate Activists

Marginalized communities are at the forefront of experiencing the negative impacts of climate change, with Indigenous peoples worldwide often the first to suffer, given their intimate relationship with the environment. This includes Indigenous peoples from sub-Saharan Africa, the Maldives, the Himalayas, Bangladesh, the Amazon, and the Arctic regions (Etchart, 2017; Haluza-Delay, 2013). Greta Thunberg (2019), the Swedish teen whose 2018 school climate strike sparked a huge wave of youth protest, consistently highlights "equity" in her speeches, including: "the people who have contributed the least to this crisis are the ones who are going to be affected the most" (pp. 39–40). Whereas the focus of mainstream climate change movements is often on reducing greenhouse gas emissions, the youth climate justice movement emphasizes disproportionate climate change impacts and insists that these inequities must be addressed at a governmental level.

Climate justice is a contested concept, developing out of policy discourses (e.g., Robinson, 2018), liberal philosophy, and the youth climate justice movement (McGregor et al., 2018). It differs from environmental racism, environmental justice, or ecojustice, though they often get grouped together or are used interchangeably in some contexts (see Haluza-Delay, 2013). Like environmental justice, many scholars have advocated the use of climate justice to describe the effects of climate change through a human rights lens and social justice framework (Haluza-Delay et al., 2009; Klein, 2014; Stapleton, 2019; Tuck & Yang, 2018). Movements focused on climate justice aim to disrupt oppressive systems of colonialism, capitalism, patriarchy, and racism, and try to reimagine the current inequitable system so those who are already underprivileged are not further disadvantaged by climate change (Kanbur, 2018; Stapleton, 2019).

As many youth activists have continuously asserted, climate injustices are not merely environmental issues but also racial injustices and gender injustices (McKibben, 2017). However, the claims of youth climate activists are not homogeneous nor are their experiences; and they may be better understood as a "polyphonic movement" (Bowman, 2020b). Nevertheless, youth climate activist messaging has a common characteristic that focuses on intergenerational injustices of climate disruption; that is, climate change will affect their futures and that adults have not acted with moral responsibility and obligation (Robinson, 2018). Given that youth are in marginalized positions (Bowman, 2020b), and that intergenerational injustice is the starting point of their climate concerns (Thew et al., 2020), the youth climate activist movement is embedded with an intersectional view, advocating for lenses of equity, anti-oppression, and anti-racism to be permanently integrated into decision-making with a focus on addressing the underlying roots of climate injustices (Damico et al., 2020; Klein, 2014; Tuck & Yang, 2018).

Youth Protests and School Strikes

After a 2018 shooting rampage in a high school in Parkland, Florida, Parkland students went on strike to denounce entrenched legislative opposition to gun reform. The strikes provided an important example for the youth climate justice movement since they showed the ability of youth to gain media attention, and thereby influence the public's consciousness and electoral politics (Bandura & Cherry, 2020, p. 947).

Inspired by the Parkland students, Greta Thunberg instigated rapid growth in the youth climate movement, which spread across the world in 2018 and 2019, the largest environmental social movement in history (Bowman, 2020a). Thunberg used Friday school strikes to demand more aggressive climate policies from governments and international organizations (Thunberg, 2019). The school strikes are a "politically motivated defiance of school attendance" (Biswas & Mattheis, 2021, p. 3) and were popularized through the use of hashtags on social media, such as #FridaysForFuture and #ClimateStrike. Her leadership has led millions of youth worldwide to take to the streets, become engaged in civic action, and demand government action to reduce greenhouse gas emissions and phase out fossil fuels. Researchers have now coined the term the "Thunberg effect" to explain how people who are familiar with Greta are more likely to think their actions are effective and meaningful (Sabherwal et al., 2021).

The tremendous success achieved by Greta Thunberg built on earlier climate action and the Fridays for Future climate strikes were propelled by the 2018 IPCC 1.5°C report, which Thunberg often refers to in her speeches (see Thunberg, 2019). The movement may have gained traction when it did in part because her voice is a strong one and it came at

46 *Rupinder Kaur Grewal et al.*

a ripe time (Beeler, 2019). Thunberg refers to her Asperger's Syndrome diagnosis as a "superpower," which she describes as seeing the world in stark terms, being able to speak directly, and to cut through lies (Birrell, 2019). We have, however, heard young people tell the truth before, such as when Anjali Appardurai scolded officials at COP 17 (Democracy Now, 2011). It is not possible to know exactly why Thunberg has become a superstar while other youth have not, but racism and Eurocentrism, leading to more media coverage, is probably a significant contributing factor (Beeler, 2019). We will come back to this shortly.

The youth climate strikes have generated unprecedented change and impact. For instance, on March 15, 2019, 1.6 million people in over 2,200 cities worldwide participated in strikes to call for policies that would follow the Paris Agreement (Haynes, 2019). The first climate emergency was declared by the British Parliament on April 23, 2019 after Jeremy Corbyn brought forward a motion to the House of Commons. In Corbyn's motion, he acknowledged how the youth climate strikes had moved him to act:

> We are living in a climate crisis that will spiral dangerously out of control unless we take rapid and dramatic action now. This is no longer about the distant future. We are talking about nothing less than the irreversible destruction of the environment within our lifetimes. Young people know this. They have the most to lose. I was deeply moved a few weeks ago to see the streets outside this parliament filled with colour and noise by children on strike from school chanting "our planet, our future." For someone of my generation it was inspiring but also humbling that children felt they had to leave school to teach the adults a lesson. The truth is they are ahead of the politicians on this – the most important issue of our times.
>
> (Labour press release, 2019)

Most likely it was the combined activism of the youth climate strikes and Extinction Rebellion in the City of London, following the release of the Intergovernmental Panel on Climate Change's special report on global warming to 1.5°C (IPCC, 2018), that together created this landmark legislation that led to other climate emergency declarations in close to 2,000 jurisdictions worldwide, covering over 800 million citizens (Climate Emergency Declarations, 2021).

The activism of the Sunrise Movement, a youth movement in the United States focused on stopping climate change, fighting against racism and the institutions built upon it, as well as creating millions of jobs in the process (Sunrise Movement, 2021), has also had immense impact. The Sunrise Movement along with Representative Alexandria Ocasio-Cortez occupied House Speaker Nancy Pelosi's office in late October

Bringing Climate Injustices to the Forefront 47

2018 (Green, 2019). Less than a year later, the group brought forward the Green New Deal, endorsed by several Democrats leading up to the US election, and has certainly inspired the Biden–Harris administration's plans to put climate change at the center of American policy (Noisecat, 2020).

Another example of the impact of the youth climate strikes comes from Denmark, where a large coalition of groups including Fridays for Future Denmark and The Green Student Movement held a massive climate march on May 25, 2019 with the slogan, "Make the election a climate election" (Folkets Klimamarch Københaven, 2019). While not exclusively a youth climate action, youth were over-represented as participants and Greta Thunberg delivered a short speech in person. The organizers demanded a fast green transition and a binding climate law, and for climate justice principles to be followed. Several weeks later in her victory speech, the new Prime Minister Mette Frederiksen said: "Dear young people. You made this election the first climate election in Danish history" (in Kallestrup & Eller, 2019, translated from the Danish). A year later, Denmark had a binding climate law to reduce greenhouse gas (GHG) emissions by 70% by 2030—more than the needed global average in order to account for climate justice and Denmark's historically high emissions (Timperley, 2020).

In response to the surge of climate protests, the United Nations Headquarters introduced its very first Youth Climate Summit in September 2019. Over 500 youth climate activists from more than 140 countries took part. In addition to participating in the Youth Climate Summit, Thunberg and 15 children (from Argentina, the Marshall Islands, France, Germany, and the USA) lodged a formal complaint under the UN Convention on the Rights of the Child (UNCRC), stating that failures to address the climate crisis violated the convention (McIntyre, 2019). This action shows the centrality of justice to these youth activists.

Youth Agency

When Thunberg and 15 children lodged a formal complaint under the UNCRC, they shone a media spotlight on society's pervasive dismissal of young people as political agents (Holmberg & Alvinius, 2020). More specifically, their actions highlighted their right to have some say over civic and political decisions that are being made about their futures. According to the UNCRC, children have a right to survival, to develop to the fullest, to be protected from harmful influences, abuse, and exploitation, and to participate fully in family, cultural, and social life (1989). Article 12 of the UNCRC also empowers children and young people to be actively involved in decisions that affect them and to have their opinions taken into account by adults. Article 12 implies that children can negotiate

48 *Rupinder Kaur Grewal et al.*

with adults and carers to determine the quality and nature of the services and infrastructure that is provided to them.

Youth climate activist speeches and the extended network of social media content demonstrate the ways in which the youth climate movement mobilizes and performs progressive resistance, demanding action from political leaders (Holmberg & Alvinius, 2020). To youth across the globe, the critical aspect of resistance is to bring about action. Although some authors suggest that youth are less knowledgeable about environmental issues than adults (e.g., Corner et al., 2015), others have found that "children's resistance in relation to the climate emergency suggests that children possess knowledge, engagement and power to act on environmental issues" (Holmberg & Alvinius, 2020, pp. 87–88).

Recognizing children as both environmental victims and actors continues to unfold in communities around the world, in the media, and in the research literature. Using a child and youth-focused theoretical lens, Biswas and Mattheis (2021) argued that climate strikes have been a powerful counterweight to formal education by allowing youth to self-educate and build agency. This emphasizes the capacity building of youth to act independently and trust their youth-driven processes of learning and acting (Andersson & Öhman, 2016) through which they have uncovered more about climate change and climate injustices.

Another important way that young people have enacted their agency to influence policymakers is through filing lawsuits as youth plaintiffs. Youth climate litigation is often made on the grounds of human rights violations wherein it is argued that children and young people's future rights are not being protected if dangerous levels of GHG emissions are not curbed. Several ground-breaking cases have created precedents that have led the way for more youth climate lawsuits. In 2015, Ashgar Leghari, a 25-year-old farmer from Rahim Yar Khan District, sued the Pakistani government for violating his human rights by neglecting to tackle the impacts of climate change (Gill, 2015). Also in 2015, a group of young people in the Netherlands sued their government for inaction on climate change and unexpectedly won, where the court ordered the government to curb carbon emissions by 25% by 2020 (Parker, 2019). In 2018 in Colombia, 25 young people argued that the government's failure to curb deforestation of the Amazon rainforest threatened their rights and those of future generations. They also won and the court ordered the government to reduce deforestation to zero by 2020 (Gerretsen, 2021). This trio of victories on three continents has built a climate litigation movement, which has proliferated with a total of 1,587 cases of climate litigation, with 37 of these cases in Asia, Africa, and Latin America (Setzer & Byrnes, 2020). The increase in climate litigation coincides with the intense advocacy and school strikes in 2019 and suggests a shift from individual agency to a sense of collective (litigation) agency as the number of cases continues to mount. A very recent case in Germany

Bringing Climate Injustices to the Forefront   49

just closed with the high court ruling that the government's 2019 climate law was incompatible with the fundamental rights of the nine German youth plaintiffs (Lombrana, 2021), strengthening the legal framework of intergenerational inequity of climate inaction that will affect children and youth around the world.

Black, Indigenous, and Racialized Youth Climate Activists

The climate strikes themselves have been important incubators for fostering youth agency. Many students worldwide, from Jakarta to New York City, have walked out of class, inspired to demand action on climate change (Marris, 2019). Climate change communications experts note how young climate activists have been using their moral authority and position as children along with their social media and tech savviness to raise adult concerns and awareness (Marris, 2019). However, the question still remains: Why has Thunberg been so effective? Curnow, who studies youth movements, thinks that it has a lot to do with race and racism: "her whiteness is very much an asset for why the media, why governments, why the UN has been willing to feature her" (Beeler, 2019, para. 28). Recognizing the media's focus on her, Thunberg asked the media at the COP25 Climate Summit in Madrid to focus on youth climate activists from developing countries instead of her, explaining that what are mostly future climate impacts for wealthy nations are current impacts in developing nations: "Our stories have been told over and over again … We talk about the future, they talk about the present" (cited in Braine, 2019). This mounting tension—between highlighting the work of Thunberg and recognizing that she may have more impact because she has ties to privileged communities and is White—is critical and will be unpacked in this section.

Autumn Peltier, Amariyanna "Mary" Copeny, Jamie Margolin, Xiye Bastida, Xiuhtezcatl Martinez, Isra Hirsi, Nadia Nazar, Vanessa Nakate, Jerome Foster II, and Leah Namugerwa. How many of these names have you heard before? These ten names were taken from a Google search conducted on May 18, 2021, for "Climate Activist People," which populated 30 names with their pictures across the top of the screen. Out of the 30 names 21 of them, or 70%, identify as Black, Indigenous, or as a person of color, which means that the majority of youth climate activists in a given sample may come from a marginalized community. They are, however, rarely represented in mainstream media.

The US youth climate movement has many young women of color at the forefront who are taking command, including Jamie Margolin, co-founder of the Zero Hour movement, and Isra Hirsi, executive director of US Climate Strike (Beeler, 2019). The problem is that not as much attention is given to youth of color—as long-time environmental justice activist, Mustafa Santiago Ali, points out—"who have been literally, not

50 *Rupinder Kaur Grewal et al.*

just standing on the front lines, but living in the front lines for decades now" (Beeler, 2019, para. 29). For example, responses to climate change in Peru are being conceptualized and enacted by Indigenous youth who are on the front lines of the latest forms of colonial devastation (Dhillon, 2018).

Racialized youth activists are striking from school, taking the issue to the streets, disrupting conferences and events, and lobbying government leaders to take action—all while seeing their own communities and families suffer. Many are connected across continents. Youth members of the Guardians of the Forest, such as Militza Flaco (aged 23), Jeffry Eduardo Torres Cortes (24), Yanisbeth González (24), and Draney Francisco Aldana Bac (22), are part of a coalition of Indigenous organizations from Asia, Africa, and Latin America called the Global Alliance of Territorial Communities (Janfaza, 2020). Advocating for inclusion and equity in global climate negotiations, this group of activists are taking an active role in fighting for the rights of forest peoples in climate change conversations (Janfaza, 2020).

Going back to the aforementioned Google search, the first person in that list is, not surprisingly, Greta Thunberg. The continuous spotlight that is given to Thunberg by the media has put her at the center of the youth-led climate justice movement. Consequently, the work and efforts of many Indigenous, Black, and Brown youth activists worldwide often get erased or obscured (Burton, 2019; McFadden, 2020; Rafaely & Barnes, 2020). As previously mentioned, Curnow noted how Thunberg "looked right" (i.e., White) for the media and prompted the UN to feature her. However, it is important to note that many youth activists, like Xiye Bastida (a Mexican–Chilean climate activist and member of the Indigenous Mexican Otomi-Toltec nation), were captured by Thunberg's school strike idea (Beeler, 2019). Bastida, one of the leaders of the US Fridays for Future movement, was invited to the Ninth UN World Urban Forum to speak on Indigenous cosmology and also received the "Spirit of the UN" award in 2018 (NPR, 2020). She is most known for organizing and mobilizing 600 students from her school for the climate strike in March 2019, and currently plays a leadership role in New York City, organizing strikes and speaking on climate justice issues in town halls (NPR, 2020).

As seen in Bastida's speech excerpt in the introduction to this chapter, she is a vocal activist who is passionate about climate justice matters. This passion stems from when she saw her hometown in Mexico suffering from a flood in 2015, which was the first time she witnessed the effects of climate change (Feller, 2019). After moving to New York with her family, she witnessed the damage caused by Hurricane Sandy, which made her realize that climate change impacts were occurring everywhere. Her passion, as she states, stems "partly from her parents' climate activism and her Indigenous roots, as she and her dad are both Otomi, part of a group of Indigenous people in Mexico" (Feller, 2019, para. 2). Then, there is

Bringing Climate Injustices to the Forefront 51

24-year-old Vanessa Nakate, who has spent more than 60 hours per week in her dad's shop, selling solar batteries in Kampala, Uganda (Marris, 2019). She speaks about the disproportionate effects of climate change on agriculture and the resulting daily struggles of Ugandans. Nakate has often protested alone; however, social media has helped to connect her with activists worldwide to amplify the message that the older generations have not done enough to combat climate change, and now youth need to clean up their mess (Marris, 2019).

Bringing awareness to and giving credit to youth of color for their hard work is important to ensure that society is "forced to reckon with the full scope of climate destruction," so that the movement is not only seen through white eyes (Burton, 2019, para. 3). From the limited information that is published in journal articles, it is clear that the experiences of Black, Indigenous, and other racialized youth activists are not comprehensively documented; however, all of these activists have social media accounts, specifically Instagram and Twitter, which is where many of these conversations are unfolding.

Youth Organizations and Social Movement Learning

Within youth-created social movement organizations, such as Fridays for Future, youth engage in various forms of informal learning, often mediated through local Fridays for Future face-to-face (pre-pandemic) and social media groups. Many youth with pro-environmental attitudes use social media platforms to engage in interest-driven learning and activism to learn and discuss environmental issues and engage in and coordinate actions in their local communities (Field, 2021). For some youth, social media platforms create unparalleled opportunities to facilitate relationships where they can join a group or discuss ideas with like-minded peers or coordinate actions around environmental or social issues they are facing (Andersson & Öhman, 2016). In this way, social media can foster relational agency, which is "a capacity to align one's thoughts and actions with those of others in order to interpret problems of practice and to respond to those interpretations" (Bohman, cited by Stevenson with Stirling, 2010, p. 231). Relational agency represents a shift from a personal sense of agency to a collective sense of agency. It can move individuals from focusing on private environmental actions (Chawla & Cushing, 2007) to advocating collective actions and policy change.

Black, Indigenous, and racialized youth activists may feel an additional burden that they need to "protest" themselves and reflexively consider their own habits and actions in light of societal dynamics and practices against which they struggle (Lowan-Trudeau, 2017b). This added burden highlights the dual responsibility that Black, Indigenous, and racialized youth activists experience—that they must do the inner work of both constantly being cognizant of, and overcoming, internal

52 *Rupinder Kaur Grewal et al.*

oppression, while also advocating their own and their community's rights. An illustrative example of exclusion within the climate justice movement is Vanessa Nakate and her first-hand experiences with racism. Nakate, the 24-year-old Ugandan activist and founder of the Rise Up Movement and Youth for Future Africa, went to a conference in Switzerland in January 2020 with other prominent climate activists, including Greta Thunberg, Loukina Tille, Luisa Neubauer, and Isabelle Axelsson (Evelyn, 2020). When the Associated Press reported on the conference, it specifically cut Nakate from the picture, showing only the four White youth activists (Dahir, 2021). The actions taken by the Associated Press exemplify how colonialism remains a lived reality for many Black, Indigenous, Brown, and other racialized communities and how it is far from over. This incident "epitomises the context in which global climate justice is itself colonised" (Malowa et al., 2020, p. 4).

Speaking up on Twitter about the omission, Nakate called out anti-Black discrimination and racism (Dahir, 2021). This resulted in an outpouring of support from other Black, Latinx, and Indigenous activists who expressed similar frustrations with being erased over for their White counterparts (Evelyn, 2020). Nakate addressed this feeling of having a greater responsibility to amplify marginalized voices who are excluded, especially those who do not have the courage to speak up. Claims of racism, such as in Nakate's case, are often prone to extra scrutiny by media and colonial institutions, within which BIPoC youth commitment to climate change activism may be challenged and a considerable amount of effort needed to demonstrate their legitimacy. Women activists, in particular, need to prove their worth, that they are more than emotional and attention-seeking, "since emotion is normatively associated with irrationality, which is seen as weakening climate activists' competence" (Rafaely & Barnes, 2020, p. 84). Despite multiple attempts by spokespersons to delegitimize her activism, Nakate has deployed alternative narratives to resist and transform discourses about her. Analyzing her interviews, Rafaely and Barnes (2020) found that whenever she was undermined, Nakate provided "evidence-based counterarguments to destabilize her interlocutors' arguments" (p. 84). Youth activists like Vanessa Nakate not only need to be knowledgeable in climate science but have to employ skills to back themselves up when being attacked with false accusations about their impact, work, and knowledge.

Indigenous, Black, and racialized youth activists are often put into boxes of what society deems appropriate to fit a certain image and narrative of who they ought to be and what they can and cannot do. Stereotyping such as this has its roots deep in the "White savior complex and its legacy of erasure" (McFadden, 2020, p. 2). The White savior complex is the idea that racialized communities who are suffering from climate change impacts are located in the "third world" and that they can only be saved by White people (McFadden, 2020). This idea is repeatedly

Bringing Climate Injustices to the Forefront   53

shown and put at the forefront of media and news outlets around the world. As Malowa et al. (2020) argue, by removing Nakate from the picture of activists, it not only seeks "to reduce her efforts to naught, but it fundamentally attempts to deny people of colour any say in the debate pitting climate-change sceptics against science-believing folks—highly reflective of the White Saviour Industrial Complex" (p. 5). Images of Black women activists are *still* highly controlled, and anything that does not fit the narrative may be opportunistically ignored, erased, and/or cropped out.

Calling out deleterious media practices can act as an antidote to the trend of cultural erasure and harmful, false narratives that continue to plague our news. Media coverage does not represent the full breadth of diversity of those who attend the workshops, conferences, and panels within the youth climate justice movement (Malowa et al., 2020; Rafaely & Barnes, 2020). As Jamie Margolin, founder of Zero Hour, put it, "a photo crop-out is an easy way to describe it, but it's really a metaphorical crop-out from the narrative of climate science in general" (Evelyn, 2020, para. 13). Social media and its accessibility as a platform allow youth worldwide to connect with each other, whereas mainstream environmentalism has not provided a platform for marginalized communities to voice their experiences to the same extent.

There is a growing interest in the new "breed" of youth activists that use social media heavily, but mainstream media has been a powerful institution that is deliberately manufacturing the cognitive path in which this activism should be perceived (Malowa et al., 2020). Unfortunately for Nakate, she "was caught up in an act purposefully intended to bequeath Greta the limelight" and her "presence was not only misconstrued as aesthetically unappealing but also unwelcome" (Malowa et al., 2020, p. 3). This illustrates how the youth climate justice movement, which has centered the intersectionality of racism, sexism, and classism with climate change—the disproportionate climate impacts for racialized communities—is also demanding *justice* for its very members. Understanding who these Black, Indigenous, and racialized youth activists are, their communities' historical pasts and passions, and seeing them as "leaders of their own revolution" (McFadden, 2020, p. 2) can help to disrupt the narrative that the only individuals working against capitalism and industrialization are white saviors.

With the COVID-19 pandemic, which brought a rapid transition to online learning in many places, and the pause of face-to-face Friday for Futures school strikes, the youth climate justice movement has adapted to online organizing. Youth have shown that fighting against climate inequities and injustices does not stop just because of physical distancing measures and lockdowns. For example, many youths have continued to fight for a livable future via Zoom gatherings with other activists around the world and even by launching court cases, such as the 15 Canadian

54   *Rupinder Kaur Grewal et al.*

youth suing the government for taking inadequate action against climate change (Crawford, 2020). Instead of bringing all activism to a halt because of the pandemic, an intergovernmental organization called the Earth Guardians Youth Council started several initiatives, such as virtual training for students who are new to activism, and Earth Day Live 2020, a three-day livestream that reached millions worldwide (Taylor, 2021). Social movement learning occurring within the movement's numerous organizations is fundamentally transgressive, allowing youth to unpack injustices, internal oppression, and complex emotions, as noted in the next section.

Emotional Work of the Climate Justice Movement

A growing body of academic research suggests that children and youth may be at a greater risk of experiencing eco-anxiety than adults (Clayton, 2020; Ojala, 2012; 2013). In US research, 82% of ten to twelve-year-olds expressed feelings of fear, sadness, and anger when discussing environmental issues (Burke et al., 2018). In Canada, 46% of 12–18-year-olds were categorized as "aware," meaning they understand that human-caused climate change is happening, but they do not believe that human efforts to stop it will be effective (Field et al., 2019). Taken together, this could indicate a burgeoning mental health crisis among youth.

Eco-anxiety among young people may also be fueled by collective senses of despair in media coverage, activism, and society at large (Nairn, 2019), as these spaces are often bereft of messaging of hopeful, though climate-altered, futures. Kelsey (2020) infers that children are suffering emotional and psychological anguish not from their lived experiences but in anticipation of an apocalyptic future they think is inevitable. Reflecting back on Bastida's speech at the Earth Summit, we were struck by her use of the word "joy": "If you want to know why youth activists are rising up, it's because we're striving for joy." This was striking because hopeful sentiment in speeches or references to potential positively framed futures from youth climate activists are very rare.

Recent research conducted in Canada with First Nations and Inuvialuit youth who attended the 2018 COP24 in Poland showed that Indigenous youth participation in climate governance offset their climate-related anxieties (MacKay et al., 2020). This ground-breaking research addresses the gap in the literature that fails to focus on and center the voices of Black, Indigenous, and racialized youth. The findings showed that Indigenous youth participation in COP24 led to personal growth and confidence. Through participating in the COP24 program youth were "heard" by Indigenous peoples in other regions, learned that their experiences were shared by others, and experienced a sense of "hope" through speaking about their communities' concerns (Mackay et al., 2020, p. 14).

Kleres and Wettergren (2017) found that youth climate activists participating in UNFCCC conferences can channel their emotions, that both fear and guilt can be managed by notions of hope to motivate action. In light of this study and its findings, it is conceivable that multiple emotions can help to motivate youth activism, despite some scholars arguing that fear can be debilitating (O'Neill & Nicholson-Cole, 2009). Black climate essayist Mary Heglar asserts that when speaking of capitalism, racism, colonialism, and climate change, rage and anger are healthy responses to these injustices (in Burton, 2020). However, Heglar also problematizes the word "hope" as a "white" concept that overwrites the actions of people of color as they respond to climate injustices out of rage or sorrow. Some groups are used to having to fight and do not need hope or optimism to engage. From this, it is clear that youth need to question their responses to climate change and how they may or may not attend to marginalized perspectives and take up issues of justice (Karsgaard & Davidson, 2021).

Key Ideas that Formal Education Should Embrace from the Youth Climate Justice Movement

In this section, we put forward key ideas from the youth climate justice movement that we believe education systems should consider in their adoption of climate change education. These ideas collectively bring together a framework that has a justice and equity orientation, focuses on youth efficacy and leadership, is pedagogically grounded in interdisciplinary action-oriented learning, and attends to youth well-being. Some of these ideas or themes are already discussed in climate change education literature and frameworks; however, we see the justice and equity orientation as an inseparable and integral aspect of climate change education. When combined with the other thematic ideas, a pedagogical framework of transformative and transgressive pedagogy is articulated for positive engagement and learning about the climate crisis.

While youth have been mobilizing, motivated by multiple injustices inherent in the causes and impacts of climate change, "education systems lag behind, preoccupied with the 'what' and 'how' of climate change, rather than engaging it as a social issue in which students themselves are implicated" (Karsgaard & Davidson, 2021, p. 1). Climate change education needs to go beyond the science classroom and begin approaching questions of "why" by critically engaging climate change as a social issue under the umbrella of critical justice education (Karsgaard & Davidson, 2021; Monroe et al., 2019; Stapleton, 2019). If children from diverse backgrounds across the world are coming together and advocating for transformative change, how can education systems be more responsive and actively participate in the biggest challenge facing humanity?

56 *Rupinder Kaur Grewal et al.*

Justice and Equity Orientation

Climate change education frameworks typically focus on understanding climate change science (Hargis & McKenzie, 2020; Læssøe, Schnack, Breiting & Rolls, 2009; Wynes & Nicholas, 2019) and have not adequately responded to the complexity the climate crisis poses to society (Field et al., 2019; Henderson et al., 2017; Lehtonen, Salonen & Cantell, 2019). With the rise of the youth climate justice movement, gaps in education have been highlighted by youth advocating climate justice curriculum reform in England by Teach the Future (2021) and in Canada by Climate Education Reform British Columbia (2021). Climate justice itself should be seen as educational content. In that case, the ideological impact of the climate justice movement "needs to extend far beyond social movement constituencies, and into schools, as well as further, higher and community-based educational institutions" (McGregor et al., 2018, p. 5).

Climate justice education should include specific curricula and strategies that educators can use in their classrooms. There is a vital need to integrate climate justice education into kindergarten to grade 12 curricula (Lowan-Trudeau, 2017a; Reid, 2019; Stapleton, 2019; Waldron et al., 2019). Climate justice education can provide a unique platform for amplifying youth voices and can be a space for the genuine activation of youth political agency within their schools and the public domain (Cutter-MacKenzie & Rousell, 2019). It would celebrate "disruptive thinking and political agency" (Kwauk & Casey, 2021, p. 9). Climate justice education, however, is still an emerging field. Stapleton (2019) proposes that climate justice should be used as a robust frame for climate change education, just as environmental justice is for environmental and sustainability education. Implementing a justice-oriented approach to climate change education will "deepen the student experience and build the commitment to act, which abstract knowledge has often failed to engender" (p. 748).

There are multiple ways a climate justice education framing could be implemented in schools. They range from extra-curricular social justice clubs focusing on climate change impacts to stories of youth climate activists integrated into Language, Arts, or English readings. A notable initiative is by Ryan Cho, a teacher who collaborated with the British Columbia (BC) branch of the Canadian Center for Policy Alternatives to develop a climate justice resource for teachers. The created modules emphasize the intersection between climate action and social justice by investigating industrial food systems, consumerism, waste, and green economies. Cho (2017) exemplifies the importance of a justice orientation by ensuring that issues are explored through the lenses of fairness and equity to help improve the lives of the most vulnerable. Framing climate change with equity and justice enables us to implicate ourselves in colonial legacies and land-extraction strategies while working to stand in solidarity with marginalized communities facing climate disparities.

Interdisciplinary Action-Oriented Learning

Understanding political, economic, sociological, and philosophical aspects of climate change, and particularly a climate justice framing, is critical to allow students to develop a comprehensive picture of the field. Manni and Knekta (2020) used thematic analysis of interviews with youth activists to demonstrate that most secondary students "expressed a lack of opportunities for real action" and stated that "this is what they want more of, i.e., more action in practice and less talk" (p. 18). A comprehensive review of countries' focus on climate change education through analyzing their Nationally Determined Contributions to the UNFCCC Secretariat showed that there are notable gaps in climate change education and communication activities, and a pronounced emphasis on cognitive knowledge over affective or action-oriented approaches (McKenzie, 2021). In terms of the research literature, Monroe et al.'s (2019) systematic review reported that very few empirical studies in climate change education have documented climate change teaching that uses both social *and* science (inter/transdisciplinary) approaches.

To ensure that climate change education is more transgressive and action-oriented, educators need to give students more opportunities to take action within their schools and communities. As we have seen, students in the climate justice movement are leaving schools to take action and learning from each other (Marris, 2019); this learning can be shared more broadly by bringing activism into schooling. There are several barriers that teachers may face when implementing this kind of transformative and transgressive approach in traditional classrooms, including packed curriculums with little time for thematic inquiry units or action projects, rigid secondary school timetables, and lack of knowledge or confidence of the teacher (Blum et al., 2013; Boon, 2010; Field et al., 2019). However, one of the first steps that educators can take is to ask students what questions they have about climate change, and invite them to be active participants to direct their learning about the questions that are most relevant to them—this can even be for as little as a few focused classes (Field, 2017; Field et al., 2020).

Haluza-Delay (2013) argued that education for environmental justice (or climate justice in this case) "should be central to environmental education theory, practice and research" (p. 400). He noted that researchers had not explored how environmental educators incorporate a justice lens into their classrooms. This gap is a weakness in the interdisciplinary field of environmental justice, and specifically climate justice, that needs to be further addressed by scholars, especially with the rise of social movements like the Youth Climate Strikes. If climate justice education is to make such advancement, there needs to be a shift in moving beyond "discipline boundaries of environmental education, education for sustainable development and education for

58 *Rupinder Kaur Grewal et al.*

sustainability" (Cutter-Mackenzie & Rousell, 2019, p. 101). Climate justice education should not simply fall into one of these disciplines or solely be identified as a sub-discipline. Instead, climate justice should be an emerging field of practice and research that is fundamentally interdisciplinary and transdisciplinary (Cutter-Mackenzie and Rousell, 2019).

Leadership and Fostering Student Efficacy

The youth climate strikes began as a political act. Greta Thunberg skipped school as an act of resistance, highlighting that for young people who could not vote and thereby push governments to take climate change seriously, she could instead not go to school. As the youth climate strikes grew, protest signs and slogans penned by youth also advocated that youth wanted an education that would teach them about the climate crisis and help prepare them for it (Bowman, 2020b). In this way, the youth climate strikes also became a clarion call for education policymakers and administrators to take leadership and integrate climate change education into education policy and practice. Some countries got to work, with Italy being the first country to make climate change education a mandatory subject, soon followed by Mexico, New Zealand, Argentina, Cambodia, and the states of Islamabad and New Jersey following suit (Hargis & McKenzie, 2020; Rodriguez & Gralki, 2020). However, given the robust scientific consensus on the need to mitigate GHG emissions and clear language in Article 12 of the Paris Agreement (2015) for signatory countries to enhance climate change education, why has educational leadership been so slow in responding? And why have Paris signatory countries focused much less on education than on public awareness or training programs (McKenzie, 2021)?

There is a strong need for drastic change at the educational policy level to address climate change and climate justice more robustly. In particular, there is a need for both top-down policy change and bottom-up cultural shifts by placing significance on youth activism while also highlighting the agency-limiting practices common in today's formal educational settings (Trott et al., 2020). This commitment should include providing opportunities for youth to learn about change-making processes, such as engaging in critical historical study, to "trace the emergence, development, challenges and impacts of collective action – including the recent youth climate strikes, along with their anti-racist and decolonizing components – rather than celebrating government leadership or focusing on heroic individuals such as Greta Thunberg" (Karsgaard & Davidson, 2021, p. 15).

In Canada, there is currently a group of 25 high school students in the province of British Columbia who are advocating educational

Bringing Climate Injustices to the Forefront   59

transformation to teach about and embody climate justice. The group—Climate Education Reform British Columbia (CERBC)—launched their campaign "Reform to Transform" in April, 2021. It consists of a list of needs for the BC Ministry of Education to respond to, and a well-organized campaign to bring pressure to bear on the Ministry. In terms of curriculum, they are advocating the following reforms:

- Understand the physical climate system and the causes and effects of climate change.
- Understand the urgency of the climate crisis and the need to act now.
- Understand the political, economic and sociological aspects of the climate emergency.
- Understand the relationship of social justice issues with climate change and climate solutions.
- Critically engage in politics.
- Feel a stronger connection to the environment through further out of classroom learning.
- Contribute to climate solutions by understanding the types of changes needed and the many ways to be involved to enact those changes.
- Envision a better world, and feel empowered and energized. (CERBC, 2021)

Beyond curriculum reforms, the group has also asked for the creation of a youth advisory committee that would work alongside the BC Ministry of Education and individual district-level committees to ensure that student voices are consistently heard.

This group initially started out of a leadership program in a Vancouver high school, which raises the question of what role developing a sense of efficacy and leadership has in fostering pro-climate behaviors. Busch's (2019) research on youth engagement provides strong empirical evidence that a young person's sense of efficacy and their engagement in social groups with social norms that support the acceptance of climate change are strong predictors of pro-climate change mitigation behaviors. In contrast, knowledge of climate change and certainty of climate science are weak to moderate predictors of pro-climate change mitigation behaviors. Busch's research and the genesis of CERBC both suggest that schooling should foster a sense of efficacy and the development of leadership skills, if cultivating pro-climate behaviors is the desired outcome of formal education systems.

We are advocating formal education systems not to shy away from focusing on teaching climate change in a meaningful way, but instead to see it as an opportunity for students to engage deeply in change-making processes. Since providing these opportunities may be antithetical to the

60 *Rupinder Kaur Grewal et al.*

ways most schooling typically functions (Aronowitz & Giroux, 1985, 1993; Giroux, 2018), we are not suggesting this will be easy. Still, this would foster conditions for youth to take leadership within their school environments, increasing student engagement, and creating the conditions in their learning environments that help attend to climate anxiety. Why should schools not be interventionist learning spaces that actively address our societal and environmental issues? We believe enough educators are, and will be, motivated by this possibility, that we will see rapid growth in the integration of climate justice into schooling in the coming years.

Activism in Education

Niblett (2017) makes a strong case for the use of activist education in schools and provides a robust pedagogical framework for educators who promote achievement, equity, and well-being. He argues that an essential task of activist education is to disrupt the social apathy that continues to infiltrate schools today. One way this can be achieved is by deliberately facilitating activist inquiry with activities that are "hands-on, minds-on, developmentally appropriate, and student-directed" (Niblett, 2017, p. 1). Activist education should incorporate three key components: environments, ideas, and actions to help youth see themselves as capable of effecting change for climate justice. Campigotto and Barrett (2017) also declare the need for more support, space, and time dedicated within pre-service programs where teacher candidates can learn about activist pedagogies. Teachers already working in schools alongside teacher candidates should implement justice frameworks to help prepare students for a more just and sustainable future. Students should not need to *leave schools* to gain education on climate justice and activism on their own.

Climate justice education must challenge teacher candidates, educators, and students alike to understand how boundaries of citizenship are negotiated and to create a space where youth activists and educators can co-construct knowledge together (McGregor & Christie, 2020). More specifically, climate justice education needs to challenge the normative, "neoliberal public pedagogy" that equates capitalism to the national interest. Again, this will not be easy in many schools. Kennelly (2009) writes about the relationship that exists between two roles of youth in Western countries—the "citizen" and the "activist." The term "citizen" embodies specific characteristics deemed desirable to the state, while being an "activist" is only sometimes seen as part of what makes a good citizen. Often, the activist is "demonized as an undesirable element undeserving of recognition," thus leading to an uneasy coexistence for youth who are navigating their relationship to the Canadian state (Kennelly, 2009, p. 128).

Bringing Climate Injustices to the Forefront   61

Indigenous, Black, and racialized youth underscore how their experiences within the Canadian school system reinforce the belief that they do not belong in the category of a "good citizen." This is because what constitutes good citizenship is deeply rooted in dominant discourses of normative liberal principles, which maintain race-based disadvantages (Kennelly, 2009). Therefore, the space which young activists navigate is restricted by nation-states that deem their expression of dissent to be threatening. This unfortunately reduces the potential for activists to generate a synergized effort to make real change happen. Consequently, how climate (in)justices are addressed in education needs to utilize collective deliberation between different stakeholders—educators, youth activists, and marginalized communities who experience these injustices first hand (Lowan-Trudeau, 2017b; McGregor & Christie, 2020). Damico et al. (2020) suggest that climate justice educators use three overlapping sets of "beneficial stories" which "emphasize Indigenous narratives of place, gender and climate justice, youth activism and civic engagement" (p. 686). By integrating the stories of marginalized groups and their important work, students will receive an enriched learning experience in schools that extends beyond the "facts" of climate science that are emphasized in traditional curricula.

Attending to Youth Well-Being

Employing critical race theory, Miller (2018) stated that although there is a growing commitment to creating more transformative learning experiences for *all* students in environmental education, there is still a large failure to uncover harmful discourses that exclude marginalized learners from equitable engagement in sustainability work. It would seem likely, then, that eco-anxiety and fear would also impact Black, Indigenous, and racialized youths' mental health. However, as Jaquette-Ray (2021) argues in *Scientific American*, eco-anxiety is predominantly a white phenomenon, trying to uphold the privileges that white communities have had for decades before recognizing the real impacts of climate change. Still, this suggests that educators may need to support and attend to the well-being of Black, Indigenous, and racialized students, specifically, as they contend with double oppression—racism *and* disproportionate climate change impacts. Mackay et al. (2020) note, however, that climate activism can be an antidote for Black, Indigenous, and racialized youth to "engage with their networks and culture, which in turn may have positive benefits to their well-being" (p. 2).

While having conversations with family and friends, students who are continually fighting for climate justice within their communities are also taking on this fight *within* themselves on an emotional and psychological level (Trott, 2021). Activism may help young people to develop a sense of agency and resiliency to counter their rising distress. In other words,

62 *Rupinder Kaur Grewal et al.*

students must be able to see themselves as capable of contributing to the transgressive change that is necessary for true climate justice. The collective, everyday actions of youth in the climate justice movement, thus, can stimulate a powerful and diffuse ripple effect—it is now time for those stories to move off social media and to be taken up by education policymakers, administrators, and teachers.

Future Directions

Understanding the implications of what *climate justice*, itself, entails, the impact and importance of youth activism, and recognizing how education can help to further the cause of equity and decolonization, provide an important lens for what needs to happen next in the climate change education field. As Klein (2019) asserts:

> Overcoming these disconnections, strengthening the threads tying together our various issues and movements are, I would argue, the most pressing task of anyone concerned with social and economic justice. It is the only way to build a counterpower sufficiently robust to win against the forces protecting the highly profitable but increasingly untenable status quo. Climate change acts as an accelerant to many of our social ills (inequality, wars, racism, sexual violence), but it can also be an accelerant for the opposite, for the forces working for economic and social justice.
>
> (p. 187)

Formal education systems can play an important role in educating children and youth, which also passes through to parents and family members (Lawson et al., 2019). Formal education can help foster leadership and efficacy and attenuate youth climate anxiety; however, how education structures engage with the type of transformative and transgressive learning that is required remains an open question:

> Rather than working to simply service this impoverished future narrative, we need education institutions that can help us to work out what intelligence and wisdom mean ... We need education institutions that can teach us how to create, draw upon and steward collective knowledge resources. We need educational institutions that can build intergenerational [and climate just] solidarity in a time of unsettled relationship between generations. We need educational institutions that are capable of nurturing the capacity for democracy and debate that will allow us to ensure that social and political justice are at the heart of the socio-[enviro]-technical futures we are building.
>
> (Facer, 2011, p. 103)

Bringing Climate Injustices to the Forefront 63

From the limited amount of research specifically dedicated to climate *justice* education, the emerging findings include a need for more professional development, educational policies, and research to be conducted on this topic to help meaningfully transform the climate change education terrain. We should not, though, wait before learning lessons from the youth climate justice movement and implementing them into schooling at every opportunity.

References

Adam, K., & Siddiqui, F. (2015, November 29). Climate change protests take place around the world on eve of summit. *The Washington Post*. https://www.washingtonpost.com/world/climate-change-protests-take-place-around-the-world-on-eve-of-summit/2015/11/29/9172b6ca-9530-11e5-befa-99ceebcbb272_story.html

Andersson, E. & Öhman, J. (2016). Young people's conversations about environmental and sustainability issues in social media. *Environmental Education Research*, *23*(4), 465–485. https://doi.org/10.1080/13504622.2016.1149551

Aronowitz, S., & Giroux, H.A. (1985). *Education under siege: The conservative, liberal and radical debate over schooling*. Routledge. https://doi.org/10.4324/9780203222034

Aronowitz, S., & Giroux, H. (1993). *Education still under siege* (2nd ed.). Bergin and Garvey.

Bandura, A., & Cherry, L. (2020). Enlisting the power of youth for climate change. *The American Psychologist*, *75*(7), 945–951.https://doi.org/10.1037/amp0000512

Beeler, C. (2019, October 10). How did teen climate activist Greta Thunberg rise to fame so quickly? *The World*. https://www.pri.org/stories/2019-10-10/how-did-teen-climate-activist-greta-thunberg-rise-fame-so-quickly

Bhattacharya, D., Carroll Steward, K., & Forbes, T. (2020). Empirical research on K-16 climate education: A systematic review of the literature. *Journal of Geoscience Education*. https://doi.org/10.1080/10899995.2020.1838848

Birrell, I. (2019, April). Greta Thunberg teaches us about autism as much as climate change. *The Guardian*. https://www.theguardian.com/commentisfree/2019/apr/23/greta-thunberg-autism

Biswas, T., & Mattheis, N. (2021). Strikingly educational: A childist perspective on children's civil disobedience for climate justice. *Educational Philosophy and Theory*, 1–14. https://doi.org/10.1080/00131857.2021.1880390

Blum, N., Nazir, J., Breiting, S., Goh, K.C., & Pedretti, E. (2013). Balancing the tensions and meeting the conceptual challenges of education for sustainable development and climate change. *Environmental Education Research*, *19*(2), 206–217. https://doi.org/10.1080/13504622.2013.780588

Boon, H.J. (2010). Climate change? Who knows? A comparison of secondary students and pre-service teachers. *Australian Journal of Teacher Education*, *35*, 104–120.

Bowman, B. (2020a, August 28). Fridays for Future: How the young climate movement has grown since Greta Thunberg's lone protest. *The Conversation*. https://theconversation.com/fridays-for-future-how-the-young-climate-movement-has-grown-since-greta-thunbergs-lone-protest-144781

64 *Rupinder Kaur Grewal et al.*

Bowman, B. (2020b). 'They don't quite understand the importance of what we are doing today': The people's climate strikes as subaltern activism. *Sustainable Earth, 3*(16). https://sustainableearth.biomedcentral.com/articles/10.1186/s42055-020-00038-x

Braine, T. (2019, December 10). Youth climate activist Greta Thunberg directs media attention elsewhere. *New York Daily News.* https://www.nydailynews.com/news/world/ny-climate-activist-greta-thunberg-media-attention-change-20191210-apt5o7eb6zfjzp3fxbr6b2f4qu-story.html

Bruno, K., Karliner, J., & Brotsky, C. (1999). Greenhouse gangsters vs. Climate justice. *Transnational Resource & Action Center.* http://www.corpwatch.org/sites/default/files/Greenhouse%20Gangsters.pdf

Burke, S., Sanson, A., & Van Hoorn, J. (2018). The psychological effects of climate change on children. *Current Psychiatry Reports, 20*(5), 1–8.

Burton, N. (2019, October 11). Meet the young activists of color who are leading the charge against climate disaster. *Vox.* https://www.vox.com/identities/2019/10/11/20904791/young-climate-activists-of-color

Burton, N. (2020, May 14). People of color experience climate grief more deeply than white people. *Vice.* https://www.vice.com/en_us/article/v7ggqx/people-of-color-experience-climate-grief-more-deeply-than-white-people

Busch, K.C., Ardoin, N., Gruehn, D., & Stevenson, K. (2019). Exploring a theoretical model of climate change action for youth. *International Journal of Science Education, 41*(17), 2389–2409.

Campigotto, R., & Barrett, S.E. (2017). Creating space for teacher activism in environmental education: Pre-service teachers' experiences. *Canadian Journal of Environmental Education, 22*(1), 42–57.

Chawla, L., & Cushing, D.F. (2007). Education for strategic environmental behavior. *Environmental Education Research, 13*(4), 437–452. https://doi.org/10.1080/13504620701581539

Cho, R. (2017). Everything is connected - Climate justice in the classroom. *British Columbia Teachers' Federation Magazine, 29*(3). https://www.bctf.ca/publications/TeacherArticle.aspx?id=44527

Clayton, S. (2020). Climate anxiety: Psychological responses to climate change. *Journal of Anxiety Disorders, 74*(102263), 1–7. https://doi.org/10.1016/j.janxdis.2020.102263

Climate Education Reform British Columbia. (2021). *Reform to Transform campaign.* https://www.climateeducationreformbc.ca/

Climate Emergency Declarations. (2021, May 4). *Climate emergency declarations in 1,935 jurisdictions and local governments cover 826 million citizens.* https://climateemergencydeclaration.org/climate-emergency-declarations-cover-15-million-citizens/

Climate Strike. (2016, March 1). Climate Strike 2015: Students skip school demanding climate actions [Video]. *Youtube.* https://www.youtube.com/watch?v=0GjdVgGfcb8

Corner, A., Roberts, O., Chiari, S., Voller, S., Mayrhuber, E., Mandl, S., & Monson, K. (2015). How do young people engage with climate change? The role of knowledge, values, message framing, and trusted communicators. *WIREs Climate Change, 6*(5), 523–534.

Crawford, T. (2020, December 19). COVID-19 may have halted massive protests, but youth are taking their fight for the future to the courts. *Vancouver Sun.* https://vancouversun.com/news/covid-19-may-have-halted-massive-protests-but-youth-are-taking-their-fight-for-the-future-to-the-courts

Cutter-Mackenzie, A., & Rousell, D. (2019). Education for what? Shaping the field of climate change education with children and young people as co-researchers. *Children's Geographies, 17*(1), 90–104. https://doi.org/10.1080/14733285.2018.1467556

Dahir, A.L. (2021, May 7). Erased from a Davos photo, a Ugandan climate activist is back in the picture. *The New York Times.* https://www.nytimes.com/2021/05/07/world/africa/vanessa-nakate-climate-change-uganda.html

Damico, J.S., Baildon, M., & Panos, A. (2020). Climate justice literacy: Stories-we-live-by, Ecolinguistics, and classroom practice. *Journal of Adolescent & Adult Literacy, 63*(6), 683–691. https://doi.org/10.1002/jaal.1051

Davenport, C., Friedman, L., & Sengupta, S. (2021, May 4). Biden's intelligence director vows to put climate at 'center' of foreign policy. *The New York Times.* https://www.nytimes.com/live/2021/04/22/us/biden-earth-day-climate-summit

Democracy Now! (2011, December 9). "Get It Done": Urging climate justice, Youth Delegate Anjali Appadurai mic-checks UN Summit [Video]. *Youtube.* https://www.youtube.com/watch?v=Ko3e6G_7GY4

Denchak, M. (2021, February 19). Paris climate agreement: Everything you need to know. *NRDC.* https://www.nrdc.org/stories/paris-climate-agreement-everything-you-need-know

Dhillon, J. (2018). Introduction: Indigenous resurgence, decolonization, and movements for environmental justice. *Environment and Society, 9*(1), 1–5. https://doi.org/10.3167/ares.2018.090101

Etchart, L. (2017). The role of indigenous peoples in combating climate change. *Palgrave Communications, 3,* 17085. https://doi.org/10.1057/palcomms.2017.85

Evelyn, K. (2020, January 29). 'Like I wasn't there': Climate activist Vanessa Nakate on being erased from a movement. *The Guardian.* https://www.theguardian.com/world/2020/jan/29/vanessa-nakate-interview-climate-activism-cropped-photo-davos

Facer, K. (2011). *Learning futures: Education, technology and social change.* Routledge.

Feller, M. (2019, September 17). What you need to know about the global climate strike. *Elle.* https://www.elle.com/culture/career-politics/a28985212/global-climate-strike-details-dates/

Field, E. (2017). Climate change: Imagining, negotiating, and co-creating future(s) with children and youth. *Curriculum Perspectives, 37*(1), 83–89. https://doi.org/10.1007/s41297-017-0013-y

Field, E. (2021). Is it all just emojis and lol: Or can social media foster environmental learning and activism? In M. Hoechsmann, P.R. Carr, & G. Thesee (Eds.), *Education for democracy 2.0: Changing frames of media literacy* (pp. 198–220). Brill/Sense Publishers.

Field, E., Schwartzberg, P. & Berger, P. (2019). *Canada, Climate Change and Education: Opportunities for Public and Formal Education* (Formal Report for Learning for a Sustainable Future). http://www.LSF-LST.ca/cc-survey

Field, E., Schwartzberg, P., Berger, P. (2020). How should climate change be taught in schools? *Ed Can Network Facts on Education.* https://www.edcan.ca/articles/climate-change/

Folkets Klimamarch København. (2019). Folkets Klimamarch København 2019: Event Description. https://www.klimamarchkbh.com/event-beskrivelse

66 *Rupinder Kaur Grewal et al.*

Gerretsen, I. (2021, April 23). How youth climate court cases became a global trend. Climate News. *Climate Home News.* https://www.climatechangenews.com/2021/04/30/youth-climate-court-cases-became-global-trend/

Gill, A. (2015, November 13). Farmer sues Pakistan's government to demand action on climate change. *Reuters.* https://www.reuters.com/article/pakistan-climatechange-lawsuit-idUSL8N1383YJ20151113

Giroux, H.A. (2018). *Terror of neoliberalism: Authoritarianism and the eclipse of democracy.* Routledge.

Green, M. (2019, October 30). Climate protesters occupy Pelosi's office over California fires. *The Hill.* https://thehill.com/policy/energy-environment/468140-climate-protestors-occupy-pelosi-office-over-california-fires

Haluza-DeLay, R. (2009). Introduction: Uncovering Canada's environmental cultural politics. *International Journal of Canadian Studies, 39,* 40.

Haluza-DeLay, R. (2013). Environmental justice and environmental education research. In R. Stevenson, M. Brody, J. Dillon, & A. Wals (Eds.), *International handbook on environmental education research* (pp. 394–403). Routledge.

Han, H., & Ahn, S.W. (2020). Youth mobilization to stop global climate change: Narratives and impact. *Sustainability, 12*(10), 4127. https://doi.org/10.3390/su12104127

Hargis, K., & McKenzie, M. (2020). *Responding to Climate Change: A Primer for K-12 Education.* Saskatoon, Canada: The Sustainability and Education Policy Network. https://sepn.ca/resources/report-responding-to-climate-change-education-a-primer-for-k-12-education/

Haynes, S. (2019, March 20). 'It's literally our future.' Here's what youth climate strikers around the world are planning next. *TIME.* https://time.com/5554775/youth-school-climate-change-strike-action/

Henderson, J., Long, D., Berger, P., Russell, C., & Drewes, A. (2017). Expanding the foundation: Climate change and opportunities for educational research. *Educational Studies,* 1–13. https://www.tandfonline.com/doi/full/10.1080/00131946.2017.1335640

Holmberg, A., & Alvinius, A. (2020). Children's protest in relation to the climate emergency: A qualitative study on a new form of resistance promoting political and social change. *Childhood, 27*(1), 78–92. https://doi.org/10.1177/0907568219879970

Intergovernmental Panel on Climate Change. (2018). Special report: Global warming of 1.5°C. https://www.ipcc.ch/sr15/

Janfaza, R. (2020, January 3). 9 climate activists of color you should know. *Teen Vogue.* https://www.teenvogue.com/story/youth-climate-activists-of-color

Jaquette-Ray, S. (2021). Climate anxiety is an overwhelmingly white phenomenon. *Scientific American.* https://www.scientificamerican.com/article/the-unbearable-whiteness-of-climate-anxiety/

Kallestrup, C., & Eller, E. (2019, June 12). Forskerne har talte: Ja, det blev et klimavalg (The researchers have spoken: Yes, it was a climate election). *DR.* https://www.dr.dk/nyheder/politik/folketingsvalg/forskerne-har-talt-ja-det-blev-et-klimavalg

Kanbur, R. (2018). Education for climate justice. *Review of Development and Change, 23*(1), 107–121. https://doi.org/10.1177/0972266120180105

Bringing Climate Injustices to the Forefront 67

Karsgaard, C., & Davidson, D. (2021). Must we wait for youth to speak out before we listen? International youth perspectives and climate change education. *Educational Review*, 1–19. https://doi.org/10.1080/00131911.2021.1905611

Kelsey, E. (2020). *Hope matters: Why changing the way we think is critical to solving the environmental crisis.* Greystone Books & David Suzuki Institute.

Kennelly, J. (2009). Good citizen/bad activist: The cultural role of the state in youth activism. *The Review of Education, Pedagogy, and Cultural Studies, 31*(2–3), 127–149. https://doi.org/10.1080/10714410902827135

Klein, N. (2014). *This changes everything: Capitalism vs. the climate.* Simon & Schuster.

Klein, N. (2019). *On fire: The burning case for a green new deal.* Knopf Canada.

Kleres, J., & Wettergren, Å. (2017). Fear, hope, anger, and guilt in climate activism. *Social Movement Studies, 16*(5), 507–519. https://doi.org/10.1080/147428 37.2017.1344546

Kwauk, C. & Casey, O. (2021). *A new green learning agenda: Approaches to quality education for climate action.* Centre for Universal Education at Brookings. https://www.brookings.edu/wp-content/uploads/2021/01/Brookings-Green-Learning-FINAL.pdf

Labour Press Release. (2019). *Jeremy Corbyn declares environment and climate emergency.* https://labour.org.uk/press/jeremy-corbyn-declares-environment-climate-emergency/

Læssøe, J., Schnack, K., Breiting, S., & Rolls, S. (2009). Climate change and sustainable development: The response from education. *International Alliance of Leading Education Institutions.* http://edu.au.dk/fileadmin/www.dpu.dk/en/research/researchprogrammes/environmentalandhealtheducation/om-dpu_institutter_institut-for-didaktik_20091208102732_cross_national-report_dec09.pdf

Lawson, D.F., Stevenson, K.T., Peterson, M.N., Carrier, S.J., Strnad, R.L., & Seekamp, E. (2019). Children can foster climate change concern among their parents. *Nature Climate Change, 9*(6), 458–462.

Leaders' Summit on Climate. (2021). [EN] Leaders summit on climate - Day 1 [Video]. *Youtube.* https://www.youtube.com/watch?v=6xa7yyypznY&t=10233s

Lehtonen, A., Salonen, A., & Cantell, H. (2019). Climate change education: A new approach for a world of wicked problems. In J.W. Cook (Ed.) *Sustainability, human well-being, and the future of education* (pp. 339–374). Springer. https://doi.org/10.1007/978-3-319-78580-6_11

Libardi, M. (2020, September 16). Amazon heroes who don't give up. *Open Democracy.* https://www.opendemocracy.net/en/democraciaabierta/guardians-of-the-forest-heroes-who-dont-give-up/

Lombrana, L.M. (2021, May 17). Teenagers are winning climate fights one court case at a time. *Bloomberg Green.* https://www.bloomberg.com/news/articles/2021-05-17/teenagers-are-winning-climate-fights-one-court-case-at-a-time

Lowan-Trudeau, G. (2017a). Gateway to understanding: Indigenous ecological activism and education in urban, rural, and remote contexts. *Cultural Studies of Science Education, 12*(1), 119–128.

Lowan-Trudeau, G. (2017b). Protest as pedagogy: Exploring teaching and learning in Indigenous environmental movements. *The Journal of Environmental Education, 48*(2), 96–108.

68 *Rupinder Kaur Grewal et al.*

MacKay, M., Parlee, B., & Karsgaard, C. (2020). Youth engagement in climate change action: Case study on Indigenous youth at COP24. *Sustainability, 12*(16), 6299. https://doi.org/10.3390/su12166299

Malowa, V., Owor, A., Merissa, E., Lado, S., & Mayelle, H. (2020, January 31). The erasure of Vanessa Nakate portrays an idealized climate activism. *Africa at LSE,* 1–8. https://blogs.lse.ac.uk/africaatlse/2020/01/31/vanessa-nakate-davos-cropped-photo-white-race-climate-activism/

Manni, A., & Knekta, E. (2020). 'A little less conversation, a little more action please': Examining students' voices on education, transgression, and societal change. *Sustainability, 12*(15). https://doi.org/10.3390/su12156231

Marris, E. (2019, September 18). Why young climate activists have captured the world's attention. *Nature, 573,* 471–472. https://doi.org/10.1038/d41586-019-02696-0

McFadden, C. (2020, December 29). Vanessa Nakate and perceptions of black student activists. *Journal of Sustainability Education General Issue, 24,* 1–3. http://www.susted.com/wordpress/content/vanessa-nakate-and-perceptions-of-black-student-activists_2020_12/

McGregor, C., & Christie, B. (2020). Towards climate justice education: Views from activists and educators in Scotland. *Environmental Education Research,* 1–17. https://doi.org/10.1080/13504622.2020.1865881

McGregor, C., Scandrett, E., Christie, B., & Crowther, J. (2018). Climate justice education: From social movement learning to schooling. In T. Jafry (Ed.), *Routledge handbook of climate justice* (pp. 494–508). Routledge.

McKenzie, M. (2021). Climate change education and communication in global review: Tracking progress through national submissions to the UNFCCC Secretariat. *Environmental Education Research,* 1–20. https://doi.org/10.1080/13504622.2021.1903838

McKenzie, M., Koushik, J.R., Haluza-DeLay, R., Chin, B., & Corwin, J. (2017). Environmental justice. In A. Russ & M. Krasny (Eds.), *Urban environmental education review* (pp. 59–67). Cornell University Press.

McKibben, B. (2017). Climate justice is racial justice is gender justice: Interview with Jacqueline Patterson. *YES Magazine.* http://www.yesmagazine.org/issues/just-transition/climate-justice-is-racial-justice-is-gender-justice-20170818

McIntyre, J. (2019, September 25). With 15 other children, Greta Thunberg has filed a UN complaint against 5 countries. Here's what it'll achieve. *The Conversation.* https://theconversation.com/with-15-other-children-greta-thunberg-has-filed-a-un-complaint-against-5-countries-heres-what-itll-achieve-124090

Miller, H.K. (2018). Developing a critical consciousness of race in place-based environmental education: Franco's story. *Environmental Education Research, 24*(6), 845–858.

Mitchell, K., & D'Onofrio, Z. (2016). Environmental injustice and racism in Canada: The first step is admitting we have a problem. *Journal of Environmental Law and Practice, 29,* 305–345.

Monroe, M.C., Plate, R.R., Oxarart, A., Bowers, A., & Chaves, W.A. (2019). Identifying effective climate change education strategies: A systematic review of the research. *Environmental Education Research, 25*(6), 791–812. https://doi.org/10.1080/13504622.2017.1360842

Munro, K. (2009, July 11). Climate warriors march behind little green book. *The Sydney Morning Herald.* https://www.smh.com.au/environment/climate-change/climate-warriors-march-behind-little-green-book-20090710-dg2t.html

Nairn, K. (2019). Learning from young people engaged in climate activism: The potential of collectivizing despair and hope. *Young, 27*(5), 435–450.

Niblett, B. (2017). Facilitating activist education: Social and environmental justice in classroom practice to promote achievement, equity, and well-being. *What Works? Research into Practice, Research monograph #66.* http://www.edu.gov. on.ca/eng/literacynumeracy/inspire/research/tips_activist_educators.html

Noisecat, J.B. (2020, July 20). Joe Biden has endorsed the Green New Deal in all but name. *The Guardian.* https://www.theguardian.com/commentis-free/2020/jul/20/joe-biden-has-endorsed-the-green-new-deal-in-all-but-name

NPR (2020, May 22). Xiye Bastida: How are young people making the choice to fight climate change? https://www.npr.org/2020/05/22/860168455/xiye-bastida-how-are-young-people-making-the-choice-to-fight-climate-change

Ojala, M. (2012). How do children cope with global climate change? Coping strategies, engagement, and well-being. *Journal of Environmental Psychology, 32*(3), 225–233.

Ojala, M. (2013). Coping with climate change among adolescents: Implications for subjective well-being and environmental engagement. *Sustainability, 5*(5), 2191–2209.

O'Neill, S., & Nicholson-Cole, S. (2009). "Fear won't do it": Promoting positive engagement with climate change through visual and iconic representations. *ScienceCommunication, 30*(3),355–379.https://doi.org/10.1177/1075547008329201

Parker, L. (2019). Kids suing governments about climate: It's a global trend. *National Geographic.* https://www.nationalgeographic.com/environment/article/kids-suing-governments-about-climate-growing-trend

Phipps, C., Vaughan, A., & Milman, O. (2015, November 29). Global climate march 2015: hundreds of thousands march around the world – as it happened. *The Guardian.* https://www.theguardian.com/environment/live/2015/nov/29/global-peoples-climate-change-march-2015-day-of-action-live

Plutzer, E., McCaffrey, M., Hannah, A. L., Rosenau, J., Berbeco, M., & Reid, A. H. (2016). Climate confusion among US teachers. *Science, 351*(6274), 664–665.

Rafaely, D., & Barnes, B. (2020). African climate activism, media and the denial of racism: The tacit silencing of Vanessa Nakate. *Community Psychology in Global Perspective, 6*(2/2), 71–86.

Reid, A. (2019). Climate change education and research: Possibilities and potentials versus problems and perils. *Environmental Education Research, 25*(6), 767–790. https://doi.org/10.1080/13504622.2019.1664075

Robinson, M. (2018). *Climate justice: Hope, resilience, and the fight for a sustainable future.* Bloomsbury.

Rodriguez, L., & Gralki, P. (2020, June 5). *New Jersey is now the 1st US state to require schools to teach climate change.* Global Citizen. https://www.globalcitizen.org/en/content/nj-introduces-climate-change-curriculum-schools/

Sabherwal, A., Ballew, M.T., van Der Linden, S., Gustafson, A., Goldberg, M.H., Maibach, E.W., ... Leiserowitz, A. (2021). The Greta Thunberg Effect: Familiarity with Greta Thunberg predicts intentions to engage in climate activism in the United States. *Journal of Applied Social Psychology, 51*(4), 321–333.

Schlosberg, D., & Collins, L.B. (2014). From environmental to climate justice: Climate change and the discourse of environmental justice. *WIREs Climate Change, 5,* 359–374. https://doi.org/10.1002/wcc.275

70 *Rupinder Kaur Grewal et al.*

Setzer, J., & Byrnes, R. (2020). *Global trends in climate change litigation: 2020 snapshot*. Grantham Research Institute on Climate Change and the Environment. https://www.lse.ac.uk/granthaminstitute/wp-content/uploads/2020/07/Global-trends-in-climate-change-litigation_2020-snapshot.pdf

Stapleton, S.R. (2019). A case for climate justice education: American youth connecting to intragenerational climate injustice in Bangladesh. *Environmental Education Research, 25*(5), 732–750.

Stephens, S. (1996). Reflections on environmental justice: Children as victims and actors. *Social Justice, 23*(4 (66)), 62–86. http://www.jstor.org/stable/29766975

Stevenson, B., with Stirling, C. (2010). Environmental learning and agency in diverse educational and cultural contexts. In Robert B. Stevenson, and Justin Dillon (Eds.), *Engaging environmental education: Learning, culture and agency* (pp. 219–237). Rotterdam, The Netherlands: Sense Publishers.

Sunrise Movement (2021). *Who we are: About the Sunrise Movement*. https://www.sunrisemovement.org/about/

Taylor, V. (2021, April 23). How youth climate activists pushed through the pandemic. *Mic*. https://www.mic.com/p/how-youth-climate-activists-pushed-through-the-pandemic-73847086

Teach the Future. (2021). *Prepare students for tomorrow, teach the future today*. https://www.teachthefuture.org/

Thew, H., Middlemiss, L., & Paavola, J. (2020). "Youth is not a political position": Exploring justice claims-making in the UN climate change negotiations. *Global Environmental Change, 61*, 102036.

Thunberg, G. (2019). *No one is too small to make a difference*. Penguin Books.

Timperley, J. (2020, July 7). The law that could make climate change illegal. *BBC Future Planet*. https://www.bbc.com/future/article/20200706-the-law-that-could-make-climate-change-illegal

Trott, C.D. (2021). What difference does it make? Exploring the transformative potential of everyday climate crisis activism by children and youth. *Children's Geographies*, 1–9. https://doi.org/10.1080/14733285.2020.1870663

Trott, C.D., Rockett, M.L., Gray, E.S., Lam, S., Even, T.L., & Frame, S.M. (2020). "Another Haiti starting from the youth": Integrating the arts and sciences for empowering youth climate justice action in Jacmel, Haiti. *Community Psychology in Global Perspective, 6*(2/2), 48–70. https://doi.org/10.1285/i24212113v6i2-2p48

Tuck, E., & Yang, K.W. (Eds.). (2018). *Toward what justice? Describing diverse dreams of justice education*. Routledge.

United Nations Convention on the Rights of the Child [UNCRC]. (1989, November 20). United Nations human rights office of the high commissioner. https://www.ohchr.org/en/professionalinterest/pages/crc.aspx

Waldron, F., Ruane, B., Oberman, R., & Morris, S. (2019). Geographical process or global injustice? Contrasting educational perspectives on climate change. *Environmental Education Research, 25*(6), 895–911. https://doi.org/10.1080/13504622.2016.1255876

Wynes, S., & Nicholas, K.A. (2019). Climate science curricula in Canadian secondary schools focus on human warming, not scientific consensus, impacts or solutions. *PloS One, 14*(7). https://doi.org/10.1371/journal.pone.0218305

2 Psychological Perspectives of Climate Equity

Reducing Abstraction and Distance through Engaged Empathy

Ananya M. Matewos, Benjamin Torsney, and Doug Lombardi

Wildfires, flooding, extreme weather storms, droughts and the subsequent water shortages; each of these environmental crises, among many others, can be tied to the impact of human-induced climate change. For many people around the world, the mental stress of the existential questions associated with the changing climate—solastalgia—has taken hold, leading to hopelessness, fear, and significant amounts of anxiety. Over-consumption of natural resources (e.g., deforestation) to burning fossil fuels contribute heavily to atmospheric carbon levels and rising average global temperatures. Ultimately those with the economic capital to overconsume resources and who are also not immediately threatened by climate-related disasters, contribute heavily to making parts of the planet uninhabitable in both the short and long term.

Many of these environmental crises have already impacted places that can least afford to mitigate those damages, making climate change an issue of global equity, policy change, and cooperative action. For example, Hurricane Dorian, a category 5 storm in 2019, resulted in the loss of many lives in the Bahamas and prompted a crisis of eco-refugees, creating political strain across global borders and which cost an estimated $3.4 billion in damage (Deopersad et al., 2020). The climate inequities do not just exist between nations, the rich and poor, but also between generations. For those in the younger generations around the world, the potential loss of a habitable planet has prompted widespread protests and demands for changes in national policies and international cooperation (e.g., Greta Thunberg's climate activism) (Bandura & Cherry, 2019).

Although climate change has already begun impacting livability across the planet, there are populations of people in wealthier countries who either do not believe in climate change occurring at all, do not accept that it is human induced, or do not believe that climate change can have a direct impact on the survival of the human race. Regardless of beliefs, people around the world are increasingly affected in disproportionate and different ways, where the poorest and most vulnerable

DOI: 10.4324/9780429326011-4

among us with the smallest carbon footprint, those who have done the least to contribute to the problem, are most impacted. This phenomenon can be seen very clearly in the case of the Bahamas, or other island nations like the Maldives and the Marshall Islands. One of the more egregious examples of environmental inequity and injustice can be found right in the USA. A study found 94% of 108 US cities within historically redlined districts in the country have hotter surface temperatures than other sites, due to higher levels of industrialization, more roadways, buildings, and de-greening (lack of tree canopy) (Hoffman, Shandas, & Pendleton, 2020). *Undoubtedly, climate change is fundamentally an issue of equity and justice.*

Further complicating the issue is the publicly confusing discourse around whether individual actions have any real impact in creating environmental progress. Some have argued that systemic change is the only way to mitigate our current situation. However, other researchers are pushing back, arguing in fact that for wealthy individuals in wealthy countries, the negative impact of individual choices is quite high. These carbon elite individuals participate in some of the highest carbon consumption practices to maintain their present lives, where two-thirds of global climate pollution can be attributed to household consumption and activity. In short, the richest 10% in the world (making more than $38,000) are responsible for around half of the carbon emissions (UNEP Emissions Gap Report, 2020).

These wealthier individuals must make choices to offset their own living, and to do so they may need to see past themselves (e.g., via large carbon offsets) so that they may help others who are not in a position to do so for a variety of equity-related reasons. In fact, many face appreciable barriers to making sustainable choices. For example, individuals in the USA living in food deserts do not have access to all the nutritious, plant based, high quality, whole foods that many wealthier individuals can routinely procure (Walker, Keane, & Burke, 2010). So not only would those living in food deserts have to spend more money (which they may not even have depending on the population), they would also have to travel further, thus negating the efforts of eating plant-based food. This is even if they plan to travel for this food at all.

Part of what makes climate change so difficult to act on is that there are significant conceptual and motivational barriers to pro-environmental behaviors. Although individual actions are necessary to address global climate issues (e.g., flying less, driving less, eating a plant-based diet), the consequences of individual actions have no immediate visible impact, and furthermore, humans are aware that even if one person makes positive changes, another person's over-consumption habits may negate those positive shifts (Wynes & Nicholas, 2017). In other words, *Why should I work to change my behavior if my neighbor could not care less about theirs?* However, we do know that people are social learners, and often mirror the actions of those in their lives that they trust (Bandura, 1977),

Psychological Perspectives of Climate Equity   73

thus one person's pro-environmental behavior could represent actions that help others to shift toward more sustainable living.

It is imperative that all countries, especially industrialized ones (i.e., the countries with the largest carbon footprint), have an educated and engaged global public, which may require a people to exhibit a greater degree of empathy. Having an educated citizenry is essential for increased shifts in individual pro-environmental choices. An empathetic person is able to understand the challenges of others, and take actions to reduce the overall burden facing everyone, even if it means taking on more personal cost and effort. Finally, an engaged person is not only doing their individual part to create change, but pushing for public change through activism and policy (both local and global) to advance systemic practices and priorities.

This chapter characterizes cognitive barriers, which may limit people's ability to accept human-induced climate change, and motivational barriers, which may prevent people from working towards climate change action and considering how climate change affects others not in their immediate environment. By understanding these challenges, we can create educational efforts and public learning interventions that can target those challenges directly.

Barriers to Learning about Climate Equity Issues

In their seminal conceptual review, Sinatra, Kienhues, and Hofer (2014b) identified epistemic cognition (the thinking, emotional, and motivational processes associated with knowledge acquisition and construction), motivated reasoning (motivations and goals that may bias thinking), and conceptual change (reconstruction of mental conceptualizations of phenomena and events) to be three major categories of challenges to the public understanding of science broadly. These challenges may make it nearly impossible for many to take any sort of meaningful action or to create progress on a topic that is misunderstood. For example, many may have difficulty understanding the climate crisis because it requires fundamental (i.e., how climate works around the world) and integrative knowledge across domains of science and complex systems (i.e., understanding that changes in climate come from changes in the whole earth system). Going even a level further, understanding the *socioscientific* impacts of a changing climate requires an individual to have a complex understanding of not only earth sciences, but also social sciences and economics. As new ideas are introduced that run counter to a learner's preexisting mental representations and beliefs, they may require *knowledge reconstruction* in order to reach an understanding of the present accepted consensus on these issues. Further, many preexisting mental representations may be inconsistent with scientific understandings and notions of social justice, and are often resistant to change (Chi, 2005, 2013).

Students today are also faced with an overflow of information from multiple sources and representations, resulting in the need to make

74   *Ananya M. Matewos et al.*

judgments about vast amounts of information in terms of its relevance, reliability, accuracy (Ferguson, Bråten, and Strømsø, 2012), and its potential impact on one's group affiliation. In such situations, students are having to form critical judgments and evaluations regarding what even constitutes knowledge or knowing, which psychologists broadly refer to as *epistemic cognition*. When confronted with competing claims, epistemic cognition is central to processing and integrating new knowledge with prior knowledge into coherent models of representation (Bråten et al., 2011).

As individuals process complex information, their values, attitudes, emotions, and beliefs converge to form unconscious biases and mental shortcuts: heuristics (Tversky & Kahneman, 1974). As such, humans are prone to *motivated reasoning*, which may interfere with conceptual understanding of evidence and its relation to new knowledge. Although individuals believe themselves to be rational, when making decisions, justifying stances, and weighing evidence, their motivations bias what information they attend to and what strategies they use to evaluate that information to form judgments. When it comes to controversial topics, such as equity issues pertaining to climate change, motivated reasoning is particularly relevant, as learners are confronted with conflicting claims and evidence (Sinatra & Seyranian, 2015). For example, most people exert extra cognitive effort to recall information they can use to refute an argument that threatens their existing ideological stance but will also suppress knowledge that contradicts a belief they prefer to hold.

Whereas knowledge reconstruction and epistemic cognition are foundational to developing a knowledgeable global public, motivated reasoning in particular is central to understanding the barriers of learning that continue to polarize societies in wealthy nations, feeding into the many controversial narratives that continue to prevent unifying policies and actions around equitable long-term solutions for climate change.

Motivated Reasoning

Motivated reasoning often stems from goals that are either accuracy driven or directionally driven (Kunda, 1990). Accuracy-driven goals require significant cognitive effort and careful reflection in order to weigh information from both sides of an issue. Directionally driven goals are pre-inclined to reach a certain conclusion, making this approach more prone to using mental shortcuts and heuristics, which could increase one's potential for cognitive biases (Kunda, 1990). Being accuracy or directionally driven on a given topic is determined and influenced by an individual's values, beliefs, social identity, message source, or framing. Many of these factors can jointly influence an individual's overall motivations for processing messages about climate change and simultaneously climate equity.

Psychological Perspectives of Climate Equity   75

The state of an individual's cognitive schema (mental patterns of thoughts and behaviors) around certain knowledge types can be seen in their values, attitudes, and beliefs about certain phenomena. And depending on the state of that individual's schemas, this person may be more or less motivated to change their conceptions and reconstruct their knowledge of a given phenomenon. In general, humans seek to balance and align their environmental stimuli with their own values, attitudes, and beliefs—learned from that environment—in order to maintain continuity with the same cognitive schemas and knowledge structures as they did before (Ajzen, 1991), because if the stimuli coming from one's environment changed, a person might encounter problems processing these new stimuli. The constant updating and refining of schemata is part of what makes learning a challenging process in general, as it may require some cognitive dissonance as it takes strategic effort to shift these fairly stable cognitive constructs (Limón, 2001).

More transient, but also necessary to facilitate, are emotions, as they affect both reasoning and learning processes, and interact with values, attitudes, and beliefs in varying ways. Negative emotions in particular may impact learning outcomes for particularly controversial topics (Heddy et al., 2017), such as climate change which includes knowledge construction around both scientific and social justice related issues. For example, if messages from home are consistent about not heeding climate change and its global impacts as real phenomena, learners will be inclined to experience negative emotions when engaging in climate related discourse at school, and likely to disengage and not trust new scientific evidence.

Values and Attitudes

Values are the sustained individual standards and socio-culturally expected behaviors derived from instrumental relations and outcomes of objects and behaviors (Rokeach, 1979). For example, one may value living a carbon neutral lifestyle, in order to minimize one's own individual impact on climate change. Generally, the values an individual holds will directly affect many of their daily behaviors. For example, the person who values being carbon neutral might choose biking as their main mode of transportation instead of using a car. Furthermore, when dealing with the climate crisis as fostering global inequities, leaders holding values in relation to the perspectives of those adversely affected by climate catastrophes will be essential to making progress.

Certain conceptual topics may also elicit certain values. Lundholm and colleagues (2013, 2018) suggested that value judgments are essential to constructing knowledge around social science topics, including environmental studies. For example, by teaching about respect for nature and promoting diverse ecosystems, students may learn to value wetlands as a resource of biodiversity. Likewise, other researchers have seen topic-specific values related to controversial and/or abstract sociosci-entific topics, such as genetically modified organisms (Mason, Junyent, & Tornatora, 2014) or biological evolution (Heddy & Sinatra, 2013).

Humans call on different types of values that may motivate them towards some goal, decision, behavior, or action. When an individual participates in a task, they have values that will motivate them toward pursuing sets of tasks. In expectancy-value theory (EVT), Wigfield and Eccles (2000) found the value construct consists of attainment value (or the importance of a task as it relates to a person's identity), interest value, utility value (or the potential utility of a task), and cost (what does it cost for me to do this task?). For example, a person might have a high utility value for learning environmental science if they are moti-vated to pursue that degree to learn skills that will benefit them after completing that degree. In another example, a person might have a high attainment value if they consider learning environmental science to be fundamentally important to whom they perceive themselves to be in a certain context. The level at which a person possesses pro-environmental values can dictate the extent to which a person takes environmental action.

Where it can become controversial and challenging is when some val-ues conflict with the values that are often self-preserving. One may not initially value environmental equity as a concept because it conflicts with what feels "fair" to their own livelihood. So, for example, convincing a wealthy individual to value taking pro-environmental actions at their own cost, while knowing poorer individuals will not be making those same choices, may initially feel unfair. However, the right intervention would help that individual recognize the barriers faced by others that do not have the access or funds to make better choices.

Related to values are *attitudes*. Whereas values are standards that behaviors are measured against, attitudes are broadly valanced evalua-tions (pro or con, like or dislike) about the world around an individual. One may have both knowledge about a particular concept (e.g., vaccina-tions) and have a positive or negative evaluation about this topic as it pertains to their values (e.g., dislike the concept of vaccinations because it impacts their personal freedom) (Sinatra & Seyranian, 2015).

Overall, climate change due to the global political polarization and misinformation campaigns of the fossil fuel industry remains a contro-versial topic. Strong attitudes are often held regarding controversial topics, whether or not deeper knowledge is present. Related to climate equity, fracking is a complex and controversial socioscientific topic. Many people have pre-existing positive attitudes towards fracking, although it is environmentally damaging, because many poorer rural communities rely on the fossil fuel industry for economic survival (Boudet et al., 2016).

Psychological Perspectives of Climate Equity   77

When individual conceptions conflict with the expert consensus, purposeful, explicit processing and reflection may be necessary to shift attitudes more permanently (Heddy et al., 2017). Thus, learners must be motivated and willing to evaluate the central message of a novel conception to deepen their thinking. This process of purposeful and elaborative thinking is a central route to attitude change (Petty & Cacioppo, 1986). This differs from peripheral routes, which rely on surface level messaging shortcuts (e.g., using celebrities), which may invoke transient attitude change. Dole and Sinatra (1998) have theorized that attitude change interventions via the central route increase the likelihood of knowledge construction consistent with experts.

Beliefs

The beliefs an individual has about a phenomenon (e.g., environmental action or the groups that differ from their group) are important motivators for action. Hofer and Pintrich (1997) pose an essential question when trying to understand why people believe what they do. This question asks: how do *"individuals come to know, the theories and beliefs they hold about knowing, and the manner in which such epistemological premises are a part of and an influence on the cognitive processes of thinking and reasoning"* (p. 88)? As such, an individual's beliefs are tied closely to their knowledge.

Beliefs differ from other components involved in epistemic cognition because belief strength is based on an individual's level of commitment to some information (i.e., strong beliefs having a high level of commitment and weak beliefs having low or no level of commitment) (Lombardi et al., 2016b). Associating beliefs with various commitment levels reflects Ajzen et al.'s (2018) notion that beliefs influence cognitive evaluations about behaviors, either implicitly (i.e., automatically with little or no conscious thought on the part of the learner) or explicitly (i.e., purposefully, with appreciable conscious thought on the part of the learner). Therefore, in the process of learning, learners may implicitly and explicitly employ their beliefs when integrating multiple representations and multiple perspectives.

Emotions

An individual's emotions also play a large role in erecting barriers to becoming more aware and participating in actions to support the environment. Emotions linked to academics and learning have been characterized across a valence of positive versus negative, and activating versus deactivating, wherein activating emotions are associated with higher levels of engagement with content (Pekrun, 2006). In essence, emotions may mediate the relationship between values and actions. Thus, emotions play a central role in dictating an individual's behaviors. Emotions

78 *Ananya M. Matewos et al.*

are powerful in that they can be elicited from a specific type of knowledge (i.e., epistemic emotions). Epistemic emotions refer to the emotional responses to knowledge and knowing, and may rely on specific epistemic criteria that govern a particular domain (e.g., science) (Pekrun & Linnenbrink-Garcia, 2014). Specifically, this relates to how one may feel regarding how knowledge is constructed and verified within a domain area.

Epistemic emotions are, as a result, commonly tied in discussion with epistemic beliefs. Muis et al. (2015) offer the example that an individual might feel surprised, curious, or confused when presented with information that is incongruous with their current knowledge set: "When individuals experience conflicting information, their first reaction may be surprise. Individuals may then experience curiosity about the conflicting information and attempt to resolve it, or they may experience confusion if the incongruence cannot be resolved" (p. 173). We can extend this quote by stating that *if the incongruence cannot be resolved then the individual's behavior and action remain constant.* This same process could explain the presence of a barrier to taking environmental action or changing individuals' perceptions about the environment.

The strength of that emotional reaction or the strength of the individual's previous knowledge will affect whether they will change their conceptions about driving a high emissions vehicle, for example. In this case, epistemic emotions are driving actions towards conceptual change. However, if this person's curiosity is thwarted, the impact of their group's collective conservatism—everyone in my group drives a large truck and global climate change is liberal propaganda—then these epistemic emotions are not likely to change this person's behavior. In sum, having emotional ties to certain pieces of knowledge can help unsettle previous knowledge and facilitate conceptual change (Dole & Sinatra, 1998).

Similar to epistemic emotions, *topic emotions* explain how specific topics elicit emotions, which has implications for conceptual change. Broughton, Sinatra, and Nussbaum (2013) found that "students come to instruction with pre-existing attitudes and ideas that have an emotional component" (p. 545). Thus, students are already emotionally connected to the topics they will cover in class. For example, a student living on a reservation might feel a sense of anger when faced with learning about American history and its sociopolitical impact on the Native peoples of the USA.

Social Identity and Group Dynamics

The psychological divisions seen on the issue of climate and environmental changes are a result of an ideologically hyperpolarized society. This hinders cooperative local and global efforts and has overall negative

Psychological Perspectives of Climate Equity 79

implications in the fight against climate inequities. Issues with tribalism and groupthink are leading to individuals devaluing reliable, valid, and scientifically supported data, and resulting in thinking and making decisions without objectivity and critical evaluation.

In today's media-heavy, on-demand world, people are now able to choose the content they want to engage with when they want to. Social media networks and the algorithms that control information reinforce certain psychological concepts, beliefs and stereotypes, and values that fit people's pre-established mental patterns or schemas (Ashley & Tuten, 2015). For example, if a person enjoys hunting and fishing, owns guns, and often shops at Cabela's then, based on the algorithms of social media sites and other websites, they will more than likely see advertisements and posts that are related to and reinforce their interest. In other words, people receive and have the same information—whether true or not—reinforced that they have learned through their daily experiences and from their existing social groups. This same idea goes for those individuals that deny or support climate and other environmental changes. In terms of the impact of environmental and climate change, understanding group psychology is essential.

Group values, beliefs, motivation, and decision making are all part of psychological processes that lead to group behavior. Groups may espouse values (e.g., fossil fuels are earth's gift to humanity and should be used freely; see, for example, Winiarski, 2019) that may be especially resistant to knowledge reconstruction and perpetuate anti-environmental outlooks. For example, organized climate denying groups tend to pose similar types of alternative explanations to warming trends, spreading disinformation about weather patterns, and other alternative models to currently accepted scientific explanations regarding the human role of climate change (Oreskes & Conway, 2011). Depending on which group we belong to dictates which information we are privy to. That is, our interests and our beliefs quickly divide us. It is necessary to understand the division between groups and the potential misinformation spread by different groups because those who are disempowered may be the ones who consistently face the life altering consequences of these tribal divisions.

Consider, for example, that in 2018 Republican federal leaders in the USA, primarily the President, famously in denial of climate change, inaccurately assigned blame to California (run by a Democratic Governor) around inadequate forest management as the primary cause of the ever-increasing firestorms in California (Byrne & Alexander, 2018). These claims were made in an effort to transfer blame to local opposition party government in order to justify slashing state budgets, even though upwards of 60% of California's forests are owned by the federal government. Using oversimplification as a way to mislead and misinform the public to gain political support, these federal leaders

80 *Ananya M. Matewos et al.*

ignored the more real climate threats such as erratic wind behavior and the severely dry conditions affecting California, its lands, and its very vulnerable residents.

Even here, the stark disparities of race and class distinguish who is really at risk and vulnerable and continue to pay the price of misinformation and inaction around climate change. Native Americans primarily along with other non-white groups are particularly vulnerable to fire hazards and other environmental disasters, and have less adaptive capacity to absorb and adjust to the damages of these disasters due to forced historic concentrations onto reservation lands that are more susceptible to brush fires, or to being stuck in rentals where mitigation strategies are beyond the purview of the residents (Davies et al., 2018). Many of these vulnerable residents are now displaced from their homes and communities and are essentially climate migrants in the USA. The media has not followed up adequately with many of the struggles of the poorer migrants that lost everything in these fires continue to face, effectively erasing their stories from the collective consciousness. These impacts are less profound for wealthy California residents, who have better insurance and more disposable income for temporary housing while their homes are rebuilt.

Furthermore, people on the opposite side of an argument often believe the others are "irrational" and "thinking against their own self-interest." Experts are very quick to throw logical fallacies (e.g., ad hominem attacks) at groups that do not use logic and rationality in their arguments. However, logical thought is often context specific and can be emotionally driven (Sinatra et al., 2014a). Often experts believe that people are thinking and acting against their own self-interest; however, their group identity *is* in their self-interest (Jacobs, 2002). This idea explains the behavior of a North Dakota soybean farmer and supporter of Donald Trump, where it has been documented that soybean farmers in North Dakota have lost up to 70% of their buyers from China due to the trade war, for example (Plume, 2019). Despite actually facing detrimental effects on their own livelihoods and economic prospects, keeping with their group identity outweighs the deeper probing of how their unwavering support is impacting their actual lives. This cognitive bias—i.e., collective conservatism—is so strong here that the emotional toll of being excluded from the group is much greater than any potential benefits of going against the group.

Collective Conservatism

Another term for the phenomenon of staying with one's group despite the need for that group to become antiquated is called *collective conservatism* (Thaler & Sunstein, 2009). According to Thaler and Sunstein, collective conservatism is:

Psychological Perspectives of Climate Equity   81

The tendency of groups to stick to established patterns even as new needs arise (e.g., environmental action). Once a practice (like wearing a tie) has become established, it is likely to be perpetuated, even if there is no particular basis for it. Sometimes a tradition can last for a long time (e.g., global climate change is not man-made), and receive support or at least acquiescence from large numbers of people, even though it was originally the product of a small nudge from a few people or perhaps even one. Of course, a group will shift if it can be shown that the practice is causing serious problems. But if there is uncertainty on that question, people might well continue doing what they have always done.

(p. 58)

The above passage explains why this idea of collective conservatism is so prevalent and detrimental when combating global environmental changes. Because people tend to stick with their pre-established patterns—which have been reinforced through their environments over long periods of time—they tend to stick to these patterns despite their negative consequences. If there is to be any change in people's thought processes regarding the environment and its impact on being able to create equitable and just societies, people will need to restructure their pre-established patterns. Because individual actions are difficult to connect meaningfully to systemic change, people struggle to shift patterns with which they are already comfortable with and benefit their present state because they see no impact from their minimal changes, and may not see others enacting similar changes. And yet, the cycle continues, because a system will not change unless the individual actors within it behave differently. According to Thaler and Sunstein (2009), changing an individual's pre-existing mental pattern would need to be the result of a cognitive nudge, or reconfigured baseline psychological input, from the individual's group where their values, motivations, actions, behaviors, and so on were learned. Unfortunately, this is not an easy task, especially when a phenomenon like the *status quo bias* is in effect.

Status Quo Bias

It is possible to explain long-standing misconceptions through an understanding of the status quo/default bias. This bias originally presented by Samuelson and Zeckhauser (1988) explains that people generally choose the default option, even if that option is not the best or more logical choice. Much of this is because people are risk or loss averse (Tversky & Kahneman, 1974). For instance, why risk switching to a green energy supplier if the current supplier has been within your budget? What if you switch and end up paying much more every month? Then you lose time and money by switching at all.

82 *Ananya M. Matewos et al.*

This same default option occurs with many groups' beliefs about the environment. The default option for many people is that their involvement in environmental action is not warranted and that the default state of the environment is perfectly fine because nothing is happening to them in the interim. The environment is always as it's been. It could be that their weather is getting better. Accepting the default state of the environment sets everyone—especially the most vulnerable—up for trouble. For this reason many default options need to be reconfigured (Thaler & Sunstein, 2009). Dominant groups in most countries with access to more resources are especially prone to the status quo bias, as the status quo generally is of benefit to their lifestyle and existence, and they are often inoculated from the harms of climate change, even if it's happening around them, because they are able to choose options that protect their lifestyle as it is but that are less available to others. Consider, wealthy coastal elites that are able to afford higher insurance premiums even as they witness worsening hurricanes each year.

Psychological Distance

According to McDonald, Chai, and Newell (2015) and Trope and Liberman (2010), "*psychological distance* is a construct referring to the extent to which an object is removed from the self—such as in likelihood of occurrence, in time, in geographical space, or in social distance" (p. 110). In this sense, when a phenomenon is psychologically close to someone—this phenomenon is occurring in their local community—they tend to view this phenomenon as more concrete (focusing on the details). Whereas, if a phenomenon is psychologically distant from someone—a person lives in Oklahoma and the phenomenon in question is occurring in Jamaica—then the phenomenon becomes more abstract (focusing on the big picture, which diminishes the need for immediate action) or initiates diffusion of responsibility on a large scale, which is fundamentally the bystander effect (Darley & Latané, 1968), wherein one hopes someone else will take action.

This spectrum from the tangible to the abstract nature of a phenomenon can have significant implications for motivation to act (Sobel, 1996). For example, if a person falls on the abstract side of the spectrum—maybe they live in Oklahoma, so rising sea levels do not have much relevance in their day-to-day lives—and they are asked to stop driving their fuel-inefficient vehicle because of the potential negative climate implications, then the likelihood of them continuing to drive that car will stay the same. However, if this same person lives in a part of Oklahoma where fracking has created constant earthquakes—maybe one in particular that damaged the foundation of their house—this person may be more motivated to take some kind of action towards policy initiatives that

Psychological Perspectives of Climate Equity 83

support anti-fracking. This person would land more towards the tangible side of the spectrum because there has been a direct impact in their lives.

There are implications for equity for the most vulnerable depending on where a person lands on this abstract/concrete spectrum. As Davies et al. (2018) indicate, environmental disasters, particularly in relation to changing climate, has the most severe and life changing outcomes for people of color and poorer communities that do not have back up options for living and resources for sustaining life, as in the aftermath of disasters. These are the individuals for whom climate change is as real as can be because their lives may have already been overturned, such as the Black community's complete upheaval in the wake of Hurricane Katrina. There is a significant amount of social privilege to having a greater amount of psychological distance from the issues and impact of climate change as of this moment.

As a phenomenon becomes more abstract and an individual's motivation to act decreases, so does their level of empathy. Some of this is due to learners emotionally disengaging from a topic (environmental problems) that causes significant distress, hopelessness, fear, and anxiety (Sobel, 1996). Furthermore, the remote, grand scale issues of climate change also invoke feelings of helplessness and inefficacy to make real change, thus creating further distance regarding taking any action at all (Bandura, 2001). We recognize the need for teaching and learning around empathy as a goal to shifting past this barrier of psychological distance and abstraction from issues of environmental equity.

Facilitating Learning about Climate Change Equity Issues

Part of what makes climate equity a topic that is particularly complex to learn about is: one must first acknowledge that humans are responsible, that some humans will benefit in the short term to the detriment of almost everyone else, and that none of that "feels" fair. Despite the numerous psychological barriers that prevent people and groups of people from taking action to combat climate and environmental changes, there are psychological facilitators that are able to guide people towards improved knowledge outcomes, at least on the human-induced nature of climate change, which is the first step towards understanding climate equity.

Communities already being impacted by environmental changes may need to move towards *adaptation and innovation* (e.g., engineering solutions). For example, the Maldives and the Marshall Islands need to be adapting toward extreme weather, whereas people in places like Oklahoma need to understand what actions, practices, knowledge, and skill sets can effect a shift towards a more carbon-free climate and a better understanding of others who are not in one's immediate community. Unfortunately, changing one's behavior to become more environmentally aware may require lifestyle changes. These lifestyle changes require

84   *Ananya M. Matewos et al.*

adopting a new set of psychological skills or a new psychological tool box. These tools may include: better reasoning skills (Lombardi et al., 2018a, 2018b), an increased sense of skepticism (García-Carmona & Díaz, 2016), a deeper understanding of what makes knowledge reliable (Chinn et al., 2014), and learning how to become more empathetic (Cheng et al., 2015).

In this section, we explain (a) the benefits of socioscientific oriented learning; (b) facilitating conceptual change despite misinformation; (c) and how to scaffold critical evaluation and reasoning processes to allow for deeper thinking on complex topics. Finally, we conclude with a discussion of how to teach for *engaged empathy* to help learners connect knowledge to real world contexts and consequences. All of these taken together are essential for combating climate change and may prompt environmental or climate-related action.

Education

Thinking occurs when confronted with a genuine problem (Dewey, 1933). In the case of environmental changes, we are confronted with a big problem, and having an educated citizenry in regard to this issue is essential. For example, what makes this point salient is that the average American would fail an 81-question test about climate related knowledge (Leiserowitz et al., 2010). Thus, it is crucial for people to have knowledge about the nature of socioscientific issues in general, the discovery process, and the iterative cycle that creates new knowledge, confirms reliable concepts, and disconfirms unreliable concepts. All of these taken together are essential for combating climate change.

Integrative Learning

Climate equity involves bringing in socioscientific knowledge such as social studies, political science, and economics to better understand how humans are impacting and impacted by changes in the climate. For example, as we consider how parts of the world are becoming uninhabitable, we also need to consider the displacement and migration of millions of people (Brzoska & Fröhlich, 2016). Entire cities in India are running out of water, which creates geopolitical crises in the region (Masih & Slater, 2019). Having an education system that can integrate these concepts and connect these ideas across classes is essential.

Even within the core domain of earth science, climate topics in particular require *systems-based* thinking and learning. It is not enough to teach science in silos of concepts, but rather how fields of science actually inform one another, and cut across to create deeper conceptual understanding of a phenomenon. In the USA, *A Framework for K-12 Science Education* (National Research Council, 2012) and the *Next Generation*

Psychological Perspectives of Climate Equity 85

Science Standards (NGSS Lead States, 2013) are a preliminary step towards this idea—wherein they have identified seven cross-cutting concepts that link different domains of science in order to provide an explicit organizational schema for how scientific knowledge is interrelated. Two of these cross-cutting concepts are systems and system models.

Although K-12 Science is certainly progressing in creating connections across domains of scientific content areas, it may be worth finding ways to further integrate across subject areas for considering the large-scale impact of climate change on humans by humans. Education programs and curricular experts may consider options such as integrative classes such as problem solving and reasoning for students as early as high school to be able to examine large-scale unstructured problems such as climate change and climate equity using multiple perspectives and interdisciplinary knowledge.

Although school-based curricula may provide foundational concepts to environmental science, school is not the only place where learning and belief formation occurs. An ongoing problem is the sheer volume of misinformation that infiltrates the internet, interfering with science-backed knowledge construction.

INOCULATION

Public beliefs and perceptions about socioscientific topics are often threatened by digital viral misinformation (e.g., the false campaign that vaccines cause autism). Scientists liken the spread of misinformation to that of an actual contagion, and to fight against it have proposed attitudinal inoculation, which is parallel to the process in medicine when a weakened form of the virus is introduced to the body to produce an immune fighting response. Similarly, inoculation theory (Compton, 2013) suggests that by forewarning people that they may be exposed to information that challenges their existing beliefs or behaviors, by pre-emptively highlighting false claims, and by pre-bunking potential counter-arguments of the anti-scientific position, learners are prepared against possible misinformation threats.

In the context of climate change, van der Linden et al. (2017) suggest that, when possible, communicating the scientific consensus (high level of agreement among experts) on human-caused climate change should be presented alongside information that forewarns the public that politically or economically motivated actors intend to undermine the findings of climate science for their own gain. In essence, public information about climate change has become "weaponized," which falls more generally within three broad categories: misinformation, disinformation, and malinformation (Wardle & Derakhshan, 2017).

Misinformation is false content shared by a person who does not realize it is false or misleading. Disinformation is content that is intentionally

86 *Ananya M. Matewos et al.*

false and designed to cause harm, and is often used for profit and/or political gains, or to cause trouble broadly. Malinformation is genuine (i.e., truthful) information that is spread with an intent to cause harm. Information "weaponization" on the internet and in social media means that nefarious actors are ramping up the sophistication of their methods for spreading misinformation and creating misinformation about non-scientific notions of climate change (Cook, 2019) and widely disseminating malinformation about climate scientists (see Pearce, 2010). To inoculate this weaponized information, learners should be provided with knowledge about the nature of disinformation campaigns to pre-emptively refute future attempts.

Knowledge Reconstruction

Even if education systems provide knowledge, classroom learning is still combatting the influx of misinformation present in the broader context of each learner's life. Past the point of inoculation, conceptions that are not consistent with scientific understanding will require knowledge reconstruction that considers the social, affective, and motivational contexts of knowledge restructuring (Sinatra, 2005). Broughton et al. (2013) found that students who demonstrated positive emotions about the reclassification of Pluto from a planet to a dwarf planet also become more accepting of this reclassification after they showed improved understanding as to why this reclassification occurred. In other words, when presented with scientifically proven information about Pluto's classification, students who felt more positively about the reclassification—because the rationale for it was understood and could easily fit into pre-existing schemas—were better able to change their conceptions. This demonstrates the importance of considering the direct affective nature of knowledge reconstruction.

What does this mean for environmental action? It means that people's emotions about a topic could determine whether they retain or change their conceptions regarding environmental phenomena. By understanding the extent to which topic emotions are congruous with pre-established thought, it is possible then to create interventions that can cater to and possibly change those pre-existing knowledge structures (Lombardi & Sinatra, 2013). For example, a person who drives a high emission pickup truck might have a positive emotional reaction when the topic of hauling timber is discussed, but may have a negative emotional reaction when they talk with their friends about people who drive hybrids. The challenge is to somehow get the person driving the truck to not think negatively of the person who drives the hybrid. The goal would be to remove the negative affiliation with the hybrid vehicle. One intervention technique that seems to be an effective method for changing people's conceptions of a phenomenon are refutation text interventions

Psychological Perspectives of Climate Equity 87

(Tippett, 2010). Somehow getting the person who drives the truck to engage in this kind of intervention could facilitate a change in their conceptions of the topic of low emission transport.

Refutation Texts

Similar to inoculation, but introduced as an intervention post-misinformation, refutation texts are designed to facilitate conceptual change by stating previously acquired incorrect knowledge and then directly refuting it while simultaneously providing the correct knowledge (Kendeou, Walsh, Smith, & O'Brien, 2014). In this way refutation texts scaffold readers to consider the plausibility of alternative explanations through co-activation and competing activation (Lombardi et al., 2016; van den Broek & Kendeou, 2008). In previous research, refutation texts have promoted knowledge reconstruction for a variety of topics, including energy (Diakidoy et al., 2003), seasons (Broughton et al., 2010; Cordova et al., 2014), and climate change (Lombardi et al., 2016a; Nussbaum et al., 2017) and shown significant benefits over other text structures. Refutation texts designed to promote both co-activation, competing activation, and critical thinking lead to better conceptual change (Hynd, 2001; Kendeou et al., 2011; McCrudden & Kendeou, 2014).

A study on refutation texts used to teach climate change found that they were effective in remedying the misconceptions they were targeting, including: (a) ozone depletion is not the cause of global warming; (b) the distinction between weather and climate; and (c) that warming oceans contribute to climate change (Nussbaum et al., 2017). Refutation texts work well because they introduce learners to a state of cognitive disequilibrium (Piaget, 1952) that is then remedied by providing the normative scientific consensus. Through the process of co-activation, learners can quickly recognize the conceptual discrepancy and overwrite the naive model with a correct one. However, the knowledge acquired through refutation texts may not be lasting and permanent without additional instructional reinforcement and rehearsal.

Critical Thinking

Given that there are significant barriers to reasoning, thinking, and judgment formation due to cognitive biases and heuristics, individuals need scaffolded instructional tools to facilitate deeper thinking and evaluative processes. Being a critical thinker (e.g., being scientifically evaluative) in socioscientific learning situations involves judgments about the relationship between evidence and alternative explanations of a particular phenomenon (McNeill et al., 2006). When being critically evaluative, an individual may weigh the strengths, weaknesses, and nuances in the connection between evidence and explanations (models

88   *Ananya M. Matewos et al.*

of natural phenomena). This may lead to collaborative argumentation, a social process wherein individuals compare, critique, and revise ideas and gauge how well evidence potentially supports both an explanation and its plausible alternatives (e.g., a counter-argument/contrary hypothesis; Chin and Osborne, 2010; Nussbaum, 2008). Students need support to critically reflect and engage in collaborative argumentation, so providing an instructional scaffold is helpful for learning (Nussbaum & Edwards, 2011). One example of this type of tool is the model-evidence-link (MEL) diagram suite of activities, which helps learners to compare a scientific model (explanation) of a natural phenomenon to an alternative model that is not scientifically accepted (Lombardi, 2016; 2018a; 2018b). In using MEL, learners draw different variations of arrows linking evidentiary data to the two models representing explanations of a particular phenomenon, only one being scientifically accurate.

Epistemic Cognition

Chinn et al. (2014) explain that to achieve epistemic ends (e.g., knowledge, understanding, useful models, explanations) individuals must call on their epistemic cognition—the cognitive processes used to achieve these epistemic ends. Chinn and colleagues posit that epistemic cognition consists of a three-component model, which they call the AIR model. AIR refers to (A)ims and values, epistemic (I)deals, and (R) eliable processes for achieving epistemic ends. The AIR model works when an individual possesses a certain value set that leads to a particular knowledge set. This value then acts as a motivator for pursuing similar types of knowledge that are already present in a person's schema. Once a person has a value set for a particular set of knowledge and that value set has been integrated into their working schemas, this person's knowledge set is under the watchful eye of a set of epistemic ideals—or "a criterion or standard that must be met for an explanation to be good" (p. 433). Essentially, this means that knowledge will continue to build, based on premises that satisfy these epistemic ideals.

Reliable processes for achieving epistemic ends consist of "schemas specifying the reliable processes by which epistemic products (such as knowledge, understanding, explanations, or models) are produced" (p. 436). In other words, a person's schemas must have continuity between their epistemic values (what is the value of the knowledge base motivating them to seek some sort of knowledge) and epistemic ideals (what is the standard of that knowledge) in order to achieve this reliable processing. A lack of continuity could cause instability in one's schemas, which would produce an emotional reaction that could then lead to some degree of conceptual change (engagement in new knowledge) or a reinforcer of that current belief (disengagement with the new knowledge). Thus, the AIR model reflects one's cognitive process for

Psychological Perspectives of Climate Equity 89

knowledge and knowing. Thus, the crux of gaining a full understanding of the AIR model is: how is this knowledge being produced? Under what premises is this knowledge being produced? Who are the people encouraging or discouraging this knowledge, and how is that affecting people's decision making and actions?

The AIR model has implications for leading to environmental action. Imagine a student who does not have much knowledge about the environment and has started studying a unit on climate change. This student's climate change/environmental science schema is not fully developed. The only knowledge this student has is from his mother and father's brief chats about the electric bill getting higher in the summers because the summers are getting hotter and they need to use the air conditioning more often. This student does not know why the summers are getting hotter. Because this student lacks this knowledge, the value of learning climate change—because his parents have been complaining about the amount of the electric bill in summer—has motivated this student to value this line of research. Because this student is a good student and understands how research and arguments are created, he trusts that climate science is really based on the data he is studying in class. Some of this student's friends do not believe climate change is real, but he sees through that argument because his friends cannot produce any reasonable argument that disproves the data offered by the scientists. This student understands the knowledge that was produced— as to why his parent's electric bill is so high in the summer—to be reliable because of what he learned in class about the hotter summers. Thus, using the AIR model of epistemic cognition has created a knowledge base that could lead to some environmental action; for example, telling his parents about smart thermometers that could be used to conserve energy.

Engagement

Once knowledge about climate change and related equity issues are structured accurately, and learners understand what is at stake, we are still left with understanding how a specific piece of information promotes engagement with the topic on a deeper level, which would ultimately encourage action both from the individual and in terms of supporting equity. Engagement has been studied ubiquitously across many learning contexts. Scholars have agreed that broad categories of engagement such as behavioral, cognitive, affective, and agentic (Fredericks et al., 2004; Sinatra et al., 2015) are imperative to learning. For learners to be behaviorally engaged, they must show activation across their behaviors in the learning environment, which could look like anything from signs of paying attention, to questioning, or demonstrated persistence on a difficult problem. We have previously discussed the role

90   *Ananya M. Matewos et al.*

that emotions play in learning and the need for positive activating emotions to support learning and engagement (Heddy & Sinatra, 2013). Social learning in classrooms may often lead to affective outcomes depending on varying qualities of social interactions (Linenbrink-Garcia et al., 2011). Cognitive engagement is often recognized as the deeper self-regulatory processing around learning, such as setting goals and meeting them. Finally, agentic engagement signifies when learners pro-actively influence the flow of instruction or knowledge construction through their contributions.

Although engagement has largely been used to promote learning and achievement outcomes, we propose considering the engagement framework as a way to reach social emotional outcomes, like empathy, which would allow individuals to feel more connected to distant parts of the world and reduce abstract suffering to tangible consequences needing personal change. Given that learning research shows that the more engaged learners are, the more likely they are to want to delve deeper into a topic, we can hope that the more engaged learners are on climate equity topics the more empathetic they will become, and ready to take action.

Moving Towards Engaged Empathy

Briefly defined, empathy allows for one person to take the perspective of another person. Empathizing involves an ability to understand other people's mental states and emotions, and be interested in the social connection with others (Hoffman, 1990). In order to have positive collective action towards the current negative environmental changes, individuals and groups must be empathetic (in their feelings and values) to those who are taking the brunt of these changes. Empathy is a cognitive, heavy, and abstract concept that does not develop without practice. Empathy is a developmental process that, for example, most people can draw on when they view negative images of disasters (Hoffman, 1990). However, having a deeper sense of empathy takes skill that is developed with practice. These communities of immense privilege that exist in ever increasing numbers due to the current hyper-capitalist globalist society (e.g., economic, geographic, knowledge) need to learn how to take the perspectives of other communities that are vastly more different and potentially under-resourced than theirs and take actions to prevent their demise. For example, a few celebrities in Los Angeles were criticized during the summer of 2015 for their exorbitant water usage during the California drought which saw water reductions of 25%. However, despite the need for water reduction and conservation, some wealthy California families figured this did not apply to them (Hackman, 2015). However, research has shown that changes can happen with some facilitation.

We propose that, for the engaged learner, empathy should be a clear outcome, though this is not something that educators actively measure as a goal. *Engaged empathy*, then, is a culmination of the various categories of engagement activated for the purpose of learning about a topic such as climate change to understand how it impacts both ourselves and others. When it comes to the environment there are many ways to teach for engaged empathy.

Environmental scholars have for a long time worked towards helping learners move away from ecophobia by encouraging local, place-based, exploratory instruction of the natural world, which can take place in one's own backyard, as well as being expanded to further places such as national parks and lands through field trips and camping excursions (Schweizer et al., 2013; Sobel, 1996). This type of instruction has the opportunity to connect the abstract concepts of climate to the tangible realities of nature, simply by reducing the distance an individual feels from the environment. In a meta-analysis of studies of the impact of marine wildlife tours, researchers found that visitors increased both emotional empathy and knowledge during guided visits with marine wildlife (Zeppel, 2008). Furthermore, they are opportunities to spark wonder and a deeper interest in nature that is connected to their own community. This form of empathy-building towards the environment itself reduces negative emotions (hopelessness), while activating positive emotions (Sobel, 1996).

Research also shows that there are ways to increase empathy by introducing learners to narratives and stories to share perspectives of other characters learning about the environment or problem solving about the environment (McKnight, 2010). Picture books and other narrative forms may encourage children to appreciate nature, but they are also access points to creating empathy for more remote environments. Science should not be so dispassionate as to not bring out stories of those in places most impacted, as those are the narratives that would not only help learners connect to abstract climate concepts, but also care deeply about making a difference right at home. Learning across other subject areas such as literacy and social studies may also be possible with story-telling of those working to not only prevent climate change now, but also those of people innovating engineering solutions to ensure human survival in a changing world.

We also propose using these same engagement strategies, discussed regarding reducing the distance to the environment, by also reducing the distance individuals feel from one another between groups and communities, both locally and around the world. The more we can understand that we all impact each other, even when that impact is not tangible and immediate, the more empathy we can generate. With more empathy we are more likely to make decisions around our individual choices, and take collective action with collective global wellbeing in mind.

Conclusion

Our present environmental state is already beginning to create unjust and inequitable outcomes for parts of the world due to the consequences of climate change. In order to move towards a more sustainable future for everyone, learners (both formally and informally) must overcome cognitive motivational barriers to engaging in empathetic actions.

Although change may seem hopeless at times, there are already those using psychological strategies to create environmental engagement. Social change relies on social diffusion of knowledge. While we have discussed educational approaches to learning about climate change and equity in the classroom, the central message of this knowledge needs to be spread in meaningful and creative ways to everyone around the world. Bandura and Cherry (2020) discuss how youth are leading social movements inspiring millions of people around the world, based on the theoretical core of social cognitive theory (increasing collective engagement and efficacy through successful symbolic models). We extend this work by adding that in setting learning outcomes and messaging for social learning, we must create opportunities of engaged empathy, to further reduce the distance one feels to the realities of climate change.

References

Ajzen, I. (1991). The theory of planned behavior. *Organizational Behavior and Human Decision Processes, 50*(2), 179–211.

Ajzen, I., Fishbein, M., Lohmann, S., & Albarracín, D. (2018). The influence of attitudes on behavior. In D. Albarracín & B.T. Johnson (Eds.), *The handbook of attitudes: Volume 1: Basic principles* (pp. 197–256). New York: Routledge.

Ashley, C., & Tuten, T. (2015). Creative strategies in social media marketing: An exploratory study of branded social content and consumer engagement. *Psychology & Marketing, 32*(1), 15–27.

Bandura, A. (1977). *Social learning theory.* Englewood Cliffs, NJ: Prentice Hall.

Bandura, A. (2001). Social cognitive theory: An agentic perspective. *Annual Review of Psychology, 52*(1), 1–26.

Bandura, A., & Cherry, L. (2020). Enlisting the power of youth for climate change. *American Psychologist, 75*(7), 945–951.

Boudet, H., Bugden, D., Zanocco, C., & Maibach, E. (2016). The effect of industry activities on public support for 'fracking'. *Environmental Politics, 25*(4), 593–612. https://doi.org/10.1080/09644016.2016.1153771

Bråten, I., Britt, M.A., Strømsø, H.I., & Rouet, J.F. (2011). The role of epistemic beliefs in the comprehension of multiple expository texts: Toward an integrated model. *Educational Psychologist, 46*(1), 48–70.

Broughton, S.H., Sinatra, G.M., & Nussbaum, E.M. (2013). "Pluto has been a planet my whole life!" Emotions, attitudes, and conceptual change in elementary students' learning about Pluto's reclassification. *Research in Science Education, 43*(2), 529–550.

Psychological Perspectives of Climate Equity 93

Broughton, S.H., Sinatra, G.M., & Reynolds, R.E. (2010). The nature of the refutation text effect: An investigation of attention allocation. *The Journal of Educational Research, 103*(6), 407–423.

Brzoska, M., & Fröhlich, C. (2016). Climate change, migration and violent conflict: vulnerabilities, pathways and adaptation strategies. *Migration and Development, 5*(2), 190–210.

Byrne, T., & Alexander, K. (2018, November). Trump on California's wildfires: 'Forest management is so poor'. *San Francisco Chronicle.* https://www.sfchronicle.com/california-wildfires/amp/Trump-on-California-s-Camp-Fire-Forest-13380388.php

Cheng, M.T., She, H.C., & Annetta, L.A. (2015). Game immersion experience: its hierarchical structure and impact on game-based science learning. *Journal of Computer Assisted Learning, 31*(3), 232–253.

Chi, M.T. (2005). Commonsense conceptions of emergent processes: Why some misconceptions are robust. *The Journal of the Learning Sciences, 14*(2), 161–199.

Chi, M.T. (2013). Two kinds and four sub-types of misconceived knowledge, ways to change it, and the learning outcomes. In S. Vosniadou (Ed.), *International Handbook of research on conceptual change* (pp. 61–82). Routledge.

Chin, C., & Osborne, J. (2010). Students' questions and discursive interaction: Their impact on argumentation during collaborative group discussions in science. *Journal of Research in Science Teaching, 47*(7), 883–908.

Chinn, C.A., Rinehart, R.W., & Buckland, L.A. (2014). Epistemic cognition and evaluating information: Applying the AIR model of epistemic cognition. In D.N. Rapp & J.L.G. Braasch (Eds.), *Processing inaccurate information: Theoretical and applied perspectives from cognitive science and the educational sciences* (pp. 425–453). Cambridge, MA, US: MIT Press.

Compton, J. (2013). Inoculation theory. In J. P. Dillard & L. Shen (Eds.), *The SAGE handbook of persuasion: Developments in theory and practice* (pp. 220–236). Sage.

Cook, J. (2019). Understanding and countering misinformation about climate change. In I. Chiluwa & Samoilenko, S. (Eds.), *Handbook of research on deception, fake news, and misinformation online* (pp. 281–306). Hershey, PA: IGI-Global.

Cordova, J.R., Sinatra, G.M., Jones, S.H., Taasoobshirazi, G., & Lombardi, D. (2014). Confidence in prior knowledge, self-efficacy, interest and prior knowledge: Influences on conceptual change. *Contemporary Educational Psychology, 39*(2), 164–174.

Darley, J. M., & Latané, B. (1968). Bystander intervention in emergencies: diffusion of responsibility. *Journal of Personality and Social Psychology, 8*(4), 377–383.

Davies, I.P., Haugo, R.D., Robertson, J.C. & Levin P.S. (2018). The unequal vulnerability of communities of color to wildfire. *PLoS ONE 13*(11), e0205825. https://doi.org/10.1371/journal.pone.0205825

Deopersad, C., Persaud, C., Chakalall, Y., Bello, O., Masson, M., Perroni, A., ... Nelson, M. (2020). *Assessment of the effects and impacts of Hurricane Dorian in the Bahamas.* Inter-American Development Bank. http://dx.doi.org/10.18235/0002582

Dewey, J. (1933). *How we think.* Boston: D.C. Heath and company.

Diakidoy, I.A.N., Kendeou, P., & Ioannides, C. (2003). Reading about energy: The effects of text structure in science learning and conceptual change. *Contemporary Educational Psychology, 28*(3), 335–356.

94 *Ananya M. Matewos et al.*

Dole, J.A., & Sinatra, G.M. (1998). Reconceptualizing change in the cognitive construction of knowledge. *Educational Psychologist, 33*(2–3), 109–128.

Ferguson, L.E., Bråten, I., & Strømsø, H.I. (2012). Epistemic cognition when students read multiple documents containing conflicting scientific evidence: A think-aloud study. *Learning and Instruction, 22*(2), 103–120.

Fredricks, J.A., Blumenfeld, P.C., & Paris, A.H. (2004). School engagement: Potential of the concept, state of the evidence. *Review of Educational Research, 74*(1), 59–109.

García-Carmona, A., & Díaz, J.A.A. (2016). Learning about the nature of science using newspaper articles with scientific content. *Science & Education, 25*(5–6), 523–546. https://doi.org/10.1007/s11191-016-9831-9

Hackman, R. (2015, May 16). California drought shaming takes on a class-conscious edge. *The Guardian.* https://www.theguardian.com

Harring, N., Torbjörnsson, T., & Lundholm, C. (2018). Solving environmental problems together? The roles of value orientations and trust in the state in environmental policy support among Swedish undergraduate students. *Education Sciences.* www.mdpi.com/2227-7102/8/3/124/pdf

Heddy, B.C., Danielson, R.W., Sinatra, G.M., & Graham, J. (2017). Modifying knowledge, motions, and attitudes regarding genetically modified foods. *The Journal of Experimental Education, 85*(3), 513–533.

Heddy, B.C., & Sinatra, G.M. (2013). Transforming misconceptions: Using transformative experience to promote positive affect and conceptual change in students learning about biological evolution. *Science Education, 97*(5), 723–744.

Hofer, B.K., & Pintrich, P.R. (1997). The development of epistemological theories: Beliefs about knowledge and knowing and their relation to learning. *Review of Educational Research, 67*(1), 88–140.

Hoffman, J.S., Shandas, V., & Pendleton, N. (2020). The effects of historical housing policies on resident exposure to intra-urban heat: A study of 108 US urban areas. *Climate, 8*(1), 12.

Hoffman, M.L. (1990). Empathy and justice motivation. *Motivation and Emotion, 14*(2), 151–172.

Hynd, C.R. (2001). Refutational texts and the change process. *International Journal of Educational Research, 35*(7–8), 699–714.

Jacobs, R.N. (2002). The narrative integration of personal and collective identity in social movements. In M. C. Green, J. J. Strange, & T. C. Brock (Eds.), *Narrative impact: Social and cognitive foundations* (pp. 205–228). Lawrence Erlbaum Associates.

Kendeou, P., Muis, K.R., & Fulton, S. (2011). Reader and text factors in reading comprehension processes. *Journal of Research in Reading, 34*(4), 365–383.

Kendeou, P., Walsh, E.K., Smith, E.R., & O'Brien, E.J. (2014). Knowledge revision processes in refutation texts. *Discourse Processes, 51*(5–6), 374–397.

Kunda, Z. (1990). The case for motivated reasoning. *Psychological Bulletin, 108*(3), 480–498.

Leiserowitz, A.A., Smith, N., & Marlon, J.R. (2010). *Americans' knowledge of climate change.* Yale Project on Climate Change Communication.

Limón, M. (2001). On the cognitive conflict as an instructional strategy for conceptual change: A critical appraisal. *Learning and Instruction, 11*(4–5), 357–380.

Psychological Perspectives of Climate Equity   95

Linnenbrink-Garcia, L., Rogat, T.K., & Koskey, K.L. (2011). Affect and engagement during small group instruction. *Contemporary Educational Psychology, 36*(1), 13–24.

Lombardi, D. (2016). Beyond the controversy: Instructional scaffolds to promote critical evaluation and understanding of Earth science. *The Earth Scientist, 32*(2), 5–10.

Lombardi, D., Bailey, J.M., Bickel, E.S., & Burrell, S. (2018a). Scaffolding scientific thinking: Students' evaluations and judgments during earth science knowledge construction. *Contemporary Educational Psychology, 54*, 184–198.

Lombardi, D., Bickel, E.S., Bailey, J.M., & Burrell, S. (2018b). High school students' evaluations, plausibility (re) appraisals, and knowledge about topics in Earth science. *Science Education, 102*(1), 153–177.

Lombardi, D., Danielson, R.W., & Young, N. (2016a). A plausible connection: Models examining the relations between evaluation, plausibility, and the refutation text effect. *Learning and Instruction, 44*, 74–86.

Lombardi, D., Nussbaum, E.M., & Sinatra, G.M. (2016b). Plausibility judgments in conceptual change and epistemic cognition. *Educational Psychologist, 51*(1), 35–56.

Lombardi, D., & Sinatra, G.M. (2013). Emotions about teaching about human-induced climate change. *International Journal of Science Education, 35*(1), 167–191.

Lundholm, C. & Davies, P. (2013). conceptual change in the social sciences. In S. Vosniadou (Ed.), *International handbook of research on conceptual change.* (2nd ed., pp. 288–304). New York: Routledge.

Lundholm, C., Hopwood, N., & Rickinson, M. (2013). Environmental learning: Insights from research into the student experience. In Brody, M., Dillon, J., Stevenson, R., & Wals, A. (Eds.), *International handbook of research on environmental education.* (pp. 242–251). New York: Routledge.

Masih N., & Slater, J. (2019, June 28). As a major Indian city runs out of water, 9 million people pray for rain. *Washington Post.* https://www.washingtonpost.com

Mason, L., Junyent, A.A., & Tornatora, M.C. (2014). Epistemic evaluation and comprehension of web-source information on controversial science-related topics: Effects of a short-term instructional intervention. *Computers & Education, 76*, 143–157.

McCrudden, M.T., & Kendeou, P. (2014). Exploring the link between cognitive processes and learning from refutational text. *Journal of Research in Reading, 37*(S1), S116–S140.

McDonald, R.I., Chai, H.Y., & Newell, B.R. (2015). Personal experience and the 'psychological distance' of climate change: An integrative review. *Journal of Environmental Psychology, 44*, 109–118.

McKnight, D.M. (2010). Overcoming "ecophobia": Fostering environmental empathy through narrative in children's science literature. *Frontiers in Ecology and the Environment, 8*(6), 10–15.

McNeill, K.L., Lizotte, D.J., Krajcik, J., & Marx, R.W. (2006). Supporting students' construction of scientific explanations by fading scaffolds in instructional materials. *The Journal of the Learning Sciences, 15*(2), 153–191.

Muis, K.R., Psaradellis, C., Lajoie, S.P., Di Leo, I., & Chevrier, M. (2015). The role of epistemic emotions in mathematics problem solving. *Contemporary Educational Psychology, 42*, 172–185.

96 *Ananya M. Matewos et al.*

National Research Council. (2012). *A framework for K-12 science education: Practices, crosscutting concepts, and core ideas.* Washington, DC: The National Academies Press. https://doi.org/10.17226/13165

NGSS Lead States. (2013). *Next generation science standards: For states, by states.* Washington, DC: The National Academies Press.

Nussbaum, E.M. (2008). Collaborative discourse, argumentation, and learning: Preface and literature review. *Contemporary Educational Psychology, 33*(3), 345–359.

Nussbaum, E.M., Cordova, J.R., & Rehmat, A.P. (2017). Refutation texts for effective climate change education. *Journal of Geoscience Education, 65*(1), 23–34.

Nussbaum, E.M., & Edwards, O.V. (2011). Critical questions and argument stratagems: A framework for enhancing and analyzing students' reasoning practices. *Journal of the Learning Sciences, 20*(3), 443–488.

Oreskes, N., & Conway, E.M. (2011). *Merchants of doubt.* Bloomsbury, USA.

Österlind, K. (2005). Concept formation in environmental education: 14-year olds' work on the intensified greenhouse effect and the depletion of the ozone layer. *International Journal of Science Education, 27*(8), 891–908.

Pearce, F. (2010, July 10). The five key leaked emails from UEA's Climatic Research Unit. *The Guardian.* https://www.theguardian.com

Pekrun, R. (2006). The control-value theory of achievement emotions: Assumptions, corollaries, and implications for educational research and practice. *Educational Psychology Review, 18*(4), 315–341.

Pekrun, R., & Linnenbrink-Garcia, L. (2014). Introduction to emotions in education. In R. Pekrun & L. Linnenbrink-Garcia (Eds.), *International handbook of emotions in education* (pp. 11–20). Routledge.

Petty R.E., & Cacioppo J.T. (1986). The elaboration likelihood model of persuasion. In: *Communication and persuasion.* Springer Series in Social Psychology. New York, NY: Springer.

Piaget, J. (1952). *The Origins of Intelligence in Children.* New York, NY: W.W. Norton & Co.

Plume, K. (2019, August 22). On the front lines: Trade war sinks North Dakota soybean farmers. *Reuters.* https://www.reuters.com

Rokeach, M. (1979). Some unresolved issues in theories of beliefs, attitudes, and values. *Nebraska Symposium on Motivation, 27*, 261–304.

Samuelson, W., & Zeckhauser, R. (1988). Status quo bias in decision making. *Journal of Risk and Uncertainty, 1*(1), 7–59.

Schweizer, S., Davis, S., & Thompson, J.L. (2013). Changing the conversation about climate change: A theoretical framework for place-based climate change engagement. *Environmental Communication: A Journal of Nature and Culture, 7*(1), 42–62.

Sinatra, G.M. (2005). The "warming trend" in conceptual change research: The legacy of Paul R. *Pintrich. Educational Psychologist, 40*(2), 107–115.

Sinatra, G.M., Broughton, S.H., & Lombardi, D. (2014a). Emotions in science education. In R. Pekrun & L. Linnenbrink-Garcia (Eds.), *International handbook of emotions in education* (pp. 415–436). New York, NY: Taylor & Francis.

Sinatra, G.M. Heddy, B.C., & Lombardi D. (2015) The challenges of defining and measuring student engagement in science. *Educational Psychologist, 50*(1), 1–13.

Psychological Perspectives of Climate Equity 97

Sinatra, G.M., Kienhues, D., & Hofer, B.K. (2014b). Addressing challenges to public understanding of science: Epistemic cognition, motivated reasoning, and conceptual change. *Educational Psychologist, 49*(2), 123–138.

Sinatra, G.M., & Seyranian, V. (2015). Warm change about hot topics: The role of motivation and emotion in attitude and conceptual change about controversial science topics. In L. Corno, E. M. Anderman (Eds.), *Handbook of educational psychology* (pp. 259–270). Routledge.

Sobel, D. (1996). *Beyond ecophobia.* Great Barrington, MA: Orion Society.

Thaler, R.H., & Sunstein, C.R. (2009). *Nudge: Improving decisions about health, wealth, and happiness.* Penguin.

Tippett, C.D. (2010). Refutation text in science education: A review of two decades of research. *International Journal of Science and Mathematics Education, 8*(6), 951–970.

Trope, Y., & Liberman, N. (2010). "Construal-level theory of psychological distance": Correction to Trope and Liberman (2010).

Tversky, A., & Kahneman, D. (1974). Judgment under uncertainty: Heuristics and biases. *Science, 185*(4157), 1124–1131.

United Nations Environment Programme. (2020). *Emissions gap report 2020.* Nairobi.

Van Den Broek, P., & Kendeou, P. (2008). Cognitive processes in comprehension of science texts: The role of co-activation in confronting misconceptions. *Applied Cognitive Psychology, 22*(3), 335–351.

Van der Linden, S., Leiserowitz, A., Rosenthal, S., & Maibach, E. (2017). Inoculating the public against misinformation about climate change. *Global Challenges, 1*(2), 1600008.

Walker, R.E., Keane, C.R., & Burke, J.G. (2010). Disparities and access to healthy food in the United States: A review of food deserts literature. *Health & Place, 16*(5), 876–884. https://doi.org/10.1016/j.healthplace.2010.04.013

Wardle, C., & Derakhshan H. (2017). *Information disorder: Toward an interdisciplinary framework for research and policymaking.* Strasbourg, Germany: Council of Europe. https://rm.coe.int/information-disorder-toward-an-interdisciplinary-framework-for-researc/168076277c

Wigfield, A., & Eccles, J.S. (2000). Expectancy–value theory of achievement motivation. *Contemporary Educational Psychology, 25*(1), 68–81.

Winiarski, D. (2019, January 30). Thank god for fossil fuels. *The Network.* https://network.crcna.org/biblical-justice/thank-god-fossil-fuels

Wynes, S., & Nicholas, K.A. (2017). The climate mitigation gap: Education and government recommendations miss the most effective individual actions. *Environmental Research Letters, 12*(7). https://iopscience.iop.org/article/10.1088/1748-9326/aa7541

Zeppel, H. (2008). Education and conservation benefits of marine wildlife tours: Developing free-choice learning experiences. *The Journal of Environmental Education, 39*(3), 3–18.

3 Public Pedagogy, Climate Change Activism and the Case for Ecosocialism

Mike Cole

Introduction

In this chapter I use public pedagogy as a theoretical lens through which to analyse discourses around climate change activism and ecosocialism. I begin by outlining the concept of public pedagogy per se (put simply educational activity and learning that occurs outside of formal educational institutions in the sense of schools, colleges and universities). I then provide examples of the ways public pedagogy has traditionally promoted progressive causes – social justice in general. Public pedagogy has also been used recently to champion regressive social change. I give some general examples, before noting the ways in which the public pedagogies of Donald Trump and the American far right are used to promote hate, racism and fascism. I move on to a consideration of public pedagogy and climate change activism, focusing on Greta Thunberg and Fridays For Future, and two variants of Extinction Rebellion in the USA. I then address public pedagogy for socialism per se, before concluding the chapter with an analysis of public pedagogy promoting ecosocialism, an ecosocialism fully informed by ecofeminism and antiracism.

What is Public Pedagogy?

Social justice educator Roger Simon (2006, p. 109) has argued that pedagogy as a concept lends itself to a variety of sites for education to take place that are 'multiple, shifting and overlapping'. *Public* pedagogy extends pedagogical analysis beyond schools, colleges and universities to learning in other institutions such as museums, zoos and libraries, as well as informal educational sites like popular culture, commercial spaces and the media, including of course, social media. It also occurs through figures and sites of activism, including public intellectuals and grassroots social movements (Sandlin, Schultz, & Burdick, 2010). It is also a widely used medium in the speeches, tweets and interviews of politicians and other public figures, and in podcasts and video lectures as well as blogs, articles and books. Public pedagogy is an important corrective to any

DOI: 10.4324/9780429326011-5

notion that pedagogy takes place only in conventional educational settings. Public pedagogy analysis can be progressive or regressive.

Public Pedagogy Promoting Progressive Social Change

While the parameters of the concept of public pedagogy are wide-ranging, traditionally the overwhelming focus of the majority of historical and contemporary public pedagogy theorists has been on the promotion of social justice for all. To this end, as Sandlin et al. (2011) point out, many have been involved in a counter-hegemonic project against neoliberalism and its multiple manifestations per se, and/or against the oppression of multiple identities based on gender, 'race', age, sexual orientation and social class that it upholds. Moreover:

> Although the context and meaning of [public pedagogy] differ in early sources from current parlance, in some ways [it] remains consistent – the term [dating back to 1894] implied a form of educational discourse in the service of the *public good*.
> (Sandlin et al., 2011, pp. 341–342)

Sandlin et al. (2011, *passim*) provide numerous examples of such public pedagogy.

Promoting Regressive Social Change

Public pedagogy has been deployed in recent times to look at ways in which regressive (or reactionary) discourses and accompanying policies are permeated. Thus Henry Giroux (2010, p. 7) refers to a 'public pedagogy of hate' in the USA, emitted by a 'right-wing spin machine', influenced by the right-wing media, in particular conservative radio talk show hosts, that 'endlessly spews out a toxic rhetoric' against Muslims, African Americans and other people of colour, immigrants and many other groups (Giroux, 2010, p. 8).

In Cole (2020a; see also 2019), I extend Giroux's public pedagogy of hate to widen regressive public pedagogy formulations. Specifically, I discuss public pedagogies of hate and threat as key components of Theresa May's 'really hostile environment', initiated and developed when May was Home Secretary and Prime Minister, and directed at ('illegal') immigrants, a toxic policy that continues under the right-wing populist government of Boris Johnson (e.g. Mellor, 2020).

I analysed how ex-president Donald Trump promoted hatred through his speeches and via Twitter in Cole (2020b, chs 2, 3 and 4; see also 2020c). Trump's public pedagogy of hate served not only to attempt to 'educate' the public at large, often to promote racism, sexism, misogyny and climate change misinformation, and to mock disability, but also to

100   *Mike Cole*

embolden and legitimise the views of individuals and groups associated with the alternative right or alt-right, and other far right groups with core fascist beliefs. Ongoing policies, I demonstrated, accompanied Trump's public pedagogy. I also referred to 'public pedagogy in reverse', this formulation referring to Trump's describing as 'fake news' any news that he claimed was published or broadcast by certain news outlets in order to undermine or discredit him: 'don't take any notice of them because you are being misinformed.' The reality is that it is the Trump administration that developed, institutionalised and weaponised the concept of 'fake news' to serve and further its own right-wing agenda (e.g. Agostinone-Wilson, 2020).

The alt-right, I argue, were, spurred on by Trump, also clearly and manifestly engaged in public pedagogies of hate, including misogyny, but in addition actively promoting a public pedagogy for fascism, both in their quest for white supremacy and a white ethno-state and in terms of policy recommendations for a neo-Nazi USA that embodies some key elements of classic fascism. Thus, Trump and the alt-right can be viewed as attempting to undermine 'liberal democracy' (e.g. Shattuck et al., 2018). Since the alt-right rally and anti-fascist response at Charlottesville in August 2017, the alt-right and its theoretical base has been in decline (see Cole, 2020b, pp. 15–16, 50–53, 94). However, the lead up to the 2020 US general election and its immediate aftermath witnessed a small consolidation of pro-Trump fascistic support that coalesced around false claims of a rigged election and a 'Biden-socialist-communist conspiracy'. The 'proud boys' (an all-male fascist political organisation that promotes violence against anti-fascists and socialists) have been a central component of this. Significant sections of Trump's non-capitalist base, the most backward and reactionary social elements in US society, remain loyal to Trump.

Public Pedagogy and Climate Change Activism

Greta Thunberg

The influence of Greta Thunberg and the many millions who are inspired by her example, including school students engaging in climate change strikes (Fridays For Future or FFF) and countless other followers world-wide, cannot be underestimated. Late in 2020, one month before her 18th birthday, Thunberg made full use of the public pedagogical opportunities afforded by social media to address her 10.5 million Instagram followers in a video in which she urged them to #FightFor1point5, an obvious reference to the Paris Agreement five years earlier in which 196 countries pledged to try to halt the average rise in world temperatures to 1.5 degrees Celsius more than pre-industrial levels (Sly, 2020). Referring to the 'distant, hypothetical targets being set' and 'empty words' continuing to be used by governments,

Public Pedagogy   101

she warned that at the rate we are heading 'our remaining CO_2 budget of 1.5 degrees will be gone within seven years'. She was keen to point out that 'we cannot solve a crisis without treating it as a crisis' and urged people to 'unite' and 'spread awareness' (cited in Sly, 2020).

The United Nations Environment Programme had warned that the 7 per cent fall in carbon pollution recorded in 2020 would have a 'negligible impact' on global warming generally, and that countries needed to undertake a rapid shift away from using fossil fuels (cited in Sly, 2020). The five years since the Paris Accord have been the five hottest years ever recorded and, in her video, Thunberg urged people to take action and stop 'living as if there was no tomorrow'. She concluded, 'There is hope ... We are the hope we, the people' (cited in Sly, 2020).

Thunberg also deserves credit for confronting arch-climate change denier Trump. Towards the end of 2019, she was named *Time* magazine's Person of the Year, prompting Trump (who was hoping to get the award himself) to tell her to 'chill out' and 'work on her anger management problem', adding that she should 'go to a good old fashioned movie with a friend' (cited in Wood, 2019). He had previously responded sarcastically to a speech she made at the UN, saying, 'She seems like a very happy young girl looking forward to a bright and wonderful future. So nice to see' (cited in Wood, 2019). Thunberg once replied to those whose public pedagogies of hate are directed at her: 'When haters go after your looks and differences, it means they have nowhere left to go. And then you know you're winning'. She went on, 'I have Aspergers and that means I'm sometimes a bit different from the norm. And – given the right circumstances – being different is a superpower' (cited in Wood, 2019). In January 2020, Trump attended the World Economic Forum (WEF) in Davos, and was involved in what Tim Cohen (2020) describes as 'surely one of the most bizarre non-confrontational confrontations in history', with a president of the United States and a young Swedish woman going toe-to-toe, without mentioning each other's names, without a meeting and without any overt acknowledgement of each other's argument. Together they symbolise the distance between climate activists and the bastions of political power (Cohen, 2020). In an audience that included Thunberg, Trump declared, 'We must reject the perennial prophets of doom and their predictions of the apocalypse', dismissing climate activists as fearmongering 'prophets of doom' who will cripple global economies and strip away individual liberties in what he described as a misguided mission to save the planet. He compared them to people who predicted an overpopulation crisis in the 1960s, mass starvation in the 1970s and an end of oil in the 1990s: 'These alarmists always demand the same thing: absolute power to dominate, transform and control every aspect of our lives. We will never let radical socialists destroy our economy, wreck our country or eradicate our liberty' (cited in Cohen, 2020). On a different panel, Thunberg responded: 'The facts are clear, but they are

102   *Mike Cole*

still too uncomfortable. You just leave it because you think it's too depressing and they will give up. But people will not give up. You are the ones who are giving up' (cited in Cohen, 2020). She argued that planting trees is good (Trump had promised to plant one trillion trees) but not enough; we need zero emissions (Cohen, 2020) (just after Trump left Davos, it was revealed that BP had successfully lobbied in favour of Trump's decision to dilute a landmark environmental law, making it easier for new major infrastructure projects, such as oil pipelines and power plants, to bypass checks – Ambrose, 2020). Thunberg was right to point out at Davos that from a 'sustainability perspective, the right, the left and the centre have all failed' and that no 'political ideology or economic structure has been able to tackle the environmental and climate emergency and create a cohesive and sustainable world', but, as will be argued in the rest of this chapter, wrong to claim that 'it's not about politics' (cited in Cohen, 2020). That no political ideology or economic structure has been able to solve climate change does not mean that it cannot. In the final part of this chapter, I will make the case that ecosocialism is the only way that we can both save the planet and harness the technological fruits of the Fourth Industrial Revolution for the good of all; but first I will consider another leading player in the global struggle for climate change emergency: the Extinction Rebellion movement.

Extinction Rebellions (XR) US and America

Like Thunberg and FFF, XR uses both street activism and radical rhetoric as media for public pedagogy to reveal the realities of climate change and the need for urgent direct action. In the United States, XR US needs to be distinguished from its offshoot XR America. Geoff Dembicki, author of *Are We Screwed? How a New Generation Is Fighting to Survive Climate Change* (2017), explains the split. Unlike the original UK version of XR, XR US embodies the demand that the needs of 'Black people, Indigenous people, people of color, and poor communities' be prioritized while transitioning to a zero-carbon economy (Dembicki, 2020). Because of this, in Spring 2020, several activists formerly with XR US or associated local chapters launched a new group called XR America, which removed the demand, replacing it with the rallying cry, 'one people, one planet, one future'. Jonathan Logan, one of XR America's founders, explains the rationale for the replacement:

> If we don't solve climate change, Black lives don't matter. If we don't solve climate change now, LGBTQ [people] don't matter. If we don't solve climate change right now, all of us together in one big group, the #MeToo movement doesn't matter … I can't say it hard enough. We don't have time to argue about social justice.
>
> (Cited in Dembicki, 2020)

Public Pedagogy 103

As Dembicki (2020) comments, remarks like this reveal:

> a fundamental divide within activist circles: Should fighting climate change mean also embracing progressive policies that prioritize people of color—who often are more at risk from global warming—or should advocates stay away from fights over inequality that might alienate some people?

The origins of this schism, he goes on, are in Extinction Rebellion UK, which holds the position that XR should transcend traditional left and right politics and operate on the more universal idea that climate catastrophe is terrible for us all. In the words of XR UK co-founder Roger Hallam, 'the main issue is everyone's gonna die in the next 30 years' (cited in Dembicki, 2020). While identity politics, he argues, have been very good at furthering the rights of minorities, 'it would be wrong to deny that it also has significant drawbacks, which is that it can't appeal to everyone' (cited in Dembicki, 2020).

While, on its plus side, within weeks of its 2018 launch, XR UK had 'succeeded in convincing thousands of people to shut down bridges and major roads in London', and while, following additional waves of protests in Spring 2019 a UK Parliament committee urged the country to achieve 'net-zero' emissions by 2050 (this became law not long after), questions arose about that organisation's approach to 'race'. This was when XR UK urged 'the police and legal system to concentrate on issues such as knife crime, and not non-violent protesters who are trying to save our planet' (cited in Dembicki, 2020) and could be seen as 'a dog whistle about crime in low-income black neighborhoods' (Dembicki, 2020).

This was why shortly after XR US was founded in the Summer of 2018, local chapters reviewed its demands and voted to add the aforementioned 'just transition that prioritizes the most vulnerable people and indigenous sovereignty'. When some activists were removed by local chapters for trying to remove this demand, XR America was born, with Logan arguing that a 'big tent' approach was needed that makes 'no judgements about race, class, politics or religion' (Dembicki, 2020). Climate change journalist and author Wen Stephenson points out that a failure to draw a clear moral line between people most affected by global temperature rise and those who profit from it has been a recurring pattern in the US climate change movement (Dembicki, 2020).

A slogan that often appears on XR demonstrates is 'system change not climate change'. A truly radical solution that advocates a post-capitalist world and calls for the redistribution of wealth is ecosocialism. This both supersedes Thunberg's lack of faith in the capability of any economic structure or political belief to solve the problem of climate change and solves the XR dilemma of whether to transcend left politics in favour of 'climate change is bad for us all'. As developed in the last section of this

104   *Mike Cole*

chapter, ecosocialism is a form of socialism that is antiracist and ecofeminist at its core. Ecosocialism is also fully inclusive of all oppressed identities. Before focusing my attention on these and other key aspects of ecosocialist transition, I make some brief comments about public pedagogy for socialism per se.

Public Pedagogy for Socialism

With respect to progressive social and socialist and ecosocialist movements and parties, a general point needs to be stressed. Public pedagogy is definitively not intended to replace more traditional struggles in the workplace, in communities and on the streets (although these of course will often encompass aspects of public pedagogy) but to complement them.

Moving beyond the traditional concerns of public pedagogy in broad social justice issues, Cole (2020a) addresses overtly *socialist* public pedagogy, primarily in the UK. In making the case for a socialist future without borders, inevitable as well as socially just, I extend the social justice concerns of traditional public pedagogy to specific and concrete socialist visions of the future.

In Cole (2020b), I introduce public pedagogies that address contemporary American political realities, including anti-fascist (pp. 94–95), anti-capitalist and pro-socialist formulations (pp. 97–115), again going beyond the social justice agenda of progressive public pedagogy theory, expanding it to include not just ongoing struggles against the growing threat of neo-Nazism, but the challenge to the capitalist system itself and the promotion of the socialist alternative in the USA. I advocate Marxism as a theory that, unlike many other progressive theories, provides both a rigorous critique of capitalism and an emblematic vision for the future (this is developed in detail in Cole, 2008, 2018). In addition, I discuss a 'public pedagogy for ecology' (Cole, 2020b, p. 111) and a 'public pedagogy of love' (Cole, 2020b, pp. 101–102), the latter based on radical Christian principles in Martin Luther King Jr. Finally, Cole (2021) addresses climate change and the Fourth Industrial Revolution (4IR). In that book, I expand the discussion of socialism that was in Cole (2020a and 2020b) to address public pedagogy for ecosocialism in a projected future that can utilise the full fruits of 4IR for the benefit of all. Ecosocialism, I argue, must be ecofeminist and antiracist.

To conclude this section of the chapter, it should be stressed that public pedagogy against capitalism and for socialism is not new, and dates back at least to the early socialists (see Cole, 2008, pp. 13–27). One of the most auspicious and powerful public pedagogical treatises, Marx and Engels's (1848) *Manifesto of the Communist Party*, has sold around 500 million copies, and is one of the four best-selling books of all time. Both the *Manifesto* and Marx's three volumes of *Capital* (1887, 1893, 1894) are UNESCO World Heritage documents (deutschland.de. 2018). However,

Public Pedagogy 105

given that Sandlin et al. (2011) limited their analysis of 'public pedagogy' to 'public pedagogy literature', that is to say to scholarly works that actually use the term or can be considered foundational texts, a discussion of Marx or Engels or socialism was not present in that literature at that time and was therefore not addressed. There is one mention of 'Marxian', when they state that 'Marxian perspectives on culture insist that all public policy, regardless of origin, is always shaped by the economic context of its production' (Sandlin et al., 2011, p. 352). It is worth noting here that during 2019, the World Socialist Web Site (WSWS), a formidable organ of public pedagogy, experienced an enormous growth in its readership. I draw on a number of WSWS articles in this chapter and in my work in general. I should point out, however, that I have reservations about the writers on the site's marginalisation of and sometimes hostility towards struggles and issues not directly related to social class. Neither do I agree totally with the WSWS's blanket rejection of the official trade union movement, although I agree that many official and/or full-time union leaders are not to be trusted. Finally I do not concur with its wholesale denunciation of other left parties and organisations as 'pseudo-left'. According to that organisation, the total number of page views increased to 20 million, from 14 million in 2018 (a growth of more than 40 per cent). The largest period of readership, with more than two million people accessing the site each month, corresponded with the General Motors strike and the auto workers' struggle in September and October in the USA (North and Kishore, 2020).

In the final section of this chapter, I turn to ecosocialism, arguably the only solution to the climate destruction and the ongoing ravages of global capitalism. Ecosocialism not only has the potential to save the planet, it can harness the technological fruits of the 4IR for the many rather than for the global elite.

The Case for Ecosocialism

It cannot be reiterated enough that an international ecosocialism for the twenty-first century must reject the anti-democratic realities of the 'actually existing socialisms' of the twentieth. Thus the core of ecosocialism is the concept of 'democratic ecological planning, wherein the population itself, not "the market" or a Politburo, make the main decisions about the economy' (Löwy, 2018). The public pedagogy of Michael Löwy (2018) makes the case for a Great Transition to Ecosocialism. Early in this transition to a new way of life with its new mode of production and consumption, some sectors of the economy must be suppressed (e.g. the extraction of fossil fuels implicated in the climate crisis) or restructured. At the same time, new sectors need to be developed. Economic transformation must be accompanied by the active pursuit of full employment with equal conditions of work and wages. As stressed by Löwy (2020),

106 *Mike Cole*

ecological goals that relate to closing coal mines, oil wells, thermal power stations and so on *must* be accompanied by guaranteed employment for the workers involved.

Such an egalitarian vision is essential both for building a just society and for engaging the support of the working class in the structural transformation of the productive forces (Löwy (2018). Ultimately, Löwy continues, this vision is incompatible with private control of the means of production and the planning process. In particular, for investments and technological innovation to serve the common good, they must be channelled towards need and not profit. In other words, decision-making must be taken away from the banks and other capitalist enterprises and put in the public domain. This will enable society as a whole and not a small oligarchy of property owners nor an elite of 'techno-bureaucrats' to 'democratically decide which productive lines are the priority, and how resources are to be invested in education, health, and culture' (Löwy, 2018). As Löwy argues, major decisions on investment priorities – such as terminating all coal-fired facilities or directing agricultural subsidies to organic production – should be taken by direct popular vote, while other, less important decisions could be taken by elected bodies, on the relevant national, regional or local scale.

The Fourth Industrial Revolution

Democratic decision-making on a local, national or even international level becomes easier and easier and more and more sophisticated as ongoing technological advances in the 4IR bring people closer and closer together in various ways. Klaus Schwab, the founder (in 1971) and Executive Chairman (*sic*) of the World Economic Forum, according to Stephan Richter, publisher and editor-in-chief of *The Globalist*, and Uwe Bott, its chief economist, 'has always naturally articulated the views of the world's economic elites' (Richter & Bott, 2019); or in the blunter words of Patrick Craven, writing in *The Daily Maverick*, serves to 'bring together the world's rich and powerful capitalist leaders to discuss how best to protect their wealth and privileges' (Craven, 2017) has differentiated 4IR from the other industrial revolutions as follows;

> The First Industrial Revolution used water and steam power to mechanize production. The Second used electric power to create mass production. The Third used electronics and information technology to automate production. Now a Fourth Industrial Revolution is building on the Third, the digital revolution that has been occurring since the middle of the last century. It is characterized by a fusion of technologies that is blurring the lines between the physical, digital, and biological spheres.
>
> (Schwab, 2015)

Public Pedagogy 107

Löwy (2018) offers three counters to right-wing fearmongering that 'central planning' takes away freedom, since 'democratic ecological planning', he argues, 'ultimately supports more freedom, not less'. First it offers 'liberation from the reified "economic laws" of the capitalist system that shackle individuals'. Freedom for workers to make their own decisions about what to produce for human need and not profit is of course greatly enhanced by the vast potentials offered by 4IR.

Löwy's second response to right-wing critics of central planning is that ecosocialism 'heralds a substantial increase in free time', since planning and the reduction of labour time 'are the two decisive steps towards what Marx (1894) called "the kingdom of freedom"' (Löwy, 2018). A significant increase of free time, he insists, must be 'a condition for the participation of working people in the democratic discussion and management of economy and of society' (Löwy, 2018).

Ecosocialism Must Be Feminist

In this regard, Mary Mellor (e.g. 2018, 2019) has criticised Löwy and other ecosocialists for their neglect of gender issues. Specifically, Mellor (2019, p. 189) argues that many ecosocialists 'fail to recognize the role of reproductive work in mediating between nature and "the economy", through the daily regeneration of human (and non-human) life'. Even with the end of alienating paid work, she stresses, there would still be 'the unrelenting nature of care work throughout the life cycle' (Mellor, 2019, p. 189). Historically and for the most part, today, she correctly asserts, this labour has mainly been performed by women. The 'kingdom of freedom', hailed by Löwy (2018), she claims, is genderless (Mellor, 2019, p. 189). She then notes that 'socialist-feminists have long pointed out, in the dreams of a coming age in which, following Marx (1845) one can hunt in the morning, fish in the afternoon and be a critic after dinner, there is never any mention of who cooks the dinner' (Mellor, 2019, p. 189). Mellor proposes an ecofeminist model of 'sufficiency provisioning' (p. 190). By 'sufficiency', she means an egalitarian organising principle whereby 'sufficiency for one must be sufficiency for all' (p. 190). 'Provisioning', she explains, is rooted in feminist economics and is concerned with both productive and reproductive labour. It is critical, she argues, in the development of 'a radical political economy that is both socially just and ecologically sustainable' (p. 190). 'Provisioning' is more comprehensive than standard political economics in that it encompasses a view of humans as 'bodily creatures' who are metabolically related to the environment and embedded in the natural conditions of the planet (p. 191):

> [Women] have a life cycle that requires nourishing, physically and emotionally. This requires constant work. Caring, cleaning, comforting, feeding, listening, watching, accompanying. There is no choice

108   *Mike Cole*

about this. If everyone is left to choose whether to carry out these activities people will die, get sick, starve, despair. Nor can this be left to democratic ecological planning. Embodied needs have to be met immediately. It is well recognized that by default this work falls mainly to women and girls whether as mothers, wives, daughters, or low-paid workers. If a red-green future will be bucolic freedom for the ex-workers/consumers, women's burden of work will never pass from them.

(Mellor, 2018)

Just as the capitalist mode of production 'treats natural resources and eco-systems – fossil fuels, water systems, forests, soils, the atmosphere, the climate system – as inexhaustible, "costless externalities"', so it also relies on a similar 'costless externality': the unpaid work of women in the gendered division of labour in reproducing the labour force with bodily needs and emotional sustenance outside the workplace (Mellor, 2019, p. 191). To which I would add, women also reproduce the next generation of female caregivers. (Mellor 2018) acknowledges that women's 'burden is also increasingly shared by men where longer lifespans and fewer children mean that many men become caregivers later in life'. Moreover, under capitalism, women often perform a double shift (if they are also in paid labour), or a triple shift (for example, if they are also students).

A solution to this oppression in an ecosocialist future would be to expand the welfare state beyond such areas as nursing, teaching and caring 'into a public/social economy that ensures that everyone has the means of sustenance' (Mellor, 2018). Sufficiency provisioning thus implies two objectives: the public sector providing goods and services through 're-gendered and non-oppressive relations' in an expansion of high quality social provision and environmental sustainability and social justice (Mellor, 2019, p. 192). Again developments in 4IR can facilitate this provision.

Löwy's (2018) third counter to the right-wing accusation that 'central planning' diminishes freedom is that in fact democratic ecological planning represents a whole society's exercise of its freedom to control the decisions that affect its destiny. If capitalist democracy in theory prevents political decision-making power being confined to a small elite, why should this not also apply to economic decisions (Kovel, 2002, p. 215; see also Bowles & Gintis, 1976)? The inclusion of 'in theory' in this sentence is pivotal. Genuinely democratic socialism, where elected leaders are permanently subject to recall democratically by those who have elected them, is the best way to safeguard against totalitarianism. While capitalist political systems are formally democratic, representative democracy, for example in the United States and Britain, in effect amounts to a form of totalitarianism. In these countries, citizens can vote every five years, having in reality a choice (in the sense of who will actually be able to form a

Public Pedagogy 109

government) of two or three main totally pro-capitalist parties, who then go on to exercise power in the interests of neoliberal global capitalism and imperialism, with little or no regard for the interests of those workers who elected them. If, for example, Bernie Sanders had been nominated for and had won the US presidential election in November 2020, this would have changed, possibly significantly. There are also, of course, some restraints on what elected leaders in capitalist 'democracies' can get away with (minimum wage and human rights legislation, for example), and importantly, the balance of class forces and the strength of working class resistance (e.g. Hill, 2020). Thus with ecosocialist central planning, production would be for need, not profit:

> Under capitalism, use-value—the worth of a product or service to well-being—exists only in the service of exchange-value, or value on the market. Thus, many products in contemporary society are socially useless, or designed for rapid turnover ('planned obsolescence'). By contrast, in a planned ecosocialist economy, use-value would be the only criteria for the production of goods and services, with far-reaching economic, social, and ecological consequences.
>
> (Löwy, 2018)

Central planning, Löwy (2018) suggests, would focus on large-scale, rather than small-scale, economic decisions: the decision, for example, to transform a plant from producing cars to producing buses and trams would be taken by 'society as a whole', but the internal organisation and functioning of the enterprise would be democratically managed by its workers. While there has been a lot of discussion about the 'centralised' or 'decentralised' nature of planning, the most important element is 'democratic control at all levels—local, regional, national, continental, or international'. Thus, planetary ecological issues such as global warming must be dealt with democratically on a global scale. 'This nested, democratic decision-making', Löwy (2018) argues, 'is quite the opposite of what is usually described, often dismissively, as "central planning," since decisions are not taken by any "center," but democratically decided by the affected population at the appropriate scale':

> Democratic and pluralist debate would occur at all levels. Through parties, platforms, or other political movements, varied propositions would be submitted to the people, and delegates would be elected accordingly. However, representative democracy must be complemented—and corrected—by Internet-enabled direct democracy, through which people choose—at the local, national, and, later, global level—among major social and ecological options. Should public transportation be free? Should the owners of private cars pay special taxes to subsidize public transportation? Should solar energy

110   *Mike Cole*

be subsidized in order to compete with fossil energy? Should the work week be reduced to 30 hours, 25 hours, or less, with the attendant reduction of production?

(Löwy, 2018)

Women, must of course, be equal partners in all such democratic endeavours. Stressing that the ecosocialist revolution is a process rather than an event, Löwy insists that the 'Great Transition' from capitalist destructive progress to ecosocialism 'is a historical process, a permanent revolutionary transformation of society, culture, and mindsets'. 'Enacting this transition', he goes on, 'leads not only to a new mode of production and an egalitarian and democratic society, but also to an alternative *mode of life*, a new ecosocialist *civilization*'. This goes 'beyond the reign of money, beyond consumption habits artificially produced by advertising, and beyond the unlimited production of commodities that are useless and/or harmful to the environment'. 'Such a transformative process' crucially 'depends on the active support of the vast majority of the population for an ecosocialist program'. 'The decisive factor', he concludes, 'in development of socialist consciousness and ecological awareness is the collective experience of struggle, from local and partial confrontations to the radical change of global society as a whole' (Löwy, 2018). This radical change must, at all stages, recognise and involve women as equal partners.

Ecosocialism Must Be Ecofeminist and Antiracist

In 1997, Mellor described ecofeminism as 'a movement that sees a connection between the exploitation and degradation of the natural world and the subordination and oppression of women' (Mellor, 1997, p. 1). Specifically, it:

> Brings together the analysis of the ecological consequences of human 'progress' from the green movement, and the feminist critique of women's disproportionate responsibility for the costs and consequences of women's embodiment, to show how relations of inequality within the human community are reflected in destructive relations between humanity and the non-human world.
>
> (Mellor, 1997, p. viii)

Some 20 years later, Leigh Brownhill and Terisa Turner, members of the ecofeminist collective associated with the journal, *Capitalism Nature Socialism*, insist, along with others writing in that journal (e.g. Barca, 2017; Feder, 2019; Giacomini et al., 2018, Kovel, 2005), that ecosocialism that is not ecofeminist is not worth its salt (Brownhill & Turner, 2020). Moreover, according to these writers, ecofeminism is inclusive of antiracism. Antiracism must, of course, be a key component of

Public Pedagogy   111

ecosocialism. In their words, 'ecofeminism is the recognition of and struggle against capitalists' racist colonization and exploitation of (that is, extraction of profits from) nature and women'. For Brownhill and Turner (2020, p. 1), in so far as ecofeminism 'is characterized by efforts to unite the exploited across historic social divisions (e.g. waged and unwaged)', it is 'the revolutionary way to an ecosocialist, post-capitalist future'. It is the ecofeminist ecosocialism or ecosocialist ecofeminism (they use the terms interchangeably) of women-led Indigenous peoples or of those women engaged in urban struggle, along with young people and people of colour, that 'reveal the depth of the crisis faced by humanity today and its resolution' rather than the 'discourse of gender equality within the bounds of neoliberal capitalism' (Brownhill & Turner, 2020, p. 3).

I agree unreservedly with Brownhill and Turner on the crucial role of the women they champion in the previous paragraph and their international significance and importance, especially in comparison with those who advocate equality under capitalism with no wish to transcend it (Brownhill & Turner, 2020, p. 3), and with Löwy (2020) that the 'workerist/industrialist dogmatism of the previous century is no longer current'; I also concur with him as to the importance of trade unions (albeit significantly de-shackled from *merely* reformist objectives) and that, 'in the final analysis, we can't overcome the system without the active participation of workers in cities and countryside, who make up the majority of the population' (Löwy, 2020).

Fundamentally changing the world economic system, of course, presents massive challenges. As Alex Callinicos argued, some 20 years ago, getting rid of capitalism is not easy. Transitioning to ecosocialism entails breaking through the 'bizarre ideological mechanism, [in which] *every* conceivable alternative to the market has been discredited by the collapse of Stalinism' (Callinicos, 2000, p. 122), whereby the fetishisation of life makes capitalism seem natural and therefore unalterable and where the market mechanism 'has been hypostatized into a natural force unresponsive to human wishes' (Callinicos, 2000, p. 125). Capital presents itself as 'determining the future as surely as the laws of nature make tides rise to lift boats (McMurtry, 2000, p. 2),

> as if it has now replaced the natural environment. It announces itself through its business leaders and politicians as coterminous with freedom, and indispensable to democracy such that any attack on capitalism as exploitative or hypocritical becomes an attack on world freedom and democracy itself.
>
> (McLaren, 2000, p. 32)

On a note of optimism, Callinicos concludes, despite the inevitable intense resistance from capital, the 'greatest obstacle to change is not ...

112 *Mike Cole*

the revolt it would evoke from the privileged, but the belief that it is impossible' (2000, p. 128). Challenging the status quo:

> Requires courage, imagination and willpower inspired by the injustice that surrounds us. Beneath the surface of our supposedly contented societies, these qualities are present in abundance. Once mobilized, ... we... can turn the world upside down.
>
> (Callinicos, 2000, p. 129)

References

Agostinone-Wilson, F. (Ed.). (2020). *On the question of truth in the era of Trump.* Boston, MA: Brill/Sense.

Ambrose, J. (2020, January 23). Trump weakened environmental laws after BP lobbying. *The Guardian.* www.theguardian.com/business/2020/jan/23/trump-weakened-environmental-laws-after-bp-lobbying?CMP=Share_iOSApp_Other

Barca, S. (2017). The labor(s) of degrowth. *Capitalism Nature Socialism, 30*(2),207–216. www.tandfonline.com/doi/abs/10.1080/10455752.2017.1373300

Bowles, S. & Gintis, H. (1976). *Schooling in capitalist America.* London: Routledge and Kegan Paul.

Brownhill, L., & Turner, T.E. (2020). Ecofeminist ways, ecosocialist means: Life in the post-capitalist future. *Capitalism Nature Socialism, 31*(1), 1–14. www.tandfonline.com/doi/full/10.1080/10455752.2019.1710362?scroll=top&neededAccess=true

Callinicos, A. (2000). *Equality.* Oxford: Polity Press.

Cohen, T. (2020, January 22). Climate crisis: A teen and a president face off in Davos – but around them the world is changing. *Daily Maverick.* https://www.dailymaverick.co.za/opinionista/2020-01-22-climate-crisis-a-teen-and-a-president-face-off-in-davos-but-around-them-the-world-is-changing/

Cole, M. (2008). *Marxism and educational theory: Origins and issues.* London and New York: Routledge.

Cole, M. (2018). Social class, Marxism and socialism. In M. Cole (Ed.), *Education, equality and human rights: Issues of gender, 'race', sexuality, disability and social class* (4th ed., 267–300). London and New York: Routledge.

Cole, M. (2019). We must never forget Theresa May's full frontal assault on families like mine. *The Huffington Post.* https://www.huffingtonpost.co.uk/entry/theresa-may-minimum-income-requirement_uk_5cfa1db5e4b06af8b506823e

Cole, M. (2020a). *Theresa may, the hostile environment and public pedagogies of hate and threat: The case for a future without borders.* London: Routledge.

Cole, M. (2020b). *Trump, the alt-right and public pedagogies of hate and for fascism: What is to be done?* London and New York: Routledge.

Cole, M. (2020c). Racism and fascism in the era of Donald J. Trump and the alt-right: Critical race theory and socialism as oppositional forces. In V. Lee and E. Shepherd W. Farmer (Eds.), *Critical race theory in the academy* (pp. 177–200). Charlotte, NC: Information Age Publishing.

Cole, M. (2021). *Climate change, the fourth industrial revolution and public pedagogies: The case for ecosocialism.* London and New York: Routledge.

Public Pedagogy   113

Craven, P. (2017, January 5). The 'fourth industrial revolution' – or socialist revolution? *Daily Maverick*. www.dailymaverick.co.za/opinionista/2017-01-05-the-fourth-industrial-revolution-or-socialist-revolution/amp/

Dembicki, G. (2017). *Are we screwed? How a generation is fighting to survive climate change*. New York: Bloomsbury.

Dembicki, G. (2020, April 28). A debate over racism has split one of the world's most famous climate groups. *Vice*. https://www.vice.com/en/article/jgey8k/a-debate-over-racism-has-split-one-of-the-worlds-most-famous-climate-groups

deutschland.de. (2018, April 27). Seven facts about Karl Marx. www.deutschland.de/en/topic/knowledge/200-years-of-karl-marx-seven-facts

Feder, H. (2019). 'Never waste a good crisis': An interview with Mary Mellor. *Capitalism Nature Socialism, 30*(4), 44–54. www.tandfonline.com/doi/abs/10.1080/10455752.2018.1499787?journalCode=rcns20

Giacomini, T., Turner, T., Isla, A., & Brownhill, L. (2018). Ecofeminism against capitalism and for the commons. *Capitalism Nature Socialism, 29*(1), 1–6. www.tandfonline.com/doi/full/10.1080/10455752.2018.1429221

Giroux, H.A. (2010). *Hearts of darkness: Torturing children in the war on terror*. London: Paradigm Publishers.

Hill, D. (2020, May 29). The good, the bad and the ugly: Coronavirus, capitalism and socialism: A Marxist response. *InsurgentScripts*. http://insurgentscripts.org/the-good-the-bad-and-the-ugly-coronavirus-capitalism-and-socialism-a-marxist-response/

Kovel, J. (2002). *Enemy of nature: The end of capitalism or the end of the world?* New York: Zed Books.

Kovel, J. (2005). The ecofeminist ground of ecosocialism. *Capitalism Nature Socialism, 16*(2). www.tandfonline.com/doi/abs/10.1080/10455750500108146

Löwy, M. (2018, December). Why ecosocialism: For a red-green future' great transition initiative: Towards transformative vision and praxis. https://great-transition.org/publication/why-ecosocialism-red-green-future

Löwy, M. (2020, February 4). Thirteen theses on the imminent ecological catastrophe and the (revolutionary) means of averting it. *International Viewpoint*. http://internationalviewpoint.org/spip.php?article6391

Marx, K. (1887). *Capital volume 1*. Moscow: Progress Publishers. https://oll.libertyfund.org/titles/marx-capital-a-critique-of-political-economyvolume-i-the-process-of-capitalist-production

Marx, K. 1893 [1967]. *Capital volume 2*. Moscow: Progress Publishers. www.marxists.org/archive/marx/works/1885-c2/index.htm

Marx, K. 1894 [1966]. *Capital volume 3*, Moscow: Progress Publishers. www.marxists.org/archive/marx/works/1894-c3/ch13.htm

Marx, K., & Engels, F. 1848 [2010]. Manifesto of the communist party. *Marxists Internet Archive (marxists.org)*. www.marxists.org/archive/marx/works/download/pdf/Manifesto.pdf

McLaren, P. (2000). *Che Guevara, Paulo Freire and the pedagogy of revolution*. Oxford: Rowman and Littlefield.

McMurtry, J. (2000). Education, struggle and the left today. *International Journal of Educational Reform, 10*(2), 145–162.

Mellor, M. (1997). *Feminism & ecology*. New York: New York University Press.

Mellor, M. (2018, December 4). Do red and green mix?: A roundtable, great transition initiative. www.greattransition.org/roundtable/ecosocialismmary-mellor

114 *Mike Cole*

Mellor, M. (2019, March/June). An eco-feminist proposal. *New Left Review*, 116/117.

Mellor, J. (2020, December 10). Hostile environment' of Home Office 'unlawfully discriminating against Windrush generation. *The London Economic.* https://www.thelondoneconomic.com/news/hostile-environment-of-home-office-unlawfully-discriminating-against-windrush-generation/10/12/

North, D., & Kishore, J. (2020, January 3). The decade of socialist revolution begins. *World Socialist Web Site (WSWS).* www.wsws.org/en/articles/2020/01/03/pers-j03.html

Richter, S., & Bott, U. (2019, January 24). Davos has learned to fake populism. *Foreign Policy.* https://foreignpolicy.com/2019/01/24/davos-has-learned-to-fake-populism/

Sandlin, J.A., O'Malley, M.P., & Burdick, J. (2011, September). Mapping the complexity of public pedagogy scholarship: 1894–2010. *Review of Educational Research, 81*(3), 338–375.

Sandlin, J.A., Schultz, B.D., & Burdick, J. (2010). *Handbook of public pedagogy.* New York: Routledge.

Schwab, K. (2015, December 12). The fourth industrial revolution: What it means and how to respond. *Foreign Affairs.* www.foreignaffairs.com/articles/2015-12-12/fourth-industrial-revolution

Shattuck, J., Watson, A., & McDole, M. (2018). *Trump's first year: How resilient is liberal democracy in the US?* Cambridge, MA: Carr Center for Human Rights Policy Harvard Kennedy School. https://carrcenter.hks.harvard.edu/files/cchr/files/trumpsfirstyeardiscussionpaper.pdf

Simon, R. (2006). Broadening the vision of university-based study of education: The contribution of cultural studies. *The Review of Education, Pedagogy, and Cultural Studies, 12*(1), 107–114.

Sly, E. (2020, December 12). Greta Thunberg criticises 'empty words' of world leaders, five years since the Paris Agreement. *The Independent.* https://www.independent.co.uk/environment/climate-change/greta-thunberg-paris-agreement-video-b1770050.html?amp

Wood, V. (2019, December 12). Greta Thunberg responds to Trump's attack after her time person of the year win. *The Independent.* www.independent.co.uk/news/world/europe/great-thunberg-trump-tweet-time-personof-the-year-bio-twitter-a9243961.html

Part II

Case Studies and Enactments of Climate Change Education for Equity and Justice

4 Equitable and Just by Design

Engaging Youth of Color in Climate Change Education

Na'Taki Osborne Jelks and Crystal Jennings

Introduction

Climate change is considered by many as the largest threat to human society in the twenty-first century. Discourse about climate change solutions centers arguments about the urgent action needed now to curb climate change's negative effects on the planet and human populations versus leaving future generations with the burden of fixing what earlier ones were unwilling to address.

The critical role of youth in advancing solutions to climate change has been highlighted in both peer-reviewed and popular literature (Alhendawi, 2014; Dapaah, 2014; O'Brien et al., 2018; Seymour, 2021; Wikler-Friday, 2021) as well as grey literature from governmental (EPA, 2018) and intergovernmental organizations (UNJFICYCC, 2013; United Nations, 2021). Youth action to elevate climate change as a defining issue of our time has spanned global acts of protest (Aronoff, 2019; Thackeray et al., 2020) and social media organizing and activism (Boulianne et al., 2020), targeted advocacy (Connect4Climate, 2020; Corbett, 2021; UNJFICYCC, 2013) as well as locally focused efforts, such as those addressing waste reduction (Bullock, 2018), food insecurity (FAO, 2019), reduced energy usage, alternative energy sources, and emission reductions implemented both in schools and the broader communities in which they are located (Fowler, 2014; NWF, 2021a; UNJFICYCC, 2013).

Programs and initiatives to educate youth about climate change, its impacts, and solutions have been implemented by a wide range of organizations at the local, national, and global scales (Connect4Climate, 2020; Earth Force, 2021; Gray, 2017; Hammonds & NWF, 2020; NWF, 2021a; Trott, 2020; WE ACT, 2021a). While some focus their approaches on teaching about personal responsibility and how individual choices can positively impact the climate crisis, others focus on youth-led solutions and civic engagement targeted at local, national, and global decision making and action (Earth Force, 2021; United Nations, 2021). To support these efforts, many climate change education curricula center their approaches on using the United Nations Sustainable Development

DOI: 10.4324/9780429326011-7

118 *Na'Taki Osborne Jelks and Crystal Jennings*

Goals (SDGs) (Mochizuki & Bryan, 2015; NWF, 2021b; UNESCO, 2010). Others emphasize a focus on examining climate change education through a social justice and/or racial equity lens (Kirkland & Poppleton, 2021; WE ACT, 2021b).

This chapter will offer reflections about the National Wildlife Federation's Earth Tomorrow® Program in terms of salient aspects of the overall program design as well as its efforts to elevate climate justice through linking climate change with social and environmental justice pursuits in the program curriculum. As one the largest conservation organizations in the United States, the National Wildlife Federation (NWF) has long focused both advocacy and education efforts on climate change solutions as it "works to prevent the causes, mitigate the impacts, and adapt to the fluctuations of a changing climate" (NWF, 2021c). In addition to NWF's focus on federal policy solutions to the climate crisis, it has also addressed climate change from an education perspective largely through its award-winning Eco-Schools USA Program (NWF, 2021b), but also through Earth Tomorrow®, a program focused on improving environmental literacy and growing youth of color into environmental stewards and leaders. Through focusing primarily on the design of one of three key elements of the Earth Tomorrow® Program, its annual summer institute, and other program components, we demonstrate the ways in which a focus on justice, equity, diversity, and inclusion shape and undergird an innovative approach to youth environmental leadership development, civic engagement, and climate change education.

The National Wildlife Federation's Earth Tomorrow® Program

Earth Tomorrow® (ET) is the longest standing youth environmental education and leadership development program of the NWF designed to help high school students empower themselves to tackle environmental justice issues in their local communities. With roots in Detroit, Michigan, the program was implemented in Atlanta, Georgia, in 2001 by staff in NWF's former Southeast Regional Center in Atlanta (now the Atlanta field office, a part of the South Central Regional Center). Although the Atlanta iteration of ET was designed, in part, with an environmental justice framework and orientation to place-based, culturally relevant, and responsive education and leadership development, the program predates NWF's Equity & Justice 2020 Strategic Plan (2020). It was created intentionally for high school-aged youth from black and brown communities "to develop environmental literacy and life skills that help them make valuable contributions to the ecological health of their communities" (Jelks, 2014a).

ET is a model program that provides year-round opportunities for young leaders to build their leadership skills, increase their understanding of environmental and environmental justice issues, gain exposure to

Equitable and Just by Design 119

environmental careers, improve environmental literacy, become more civically engaged, and, ultimately, become well-informed and effective stewards of their environments (NWF, 2021d). The ET program uses its three foundational components—ET school-based clubs, community action and service-learning projects, and the annual ET Summer Institute (ETSI)—to help create opportunities for youth living in urban areas to empower themselves to affect positive environmental change in their communities. Supporting these three foundational components are three critical steps that NWF incorporates in an effort to cultivate the leadership of urban youth of color: (1) broadening youth's understanding of the environmental issues affecting their communities; (2) training youth to develop their skills in community needs assessment and project planning; and (3) supporting youth in using increased awareness of honed leadership skills to transfer knowledge to action in youth-led community action projects (Jelks, 2014b).

Inspiration for the ET Program design comes from a diverse set of frameworks and approaches. In addition to using an environmental justice framework, ET also draws from principles of service-learning (Kaye, 2010) and a commitment to placed-based and culturally relevant and responsive experiential education. The program was crafted in response to the unique cultural, ecological, and social needs of local communities. Youth from neighborhoods highly impacted by pollution and economic disparities are equipped with tools and resources to identify environmental challenges in their communities and develop and implement youth-led solutions that advance urban sustainability and environmental justice. ET cultivates youth leadership in the following ways:

- *Facilitating youth empowerment with tools and processes.* Youth leaders are exposed to a community action planning process and develop key leadership skills they can use to effectively impact community issues.
- *Youth as local agents of change.* NWF believes that young people have the knowledge and awareness to identify issues of importance in their communities. By allowing teens to identify their own community issues and equipping them with useful tools and processes, youth empower themselves to find solutions to local problems and build confidence and voice.

Connecting Theory to Behavior Change

The Environmental Citizenship Behavior Model (Hungerford & Volk, 1990) posits that in order to influence behavior change resulting in responsible citizenship behavior, environmental education and outreach programs must extend beyond raising awareness and increasing knowledge. Research on environmental behavior demonstrates that increased awareness and knowledge are not the only precursors to taking action.

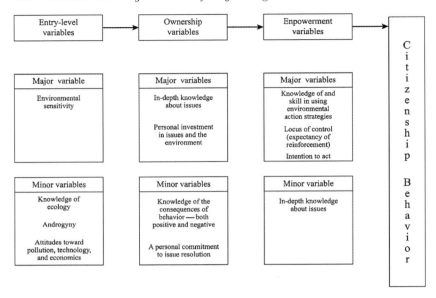

Figure 4.1 Environmental Citizenship Behavior Model (Hungerford & Volk, 1990).

According to Hungerford & Volk, there are three categories of variables that influence behavior: entry level, ownership, and empowerment. Each category of variables is divided into major and minor elements or variables as depicted in Figure 4.1. A brief discussion of the major variables that help undergird the ET program design also follows below.

Entry Level Variables

According to Hungerford &Volk (1990) entry level variables (described below) are good predictors of citizenship behavior and are variables that enhance a person's decision making.

Environmental Sensitivity

In previous studies environmental sensitivity (Goldman et al., 2013) and engagement in youth groups (Arnold et al., 2009) has shown a positive relationship to behavior that supports environmental citizenship. Through ET, the local urban environment is used as a living laboratory and teaching tool to connect students to their environment through hands-on field study activities, service-learning, and community action projects—thereby fostering a sense of place and environmental sensitivity in participants. This approach has also been used in

Equitable and Just by Design   121

other efforts (Barnett et al., 2006) to engage youth in urban ecology studies that have been found to positively impact and improve students' sense of environmental stewardship. In the following sections, we describe activities that are designed to engage ET youth in: exploring and reflecting upon the conditions in their local environment; understanding how these conditions impact the health of ecosystems, human health, and quality of life; and learning about the ways that community-based groups and non-profits are taking actions to address local challenges.

Ownership Variables

In this model, the factors related to ownership are those that make the issues and concerns of the environment personal. Such factors can build on environmental sensitivity, especially as it relates to sense of place and feelings of ownership with respect to addressing issues and problems in one's communities.

In-Depth Knowledge About the Issue

In order for the students to take ownership of local environmental issues, they reflect upon the challenges impacting their schools and surrounding communities. Curricular components focus on ensuring that the students understand the issues in their neighborhoods and both the ecological and human implications as well as the root causes of these issues.

Personal Investment in the Environment

Hungerford and Volk (1990) stipulate that while the categories of variables (entry-level, ownership, and empowerment) probably operate in a linear fashion, the major and minor variables under these categories are more likely to be synergistic in their operations; personal investment in the environment can truly only occur when participants have an in-depth knowledge about the relevant issues.

Empowerment Variables

When citizens/students feel empowered to make changes in their neighborhoods and surroundings, important environmental challenges can be resolved.

Perceived Skill in Using Environmental Action Strategies

To build ET student confidence in their ability to enact environmental action strategies, they are both engaged in community action projects

122 *Na'Taki Osborne Jelks and Crystal Jennings*

designed by NWF staff (to model what a successful project entails) and given training in community action planning to develop their own projects from the issue identification to the implementation stage. When students see that their efforts can make a difference in their local communities, they believe that positive change is possible even when the challenges seem daunting. This belief that beneficial change can happen is reinforced when ET leaders interact with local and national environmental justice leaders who, through storytelling, share their own experiences with fighting environmental injustices and advancing community, environmental, and systems change. Also, when funding is available, NWF supports ET clubs with community action project mini-grants to help carry out their plans, thereby making some projects more feasible. Fundraising training is also a part of the community action project planning process along with training on how to develop communications strategies to help engage and get the support of key school or community decision makers and influencers.

Intention and Ability to Act for the Environment

The synergy of the variables is evidenced when we consider the second major variable related to intention to act. When a person has an intention to act the likelihood of the action occurring increases. NWF makes training and support available for ET club leaders and general members alike to amplify the collective efforts of youth from the same schools and communities.

When the Atlanta ET Program started, there were not many youth programs that connected leadership development, citizenship behavior (action), education, and the environment to social issues in the Atlanta Metropolitan area. ET provides a framework to help youth connect the dots between big global issues like climate change and local issues unevenly and disproportionately impacting communities of color, such as asthma rates. For example, a report from the Asthma and Allergy Foundation of America found that Black, Hispanic, and American Indian/Alaska Native people were most burdened by asthma, with not just the highest rates but also the highest deaths and hospitalizations (AAFA, 2020). In a 2016 study, Atlanta, in particular, was identified as one of three geographic locations in a multi-city study on ambient air pollution and emergency department (ED) visits for asthma in which short-term concentrations of ambient O_3, CO, NO_2, and $PM_{2.5}$ were positively associated with ED visits in children and youth (0–18 years). The greatest mean daily ED visits were identified for non-White populations (Alhanti et al., 2016). Dr. Anthony Fauci, Director of the National Institute of Allergy and Infectious Diseases, has been quoted as indicating something strikingly similar when talking about COVID-19 killing Black people at a high rate: "Health disparities have always existed for

Equitable and Just by Design 123

the African American community. Here again with the crisis … it's shining a bright light on how unacceptable that is because, yet again … you have a situation like the coronavirus, [and] they are suffering disproportionately" (Vergano & Goba, 2020).

As disheartening as it likely is to constantly hear that one's community will suffer more than other communities from challenges like climate change or from a broad range of health disparities associated with systemic racism and the social determinants of health, it can also create a sense of urgency for youth (CBE, n.d.), and, in particular, for participants of ET to investigate the root causes of environmental problems and to initiate student-led solutions to address them. ET staff and partners work side-by-side with students from these frontline communities—making them increasingly aware of the impacts of climate change, and how disparities in access to nature, healthy food, clean air and water, healthy living conditions, and other factors have a detrimental effect on human health and quality of life.

Aida Eyasu, a Tucker High School ET club member (Tucker, Georgia) shared her personal story for why she got involved with the program:

> I was raised in a low-income home, and so watching my community go through gentrification has inspired me to speak out for my community. It's never been about what is good for the people who reside here, in fact the only reason why people are building sidewalks, planting trees, etc. is for the people who are now just moving here to change the area. I think it's very important to care about the environment, but because of money and resources it seems that it's not attainable. Though it is really hard, I'm sure making an effort will still land us somewhere.

Aida's willingness to speak out and share her perspective on challenges in her community is one representation of youth voice and leadership on pressing environmental problems, particularly those that impact low-income and communities of color. While the ET Program's parent organization has its roots in concern for wildlife and wild places, the design of the program encourages participants to draw connections between the social, political, and economic issues that undergird environmental challenges, particularly in urban spaces.

ET also serves as a gateway and connector between teen-aged youth and other environmental and social justice organizations and causes. Aida is also active in the Youth Climate Action Coalition in Clarkston, Georgia, where there are the highest number of refugees per capita in the United States. Her interest in the environment stemmed from her own personal experience with gentrification in her community. Seeing first-hand how low-income residents were losing their homes propelled Aida to find ways to mitigate the social impacts of gentrification, using an

124 *Na'Taki Osborne Jelks and Crystal Jennings*

environmental lens. Through her involvement in ET, Aida has also led projects to remove invasive species, pick up recycling, and get petitions signed about combatting racial injustice and taking steps in her local community to address climate change. She has also used social media platforms to spread awareness about local issues in her community among her peers. Aida understands how daunting it is to undo the impact of social injustices rooted in years of unjust and outright racist policies, but she feels that we can still make some progress. Aida's story is very similar to many other students and alumni of the ET PPogram— once their environmental sensitivity is heightened, they gain in-depth knowledge about environmental issues and are armed with skills and tools to make an impact on community challenges and so they turn their awareness into action.

The Earth Tomorrow® Summer Institute

A key element of the ET Program is ETSI, which serves as a pivotal training ground for ET club officers and other students interested in taking on leadership roles in ET activities both at the school and immediate community level and in collaboration with ET leaders from across the Atlanta Region. ETSI is an annual five to seven day residential "environmental leadership bootcamp" held on a local college campus at which students engage in developing and strengthening leadership skills, investigating their local environment, interacting with environmental leaders, and enjoying the "great outdoors." An experience in which ET teens are guided by NWF staff with the support of ET graduates (typically enrolled in college) serving as peer mentors, ETSI exposes students to current global and local environmental issues; provides students with skills training in community needs assessment and problem solving; and engages students in outdoor field study experiences and outdoor recreation, including an overnight camping experience.

The goals of ETSI are:

1. Help teens develop a greater sense of self-esteem, comfort, and sense of pride in their local environment.
2. Provide outdoor experiences for high school students that foster enjoyment of, and appreciation for, the natural world while learning about their local environment and local conservation issues.
3. Engage teens in the research, development, and implementation of projects that benefit the local community.
4. Improve environmental literacy of high school students so they understand their local environment and improve their critical thinking skills on environmental issues that affect their everyday lives, specifically urbanization, watersheds and water conservation, climate change, land and aquatic species, and environmental justice issues,

Equitable and Just by Design 125

5. Ignite enthusiasm for further participation in environmental stewardship activities and build leadership skills to enable such participation,
6. Introduce students to a diverse set of environmental careers and career paths.

While varied themes populate the annual ETSI agenda, justice, equity, diversity, and inclusion undergird the approach to each topic represented from those that focus on urban ecosystems and enjoying the great outdoors to those specific to environmental careers and climate change causes and solutions. With great intentionality, the week is curated to center the experiences of people of color in the outdoors, in environmental and conservation careers, and in terms of historical and present-day perspectives on the roles and contributions of people of color to addressing pressing environmental issues and their related social challenges. In addition to NWF staff, who lead ETSI, the community-based nature of the overall ET Program shows up through a diverse set of facilitators and presenters, such as like-minded non-profits, government agencies, academic institutions, and community-based organizations. These facilitators and presenters represent a wide range of disciplinary backgrounds such as wildlife biology, ecology, watershed science, environmental engineering, urban agriculture, environmental education, marine science, and environmental health, and they are primarily people of color. By design, ETSI exemplifies the 16th Principle of Environmental Justice which calls for the "education of present and future generations which emphasizes social and environmental issues, based on our experience and an appreciation of our diverse cultural perspectives" (First National People of Color Environmental Leadership Summit, 1991). Climate change education for ET leaders is therefore approached from culturally relevant and responsive viewpoints.

Climate Change Education: An Imperative for Earth Tomorrow® Leaders

NWF has published numerous reports and fact sheets on climate change, fought for policies to address climate change, and has partnered with a number of like-minded organizations to create climate education resources. For example, NWF teamed up with filmmakers as the educational partner for Showtime, the American premium cable television station, on its docuseries, *Years of Living Dangerously*, a groundbreaking documentary exploring the true stories of people impacted by, and seeking solutions to address, global climate change (NWF, 2016). Climate change education is an organizational priority for NWF, and in the context of youth, climate change education is a major way that NWF has been and will continue to confront the climate crisis.

126 *Na'Taki Osborne Jelks and Crystal Jennings*

Climate change education is critical for ET participants for a number of reasons. Scholarly articles have reported about the potential for climate change education and the implementation of active learning pedagogy in environmental science to improve students' literacy, boost student engagement, and increase academic achievement in science, technology, engineering, and math (STEM) (Derevenskaiaa, 2014; McCright, 2012; McCright et al., 2013; Soper et al., 2015; Theobald et al., 2020). According to the NWF's Green STEM Guidebook, "students are more motivated to learn and do better in school when they feel that their learning is connected to a larger purpose" (Soper et al., 2015). ET participants are introduced to STEM and related careers, in part through: climate change education presentations; engagement with guest speakers; experiential activities; group discussions; and introductions to videos, reports, and other curated resources as a part of ETSI and other ET activities. If one thinks of STEM disciplines as doors to broadening student engagement and exposure to an expanded set of career opportunities, then climate change education can be considered as unlocking multiple pathways to career and societal success.

Lastly, climate change education prompts civic engagement and student action. This sort of education and action is important for communities of colors to survive and, better yet, to thrive. Taking into consideration the lives that can be improved or even saved through the application of science-based knowledge about climate change, climate education has been central to the ET Program for over 20 years. In this context, the link between climate change and environmental justice has always been underscored for participants. Therefore, climate justice—sitting at the intersection of climate change and environmental justice—is discussed, investigated, and addressed through student-led action by ET participants. As previously mentioned, climate change is an existential threat to human society, but it has a disproportionate impact on communities of color, who are direct beneficiaries of ET-led service learning and community action projects.

Participation in service-learning and community action projects also promotes teenage civic engagement by providing interested youth with the tools needed to research, design, and implement effective solutions focused on environmental and climate justice as well as environmental stewardship projects in their communities. By assessing community needs, implementing projects, and getting the community involved, students are playing a critical role in educating and strengthening their communities.

An Environmental Justice Framework

As defined by the United States Environmental Protection Agency (EPA), environmental justice is "the fair treatment and meaningful involvement of all people regardless of race, color, national origin, or income, with

Equitable and Just by Design 127

respect to the development, implementation, and enforcement of environmental laws, regulations, and policies" (2020). Accordingly, the US EPA asserts that environmental justice is realized when all people can achieve "the same degree of protection from environmental and health hazards, and equal access to the decision-making process to have a healthy environment in which to live, learn, and work" (2021).

Grassroots environmental justice organizations and environmentally overburdened communities often elevate a more expansive definition of environmental justice that emphasizes protection from environmental harms for all people in the environments and associated locations in which they live, work, play, worship, and learn, in both the built and natural environments—emphasizing accountability, democratic practices, equitable treatment, and the self-determination of impacted communities to identify and address their environmental challenges and to determine their own futures, free of toxic exposure, discriminatory planning, the devaluation of low-income and communities of color, and exclusion from decision-making processes that affect health and quality of life. According to one such environmental justice organization, "environmental justice provides a framework for communities of color to articulate the political, economic and social assumptions underlying why environmental racism and degradation happens and how it continues to be institutionally reinforced" (APEN, 2002). Within this context, environmental racism refers to any environmental policy, practice, or directive that intentionally or unintentionally differentially impacts or disadvantages individuals, groups, or communities based on race, color, or ethnicity (Bullard, 1993).

The disproportionate impacts of climate change on communities overburdened by exposure to environmental toxicants and locally unwanted land uses are thereby viewed from this perspective. Grassroots community groups and other community-based organizations and social-justice-focused non-profits teach and engage youth and adults in climate change education and action through the lens of environmental and climate justice. Though NWF is neither a community-based organization or social-justice-focused non-profit, this same approach has been adopted in the ET Program.

Climate Justice is Environmental Justice

Climate change is an existential threat with both current and projected future global impact. While climate change is largely treated as an issue about the natural environment, it also has undeniable implications for social justice and human rights (Bhardwaj, n.d.; Levy & Patz, 2015). Climate change is a human and civil rights issue. Nearly 20 years ago the Congressional Black Caucus (2004) documented the disproportionate health effects associated with climate change experienced by Black communities in the United States. Other important findings of this research were that Black populations in the USA were less responsible for greenhouse gas emissions and that policies designed to mitigate climate change impacts have the potential to result in substantive health and economic benefits for Black communities if intentionally structured to produce just outcomes (CBCF, 2004).

Many of the extreme weather events that have been attributed to or associated with climate change are considered natural disasters; however, they are also unnatural disasters of grand proportion—fueled by anthropogenic activities and leaving behind devastating and far-reaching effects for the most vulnerable populations worldwide (Woetzel et al., 2020). While no one will be able to escape the impacts of climate change, some groups are and will continue to be disproportionately impacted without bold action to change this current trajectory. Not only are these groups, who are largely people of color and low-income populations across the globe, more likely to suffer from the health, economic, and environmental impacts of climate change, but long-standing injustice has left them with compromised abilities to recover and adapt (Kaplan, 2020; Thomas et al., 2019).

Some refer to the multiplier effect of climate change in that it will layer on top of existing inequities in the context of economics, public health, and racial injustices (Causevic, 2017; Howeth, 2020; Huntjens & Nachbar, 2015; WE ACT, 2021c). The COVID-19 pandemic has more than amplified this phenomenon as communities of color in the United States bearing the burden of unequal climate change impacts are also disproportionately affected by deaths from complications due to COVID-19 (Holmes et al., 2020; Koons & Ivry, 2020). Studies have demonstrated the association between living in communities affected by air pollution and contracting COVID-19, and some show that other environmental factors may also affect disease severity (Kumar et al., 2021). Poor air quality, in particular, is associated with more severe health outcomes in infected individuals. Specifically, researchers found in an initial cross-sectional study that long-term exposure to fine particulate matter ($PM_{2.5}$) is linked to increased risk of death from COVID-19 (Wu et al., 2020).

The disproportionate impacts of climate change on low-income and communities of color have long prompted calls for climate justice by impacted populations. One definition of climate justice asserts:

> As a form of environmental justice, climate justice is the fair treatment of all people and the freedom from discrimination in the creation of policies and projects that address climate change as well as the systems that create climate change and perpetuate discrimination.
>
> (Bartholomew, 2015)

The discourse on climate justice shifts the conversation about climate impacts from melting ice caps and other impacts on wildlife to the very real and perhaps more relatable experiences with climate change also borne by human populations (Schlosberg & Collins, 2014). This discourse also raises the assertion that unjust political and economic systems produce both climate change and social inequities that plague low-income and people of color (Public Health - Seattle & King County, n.d.; BCJN, n.d.). By focusing on the root causes of climate change, those who advocate for climate justice call for a systemic approach to addressing the glaring racial and economic injustices that have resulted in an unequal climate burden for Black and other communities of color as well as low-income populations (BCJN, n.d.; Simmons, 2020). Climate justice advocates also emphasize the co-benefits to communities made vulnerable to climate change, through systemic injustice, when the use of fossil fuels is reduced—both climate change and the health effects associated with it are mitigated (CBCF, 2004; Smith et al., 2014). As one precursor to achieving climate justice, the study of climate science integrated with the investigation of related social factors is critical to advancing the intersectional approaches needed to adequately address the complex challenge of climate change (Kaijser & Kronsell, 2014; Kirkland & Poppleton, 2021). The section that follows details the unlikely approach to climate change education delivered to youth of color through NWF and its community partners. The annual ETSI will be used as a focal point for this illustration.

A Pedagogy of Transformation: Climate Change Education as Social Justice Empowerment

Approaches to teaching climate change vary state-by-state and from classroom to classroom; therefore, it is advantageous to provide youth with STEM-supported, interdisciplinary climate change programming to supplement what they may or may not be receiving in the classroom. According to a poll by National Public Radio (NPR), 86% of teachers, in theory, believe that climate change should be taught in the classroom but, in practice, 55% of teachers do not cover it because they believe it is not related to the subjects they teach (Kamenetz, 2019). Fortunately, informal education programs like ET are able to help fill the gap, especially for minority and female students who are under-represented in STEM career fields (National Center for Education Statistics, 2017; Noonan, 2017; Wu & Jing, 2013), and who also make up a large percentage of ET participants. Pedagogically, ETSI participants engage in inquiry-based, experiential learning about climate change through the contexts of climate science, climate impacts, and climate change solutions. Intertwined in the science, impacts, and solutions is the imperative to teach students about and give them tools to help advance environmental

130 *Na'Taki Osborne Jelks and Crystal Jennings*

justice. Climate change and environmental justice are taught together because the fight against climate change and the fight for environmental justice are intricately linked. While everyone will suffer from climate change in terms of mental and physical health effects, economic impacts, and potential disruption to our lives, communities of color and low-income populations are often impacted first and worst (Schlosberg & Collins, 2014). The same strategies used to advance environmental justice are the strategies needed in the climate fight. It is important to note that climate solutions cannot stop at reducing overall carbon emissions; rather they must achieve both the overall reductions as well as remedy the disproportionate impacts to vulnerable populations who often bear the brunt of exposure to the same polluting facilities whose emissions help to drive climate change.

In contrast to a purely didactic approach to engaging youth in foundational content about climate change and environmental justice during classroom sessions, youth are invited to share what they know, have observed in their communities, and the salient experiences they have had in their everyday lives that connect to topics addressed in the interactive learning space created for ETSI. This helps to deepen and foster common understanding of important terminology, impart new information, correct misconceptions, and build on personal experiences as an introduction to ongoing dialogue and engagement. Not only are ET leaders introduced to the aforementioned definitions of environmental justice from the US EPA (2020) and grassroots environmental justice organizations such as the Asian Pacific Environmental Network (2002), but they also create their own working definitions of the term, informed by their own experiences in their communities as well as observations about the Atlanta Region, the United States, and the planet.

Teaching about climate change and environmental justice concurrently with an emphasis on developing solutions to both climate change, itself, and the differential impacts to vulnerable populations has been the basis of the ET approach to climate change education. The 17 Principles of Environmental Justice (First National People of Color Environmental Leadership Summit, 1991), the Principles of Climate Justice (EJLFCC, 2009), and the 10 Principles for Just Climate Change Policies in the USA (EJCC, 2002) are key texts to which ET leaders are exposed and challenged to apply the principles contained therein as they analyze and reflect upon potential climate change impacts in their communities and in case studies about other geographic locations.

Through exploration of the 12th Principle of Environmental Justice (EJ), ET leaders learn that:

> Environmental Justice affirms the need for urban and rural ecological policies to clean up and rebuild our cities and rural areas in

balance with nature, honoring the cultural integrity of all our communities, and provided fair access for all to the full range of resources.

Through the study of urban ecosystems and direct engagement in hands-on land and water stewardship and restoration activities in the local Atlanta community, participating youth connect the dots between the EJ Principles and youth-engaged action on the ground to help transform environmentally impaired communities into healthy landscapes. NWF partners with like-minded community-based and non-profit organizations to provide experiences for ET leaders to engage with local urban agriculture initiatives and organizations as well as habitat restoration projects in Atlanta's urban forests and watersheds. These stewardship and restoration activities take place both during ETSI and at other points in the program's year-long cycle of leadership training, issues exploration, civic engagement, experiential environmental education, community outreach, service learning, and career development (Jelks, 2014b) (Figure 4.2).

As a part of the ETSI, participants engage in an annual Toxics Tour, a half-day field study to increase awareness of the layered sources of pollution, poor environmental conditions, infrastructural neglect, inadequate city services, and impact of racialized policies such as redlining that are experienced by low-income and communities of color in Atlanta. During

Figure 4.2 ET leaders engaging in an urban agriculture community action project during an ETSI.
Photograph by © Charles M. Brown.

these field studies, ET leaders visit combined sewer overflow and wastewater treatment facilities, the fence lines of polluting facilities, illegal dumps and polluted creek sites, sites of green gentrification, and areas that amplify the neglect and divestment of public resources with respect to community infrastructure. Hands-on data collection and community action projects provide ET participants with the opportunity to monitor water quality, clean up plastics pollution and other debris from urban streams, contribute to the success of urban agriculture efforts, and help restore trails and remove invasive species from urban forests and other greenspaces. The reinforcement of local examples and engagement with community leaders and grassroots organizations working on climate and environmental justice issues tends to leave a significant impression on ET leaders. Through the Toxics Tour, they also engage with and hear the personal stories of local residents, environmental justice activists, and community-based organization (CBO) leaders who work to hold government officials, developers, and other entities accountable for toxic pollution, gentrification and displacement, and the inadequate enforcement of environmental regulations and policies in their neighborhoods (Figure 4.3).

While there is significant attention to community characteristics and factors that render these neighborhoods vulnerable with respect to environmental and health risks, community assets are also elevated. While

Figure 4.3 ET leaders clean up a polluted creek site after learning about water infrastructure challenges in Atlanta's communities of color.
Photograph by © Charles M. Brown.

Equitable and Just by Design   133

doing so, ET leaders are encouraged to see and consider even environmentally impacted communities for their strengths and positive attributes and not just their problems and challenges. These assets and strengths include grassroots organizations and the community responses to environmental and social injustices that these organizations lead as well as natural resources such as urban farms, parks, greenspaces, and green infrastructure, in many cases established by and maintained by community residents alone or in collaboration with supporting non-profits. Other assets that ETSI participants get exposed to include academic institutions such as schools in the Atlanta University Center, the world's oldest and largest association of historically Black colleges and Universities (HBCUs). Community-led urban sustainability and environmental justice projects are showcased along with aquaponics systems, schoolyard wildlife habitats, traditional school gardens, and other student-led projects designed to address community and school challenges identified by ET leaders and their peers.

Environmental Justice Community Dinner

Through an annual Environmental Justice Community Dinner, held during the ETSI, ET leaders are connected to local and national environmental and climate justice heroes and sheroes. This dinner, a culminating event for the thematic day dedicated to climate change and environmental justice, gives ET youth the opportunity to learn from and be inspired by the struggles and triumphs of grassroots community leaders, officials who have worked to advance environmental justice through posts in local and national government agencies, and well-known US figures in the environmental and climate justice movements. NWF staff and ET peer mentors prepare ET youth, through communications training, for table conversations with local and national EJ and climate justice leaders. Students are encouraged to ask specific questions of the leaders about their interests in and history of activism and engagement to advance environmental and climate justice. Each dinner also features a keynote speaker—usually a nationally recognized leader who covers a wide range of current-day environmental and climate justice themes and case studies in their keynote addresses, from water shutoffs in Detroit, Michigan, to the impacts of Hurricane Katrina on the Gulf Coast Region, and living along the fence line of polluting industries in Louisiana's Cancer Alley Corridor. Students commonly end this day reflective, inspired, and ready to be warriors for environmental and climate justice.

In sharing some of their thoughts and reflections with speakers and other presenters and facilitators for the environmental justice and climate change day of the ETSI, one participant wrote the following in a thank you letter to one of the Environmental Justice Community Dinner keynote speakers:

134 *Na'Taki Osborne Jelks and Crystal Jennings*

Hearing you speak about the injustice in Flint and Detroit really struck a chord with me. It is a shame that corporations think they can get away with poisoning our people and tearing apart our communities. Without activists like you, we would never hear about the injustice that the media does not cover. I feel inclined to tell others and impact transformation with them. We are the leaders of today and we need to keep up the efforts that you and your co-workers have begun.

Another wrote:

Thank you for taking the time out of your day to help me learn about the impacts that climate change has on the environment. I had fun learning about environmental justice and how communities need to come together and use their power and voice to fight for the environment. It really inspired me when you talked about how the youth are the future and how we have the power to change the world ... thank you for helping me to learn more about the environment and giving me the motivation to help have an impact on the world.

Increasing Efficacy for Action: Civic Engagement

Through various field study experiences held outside of the ETSI, ET leaders are also exposed to opportunities to deepen their understanding of how policy is formed and the political and civic engagement processes that undergird it. For more than 15 years, ET leaders have engaged in an annual ET Day at the State Capitol, a field study experience designed to provide youth with the opportunity to observe the lawmaking process, and to provide a setting in which students meet and practice their communication skills with state lawmakers. Participants gain a better understanding of the legislative process, state legislators' role in state policy making, as well as a sense of how policy is shaped by passionate community leaders, inclusive of youth. In addition, this field study experience creates a connection for participating youth between policy and environmental issues that range from habitat protection and energy efficiency to environmental justice and public health. In groups of school-based ET Club delegations, ET leaders study current environmental policy measures being undertaken by the state legislature, and they develop questions for their own state legislators and their staff, to help them understand some of the nuances of these bills and the direction in which policy debates are moving around specific pieces of legislation that will

Equitable and Just by Design   135

impact Georgia's environmental future. In coordinated meetings with their state senators and representatives at the Capitol, ET leaders ask legislators and their staff questions about their policy positions and also educate decision makers about the concerns in their communities with an emphasis on issues that can be addressed by state-level elected officials.

In addition to this annual field study experience, ET leaders gain opportunities to attend local environmental leadership summits, coordinated by NWF and partner organizations, focused on supporting youth engagement in environmental stewardship (Jennings, 2014) as well as travel to national convergences focused on developing the voice and environmental leadership skills of youth, such as Power Shift, a convening focused on "mobilizing the collective power of young people to mitigate climate change and create a just, clean energy future and resilient, thriving communities for all" (The Power Shift Network, n.d.). Through exposure to these and other activities curated to activate civic engagement in ET youth, they speak out to educate and influence their peers and the general public about causes and solutions of environmental challenges facing their schools and communities.

Expanding Civic Engagement: The 2020 Elections

ET leaders stepped up their efficacy for action in 2020 and 2021 by participating in a voter engagement initiative. With support from Clean and Prosperous America and the NWF Action Fund, ET students assisted in coordinating a Voter Rally Drive-Through to get out the vote for the historic Georgia Senate Runoff election, which determined the balance of power in the US Senate. The ET leaders' objective was to encourage as many people as possible to vote early, and they contributed to a host of voter mobilization efforts throughout the state. Based on voter turnout, the collective efforts of engaged groups paid off. Coupled with the rally was an engaging and effective social media campaign to get the word out about important voter registration deadlines, polling locations and times, voting by mail procedures, candidate information, and candidate stances on climate legislation. Prior to the Senate Runoff Election, ET participants attended a series of virtual meetings with local elected officials, college professors, and NWF staff to learn more about the importance of voting. While many ET students were not able to participate in the general election in 2020, some turned 18 just in time to vote in the runoff election in January 2021. ET leaders were fully aware of how important this particular election was for climate justice, and they took action to make their voices heard (Figure 4.4).

Figure 4.4 ET leader encouraging motorists in DeKalb County, Georgia, to vote. Photograph by © Travis Brown.

Being the Change

In a 2003 speech, Nelson Mandela said: "Education is the most powerful weapon which you can use to change the world." ET participants are doing their part to change the world for future generations. Joshua Bellamy, an ET alumni member from DeKalb Early College Academy (DECA) in Stone Mountain, Georgia, joined ET as a freshman in high school. At a minimum, Joshua was skeptical about engaging in outdoor activities, and he was not very familiar with environmental justice issues. He had a basic understanding of climate change but not a full picture of how climate change was impacting local communities of color. After attending his first ETSI, Joshua developed a newfound interest in environmental causes, and he started to gear his career pathway towards environmental education. After graduating from high school, Joshua served as an ET Peer Mentor. Peer Mentors are former ET student leaders who are provided with a unique opportunity to hone their leadership skills and share their enjoyment for the program with new participants as Summer Institute facilitators and guides. Joshua understands the importance of encouraging younger generations and his peers to join the environmental justice movement and it starts with sparking their interest through education and action. Joshua now attends Morehouse College where he will earn his Bachelor of Science degree in psychology with a

Equitable and Just by Design 137

focus on animal behavior. He credits much of his success to ET. He had this to say about his career pathway:

> A couple of weeks before going to college, I was offered and took a position as a lab assistant in animal behavior, which is a career that I am currently working towards. Within the same year I received an internship at Zoo Atlanta for the Conservation Education Department ... Currently, I am Vice President of Morehouse Moregreen, a sustainability based non-profit organization based at one of the most prominent HBCUs in the country, Morehouse College. All of these accolades wouldn't have been achieved without the engagements, lessons, and exposure from the Earth Tomorrow Summer Institute.

Joshua alluded to the role that the ET Program has had on his journey and trajectory since he first became involved. Given the interests that he'd started to articulate and develop in animal behavior and conservation, at an ETSI Environmental Justice Community Dinner, he met and was paired during table conversations with the director of the Morehouse College lab that he later joined. This same professor was able to provide guidance for Joshua as he applied for his internship at Zoo Atlanta. In addition, Joshua started Moregreen on his college campus, located in Southwest Atlanta, Georgia, as a result of being an ET participant. Joshua's story is not an anomaly. ET alumni typically go on to start businesses, organize community-wide projects, major in environmental or social sciences, organize climate strikes, take on board leadership roles, coordinate voter engagement events, and take on other significant action to help mitigate the impacts of climate change in their communities both directly and indirectly. Climate change education provides the foundation for ET students to deepen their understanding of environmental justice issues and emerge as confident leaders ready to make a positive impact.

Conclusion

For two decades NWF has inspired and equipped youth of color to be environmental leaders through engagement in the ET Program. The program's impact can be seen in students' lives not only in the understanding that they gain about critical environmental challenges affecting their communities, but also in the affinity they develop for addressing these problems. The program's unique approach to climate change education centers justice, equity, diversity, and inclusion, and it elevates the voices of often marginalized environmental and climate justice leaders and organizations. Lessons from this and similar efforts can inform other programmatic initiatives—particularly those that are place-based and those that strive to include diverse perspectives in framing root causes as well as solutions to climate change. Engaging youth leaders of color as

138 *Na'Taki Osborne Jelks and Crystal Jennings*

agents of change with respect to pressing environmental challenges with local and global implications is critical to the health of the communities from which these youth come and the success of community-based environmental initiatives across the country and globe.

References

Alhanti, B., Chang, H., Winquist, A. Mulholland, J.A., Darrow, L.A., & Sarnat, S.E. (2016). Ambient air pollution and emergency department visits for asthma: A multi-city assessment of effect modification by age. *Journal of Exposure Science and Environmental Epidemiology, 26,* 180–188. https://doi.org/10.1038/jes.2015.57

Alhendawi, A. (2014). Why young people are key to tackling climate change. Retrieved April 24, 2021, from https://www.weforum.org/agenda/2014/07/young-people-tackling-climate-change/

Arnold, H.E., Cohen, F.G., & Warner, A. (2009). Youth and environmental action: Perspectives of young environmental leaders on their formative Influences. *The Journal of Environmental Education, 40*(3), 27–36.

Aronoff, K. (2019, March). How Greta Thunberg's lone strike against climate change became a global movement. *Rolling Stone.* Retrieved April 24, 2021, from https://www.rollingstone.com/politics/politics-features/greta-thunberg-fridays-for-future-climate-change-800675/

Asian Pacific Environmental Network. (2002). Environmental justice & API issues. *What is EJ?* Retrieved April 24, 2021, from http://archive.apen4ej.org/issues_what.htm

Asthma and Allergy Foundation of America. (2020). Asthma disparities in America: A roadmap to reducing burden on racial and ethnic minorities. Retrieved April 24, 2021, from https://www.aafa.org/asthma-disparities-burden-on-minorities.aspx#pdf

Barnett, M., Lord, C., Strauss, E., Rosca, C., Langford, H., Chavez, D. & Deni, L. (2006). Using the urban environment to engage youths in urban ecology field studies. *The Journal of Environmental Education, 37,* 3–11.

Bartholomew, S. (2015). What does climate justice mean to you? Retrieved April 24, 2021, from https://www.climategen.org/blog/what-does-climate-justice-mean-to-you/

Bhardwaj, M. (n.d.). The role and relationship of climate justice and common but differentiated responsibilities & respective capabilities (CBDR-RC) principle in the international climate change legal framework: Historical evaluation, developments, challenges & future outlooks of CBDR-RC principle & climate justice. *Connect4Climate.* Retrieved April 24, 2021, from https://www.connect4climate.org/sites/default/files/files/publications/Climate%20Justice_Manuj%20Bhardwaj%20India_0.pdf

Boulianne, S., Lalancette, M., & Ilkiw, D. (2020). "School strike 4 climate": Social media and the international youth protest on climate change. *Media and Communication, 8*(2), 208–218. http://dx.doi.org/10.17645/mac.v8i2.2768

Bronx Climate Justice North (BCJN). (n.d.). What is climate justice? Retrieved April 24, 2021, from https://bronxclimatejusticenorth.wordpress.com/about-us/climate-justice/

Equitable and Just by Design   139

Bullard, R.D. (1993). The threat of environmental racism. *Natural Resources & Environment*, 7(3): 23–26, 55–56.

Bullock, S. (2018). Meet the terrific teens with pollution solutions! Retrieved April 24, 2021, from https://www.greenpeace.org/usa/stories/meet-terrific-teens-pollution-solutions/

Causevic, A. (2017). Facing an unpredictable threat: Is NATO ideally placed to manage climate change as a non-traditional threat multiplier? *Connections*, 16(2), 59–80. Retrieved April 24, 2021, from http://www.jstor.org/stable/26326481

Communities for a Better Environment (CBE). (n.d.). Youth for environmental justice (YouthEJ). Retrieved April 24, 2021, from https://www.cbecal.org/organizing/southern-california/youth-and-adult-groups/#:~:text=Youth%20for%20Environmental%20Justice%20(YouthEJ)&text=Youth%20EJ%20is%20committed%20to,%2C%20organizing%2C%20and%20leadership%20development

Congressional Black Caucus Foundation, Inc. (CBCF). (2004). *African Americans and climate change: An unequal burden.*

Connect4Climate. (2020). Connecting the world to take on climate change. Retrieved April 24, 2021, from https://www.connect4climate.org/about

Corbett, J. (2021). Youth demand US action on climate-induced loss and damage in global south. Retrieved April 24, 2021, from Youth Demand US Action on Climate-Induced Loss and Damage in Global South | Common Dreams News.

Dapaah, B. (2014). How bamboo bikes gave women a new future in Ghana. Retrieved April 24, 2021, from https://www.weforum.org/agenda/2014/03/bamboo-bikes-ghanas-women-riding-high/

Derevenskaiaa, O. (2014). Active learning methods in environmental education of students. *Procedia - Social and Behavioral Sciences*, 131, 101–104.

Earth Force. (2021). Our model. Retrieved April 24, 2021, from https://earth-force.org/caps/

Environmental Justice Climate Change Initiative (EJCC). (2002). 10 Principles for Just Climate Change Policies in the U.S. Retrieved April 24, 2021, from https://www.ejnet.org/ej/climatejustice.pdf

Environmental Justice Leadership Forum on Climate Change (EJLFCC). (2009). Principles of climate justice. Retrieved April 24, 2021, from https://www.ejnet.org/ej/ejlf.pdf

Food and Agriculture Organization of the United Nations (FAO). (2019). Youth in motion for climate action! - A compilation of youth initiatives in agriculture to address the impacts of climate change. Retrieved April 24, 2021, from http://www.fao.org/3/ca5746en/ca5746en.pdf

Fowler, M. (2014). Green school challenge a success. Retrieved April 24, 2021, from https://blog.nwf.org/2014/04/green-school-challenge-a-success/

First National People of Color Leadership Summit. (1991, October). Principles of environmental justice. Retrieved April 24, 2021, from http://www.ejnet.org/ej/principles.html

Goldman, D., Ben, O., Assaraf, Z., & Shaharabani, D. (2013). Influence of a non-formal environmental education programme on junior high-school students' environmental literacy, *International Journal of Science Education*, 35(3), 515–545.

Gray, J. (2017). These youth of color are organizing to address climate change. *PBS News Hour Weekend.* Retrieved April 24, 2021, from https://www.pbs.org/newshour/science/youth-color-organizing-address-climate-change

Hammonds, J., & National Wildlife Federation (NWF). (2020). Climate change: Building climate science knowledge to enact local change. Retrieved April 24, 2021, from https://flexbooks.ck12.org/user:agftbw9uzhnqqg53zi5vcmc./cbook/national-wildlife-federation-climate-change-education/

Holmes, L., Jr, Enwere, M., Williams, J., Ogundele, B., Chavan, P., Piccoli, T., ... Dabney, K.W. (2020). Black-White risk differentials in COVID-19 (SARS-COV2) transmission, mortality and case fatality in the United States: Translational epidemiologic perspective and challenges. *International Journal of Environmental Research and Public Health, 17*(12), 4322. https://doi.org/10.3390/ijerph17124322

Howeth, I. (2020, November 14). Climate change is a threat multiplier. *Alliance for Climate Education (ACE).* Retrieved April 24, 2021, from https://acespace.org/2020/11/14/threat-multiplier/#:~:text=That%20means%20that%20the%20direct,Famine

Hungerford, H.R., & Volk, T.L. (1990). Changing learner behavior through environmental education. *The Journal of Environmental Education, 21*(3), 8–21.

Huntjens, P., & Nachbar, K. (2015). Climate change as a threat multiplier for human disaster and conflict. The Hague Institute for Global Justice. Working Paper 9. Retrieved April 24, 2021, from https://www.thehagueinstituteforglobaljustice.org/wp-content/uploads/2015/10/working-Paper-9-climate-change-threat-multiplier.pdf

Jelks, N.O. (2014a). Urban environments provide context and inspiration for 21st Century conservation leaders. Retrieved April 24, 2021, from https://obamawhitehouse.archives.gov/blog/2014/03/24/urban-environments-provide-context-and-inspiration-21st-century-conservation-leaders

Jelks, N.O. (2014b). *Fostering environmental stewardship in youth of color through the urban environment: Earth tomorrow® in connecting children to nature: Ideas and activities for parents and educators* (M.L. Bentley, M.P. Mueller & B. Martin, Eds.). Bethany, OK: Wood 'N' Barnes Publishing.

Jennings, C. (2014). National Wildlife Federation and the Atlanta Woman's Club host youth conservation leadership summit. Retrieved April 24, 2021, from https://blogNational Wildlife Federation and the Atlanta Woman's Club Host Youth Conservation Leadership Summit/

Jennings, C. (2021). Earth tomorrow Atlanta program helps get out the vote for Georgia senate runoff election. Retrieved April 24, 2021, from https://blog.nwf.org/2021/01/earth-tomorrow-atlanta-program-helps-get-out-the-vote-for-georgia-senate-runoff-election/

Kaijser, A., & Kronsell, A. (2014). Climate change through the lens of intersectionality. *Environmental Politics, 23*(3), 417–433, https://doi.org10.1080/09644016.2013.835203

Kamenetz, A. (2019). Most teachers don't teach climate change; 4 in 5 parents wish they did. Retrieved April 24, 2021, from https://www.npr.org/2019/04/22/714262267/most-teachers-dont-teach-climate-change-4-in-5-parents-wish-they-did

Kaplan, S. (2020, June). Climate change is also a racial justice problem. *The Washington Post.* Retrieved April 24, 2021, from https://www.washingtonpost.com/climate-solutions/2020/06/29/climate-change-racism/

Equitable and Just by Design   141

Kaye, C.B. (2010). *The Complete Guide to Service Learning: Proven, Practical Ways to Engage Students in Civic Responsibility, Academic Curriculum, & Social Action* (2nd ed.). Free Spirit Publishing.

Kirkland, L., & Poppleton, K. (2021). Climate change education: A model of justice-oriented STEM education. *Connected Science Learning, 3*(1). Retrieved April 24, 2021, from https://www.nsta.org/connected-science-learning-january-february-2021/climate-change-education-model-justice-oriented

Koons, C., & Ivry, B. (2020). Covid plus decades of pollution are a nasty combo for Detroit. *Bloomberg Businessweek.* Retrieved April 24, 2021, from https://www.bloomberg.com/news/features/2020-10-21/covid-pandemic-southwest-detroit-faces-pollution-covid-19-outbreaks

Kumar, S., Singh, R., Kumari, N., Karmakar, S., Behera, M., Siddiqui, A.J., ... Kumar, N. (2021). Current understanding of the influence of environmental factors on SARS-CoV-2 transmission, persistence, and infectivity. *Environmental Science and Pollution Research, 28*, 6267–6288. https://doi.org/10.1007/s11356-020-12165-1

Levy, B.S., & Patz, J.A. (2015). Climate change, human rights, and social justice. *Annals of Global Health, 81*(3), 310–322. https://doi.org/10.1016/j.aogh.2015.08.008

McCright, A.M. (2012). Enhancing students' scientific and quantitative literacies through an inquiry-based learning project on climate change. *Journal of the Scholarship of Teaching and Learning, 12*(4), 86–102.

McCright, A.M., O'Shea, B.W., Sweeder, R.D., Urquhart, G.R., & Zeleke, A. (2013). Promoting interdisciplinarity through climate change education. Retrieved April 24, 2021, from https://www.researchgate.net/profile/Gerald-Urquhart/publication/260629500_Promoting_interdisciplinarity_through_climate_change_education/links/54f3c63b0cf299c8d9e558c0/Promoting-interdisciplinarity-through-climate-change-education.pdf

Mochizuki, Y., & Bryan, A. (2015). Climate change education in the context of education for sustainable development: Rationale and principles. *Journal of Education for Sustainable Development, 9*(1), 4–26. https://doi.org/10.1177/0973408215569109

National Center for Education Statistics. (2017). U.S. Department of Education "table 318.45: Number and percentage distribution of Science, Technology, Engineering, and Mathematics (STEM) degrees/certificates conferred by postsecondary institutions, by race/ethnicity, level of degree/certificate, and sex of student: 2008–09 through 2015–16," *Digest of Education Statistics*: 2016 Tables and Figures. Retrieved April 24, 2021, from https://nces.ed.gov/programs/digest/d17/tables/dt17_318.45.asp?referer=raceindicators

National Wildlife Federation (NWF). (2016). Bringing climate to the classroom: Years of living dangerously. Retrieved April 24, 2021, from www.climateclassroom.org

National Wildlife Federation (NWF). (2020). Equity & justice strategic plan. Retrieved April 24, 2021, from https://www.nwf.org/-/media/Documents/PDFs/Equity/NWF-Equity-and-Justice-Strategic-Plan.ashx

National Wildlife Federation (NWF). (2021a). Cool school challenge. Retrieved April 24, 2021, from https://www.nwf.org/Eco-Schools-USA/Resources/Activities/Projects/Cool-School-Challenge

142 *Na'Taki Osborne Jelks and Crystal Jennings*

National Wildlife Federation (NWF). (2021b). About Eco-Schools USA. Retrieved April 24, 2021, from https://www.nwf.org/Eco-Schools-USA/Framework/About

National Wildlife Federation (NWF). (2021c). Climate change education. Retrieved April 24, 2021, from https://www.nwf.org/Eco-Schools-USA/Resources/Curriculum/Climate-Change#:~:text=Climate%20Change%20Resources&text=The%20National%20Wildlife%20Federation%20works,fluctuations%20of%20a%20changing%20climate

National Wildlife Federation (NWF). (2021d). Earth tomorrow. Retrieved April 24, 2021, from https://www.nwf.org/Educational-Resources/Education-Programs/Earth-Tomorrow

Noonan, R. (2017). Women in STEM: 2017 update (ESA Issue Brief #06-17). Office of the Chief Economist, Economics and Statistics Administration, U.S. Department of Commerce (November 13, 2017). Retrieved April 24, 2021, from https://www.commerce.gov/news/fact-sheets/2017/11/women-stem-2017-update

O'Brien, K., Selboe, E., & Hayward, B. (2018). Exploring youth activism on climate change: Dutiful, disruptive, and dangerous dissent. *Ecology and Society*, *23*(3). https://doi.org10.2307/26799169

Public Health - Seattle & King County (n.d.). Blueprint for addressing climate change and health. https://kingcounty.gov/depts/health/~/media/depts/health/environmental-health/documents/publications/blueprint-climate-change-and-health.ashx

Schlosberg, D., & Collins, L.B. (2014). From environmental to climate justice: Climate change and the discourse of environmental justice. *Wiley Interdisciplinary Reviews: Climate Change*, *5*(3), 359–374. https://doi.org/10.1002/wcc.275

Seymour, S. (2021). *Climate Change: What happened and What We Can do*. New York: HarperCollins Publishers.

Simmons, D. (2020). What is climate justice? Yale climate connections. Retrieved April 24, 2021, from https://yaleclimateconnections.org/2020/07/what-is-climate-justice/

Smith, K.R., Woodward, A., Campbell-Lendrum, D., Chadee, D.D., Honda, Y., Liu, Q., ... Sauerborn, R. (2014). Human health: Impacts, adaptation, and co-benefits. In C.B. Field, V.R. Barros, D.J. Dokken, K.J. Mach, M.D. Mastrandrea, T.E., Bilir, ... L.L. White (Eds.), *Climate change 2014: Impacts, adaptation, and vulnerability. Part A: Global and sectoral aspects* (pp. 709–754). Contribution of Working Group II to the Fifth Assessment Report of the Intergovernmental Panel on Climate Change. Cambridge, UK and New York, NY: Cambridge University Press.

Soper, E., Fano, E., Hammonds, J., & the National Wildlife Federation (NWF). (2015). Green STEM: How environment based education boosts student engagement and academic achievement in science, technology, engineering and math. Retrieved April 24, 2021, from https://www.nwf.org/-/media/Documents/PDFs/Eco-Schools/Green-STEM-Guidebook.ashx

Thackeray, S.J., Robinson, S.A., Smith, P., Bruno, R., Kirschbaum, M.U.F., Bernacchi, C.,... Long, S. (2020). Civil disobedience movements such as School Strike for the Climate are raising public awareness of the climate change emergency. *Global Change Biology*, *26*, 1042–1044. https://doi.org/10.1111/gcb.14978

Equitable and Just by Design 143

Theobald, E.J., Hill, M.J., Tran, E., Agrawal, S., Arroyo, E.N., Behling, S.,... Freeman, S. (2020). Active learning narrows achievement gaps for underrepresented students in undergraduate science, technology, engineering, and math. *Proceedings of the National Academy of Sciences, 117*(12), 6476–6483. https://doi.org10.1073/pnas.1916903117

The Power Shift Network. (n.d.). Power shift convergences. Retrieved April 24, 2021, from https://www.powershift.org/convergences

Thomas, K., Hardy, R.D., Lazrus, H., Mendez, M., Orlove, B., Rivera-Collazo, I.,... Winthrop, R. (2019). Explaining differential vulnerability to climate change: A social science review. *WIREs Climate Change, 10*, e565. https://doi.org/10.1002/wcc.565

Trott, C. (2020). Children's constructive climate change engagement: Empowering awareness, agency, and action, *Environmental Education Research, 26*(4), 532–554, https://doi.org10.1080/13504622.2019.1675594

United Nations. (2021). To the Secretary-General: Youth press for climate priorities. Retrieved April 24, 2021, from https://www.un.org/en/climatechange/yag-meeting

United Nations Educational, Scientific, and Cultural Organization (UNESCO). (2010). Climate change education for sustainable development: The UNESCO climate change initiative. Retrieved April 24, 2021, from https://unesdoc.unesco.org/ark:/48223/pf0000190101

United States Environmental Protection Agency (EPA). (2018). Youth perspectives on climate change best practices for youth engagement and addressing health impacts of climate change. Retrieved April 4, 2021, from https://www.epa.gov/sites/production/files/2018-10/documents/nejac_youth_perspectives_on_climate_change_report.pdf

United States Environmental Protection Agency (EPA). (2020). Learn about environmental justice. Retrieved April 24, 2021, from https://www.epa.gov/environmentaljustice/learn-about-environmental-justice

United States Environmental Protection Agency (EPA). (2021). Environmental justice. Retrieved April 24, 2021, from https://www.epa.gov/environmentaljustice

United Nations Joint Framework Initiative on Children, Youth and Climate Change (UNJFICYCC). (2013). Youth in action on climate change: Inspirations from around the world. Retrieved April 24, 2021, from https://unfccc.int/resource/docs/publications/publication_youth_2013.pdf

Vergano, D., & Goba, K. (2020). Why the Coronavirus is killing Black Americans at outsize rates across the US. Retrieved April 4, 2021, from https://www.buzzfeednews.com/article/danvergano/coronavirus-black-americans-covid19

WE ACT. (2021a). Environmental justice education. Retrieved April 4, 2021, from https://www.weact.org/environmental-justice-education/

WE ACT. (2021b). Environmental health and justice leadership training. Retrieved April 14, 2021, from https://www.weact.org/home-3-2/getinvolved/education/ehjlt/

WE ACT. (2021c). Climate change: The climate multiplier in frontline communities. Retrieved April 24, 2021, from Climate Justice | WE ACT for Environmental Justice

Wikler-Friday, M. (2021). 3 youth living and organizing on the frontlines of the climate crisis. Retrieved April 26, 2021, from 3 Youth Living and Organizing on the Frontlines of the Climate Crisis (msn.com)

Woetzel, J., Pinner, D., Samandari, H., Engel, H., Krishnan, M., Boland, B., & Powis, C. (2020). Climate risk and response: Physical hazards and socioeconomic impacts. Retrieved April 24, 2021, from https://www.mckinsey.com/~/media/McKinsey/Business%20MacFunctions/Sustainability/Our%20Insights/Climate%20risk%20and%20response%20Physical%20hazards%20and%20socioeconomic%20impacts/MGI-Climate-risk-and-response-Full-report-vF.pdf

Wu, L., & Jing, W. (2013). Leadership hurdles. *Nature, 493*, 125–126. https://doi.org/10.1038/nj7430-125a

Wu, X., Nethery, R.C., Sabath, M.B., Braun, D., & Dominici, F. (2020). Air pollution and COVID-19 mortality in the United States: Strengths and limitations of an ecological regression analysis. *Science Advances, 6*(45), eabd4049. https://doi.org/10.1126/sciadv.abd4049

5 A Course on Natural Disasters Gets Real

Living the Impacts of Climate Change in the US Virgin Islands

Michele L. Guannel, Gregory Guannel, Imani Daniel, Nailah Copemann, Angelisa Freeman, and Bethany Good

Author note: All authors experienced Hurricanes Irma and Maria (on the islands of St. Thomas or St. Croix, United States Virgin Islands, or on St. Kitts) and Hurricane Dorian (which unexpectedly strengthened to a Category 1 hurricane over St. Thomas in 2019). We gratefully acknowledge the assistance of Dr. Christopher Plyley for guidance on the analysis of the disaster preparedness pre- and post-survey data.

After a 12 day-span, as Hurricane Irma opened the pathway and left us exposed, Hurricane Maria arises from thin air and tumbled into the already razed Virgin Islands with more destruction in its path … Throughout the storm, I was terrified as the house had shaken from side to side, making me fear that the house was going with us inside … And behold the water was inching towards entering inside the house, but by God's grace and mercy, the water didn't enter the house, possibly enduring more trials.

Science 100 student

The Story of 'IrMaria'

In September 2017, the United States Virgin Islands (VI) were devastated by two Category 5 hurricanes, Irma and Maria. Irma impacted the islands of St. John and St. Thomas on the afternoon of September 6, leaving a nearly barren landscape as intense winds stripped the majority of leafy vegetation from trees, and destroyed or severely damaged many structures. Just two weeks later, through the dark hours of September 19–20, Maria moved more slowly over the VI, causing rain-induced flooding on all major islands and impacting St. Croix most heavily, where inds and rains damaged many more structures. Hurricane Irma alone was notable in that ground wind stations measured wind speeds and gusts reaching 130–140 mph, and sustained wind speeds above 120 mph (Watlington, 2018). However, most stations were destroyed by the hurricane itself. Models indicated that winds probably reached speeds above 174 mph

DOI: 10.4324/9780429326011-8

146 *Michele L. Guannel et al.*

over flat terrain areas, and more than 250 mph on mountainous areas (ARA, 2018). Hurricanes Irma and Maria are also notable because, together, they contained more accumulated cyclone energy than the 1981–2010 average value, and caused the 2017 hurricane season to be in the top five most energetic since 1950 (NOAA, 2018). Note, however, that since then the Atlantic hurricane season has only intensified, including the massive devastation wrought by Hurricane Dorian in 2019 across regions of the Bahamas (Shultz et al., 2020).

Based on an analysis of the post-storm roof survey done by the Federal Emergency Management Agency (FEMA), the storms destroyed or severely damaged more than 8% of the housing stock (approximately 3,530 structures), flooded numerous structures, heavily damaged the two hospitals in the Territory, obliterated the above ground electric grid (such that most residents were without consistent power for nearly three months), as well as numerous telecommunication towers, roads, and other critical infrastructure, including ports and airports. As a result, the hurricanes caused approximately $10.7 billion in damages, including $6.9 billion in infrastructure, $2.3 billion in housing, and $1.5 billion in economic damage (USVI HRRTF, 2018). It was not long before the combined experience of these two historic hurricanes, experienced by only a small fraction of humans on Earth, was described as "IrMaria," also known as "IrMariageddon," and for good reason.

The infrastructure damage resulted in a steep loss of economic vitality and competitiveness. The combined impacts of Irma and Maria on the VI have been described as second only to Hurricane Katrina (a loss of nearly 12% of all jobs at maximum; Bram, 2018). Of the top five most devastating natural disasters in the USA, four of these events (all hurricanes) occurred in the USVI and Puerto Rico (Bram, 2018). For the VI, the severity of the employment losses can be linked largely to the Territory's heavy reliance on tourism (70% of gross domestic product), which plummeted after the hurricanes due to the destruction of major hotels and island-wide devastation (USVI HRRTF, 2018).

It is critical to place these damages in the context of the already vulnerable, and now hurricane-devastated, educational structure of the USVI. Pre-hurricanes, the USVI were characterized by SAT scores that are lower than those of all 50 states (College Board, 2018), as well as a poverty rate that is higher than all 50 states (Austin, 2018). Hurricanes Irma and Maria heavily damaged over 50% of Virgin Islands schools (USVI HRRTF, 2018). For example, on the island of St. Thomas, two of the four public middle/high schools were combined in one building to compensate for the loss of one school building; these and other schools on St. Croix were delayed in reopening by multiple weeks, and operated on split sessions where the majority of preteen and teenaged students received just four hours of instructional time per day, over the 2017–2018 school year (USVI HRRTF, 2018). Impacts continued throughout the 2018–2019 school year, such as the mid-October opening of a junior high school that was moved to a modular unit. Facilities at the Territory's only university, the University of the Virgin Islands, suffered at least $60 million in damages with insurance covering only $23 million (USVI HRRTF, 2018); as a result, most damage has not been repaired. Many faculty and staff remain displaced, three years after the hurricanes, with planned new buildings not constructed as yet. The same holds true for K-12 schools that have not been rebuilt, three years later. Furthermore, these disruptions and losses occurred prior to the 2020 COVID-19 pandemic, during which all public schools became completely or partly virtual in a Territory with limited and sporadic power, internet, and electronic devices.

(Un)natural History of the VI: Climate Change Impacts

IrMaria fits into the pattern of expected stronger hurricanes that climate science long predicted to occur, as the impacts of climate change continue to unfold. And, as with everywhere on the planet, the VI will be greatly impacted by the consequences of climate change.

First, in the VI, temperatures are increasing, and they are likely to increase by more than 1.1°C on average by the 2050s, leading to extremes not experienced previously in the Territory. More importantly, the number of days with maximum daily temperatures above 32°C and warmer nights will also increase. In addition, the VI will likely become drier, during both the wet and dry seasons (Stephenson et al., 2014; USGCRP, 2018). These changes will present increasing health (Campbell-Lendruma et al., 2007) and financial stresses for vulnerable populations (including the economically depressed, the very young and the very old, and people with disabilities) who will likely pay more for cooling technologies and for water. Although most households have cisterns that collect rainfall from roofs, residents often pay for water deliveries during drought conditions, after cisterns run dry. These changes will impact the health of various members of our community, especially vulnerable populations.

Another impact of climate change is an increased risk of flooding. Even though the VI is likely to experience longer droughts and drought-like conditions, it is also expected that rainfall intensity will increase: higher volumes of water will fall per unit of time, which will lead to flash-flooding situations and will likely overwhelm most drainage infrastructure. Rainfall-induced flooding conditions are likely to occur during the rainy season as well as during hurricanes. Indeed, as temperatures increase and moisture levels increase, it is expected that rainfall during hurricanes will increase, leading to more widespread flooding (Patricola & Wehner, 2018). In addition to rain-induced flooding, coastal flooding during hurricanes is predicted to become more widespread, as stronger hurricanes—but not necessarily more hurricanes in general—are

148 *Michele L. Guannel et al.*

expected, and also as the sea level continues to rise. Specifically, in the VI, the sea level has risen by more than 7.7 cm in 40 years, and the US Army Corps of Engineers (2014) predicts a mean sea-level increase of more than 50 cm by 2050, and more than 1.3 m by 2100.

In addition to increasing flooding risks, sea-level rise will also lead to the loss of coastal habitats, especially beaches, which are the main economic engine of the Territory. For example, iconic beaches such as Magen's Bay on St. Thomas, Trunk Bay on St. John, or Sandy Point on St. Croix are all at risk of being lost to the sea by the middle of the century (NOAA, 2019). Unmanaged, these losses will likely lead to economic distress for the hundreds of people employed by the hospitality and recreation businesses.

Sea-level rise will also lead to an increased stress on the infrastructure (USVI HRRTF, 2018). Like most islands, most of the population and infrastructure in the VI is coastal. As a consequence, an approximately 30 cm of sea-level rise will lead to the flooding of nearly 16 critical facilities (government buildings, schools, airports, power plants, wastewater treatment plants, etc.), 19 km of underground electric lines, 106 public and private buildings, and 4% of the roads—most of them in St. John (USVI HRRTF, 2018). Finally, in addition to impacts to tourist attractions and the built environment, sea-level rise might cause potential problems for drainage, as outfalls could become submerged, and thus exacerbate flooding in urban areas.

More broadly, the experience of climate-driven disasters in the VI and other Caribbean islands is becoming commonplace as "climate change" becomes "climate catastrophe." In 2017, natural disasters impacted a staggering number of US citizens: 8% of the population, or 25 million people (FEMA, 2018). Together, during the years of 2017 and 2018 alone, US disaster damages exceeded all of the previous 37 years (Long, 2019). Evidence for climate-change-exacerbated hurricane impacts is mounting; for example, the extreme rainfall of Hurricane Harvey, just weeks before Irma arose, has been attributed in part to rising global temperatures (Simon Wang et al., 2018; USGCRP, 2018). The intensity and severity of extreme weather events are predicted to increase (USGCRP, 2018), which holds dire predictions for the VI and for communities throughout the USA.

Territorial and Demographic Contexts of the VI

The 2017 hurricane impacts must be contextualized within the Territorial status, building on a series of colonial powers, of the VI. For example, languages, cuisine, and music have become a blended collaboration of native Caribbean, African, and European influences (Krigger, 2017). On the one hand, this dynamic existence has led to a culturally diverse community and culture, with a deep understanding of pluralism and nuanced

A Course on Natural Disasters Gets Real   149

sub-communities within larger ones. On the other hand, ancestral Virgin Islanders experience resultant inconsistencies in urban planning, poor land and water use management, and in the opinions of some—unsuccessful self-determination.

Today, VI residents number approximately 100,000 in total (U.S. Census Bureau, 2013) and represent a rich cultural diversity. VI communities are primarily people of color, just as the top five most devastating natural disasters (Bram, 2018) disproportionately impacted people of color. Racial and ethnic demographics of the VI are approximately 79% African Caribbean and 17% Latinx of any race, including richly diverse religions (denominations of Christianity, Islam, Judaism) and different countries of parental or ancestral origin (outside of the USVI, the Dominican Republic, Haiti, Dominica, St. Kitts/Nevis, Anguilla), with major languages including English, Spanish, and Haitian Creole (Krigger, 2017). As a consequence, the VI have been led by an African Caribbean, West Indian majority since 1970. The VI are also lacking youths. With a median age of 43.5 years, 20% of the population is less than 18 years old, and 62% is over 35 years old. In addition, the VI is also relatively poor, with nearly 20% of the population living below poverty, and a median income of $37,254 (Austin, 2018). However, economic stability is starkly divided by race, with 57% of the Black households earning less than $50,000 per year, while 50% of white households earn less $75,000. In addition, 12% of Black households earn more than $100,000 per year, but this number increases to 32% for white households (U.S. Census Bureau 2013, USVI CS 2017).

"Post-colonialism" may be too outdated to accurately describe the current reality of modern life for locals in the islands. It is the observation of some authors that generational residents are subjected, time and time again, to gentrification, outside influences determining their destiny, and to the increasing destruction of their natural resources for the promotion of capitalism. Often, outside "experts" are brought in to solve issues of which they have very little practical knowledge or nuanced understanding. These experts bring their preconceptions of what marginalized communities need and want, while draining resources and funding from the people who need it most. The issues compound when viewed through the lens of disaster response and mitigation planning.

#VIStrong: Initial Response to IrMaria

Irma and Maria caused widespread devastation to both the built and natural environments, as well as to VI people. The impacts of this devastation were felt harder in the VI than in parts of the continental United States. The people of the VI face several fundamental challenges that have compounded the negative impact of the hurricanes. First, the territorial government structure lacks a municipal component, making it

150   *Michele L. Guannel et al.*

harder to access heavily monitored federal funds needed to implement comprehensive recovery projects. Second, the geographic isolation forces the economy to be increasingly reliant on imports and outside distribution chains, leading to less market autonomy and local production. Finally, the high-risk, marginalized, and poverty-stricken population was incredibly vulnerable before the storm and is finding very few resources available to access and adequately fill their current unmet needs. Many of their vulnerabilities, like poor health, low education levels, low income, and/or undocumented status, have been compounded, making the chances of full individual recovery highly unlikely.

These three aforementioned disadvantages facing the average residents in the VI forced the hand of the private sector: businesses, nonprofits, and individuals alike sprang into action before, during, and after Hurricanes Irma and Maria. The fractured and under-resourced local government was not prepared to respond to the widespread unmet needs of the people. Consequently, informal grassroots networks began to organize and focus intently on protecting the life and property of the most vulnerable residents.

Volunteers—all VI residents—came together as the island's real first defense, from boarding up neighbors' homes to shuttling vulnerable people to shelters as Irma crashed through the Northern Antilles, heading for the USVI. Before Irma had truly passed the islands, as rain still fell, volunteers began to chainsaw people out of their homes, perform wellness checks on neighbors, and set up low-tech systems of communication and coordination. These local volunteers spent their days immediately after the storms searching for ice and insulin to deliver to medical patients, sourcing food and water to bring to nursing homes and shut-in individuals, and creating daily records of who needed what and where.

These informal groups were forced to learn a lot, quickly. Lessons like "every donated generator also needs a gas can and extension cord" "several thousands of people needed a way to keep medication and breast milk cool to stop them from spoiling," and "when our only air and freight ports are severely damaged, scarcity and desperation set in quickly" were especially hard lessons to stomach. Early on, it became clear that local knowledge must be preserved and appreciated. Many federal and local government resources were squandered by bringing in outside "experts" who had to climb very steep learning curves related to the islands' unique cultures and topography. On the other hand, the local youth learned how to cook outside from their elders, some got into the best shape of their life hauling buckets of water out of the cisterns, and many mastered time management by prioritizing their needs during the months-long curfew which only allowed people outside for six hours. The darkness, both electrical and communication, framed life in the context of going back to how the islands used to do things culturally, decades before. Information spread like wildfire on Facebook messenger, WhatsApp, and old fashion community bulletin boards. The islanders learned patience, community, and most saliently disaster response that occurs immediately following an extreme event.

As Virgin Islanders continued to collectively respond to Hurricanes Irma and Maria, volunteers, faith-based organizations, non-governmental organizations, and small businesses were coming together to develop a more coordinated framework. By November 10, 2017, early acting local leaders had established the St. Thomas Recovery Team (STRT) (a Long-Term Recovery Group; LTRG). Traditionally, an LTRG acts as a coordinating and collaborative umbrella organization between its organizational members, but the lack of local capacity and high service demand led the STRT to commit to two parallel missions. First and foremost, the STRT assessed the unmet needs of vulnerable homeowners in St. Thomas and provided spiritual, physical, financial, and emotional support, as they were able, to facilitate rehabilitation. Second, the STRT worked with local government, federal government, and community partners to boost community engagement and facilitate longer term community-based sustainability projects revolving around food security, solarization, cultural and artistic preservation, and public and mental health initiatives.

Within three years of Hurricanes Irma and Maria, the STRT satisfied hundreds of client cases through donations management, home garden installation, or larger home rebuild projects. Additionally, the STRT hosted several large community meetings where citizens, local and federal government officials, and volunteers contributed by laying out nearly one hundred different priorities or gaps in the current quality of life. From there, priorities were reorganized and developed into projects to address these notable gaps. As a result, the St. Thomas Community Recovery Plan was published in late 2018. Through a similar process, the St. Thomas Community Response Plan (with detailed asset maps) was published in 2019 and continues to be updated yearly.

Youth Voices and Leadership: The Hurricane Essay

Starting just months after the hurricanes, at the University of the Virgin Islands (UVI), we developed an enhanced resilience focus in the general education science course, Science 100. UVI is the only Historically Black College or University (HBCU) outside of the mainland United States. Originally inspired by Hurricane Marilyn in 1995, Science 100 has focused on natural disasters and local ecosystems in the Caribbean (Jones et al., 2018; Paul & Watlington, 1997). Science 100 is the largest class on the two main UVI campuses on St. Thomas and St. Croix, and it is also a required general education course for freshman students. As such, it is the largest formal learning environment for adults in the Territory. In addition to education regarding the major natural hazards of the Caribbean—hurricanes, volcanic eruptions, earthquakes, and

152 *Michele L. Guannel et al.*

tsunami waves—the course addresses climate change and climate disasters. One addition to the class (discussed in more detail in pp. 000–000I) has been to offer an alternative to a traditional research paper assignment, in which students engage in service learning related to hurricane recovery or other local scientific problems.

The course is supported by a large instructional team: a Lead Instructor (M. Guannel, since January 2018) who prepares twice-weekly lectures, oversees curricula, and manages all staff; several Lab Instructors who teach the required practical three-hour lab component; and around ten Peer Instructors who are current students and assist with lab instruction and grading, run tutorial sessions, and provide support on perhaps a more relatable level than older instructors. Co-author N. Copemann was a Peer Instructor and then Lead Peer Instructor for a total of three years.

By virtue of the course content alone, course instructors were concerned that, without proper support, there would be a risk that reliving traumatic events such as the 2017 hurricanes would increase symptoms of post-traumatic stress disorder, or PTSD (e.g., Baker et al., 2016). In general, trauma, including natural disasters, combat, terrorism, domestic violence, and sexual assault can result in a range of biological, psychological (e.g., PTSD), and social impacts (Baker et al., 2016). Symptoms of PTSD can arise through disaster-related exposure and numerous stress factors such as witnessing homes being damaged; being forced to evacuate; injury or death; the shortage of food and water; and loved ones leaving the region. Specifically, people who have experienced major disasters naturally experience distressing emotions that can vary depending on the intensity, severity, and duration of physical threat or suffering, as well as individuals' personal backgrounds, support systems, and coping mechanisms. These emotions range from disbelief, numbness, sadness, guilt, anger, irritability, yearning for the deceased, wishing that things could be different, repetitive thoughts and images of the event, as well as a range of changes in everyday behaviors such as eating and sleeping (SAMHSA, 2013).

Simultaneously, many disaster-impacted individuals develop various coping mechanisms to manage the trauma they faced—which can develop into post-traumatic growth (PTG). The trauma experienced can eventually result in positive outcomes of individuals' lives (Tedeschi et al., 1998). While many are recovering, they recount the lessons learned, including individual growth that arises. Therefore, PTG is a process that can be triggered by a disastrous event, and further encompasses positive outcomes that are attributed to individuals and communities who experience traumatic events (Tedeschi & Calhoun, 1995, 1996). PTG is the individual's struggle with the new reality in the aftermath of trauma (Tedeschi & Calhoun, 2004).

Given the intensity of emotions and behavioral changes that can occur in disaster survivors, a long-standing assignment of the course, the

A Course on Natural Disasters Gets Real   153

hurricane essay, took on new complexities following Hurricanes Irma and Maria. For this assignment, students were given three choices: (1) describe your own experience with a hurricane; (2) interview a hurricane survivor and summarize their experience; or (3) research any hurricane and write an objective description with appropriate citations. Overwhelmingly, students chose option (1). Specifically, for the Spring 2019 semester, over 90% of students wrote about their own experiences.

From reading through all hurricane essays completed in three semesters (totaling near 300 essays), it was striking that, despite the tribulations detailed with vivid imagery by most students, the majority chose to end their hurricane essay with statements of pride and strength. Therefore, our overarching framework for analysis was the extent to which the narratives tell a story of PTG.

We requested informed consent from most lecture sections taught during the Fall 2018 and Spring 2019 semesters, in accordance with a larger Institutional Review Board-approved research study on effective pedagogical strategies within Science 100. For the purposes of this work, 19 hurricane essays were volunteered for analysis. These included essays by thirteen females and six males, which is representative of the predominantly female UVI student body. Most of the study participants are students who completed their senior year of high school during/ after the 2017 hurricanes. Seventeen of the 19 students wrote about their own experiences with Irma, Maria, or another hurricane, for the assignment.

We utilized a phenomenological approach (Eatough & Smith, 2008), in which authors N. Copemann and M. Guannel analyzed student essays for emergent themes related to processes of individual- or community-level PTG. N. Copemann, an ancestral Virgin Islander, drew upon her experience with Hurricane Irma on St. Thomas and Hurricane Maria on St. Croix; she also contributed a student perspective as a recent UVI graduate and a former Science 100 Peer Instructor for multiple semesters. M. Guannel, hailing from the northeastern United States, was informed by her teaching and reading of hundreds of previous Science 100 student experiences of Hurricanes Irma and Maria, as well as her experiences of Irma and Maria on St. Thomas. In accordance with a hermeneutic cycle (Bontekoe, 1996), the essays were read and re-read multiple times until no additional meaning was identified. Each essay was coded independently by N. Copemann and M. Guannel. Some of these codes were entitled "Remembering Details," "Community Panic," "Learning from Experience," among others. While reading each essay, we identified direct quotes from the students' writing that were representative of individual codes. These quotes were then organized on charts under the specific code they represented. Minor text modifications, noted inside brackets, were made to some student quotes if one of two cases applied: (1) if the details might identify the author or (2) if

154 *Michele L. Guannel et al.*

major misspellings or text omissions complicated the meaning of the words. The pronouns "they" or "them" were used in the singular case to further protect the identity of the authors. Virgin Islands dialect was not edited in order to preserve student voice and culture.

Researchers N. Copemann and M. Guannel discussed codes and emergent themes to identify a large number of codes, finally collapsing similar codes down to those described below in the individual "Youth Voices" sections. These final "Youth Voices" codes address the themes identified in the writing of most students, which was voiced by individual students across multiple time frames (before, during, and after the hurricanes), and which appear to describe PTG processes. The summative analysis below, not the essays as written, was shared with co-authors in order to honor student confidentiality.

Youth Voices: Ignorance of the Severity and Possible Impacts of Irma and Maria

For most students, this was the first major hurricane they had experienced. Therefore, ignorance of hurricane preparedness and safety was echoed in their essays. There were students who did not take the news of two major Category 5 hurricanes seriously. This left many families ill-prepared for the storms. One student suggested: "People home were really damaged, more than half of the people weren't prepared because they didn't [take] the hurricane seriously." Another student, who was familiar with hurricanes due to having previously lived in a different hurricane-prone region, decided to seek shelter by a friend's apartment. They said: "While doing this preparedness checklist, I was informed nobody there had been through a hurricane ever." Another student, in their essay, claimed they took the storm seriously, while others around them did not. They said:

> I felt like I was one of the only few people that took the coming of this hurricane seriously. Everyone around me, from friends to some people talking about it on the streets, felt like the Virgin Islands wasn't touched by a natural disaster in years and was overdue for a tsunami that never came. This made them overly confident and began to support their ignorance with outlandish claims such as, we were untouchable because we were lucky, or that we were to[o] small to attract such a big natural disaster, or that we were to[o] blessed or special to be hit with so much force.

Again, a common denial of the potential impact left many residents ill-prepared for Irma and Maria.

Nine of the nineteen essays noted the disruption of students' preparations for their senior years in high school. When news of an incoming

Category 5 hurricane broke, they described feelings of worry, denial, and shock. One student said:

> I remember that I was making sure that I had everything for school, because I was excited to be a senior. I made sure that my hair and my nails were done. I then went on social media and saw that everyone was posting about hurricane Irma. I was totally upset because I was hoping that it didn't come so that I would be able to go to school.

In many essays, students described their preparation for Hurricane Irma. Part of last-minute preparations included going to the grocery stores to buy non-perishable goods. One student in their hurricane essay claimed: "The lines in the stores were longer than ever because everyone needed to get supplies in order to stay safe for this Hurricane." This is just one example of the actions people took to prepare for the incoming storms. The students described the physical labor of bolting down windows. One student described their preparation methods by saying:

> Nonetheless I prepared, I had sought out nonperishable food items, canned foods, drinking water, batteries, torch lights, water for household use, stored away clothes and electronic items, had the house boarded with plywood sheets and took all necessary precautionary measures I could to make my family feel safe in the comfort of our home.

For example, after Irma approached, many residents found themselves in positions in which they needed to take risky actions—during the high points of this historic Category 5 hurricane. In several instances, students recounted times when they, or neighbors, had to quickly escape from their residences during the hurricane. One student wrote:

> With winds clocking in at 185 mph, [our family of four, our tenant, and our dogs] had to make it down the hill of our driveway. The force of the winds kept shoving us to and fro as we made our way down hill towards our yard's gate.

Another student admitted to making a last-minute decision to escape their house. This student stated:

> At which point we decided it would've been safer to evacuate to our neighbor's home, which wasn't directly being hit by the storm as it was sheltered by neighboring houses. We thought of the danger outside, the possibility of being struck by flying objects. We gathered some food and change of clothes and timed when the winds weren't so heavy and then we would dash across to the next house. We made it across and finally felt somewhat safe throughout the night.

Another risky action, described in the essays, was when a student mentioned someone placing sandbags by the door. They said: "I even witness my mother's co-workers risking their lives in the storm trying to put sandbags behind the door to keep it from banging." Some of these actions or behaviors could have been prevented if there had been greater understanding of the potential impacts of a Category 5 hurricane. Throughout the essays, there was a prevalent use of the word "evacuate"—when in reality students and their families were escaping during one of the most powerful hurricanes the Earth has ever seen, to seek safer shelter (rather than proper evacuation over one day in advance of the storm's arrival).

In vivid detail, students recount the damages they witnessed during the storm. In one essay, a student mentioned:

> Watching through window we saw winds pushing its way through every nook and cranny it could get through, it blew out the roofs, doors and plywood sheets that neighbors had bolted to keep their homes safe. In addition to heavy winds, floods of water came rushing into our home.

Another student reflected:

> When the hurricane force winds arrived, the roof screamed as the galvanize was being ripped off of it. Looking out the window I saw galvanize from surrounding houses being thrown in the air. As the wind intensified the windows in my bedroom blew out and water started rushing in the house.

These descriptions demonstrate the extent of the damage people's houses sustained, and the dramatic impacts upon people who were inhabiting their homes during the hurricanes. Again, as described earlier, the hurricane impacts prompted risky actions, such as escaping homes that were failing under Irma's strong winds.

Based on the essays, some people experienced a reality check right after the storms. When they saw the damage, they appeared to acknowledge the severity of one (or two) Category 5 hurricanes. One student described the shock they experienced when they saw the change in the environment:

> Trees were on top of each other, the roads were blocked, when I went outside after Irma I was shocked when I saw the results, I never thought that a hurricane could cause so much damages, I was really shocked.

A Course on Natural Disasters Gets Real   157

Students described an increased understanding of the power of Mother Nature, and of the importance of preparation. For example, one student ended their essay with the statement:

> The lesson we might learn from similar event is that always prepare and don't take issues like this as a joke because in situation like those you will know it is always better to be always be ready for anything since we have experience it and the memories is fresh in our mind we will always be prepare for something like this.

Some took the initiative to learn more about hurricane preparedness so they could apply that knowledge in the future. Most students recognized in their essays that Hurricanes Irma and Maria had changed their lives forever. One student ended their essay with:

> From the governor to the residents, I believe that proper preparedness will be put into play before hurricane season. Without the help of the mainland United States, this territory would still be a wreck. This hurricane season was for the books, but I do believe it has made me, my new-found hurricane family, and this island realize preparation is everything with a backup plan.

Another student claimed:

> Other lessons we might learn from similar events that may happen in the future is to always be prepared no matter what, serious or not because we might have get less damage if we were at least eighty percent prepared. It's better to be over prepared than sorry.

Youth Voices: Collaboration and Cooperation During and Following Irma and Maria

After Irma, individuals experienced shock over the broad extent of the impacts, and they reflected on the immediate responses to the disaster. Such responses encompassed both collective acknowledgment of community-level losses, as well as cooperation with family and neighbors to check on everyone's well-being and to move debris—the creation of that "new-found hurricane family," as so aptly described in the previous quote. One reflection spoke of both the range of losses experienced by individuals and the shock of togetherness after this massive hurricane:

> Some lost family members while more people lost their homes and personal belongings. It was total chaos and many were on edge with themselves and others. That morning as I went outside, it was foggy

158   *Michele L. Guannel et al.*

and grey; the roads were flooded with water that people were unable to move around to check on neighbors and family members.

A commonly described day after the storm would be filled with cleaning and throwing away debris left by the hurricanes. Some students had to adjust to not having electricity and the internet. Many students reported an increased appreciation of things that they described as more meaningful. This meant increased interaction with their family members and neighbors.

Indeed, many residents found importance in cooperating and assisting one another—whether out of necessity, or out of desire, or both. The students, in their essays, expressed this theme. Often, it would be one family helping their neighbors and vice versa. One example of this is: "The neighbor on top of us could not stay in their apartment because the hurricane take their roof of their apartment off. So they had to come down stairs to my house to find shelter." In another example, the student's family sought shelter claiming: "Throughout Hurricane Irma, my family and I relocated to a family's friend's concrete house, to shelter the storm, thinking that our house was unsafe for that task." People were more than willing to open their doors to help others whose houses were damaged heavily. In their essay, one student wrote: "During the hurricane, we even had to open the doors to let some people in that house got destroyed."

When Hurricanes Irma and Maria left the VI, the community took the opportunity to come together. As described earlier, initial response efforts were led, informally, by those on the ground: VI residents. One student mentioned:

> Many people were very cooperative and supportive, they help and support neighbors, and they share water, food and etc. Federal leaders help pretty good as well, they made sure people get home safe because we had curfews, with n[o] power we couldn't be on the road at any time, not everybody followed the rules but a lot of us listened and do the right thing. Many local people provide water and food to people with necessities.

The same student continued by relating: "We got a lot of help from everybody, everybody was helping which was really appreciated." In another essay, one student stated that:

> The government made sure to keep local stores from raising prices, FEMA provided financial need and places to stay as well as household supplies; the National Guard provided assistance by giving out MRE's, bottles of water, and baby supplies; we were also helped with funding and quickly regained power and roads to drive on by workers provided by the states.

A Course on Natural Disasters Gets Real   159

Although there was expressed appreciation for formal aid efforts, criticism existed as inefficiencies meant that residents spent a great deal of their curfew-limited time waiting in lines for supplies that would be exhausted by the time they reached the front.

At the same time as collaboration seemed to buoy the spirits of many individuals, major life changes occurred for residents whose homes were heavily damaged or completely destroyed (some while families were inhabiting them). Territory-wide, residents grappled with inconsistent access to telecommunications, power, and key services such as schooling and medical care. Everyone within Irma's and Maria's paths experienced life-altering changes.

Youth Voices: From Fear to Strength

> I didn't come ... out of the storm the same way I went in. I came out stronger and wiser. What I experienced was a once in a lifetime experienced t[o] have two category 5 hurricanes a week apart. My mom and dad went through hurricanes Hugo and Marylyn everyone says Irma and Maria were way worse. If I can give any advice about ... a big hurricane be prepared for the worst and don't give up.
>
> —Science 100 student

Physical changes to the built and natural environments were inevitable, and students also expressed their emotional journeys, which sometimes reflected changes in mindsets and attitudes. For example, while many students could have (and did) title their essays simply "Hurricane Essay," the titles of others foreshadowed the strong emotional impacts of Hurricanes Irma and Maria on these students: "#Irmaria2017," "My Mixed Feelings Towards Hurricane Irma," "Hurricanes Irma and Maria: The Fight for Survival and Defeating Tribulations," "What I Gained from the Two Hurricanes." The power that these two Category 5 hurricanes hold for students was conveyed in multiple essays through a personification of either one or both hurricanes. For example:

> On September 6th, an unwelcomed guest known as Irma decided to have a vacation on this beautiful island. Unfortunately, she couldn't help but wreak havoc. To make matters worse, she recommended her friend Maria to vacation here as well, and she quickly came on September 20th ... Irma ran off with the island's power, which means her bag was filled with our televisions, computers and phones.

Given the expressed emotions and ferocious power attributed to IrMaria, we noted emotional responses of students that could be attributed to PTSD or trauma. Most students wrote about the fear they experienced

160 *Michele L. Guannel et al.*

before, during, and just after one or both hurricanes. For example: "I couldn't contact anyone to make sure that they were okay. That was the most upsetting thing that could have ever happen to me." In addition to the distress caused by not knowing whether loved ones were safe, the same student describes the emotional impact of viewing the destruction of Irma: "I literally wanted to cry when I went outside, because it was so bad." Of the several students who discussed the comparative impacts of experiencing Irma and then Maria, a slight majority described intensified fear or being "restless" during the second Category 5 hurricane: "It felt like living through another nightmare." In contrast, there may have been some fortitude (or numbness) that was gained from the experience of Irma: "Hurricane Maria experience wasn't as terrifying as Hurricane Irma. Reason behind my opinion is that the damage was already done to my island with Hurricane Irma." Notably, most students in the class experienced both Irma and Maria on St. Thomas; where Irma impacted St. Thomas and St. John severely, and Maria (though it impacted St. Thomas) had a more southerly route and was generally more damaging to St. Croix.

However, despite the fear expressed during the hurricanes or their aftermath, most essays did not describe experiences that were suggestive of potential PTSD. Only five students described experiences that could possibly be attributed to direct trauma, shock, depression, or PTSD. Such experiences included changes in lifestyle functions: "Personally, after hurricanes Irma and Maria, I did not want to eat or speak to anyone for several weeks." Another student describes mixed emotions in a role as a first responder, repeatedly stating never wanting to experience a disaster again: "The hurricane did not affect me that much at first I was very shock because of the situation but [as] time pas[sed], helping my community and other stuff and kind of did not bother me very much," ending their essay with: "The hurricane was not fun and it is something that is very scary especially for a small island like the virgin island. I hope to never ... experience something in this magnitude ever again in my life."

Each semester in Science 100 since Irma and Maria, there have been a handful of students who self-identify as survivors of previous natural disasters. These previous disasters include those that have occurred in the states, elsewhere in the Caribbean, or (for more mature students) in the VI with Hurricanes Hugo (1989) and Marilyn (1995). The subset of essays, presented in this chapter includes some of these survivors who had experienced Hurricane Katrina and the 2010 Haiti earthquake. These experiences no doubt influenced their experiences of Irma and Maria, in terms of being knowledgeable about preparation and the extent and complexities of the aftermath of disasters. It is possible that those previous experiences may have allowed these students to more clearly articulate their emotions, such as "the feeling my stomach felt was unforgettable." Another student stated:

A Course on Natural Disasters Gets Real   161

> Personally this hurricane bring sad memories, I don't do well with natural disasters, [the previous disaster] was nothing fun, it was tragic, but I survive ... [after Irma and Maria] I just felt really off, I missed going school, I missed lunch times, I was really sad.

One previous disaster survivor was able to identify the severity of emotional impact on another community member and got help for her: "She didn't eat, drink, or sleep for a few days after. We got her on the Mercy ship to Puerto Rico as soon as we could." Unfortunately, in the instance of this person as well as for many others, mercy ship evacuations from St. Thomas and St. John were going to Puerto Rico, St. Croix, and other locations—which were destined to soon be hit by Maria.

A subset of students told their very tumultuous, impactful hurricane stories without much expression of emotions. Those stories are too detailed to reprint here, as they include identifying information, and so we do not include them out of respect for the students. It is impossible to know for sure how their intense experiences have impacted their mental health, now or in the future. We do know that broader studies in the VI have revealed widespread trauma and PTSD, with an estimated 42.5% of secondary school students at risk of PTSD and 60% of adults showing symptoms of depression (Michael et al., 2019). In early 2019, USVI Governor Albert A. Bryan declared a state of emergency in terms of mental health (Executive Order No. 486-2019, 2019).

In contrast, the real "hurricane story" of the VI may be a positive one—or at least this is the story that overwhelmingly IrMaria survivors choose to tell, and to live, by continuing to embrace positive skills and outcomes of these devastating events. The majority of hurricane essays (at least 11 of the 19) framed the events of IrMaria, including the prolonged aftermath, in an overwhelmingly positive manner, consistent with PTG. Here we identify evidence of PTG through expressions of strength and identity, and/or discussion of coping strategies (coping with trauma/PTSD) that students recognize to be productive and a lifelong lesson. The descriptions of the positive outcomes from Irma and Maria can be categorized into both individual outcomes and community outcomes.

Positive individual outcomes included skills that students developed out of need, or activities done in the absence of school attendance, which, in their essays, students also recognized as beneficial in the long term. Their insights and skills included a greater strength and ability to persist, a greater appreciation of life, development of hobbies such as writing and video-making, social skills, survival skills, and a determination to succeed in their studies and career goals. One of the top-achieving students on island remarked: "This experience made me a stronger and unwavering individual who wouldn't let anything hinder me from

162 *Michele L. Guannel et al.*

accomplishing my dreams." Students credited their enhanced capabilities to problem-solve and persevere. One student stated: "Persisting through Hurricanes Irma and Maria strengthened my ability [to] critically think about situations and create solutions." Another commented: "I learned to surrender, be patient, and kind in any way possible."

Several students did not discuss fear or related emotions at all in their essays. In some of these hurricane stories, students made strong statements such as:

> It didn't bring me down, or prevented me from cracking jokes over the candle or taking the opportunity for more sleep because of no light and no phone with a charged battery; it allowed me to find myself and see how adaptable I could be when people have to depend on me.

Another student's entire hurricane essay detailed her PTG process, and she described her positive mindset, and skills gained, as an active choice:

> Many people were traumatized and might never be the same again. Although, I took advantage of the situation and decided I would have post traumatic growth. When the hurricanes hit in my senior year, I considered how their effects would cause me to be a positive asset to various universities.

Throughout the descriptions of PTG, there was recognition that these gains have not been individual. Students reference a larger-scale growth of positivity and strength, including references to VI identity:

> "Society has realized how strong the residents of the United States Virgin Islands [are]."
>
> "This island is so resilient in so many ways ... I understand that people had obligations that forced them to leave [the] island, but I am proud to say I was here for the whole deal. We rose together and I saw some of the most beautiful acts of kindness".
>
> "From going out as a group searching for food and items we needed daily, sharing any and everything we had, or just hanging out together entertaining each other, the neighbors and our families have grown bonds we've never had before. We've learned to have a natural sense of sincerity to each other and we all feel like one big family."

This community-level growth is likely linked to this shared experience: "I never imagined having a conversation with an unfamiliar person, *but our conversation flowed because it was based on our hurricane experience*" (emphasis added).

A Course on Natural Disasters Gets Real   163

Synthesis of Hurricane Essays

> Robert Jordan once stated that "The oak fought the wind and was broken, the willow bent when it must and survived." Surviving natural disasters is quite impressive. Not because one must manage to stay alive, but because of the various experiences that one goes through and lessons that one learns while surviving the natural disasters.
>
> —Science 100 student

Much of this chapter was originally inspired by nearly 300 hurricane essays written since IrMaria. The most striking common thread among them has been the prevalence of personal essays ending on a positive expression of strength and identity. Similarly, of the individuals who consented for analysis of their assignments for this research study, which we believe to be a representative subset of Science 100 students, the majority of students ended their hurricane essays on a positive note. Early on in the response and recovery process, VI residents exhibited many expressions of being "#VIStrong," similar to other communities who have experienced community-wide trauma or tragedy. Even the USVI Hurricane Recovery and Resilience Task Force (2018) prefaced their 273-page September 2018 report on the 2017 hurricane impacts with: "[t]hese pages ... recognize the strength, resilience, and resourcefulness of the Virgin Islanders working hard to rebuild and recover. *We are Virgin Islands Strong*" (emphasis included by Task Force authors). These stories echo those told in the film *Paradise Discovered: The Unbreakable Virgin Islanders* by Peter Bailey (Bailey, 2018), and those told by our neighbors on the British Virgin Islands, in *The Irma Diaries* (Burnett, 2017), which link Hurricane Irma experiences to climate change impacts.

Despite the overwhelming trend of PTG, we also hear in these essays the great divide among students who experienced vastly different impacts. Some students speak of being displaced by the hurricanes. For example, one student attended three high schools, two in the states. Some essays are a recitation of the heavy impacts to the student's home, without a statement of "growth" that resulted. In individual essays, some students repeat feelings of shock and never wanting to experience such disasters again—again without a "positive" resolution. Despite, as one student states, losing "everything," she says, "we were able to find a few laughs" after her family member made a joke. The variability in experiences underscores the fact that not all people who experience traumatic events will develop PTSD. As one student astutely noted: "A hurricane could break the spirits of a strong man and build the strength of a young child."

Looking to a future that will almost certainly contain more natural hazards, what are the factors that have evidence of minimizing the emotional toll on Virgin Islanders? Certainly, humor is one. In addition to the student who mentioned a sibling's joke, one student's humor is

164 *Michele L. Guannel et al.*

apparent in this description of PTG: "I can thank Irma and Maria for the kind exchange: attempt at murder for strengthen social skills." Additionally, a subset of students describe their reliance on spiritual faith: before, during, and after the hurricanes. The VI are known for strong and diverse religious communities. Multiple students made reference to sending prayers, singing choruses, and thanking God, and usually for these essays, the references to faith were repeated across the timeline of the hurricane story.

However, it is critical to remember that PTSD and PTG can co-occur in individuals. In terms of PTG following natural disasters, one of the first studies to document evidence of PTG in children was published just over ten years ago (Cryder et al., 2006), while the same event, Hurricane Floyd, was documented to have caused at least mild PTSD symptoms in 95% of children six months post-disaster (Russoniello et al., 2002). In some of the essays described herein, we have heard students describing experiences that could reflect both PTSD and PTG. Given the stigma associated with PTSD, depression, and other types of mental illness, it is likely that any mention of PTSD-like experiences, within the hurricane essays, are under-reported. There are possible cultural factors at play, encouraging Virgin Islanders to emphasize strength over fear and trauma. Furthermore, students who were experiencing (and writing about) PTSD may not have consented to examination of their assignments for research purposes.

In addition, although Science 100 students are mainly traditional-age and did not disclose health issues or other vulnerabilities, we heard echoes of the needs of vulnerable populations in a subset of the essays. A few students shared their own or loved ones' experiences with having special needs that were threatened by the 2017 hurricanes, including serious health conditions of the students as well as caretaking responsibilities for younger children. Additionally, it can be argued that nearly all of the traditional-age students were members of vulnerable groups at the time of Irma and Maria, as most of them were 17 or younger at the time of the hurricanes.

How do students' stories describe the VIs journey from overwhelmingly unprepared to a greater awareness of preparedness and resilience? The essays describe mostly instances of informal helping by VI residents, while opinions of external aid efforts varied, from appreciative to highly critical. Regardless of students' opinions of formal aid, the prevalence of "neighbors helping neighbors" was experienced widely. Furthermore, in geographically isolated regions such as islands or rural communities, it will always be the case that residents "on the ground" are the first responders—whether they are trained or experienced in any way, or not. Overwhelmingly, UVI students voice a willingness and ability to face future challenges, including natural disasters on the order of IrMaria.

A Course on Natural Disasters Gets Real   165

Education in the Post-IrMaria Landscape

> If there is no transportation to classes, I'll walk. If there is no washing machines, I'll wash it myself. If there is no power I can survive without my phone and other technologies. If I can survive two category five hurricanes then I can survive anything.
>
> — Science 100 student

Based upon the experiences of Irma and Maria, Science 100 utilizes several assignments to expand preparedness education and to communicate the scientific evidence that climate change is exacerbating natural disasters such as those experienced by students. These course-based assignments include:

1. An enhanced importance and introduction to the writing of the hurricane essay—which now is described as the "resilience essay." The essay options now total four, with an additional option to write about changes observed in the natural environment. The intent is to more clearly communicate that students have a choice not to write about their own hurricane experiences.
2. Scaffolded content on climate change, which often starts with watching the documentary *Chasing Coral* (that describes the causes of climate change and its impacts on one of the major Caribbean ecosystems, coral). Later, during the hurricane unit, evidence of climate impacts on hurricane intensification, frequency, and rainfall is presented. Finally, a climate change lecture is now framed as "climate crisis," in which students are asked to identify the most significant local climate change issue and suggest one solution; lecture and activities are also related to local renewable energy sources.
3. Individualized emergency preparedness plans—each student assesses their own household vulnerabilities and creates plans in terms of survival preparedness, planning preparedness, and structural preparedness.
4. A new pre- and post-survey to assess the course's contribution to understanding of disaster safety and preparedness (described below).
5. A service learning initiative to get students active in their communities, in order to contribute to hurricane recovery and ongoing resilience-building (described below).

For the purposes of this chapter, we will focus on initial assessment of the disaster safety and preparedness survey as well as the service learning initiative. These and other changes represent culturally sustaining pedagogy (Paris, 2012)—in which course curricula are continually revised in

166   *Michele L. Guannel et al.*

order to encompass our community members' changing perceptions of IrMaria impacts (and the PTG process) and new hazards including the COVID-19 pandemic.

Education in the Post-IrMaria Landscape: Assessment of Disaster Preparedness

Starting in Fall 2019, we initiated a new pre- and post-survey to gauge students' understanding of disaster safety and their use of resources to learn about natural hazards. This survey grew out of two major observations in these essays and in other parts of the class over several semesters since Spring 2018. First, students repeatedly reported feeling unprepared for hurricanes. Second, their emergency preparedness plans sometimes included potentially dangerous actions and a lack of knowledge of other hazards that influence the VI, such as earthquakes and tsunami waves.

The new Disaster Preparedness and Safety Survey is now given to students at the beginning and at the end of the semester. It consists of nine true/false questions that test common disaster preconceptions (e.g., the myth that it is safest to stand in a doorway during an earthquake) and two short open-ended questions. The data that we analyzed are from the Fall 2019 semester on the St. Thomas campus, and included 53 students who completed both pre- and post-surveys out of the total 95 students who completed the class.

First, to analyze students' understanding of disaster safety, we assigned each true/false question with a value of 0 if it was incorrect and 1 if it was correct. For example, true/false questions related to hurricanes included X (Correct Answer = True) and Y (Correct Answer = False). We then calculated each student's score (from 0–9) depending on how many questions they got correct; pre–post differences were assessed using a paired samples t-test. The results revealed that there was a significant difference in the number correct ($p < 0.0001$) between the pre- and post-surveys. We can conclude that it is likely that the better performance of the students on the true/false portion of the survey was due to the completion of the Science 100 class.

Second, we analyzed the open-ended survey question that asked: "What are up to three sources of information that you use to learn about possible natural hazards that may impact the VI?" Answers were separated into seven categories: Social Media/Apps, Websites, TV/Radio/Text Programs, School/People, Paper Sources, Disaster Response/Recovery Organizations, and Other Responses. The replies were quantified in terms of percentage of total responses. To test for statistically significant trends, a McNemar's chi-square test on a 2 x 2 contingency table was utilized to check the marginal homogeneity of two dichotomous variables (Glen, 2015). Here, the chi-square test was used to analyze tests performed before and after treatment in the population, where the treatment was the Science 100 course material and the population was the 53 respondents. The two variables were whether each student included or did not include a response in each category while completing the pre-survey and the post-survey. We ran the McNemar tables with a significance level of $p < 0.05$. For example, the post-survey responses in the category of Disaster Response/Recovery Organizations had the largest pre–post change, representing 5% of all pre-survey responses to 25% of all post-survey responses (p = 0.00001).

Furthermore, we found that students included more specific, reputable sources for information regarding natural hazards in the post-survey as compared to the pre-survey. The Virgin Islands Territorial Emergency Management Agency (VITEMA) provides the USVI with the primary response to prepare before, during, and after a hazard occurs. Only four students included VITEMA in their pre-survey responses, whereas that amount increased to 21 students in the post-survey. This increase shows that students are more knowledgeable about reputable alert sources related to hurricanes and other disasters based on the sources they use prior to a hazard occurring. It is also shown in the Website category where students' responses shifted from the general answer of "Internet" in the pre-survey to "National Oceanic and Atmospheric Administration (NOAA)" and the "National Hurricane Center (NHC)" in the post-survey.

Based on the incorporation and analysis of new disaster safety surveys, we conclude that the course is increasing student understanding of reliable sources related to natural hazards. We hope that this increased knowledge will lead to greater preparedness. Similarly, the hurricane essay (resilience essay) seems to serve to remind students of the strength they found to overcome IrMaria—which is part of feeling prepared for future impacts of climate change.

Education in the Post-IrMaria Landscape: Service Learning as a Pathway

We posit that, just as students voiced strength related to their participation in relief and response efforts, course-embedded opportunities to contribute to recovery and resilience efforts can have a healing effect on participants. Between the Spring 2018 and the Spring 2021 semesters within Science 100, over 100 students have pursued service learning and other project-based learning experiences, related to hurricane recovery or stewardship of local ecosystems (Guannel, 2018; Guannel et al., 2019). These projects have included donation management, note-taking during recovery meetings, and development of removable home garden prototypes as part of the STRT's Food Security Program. Projects have also matched students with science, engineering, and community engagement professionals to work towards drainage mapping, solar

168   *Michele L. Guannel et al.*

energy development, and restoration of mangroves that were damaged heavily by Hurricane Irma.

Similarly, one Puerto Rican resident, Yarimar Bonilla, observed: "the people who seem to be doing the best are those who are helping others, those who are involved in community efforts," as reported by Naomi Klein in her book on the impacts of Hurricane Maria on Puerto Rico (Klein, 2018). Klein also noted expressions of strength and pride from youth who were working, amidst the lack of electricity and water, to provide food for their families. Within the field of resilience, there is acknowledgment that inherent psychological components can empower an individual to be more or less flexible in the face of changes, including traumatic events such as natural disasters. From informal self-reporting polls taken in Science 100 during each semester since January 2018 (including the semesters of student voices in this study), the majority of students self-identified as having either a high resiliency trait or a very high resiliency trait according to the ego resiliency scale (Block & Kremen, 1996). Furthermore, the title of Rebecca Solnit's book, *A Paradise Built in Hell: The Extraordinary Communities that Arise in Disaster* (2009), speaks to positive community pride and strength that has been documented as a result of past tragedies, including the 1906 San Francisco Earthquake, Hurricane Katrina's 2005 impacts on the New Orleans metro region, and the 9/11 terror attacks on the United States. Similarly, we hear strong statements of individual and community pride and strength in UVI student essays, through the trials endured by the 2017 hurricanes.

Additional potential positive impacts of service learning, within a course on natural disasters taken by mainly disaster survivors, are multifaceted. First, service learning has been described as a high-impact activity (Kuh, 2008) that has the capacity to increase retention (Yob, 2014) and requires students to demonstrate "21st century skills" that comprise a cornerstone of education reform (Bellanca & Brandt, 2010). These 21st-century skills include those that are echoed by the descriptions of PTG: collaboration, creativity, critical thinking, and communication; assessment is being conducted both quantitatively (S-STEM instrument; Unfried et al., 2015) and through qualitative analysis of themes voiced in students' products, including written reflections on their service learning experiences.

We are currently pursuing an expanded service learning initiative, across the two major general education courses for UVI freshmen (Science 100 and Social Science 100)—both of which focus on Caribbean life. The goal is to increase retention and persistence of UVI graduates, as part of an integrated Freshman Year Experience (Upcraft & Gardner, 1989). For example, for the 2016–2017 academic year, 67% of the freshman class returned to UVI after the first year (UVI's metric of retention), and only 23% of students graduated after six years of undergraduate education. Clearly, based on the stories shared here that are representative of hundreds of more newly matriculated students, UVI students have much more to offer that can also be supported through a bachelor's level education.

Conclusion

> Maria and Irma is an experience everyone needed to prepare for a changing society and changing climate.
>
> — Science 100 student

Nearly four years later, after reading additional hurricane essays that consistently tell similar stories, we have evidence of massively resilient and experienced Virgin Islanders, uncertainties about the recovery process under a newly appointed governor, and a federally unchecked pathway, with the world traveling full-speed ahead to the Intergovernmental Panel on Climate Change's worst nightmare scenario of increased heat, rainfall changes, sea level rise, and increased likelihood of another IrMaria.

The people of the VI have many questions:

- Will the 2017 hurricanes end up being unparalleled opportunities for the VI to reinvent itself, or will this opportunity be squandered?
- Will the Territory suffer additional challenges of new hurricanes, over the decade-long recovery?
- What will the story of the VI and IrMaria give to the world?

Emergency preparedness education is a critical component of climate change education. Based upon the extent and severity of challenges described in students' stories, some of which hold elements of possible PTSD, it is critical that such education be couched as part of a trauma-informed practice (DeCandia & Guarino, 2020). We invite psychologists as guest speakers, provide and discuss informational resources on mental wellness such as those published by SAMSHA (Substance Abuse and Mental Health Services Administration), and students are given a choice to write about ecosystem changes rather than disasters in the former "hurricane essay." Furthermore, any instructors who may be new to the VI and to the course must strive to become culturally competent, especially as it relates to the impacts of Hurricanes Irma and Maria, in order to support the mental wellness needs of students who are studying the very natural disasters that they survived.

We believe that the pedagogical technique of service learning will not only enhance retention and persistence at UVI, but more importantly, it will develop VI residents who are skilled and cross-trained in designated areas of need, post-hurricanes, and sustainable economies moving forward to develop greater resilience on-island. Engagement of students in

170   *Michele L. Guannel et al.*

recovery and resilience efforts diversifies the voices and needs that feed into missions of recovery organizations. By directly linking students to leadership in recovery and resilience, this initiative will expand community engagement and extend/diversify the visioning initiatives and integration of ever-evolving community needs.

Indeed, as natural disasters disproportionately impact people of color, there is a great need for cultural competency within formal emergency management programs. VI residents, knowledgeable of the islands' distinct terrain and cultures, are the best responders for future disasters in the VI—and, we would argue in many other locations. VI residents represent the small percentage of humans on the planet who are experienced in survival of two Category 5 hurricanes. They are primarily people of color who speak English, Spanish, Haitian Creole, and various dialects. They are familiar with the challenges of colonized and poverty-stricken communities. As heard here in their voices, VI youth are the best and brightest of a new wave of climate change and disaster responders, and are well-positioned to assist those who look like them, who speak their languages, and who are marginalized peoples.

References

2014 United States Virgin Islands Community Survey (USVI CS). (2017). St. Thomas, USVI: Eastern Caribbean Center, University of the Virgin Islands.

Applied Research Associates (ARA). (2018). Development of wind speed-ups and hurricane hazard maps for the United States Virgin Islands., Draft Final Report, FEMA TASK ORDER NUMBER: 70FBR2-18-F-00000012.

Austin, R. (2018). Economic and fiscal conditions in the U.S. Virgin Islands, congressional research service report no. R45235.

Bailey, P. (2018). Paradise discovered: The unbreakable virgin islanders. Film produced by Nite Cap Media.

Baker, C.N., Brown, S.M., Wilcox, P.D., Overstreet, S., & Arora, P. (2016). Development and psychometric evaluation of the attitudes related to trauma-informed care (ARTIC) scale. *School Mental Health, 8,* 61–76.

Bellanca, J., & Brandt, R. (Eds.). (2010). *21st century skills: Rethinking how students learn.* Bloomington, IN: Solution Tree Press.

Block, J., & Kremen, A.M. (1996). IQ and ego-resiliency: Conceptual and empirical connections and separateness. *Journal of Personality and Social Psychology, 70*(2), 349–361.

Bontekoe, R. (1996). *Dimensions of the hermeneutic circle.* Humanities Press.

Bram, J. (2018, June 21). *Puerto Rico & the US Virgin Islands in the aftermath of hurricanes Irma and Maria.* Federal Reserve Bank of New York Presentation to Community Advisory Group.

Burnett, A. (2017). The Irma diaries: Compelling survivor stories from the Virgin Islands. e-publication available through Amazon Digital Services LLC.

Campbell-Lendrum, D., Corvalan, C., & Neira, M. (2007). Global climate change: Implications for international public health policy. *Bulletin of the World Health Organization, 85*(3), 161–244.

A Course on Natural Disasters Gets Real   171

College Board. (2018). *SAT suite of assessments annual report.* New York: College Board.

Cryder, C.H., Kilmer, R.P., Tedeschi, R.G., & Calhoun, L.G. (2006). An exploratory study of posttraumatic growth in children following a natural disaster. *American Journal of Orthopsychiatry, 76,* 65–69.

DeCandia, C., & Guarino, K. (2020). Trauma-informed care: An ecological response. *Journal of Child and Youth Care Work, 25,* 7–32.

Eatough, V., & Smith, J.A. (2008). Phenomenological psychology. In A.P. Giorgi & B. Giorgi (Eds.), *The SAGE handbook of qualitative research in psychology* (pp. 165–179). Thousand Oaks, CA: Sage.

Federal Emergency Management Agency. (2018, January 3). Disasters affected 8% of U.S. population in 2017, FEMA notes in review of historic year. *Insurance Journal* [Web article]. https://www.insurancejournal.com/news/national/2018/01/03/476001.htm

Glen, S. (2015, July 17). McNemar test definition, examples, calculation. https://www.statisticshowto.com/mcnemar-test/

Guannel, M.L. (2018, October 18). Service learning and hurricane recovery: A reflection. [Web log post]. https://viepscor.org/news/2018/10/18/service-learning

Guannel, M.L., Peterson, M., Daniel, I., Guannel, G., & Jaeger, E. (2019). *University youth leadership in hurricane recovery in the Virgin Islands. Conference proceedings: 21st annual emergency management higher education symposium,* Emmitsburg, Maryland.

Jones, N.N., Cummings, L., Guannel, M.L., & Abdallah, S. (2018). *Reforming science education to a place-based focus: Cultural congruence and 21st Century Skill development. Conference proceedings: Arts, humanities, social sciences, & education, 2018 Hawaii University International Conferences,* Honolulu, Hawai'i.

Klein, N. (2018). *The battle for paradise: Puerto Rico takes on the disaster capitalists.* Chicago, IL: Haymarket Books.

Krigger, M.F. (2017). *Race relations in the U.S. Virgin Islands.* Durham, NC: Carolina Academic Press.

Kuh, G.D. (2008). *High-impact educational practices: What they are: Who has access to them, and why they matter.* Washington, DC: Association of American Colleges & Universities.

Long, B. (2019, June 3). Why will FEMA spend as much in past 2 years as the previous 37? Here's how disaster aid works. *The Hill* [Web article]. https://thehill.com/opinion/energy-environment/446635-why-will-fema-spend-as-much-in-past-2-years-as-the-previous-37

Michael, N., Valmond, J.M., Ragster, L.E., Brown, D.E., & Callwood, G.B. (2019). *Community needs assessment: Understanding the needs of vulnerable children and families in the US Virgin Islands Post Hurricanes Irma and Maria.* St. Thomas, USVI: Caribbean Exploratory Research Center, School of Nursing, University of the Virgin Islands.

NOAA 2019 Sea Level Rise Viewer. (2019). https://coast.noaa.gov/digitalcoast/tools/slr.html

NOAA National Centers for Environmental Information, State of the Climate: Tropical Cyclones for Annual 2017, published online January 2018, retrieved on October 7, 2021 from https://www.ncdc.noaa.gov/sotc/tropical-cyclones/201713/

Paris, D. (2012). Culturally sustaining pedagogy: A needed change in stance, terminology, and practice. *Educational Researcher, 41*(3), 93–97.

Patricola, C.M., & Wehner, M.F. (2018). Anthropogenic influences on major tropical cyclone events. *Nature, 563*(7731), 339–346.

Paul, D.F., & Watlington, R.A. (1997). Development and initial implementation of the general education reform: Creating the UVI graduates of the 21st century: A general education reform project. Internal committee report: unpublished.

Russoniello, C.V., Skalko, T.K., O'Brien, K., McGhee, S.A., Bingham Alexander, D., & Beatley, J. (2002). Childhood posttraumatic stress disorder and efforts to cope after Hurricane Floyd. *Behavioral Medicine, 28*, 61–70.

Shultz, J.M., Sands, D.E., Kossin, J.P., & Galea, S. (2020). Double environmental injustice - climate change, Hurricane Dorian, and the Bahamas. *New England Journal of Medicine, 382*(1), 1–3.

Simon Wang, S-Y, Zhao, L., Yoon, J-H, Klotzbach, P., & Gillies, R.R. (2018). Quantitative attribution of climate effects on Hurricane Harvey's extreme rainfall in Texas. *Environmental Research Letters, 13*(5), 054014.

Solnit, R. (2009). *A paradise built in hell: The extraordinary communities that arise in disasters.* New York: Viking.

Stephenson, T.S., Vincent, L.A., Allen, T., Van Meerbeeck, C.J., McLean, N., Peterson, T.C., & Trotman, A.R. (2014). Changes in extreme temperature and precipitation in the Caribbean region, 1961–2010. *International Journal of Climatology, 34*(9), 2957–2971.

Substance Abuse and Mental Health Service Administration. (2013). Tips for survivors of a disaster or other traumatic event: Managing stress. SAMHSA Publication ID SMA13-4776. https://store.samhsa.gov/product/Tips-for-urvivors-of-a-Disaster-or-Other-Traumatic-Event-Managing-Stress/SMA13-4776

Tedeschi, R.G., & Calhoun, L.G. (1995). *Trauma and transformation: Growing in the aftermath of suffering.* Thousand Oaks, CA: Sage.

Tedeschi, R.G., & Calhoun, L.G. (1996). The posttraumatic growth inventory: Measuring the positive legacy of trauma. *Journal of Traumatic Stress, 9*, 455–471.

Tedeschi, R. G., Park, C. L., & Calhoun, L. G. (Eds.). (1998). *Posttraumatic growth: Positive changes in the aftermath of crisis.* Routledge.

Tedeschi, R.G., & Calhoun, L.G. (2004). Posttraumatic growth: Conceptual foundations and empirical evidence. *Psychological Inquiry, 15*(1), 1–18.

Unfried, A., Faber, M., Stanhope, D.S., & Wiebe, E. (2015). The development and validation of a measure of student attitudes toward science, technology, engineering, and math (S-STEM). *Journal of Psychoeducational Assessment, 33*(7), 622–639.

Upcraft, M.L., & Gardner, J.N. (1989). *The freshman year experience: Helping students survive and succeed in college.* San Francisco, CA: Jossey-Bass, Inc., Publishers.

US Army Corps of Engineers (USACE). (2014). Procedures to evaluate sea level change: Impacts, responses, and adaptation, Technical Letter No. 1100-2-1.

U.S. Census Bureau. (2013). US Virgin Islands 2010 census. https://www2.census.gov/census_2010/10-Island_Areas_Detailed_Cross_Tabulations/Virgin_Islands

U.S. Global Change Research Program (USGCRP). (2018). *Impacts, risks, and adaptation in the United States: Fourth national climate assessment, volume II* (1515 p). (Reidmiller, D.R., Avery, C.W., Easterling, D.R., Kunkel, K.E., Lewis, K.L.M., Maycock, T.K., and Stewart, B.C., Eds.). Washington, DC, USA: U.S. Global Change Research Program.

USVI Hurricane Recovery and Resilience Task Force (USVI HRRTF). (2018). USVI hurricane recovery and resilience task force report. [Web report]. https://first.bloomberglp.com/documents/257521_USVI_Hurricane+Recov ery+Taskforce+Report_DIGITAL.pdf

Watlington, R. (2018). Personal communication of wind speeds measured from OCOVI weather stations. http://ocovi.org/

Yob, I.M. (2014). Keeping students in by sending them out: Retention and service-learning. *Higher Learning Research Communications, 4*(2), 38–57.

6 "A Different Kind of Middleman"

Preservice Science Teachers' Agency for Climate Change Education

Asli Sezen-Barrie and Lucy Avraamidou

Introduction

> I still care about climate change a lot and I try to do things to, you know, reduce my carbon footprint as best way that I could because I feel like that's what is going to help. But, in terms of, like—and I am not that into politics that much—I feel as if it's a bigger problem.
>
> Not enough people are thinking about it GLOBALLY and they are more thinking INDIVIDUALLY. And that's why, for me, I feel like I'm more ALONE in it because I feel like I'm the minority who's thinking about the majority, like the global scale. But, I don't think that a lot of people do that.
>
> (Ms. Cassy Crawford, Middle School Science Teacher)

This excerpt from the focal participant of the study reported in this chapter serves to illustrate one of the moral and ethical dilemmas the world has been facing in relation to climate change crisis. On the one hand, people who believe in climate change think that it is rational for every agent to cooperate in taking actions to solve climate change problems. On the other hand, if people act based on their individual interests, it is rational to undermine the problem. Stephen Gardiner (2006) relates this paradoxical situation to the idea of the "Tragedy of the Commons," an article published by the ecologist Garrett Hardin in 1968 in *Science*. Since climate change is an international problem, Gardiner describes nations as the relevant parties "who represent the interests of their citizens in perpetuity" (p. 400). While many countries agree that measures need to be taken to solve the climate change problem, such as restricting greenhouse gas emissions, every nation wants to rely on other countries' actions. In this way, countries are able to protect the individual, often short-term economic and political interests of their own citizens. This creates a paradoxical situation which adds to the complexity of addressing the climate change crisis.

As we are still in debate on how to deal with this paradoxical situation across different communities or nations, climate scientists are calling for urgent action. As of 2018, human-made climate change has

DOI: 10.4324/9780429326011-9

"A Different Kind of Middleman" 175

caused a 0.87 degrees Celsius increase in average global temperature over historic averages (International Panel for Climate Change—IPCC). This change has led to drastic impacts on ecosystems and organisms, such as increased acidification in oceans, which challenges oyster larval development, or intense rain in parts of the world and drought in other regions. To further complicate the problem, the most devastating impacts of climate change are unfairly experienced by people who live in poverty. What this means is that climate change is not only an ecological issue, but it is also a political issue with implications for equity and social justice. The recent IPCC report (2018) calls for collective action, such as a 45% decrease in global carbon emissions by 2030 so that we can limit disastrous impacts of climate change.

As two midcareer, international scholars of science education, we observed climate change impacts in different communities across the world, such as heat waves and drought in Europe, and the polar vortex, hurricanes, and wildfires in the USA. These extreme weather events led to destruction of houses, damage to crops and feeders for animals, and even death of humans. We witnessed practical solutions our communities wanted to act on such as creating bike friendly communities, recycling programs, reducing one-time-use plastics, and so forth. Yet, the bigger, global problem still persists. Our work as science education scholars has a focus on teachers as they are critical social agents (e.g., Avraamidou, 2019). Other scholars in the field also explored Preservice Science Teachers (PSTs) as the subject of climate change studies. These studies looked at PSTs' scientific background knowledge to understand the climate change evidence (e.g., Boon, 2010), their misconceptions (e.g., Plutzer et al., 2016), emotions about climate change issues (e.g., Lombardi & Sinatra, 2013), and use of argumentation in scientific practices to improve PST's sensemaking of climate science (e.g., Lambert & Bleicher, 2017).

Previous studies highlighted the potential role of PSTs as agents of taking action to solve the climate change problem (McNeill & Vaughn, 2010). Science educators then raised the question of how PSTs' sense of agency might be enhanced in order to enable them to feel a part of the solution to climate change (e.g., Rivera Maulucci, Brotman, & Fain, 2015). However, there is still a dearth of studies that looked at PSTs' agency in effectively communicating climate change and encouraging people to act on this urgent problem. Therefore, in this chapter, we are interested in exploring PSTs' agency through a single case study of Ms. Cassy Crawford. In this four-year-long study, we were able to trace Ms. Crawford across spaces such as workshops, research meetings, and middle school classrooms, and across time from a junior in college to science teacher at a public school.

What is Teacher Agency and Why Does It Matter?

The study is framed within the construct of "agency" which is generally used to refer to the ways in which teachers might see themselves and be recognized by others as agents of change. In science education, the construct of agency has been conceptualized as a dimension of teacher identity, which refers to "the ways in which a teacher represents herself through her views, orientations, attitudes, content knowledge, knowledge, and beliefs about science teaching, and the ways in which she acts within specific contexts" (Avraamidou, 2014, p. 224). The construct of identity has been mostly framed within cultural-historical activity theory (Engeström, 1999), initially formulated by Vygotsky's idea of activity systems where subjects reach their objects through social interaction with their mediating artifacts. As Roth et al. (2004) argued:

> Social analysis in terms of cultural historical activity theory focuses on what people (subjects) actually do, the objects that motivate their activity, the tools they use, the community of which they are part, the roles that pattern their actions, and the division of labor they take in activity.
>
> (p. 50)

This emphasis on the dialectical relationship between teachers and the contexts in which they develop and enact their identities are of special interest in this study. As Luehmann (2008) argued, the construct of identity is particularly important within the field of teacher education because it offers a comprehensive construct for studying teacher learning and development, which goes beyond knowledge and skills:

> The sole focus on knowledge, understanding or other purely cognitive constructs in teacher education, has been criticized as limited as it leaves the novice teacher alone to figure out how to develop, integrate, and reconcile emotions and physical aspects with the understandings involved in becoming a teacher.
>
> (p. 827)

Beyond the emphasis on the affective domains of teacher learning and development, the sociocultural nature of identity is also important for the purpose of conceptualizing agency because it highlights the value of paying attention to the social contexts and communities in which teachers learn, develop, and act. As Shanahan (2009) argued, agency refers to each individual's ability to shape the world around them. Our interest on agency goes beyond understanding what agency is to also include what agency looks like in practice. Hence, we focus our attention on characterizing the participant's practices. This is rooted in Biesta and

Tedder's (2007) ecological conceptualization of agency, which places emphasis on its enactment:

> [T]his concept of agency highlights that actors always act by means of their environment rather than simply in their environment [so that] the achievement of agency will always result from the interplay of individual efforts, available resources and contextual and structural factors as they come together in particular and, in a sense, always unique situations.
>
> (p. 137)

The construct of teacher agency remains largely unexplored in science education research with only a few notable exceptions. For example, Moore (2008) examined how teachers' identity and agency were connected, influenced, and shaped by each other. In a study with a group of 23 preservice elementary teachers, she examined how elementary preservice teachers' conceptions as "agents of change" shape their identities and agency as science teachers, and the ways in which their perceptions as change agents frame their understanding of teaching science for social justice in urban elementary classrooms. The participants of this study enrolled in a 16-week science methods course in the northeastern United States. Data consisted of the participants' reflections from a semester-long Book Club in which they participated and two diversity surveys (before and after the Book Club). In this Book Club, the preservice teachers read the book *Ways with Words* and met in class three times in small groups to discuss questions about the book, issues of diversity, teacher identity, and science teaching. Five of these teachers also participated in semi-structured interviews at the end of the semester where they were asked questions about their positional identities. The analyses of these data revealed how identity and agency connect, influence, and shape each other as preservice teachers become agents of change in elementary science classrooms. These findings highlight the need to address agency and science teacher identity in supporting preservice teachers in learning to teach science for social justice.

Another example of research that explores agency is found in Richmond's (2016) study which explores the interplay between professional identity and contextual factors and how those contribute to a sense of agency. In this work, using interviews, journals, course and field assignments, and related artifacts, the author reports on efforts to elucidate how PSTs preparing to work in high-poverty schools in the United States make sense of their multiple contexts, and how this sense-making shapes their professional identity and agency as science educators committed to working in challenging settings on climate change topics that offer unique challenges due to their assumed controversial, interdisciplinary, and complex nature. In this, Richmond shares what she calls

178 *Asli Sezen-Barrie and Lucy Avraamidou*

"re-constructed" narratives, comprised of first-, second-, and third-person narratives that are constructed from a variety of data sources collected during the participants' final two years of the teacher preparation program. The purpose of these reconstructed narratives, as Richmond argues, is to illustrate, and at the same time problematize, the relationship between agency and identity, and point to ways in which various kinds of contexts can serve to help move an individual's identity as a teacher forward or can serve as obstacles to growth. Essentially what the findings of this study show is: (a) the consonance between the professional identity one sculpts and the agency one has for making intentional moves likely to have positive outcomes is critically important for creating the conditions for success, in the immediate present and into the future; and (b) contextual factors matter, not only for that sense of agency to develop initially, but to be maintained. The ways in which identity intertwines with agency and how contextual factors might shape agency are at the heart of the account of this study in the context of climate change.

Preservice Teacher Agency from an Ethical and Moral Lens for Climate Change Education

Our fields are starting to recognize PSTs' potential to be the critical agents in engaging the public to act on solutions towards climate change. Due to their close connections to the next generation and the many years of teaching ahead of them, each PST has the potential to create an immense impact on K-12 students. According to Lawson et al. (2019), these K-12 students can then impact the views and even actions of their parents. By working with 238 families in coastal North Carolina, Lawson et al. found that children who developed more concern towards climate change through new instructional strategies also impacted their parents such that their parents had significantly increased concern for the climate change problem. Interestingly, they found that the impact was higher among families who had initially refused to engage in climate change related issues. Therefore, the impact of PSTs' practices might extend beyond their students, and potentially influence their parents as well as stakeholders. In what follows, we examine the ethical and moral reasons and dilemmas that PSTs might experience during the process of developing a sense of agency.

What Leads to Preservice Teachers' High Feeling of Agency to Teach Climate Change?

We will draw from two recent theories to show why some PSTs develop a high feeling of agency for teaching climate change, particularly when they are engaged in working with K-12 students. One is a few decades old

"*A Different Kind of Middleman*" 179

theory of "the ethics of care" (Gilligan, 1982; Held, 2006; Noddings, 1984). The ethics of care looks at the relationship between two parties: one is the carer and the other is cared for (Buber, 1965). This theory suggests a moral dimension that the carer is responsible for listening and attending to the needs for the cared for (Noddings, 2012). By using ethics of care, scholars explored the relationships between teacher as the carer and the students as the cared for (e.g., Noddings, 2012) or the human as the carer for the place (the environment) as the cared for (e.g., Schindel & Tolbert, 2017). Despite highlighting a moral responsibility in relationships, the ethics of care scholars are against the common views of traditional moral theories that aim to eliminate bias, personal values, and emotions from their claims. Hence, the ethics of the care view acknowledges personal or family stories and moral emotions, such as empathy and sensitivity, to examine what shapes reasoning and decision making (Held, 2016).

Both human–human and human–nonhuman relationships might relate to how PSTs see themselves as important agents in climate change education. As future teachers, they learn to care about their students and feel the moral responsibility to raise climate literate generations who can make decisions for the world they will be living in. PSTs might feel the moral responsibility for youth to be prepared for living in an environment where worsened climate impacts are highly possible. This statement assumes that youth need help to deal with climate change problems in the future. Ethics of care scholars argue that there is a difference between "assumed" vs. "expressed needs" by the cared for (Noddings, 2012, p. 773). It is necessary that the students' need should be expressed in interactions with teachers and that PSTs listen to their students' needs. Moreover, the ethics of care perspective can help us understand how students can engage in climate change learning thanks to the relationship between PSTs (and their students) and the environment. In this case, PSTs and their students are the carer, and the environment or the local place is in need of protection from climate change impacts. In their study, Schindel and Tolbert (2017) found that a male science teacher's explicit carework for the place led his students to positively connect to nature and to their teachers. Moreover, their study emphasized that the teacher's carework better engaged marginalized students in formal school work.

Another theory we see as influential in PSTs' feeling of agency for the climate change problem is the theory of intergenerational equity. This theory considers that the right of future generations to inherit the planet in "at least as good condition as every other generation receives it and to be able to use it for its own benefit" (Weiss, 2008, p. 622). The theory of intergenerational equity runs on three major principles: (a) conservation of options that requires the future generation inheriting the same diversity of natural resources as we have now; (b) conservation of quality suggests that the Earth will not be in a worse condition for future

180   *Asli Sezen-Barrie and Lucy Avraamidou*

generations; and (c) conservation of access recommends that different populations on Earth will have fair access to nature's resources (Weiss, 1983, 2008).

We view PSTs as being at the center of a social justice issue of intergenerational phenomena in acting on the climate change problem. Gardiner (2006) sees this intergenerational aspect of climate change as a bigger problem than the "Tragedy of the Commons" problem that nations face due to dilemmas about global vs. individual interests. This is because we have no other option but to come into an agreement with the generations before us who initiated many of the drivers of climate change, or future generations who might experience the worst impacts. Scientists have been in strong agreement that the excess amount of atmospheric CO_2 has been the major driver of climate change. CO_2 can stay in the atmosphere close to 200 years (Archer, 2005). Due to this long life, it makes it harder to reverse this backloaded problem for future generations. Moreover, it is often hard to understand the impacts of climate change. For example, sea level rise is a process that plays out over decades, or even centuries. As a result, leaders with short-term horizons will have a hard time responding to these threats. These threats will be worse for the disadvantaged regions of the world if our generation does not develop guidelines or laws for conservation of access for future generations (Weiss, 2008). As opposed to working with people whose concerns are the urgent problems of our generation, PSTs have an advantage of working with the students who are closer to the next generation and might have more concerns for the quality and options of resources that will be inherited by these next generations. Working with youth can inspire PSTs as they think of themselves impacting future generations; and this expands their horizons.

From a High Feeling of Agency to Taking Action: What Do Preservice Teachers Need?

A review of the literature provides evidence that a feeling of agency is necessary for taking action; however, a feeling alone is not sufficient to initiate action (Haggard & Tsakiris, 2009). Instead, a high feeling of agency can lead to individual action only if the social structures are in place and the trust is established for the actors in positions of power, such as scientists and politicians, so that they are willing to solve the climate change problem on a broader scale (Tayne et al., 2021; Walsh & Cordero, 2019). Similarly, PSTs might have a high feeling of agency; however, they often do not have enough opportunities to develop identities to take on the challenge of teaching climate change once they become a practicing teacher. *Climate Change and Sustainable Development: The Response from Education* (Læssøe et al., 2009) blames the inadequacy of preservice teacher education programs as the reason for the lack of

"A Different Kind of Middleman" 181

effective climate change education. In this regard, some studies focused on threading the climate change issue through methods courses (e.g., Matkins & Bell, 2007) and emphasizing the moral and ethical issues related to climate change (Hestness, McGinnis, Riedinger, & Marbach, 2011). Matkins and Bell (2007) found that teachers who were exposed to a climate change unit were more likely to integrate climate change in their future classrooms.

Carter (2012) draws attention to the complexity of preservice teachers' engagement in climate change issues due to their still developing sense of their own professional identities as becoming a teacher. To add to this complexity, studies found that preservice teachers focus on individualistic solutions to climate change while not highlighting collective actions towards solutions to it. This was the issue that Ms. Crawford highlighted in a recent interview (see opening quotation). A study by Kenis and Mathijs (2012) found that young adults might not see such individual behavior as effective, but continue to do it as they might not know how to work towards systemic, collective efforts. This raises an ethical issue as teachers are constrained in their ability to contribute to large institutional or infrastructural efforts to take action. The sociopolitical context of recent years limits the contributions to climate change adaptations to only a few, while educators from high poverty neighborhoods do not typically have access to work towards these broad scale solutions (Walsh & Cordero, 2019).

Another burden PSTs need to shoulder is working with students in uncertainties involved in climate change claims. Despite the certainty on what causes climatic changes, the uncertainties remain regarding its future impacts, making it harder for novice teachers to make sense of climate change and to attend to students' questions. Although climate scientists have a consensus on human-caused climate change (Cook et al., 2016), there remains the "scientific uncertainty about the precise magnitude and distribution of effects" (Gardiner, 2006, p. 401). Therefore, it will be hard to infuse these uncertain ideas into the dynamics of a traditional science classroom environment that prioritizes facts and accurate findings from canonical science. These uncertainties can put PSTs in vulnerable positions as they are learning to promote students' epistemic agency, that is, students' participation in knowledge construction through scientific practices in their classroom (Damsa, Kirschner, Andriessen, Erkens, & Sins, 2010; Stroupe, 2014). The increased student epistemic agency in science classrooms has been recently emphasized by scholars in the USA (e.g., Miller et al., 2018; Stroupe, 2014) who view it as a necessary move for meaningful engagement in scientific practices as suggested by the most recent standards (NGSS, 2013). Examples of how PSTs can promote students' epistemic agency are recognizing students' background or local knowledge (Campbell, Schwarz, & Windschitl, 2016), designing activities where

182 *Asli Sezen-Barrie and Lucy Avraamidou*

students collect their own data and make decisions about the validity of this data, formulating scientific questions, and designing investigations to respond to these questions (Miller et al., 2018; Sezen-Barrie et al., 2020). While working with climate data and claims and being active epistemic agents, students will explicitly notice the uncertainties. PSTs will need to navigate students' perspectives regarding uncertainty, which is an ethical dilemma considering the current public denial over climate change action (Gardiner, 2010). Furthermore, the current model of STEM education in many schools requires science teachers to work on already established claims with high scientific certainty (Plutzer & Hannah, 2018). This model might limit PSTs to working on recent questions about climate change impacts, mitigation, and adaptation, or give students opportunities to raise their questions.

Our aim with the study reported in this chapter is to contribute an in-depth exploration of how a PST, Ms. Crawford, conceptualizes her sense of agency in relation to climate change. We do so through an exploration of her learning and teaching of climate change in multiple contexts across time: middle-school classrooms, professional learning environments, family gatherings, and climate change education research meetings.

Modes of Inquiry

For the purpose of the study we used an ethnographic perspective where the participant observations and iterative cycles of ethnographic interviewing have been utilized (Spradley, 2016). We intentionally selected Ms. Crawford as a potentially illustrative case from which we can unpack the affordances and tensions a dedicated preservice teacher might have in developing a sense of agency in contributing to solving the problem of climate change. We also looked at intertextualities (Gee, 2014) among interview data and teacher and student produced artifacts to make sense of the reason for changes in the conceptualization of agency (Strauss & Feiz, 2013).

Focal Participant and Her Relationship with the Research

The study has the characteristics of a single case study (Stake, 2010) as an exploration of a phenomenon (i.e., teachers' development of agency) through detailed, in-depth data collection involving multiple sources of information rich in context (Creswell, 2007). The value of a single case lies in the opportunities for readers "to experience vicariously unique situations and unique individuals" (Donmoyer, 1990, p. 193). Focusing on only one participant allowed for deep and detailed explorations of the complex processes and dynamics of the development of her sense of agency as well as the factors that were critical to the development of her agency.

"A Different Kind of Middleman"   183

This single case study is a part of a larger, five-year-long National Science Foundation (NSF) funded project, which aims to improve and assess climate change education at K-16 classrooms. As a part of this project, scientists, education researchers, and teachers work together to prepare Climate Literacy Workshops (CLWs) for preservice teachers. CLWs aim to strengthen preservice teachers' conceptual and epistemic sensemaking of the science behind climate change as well as to provide rigorous and responsive teaching tools. CLWs had two main parts: (1) a one-day-long workshop to introduce teachers to the core concepts and epistemic ideas of climate change; (2) preservice teachers' implementation of a climate change unit in a middle school classroom. Ms. Crawford was recruited for a CLW while she was a junior student in the first author's (Asli Sezen-Barrie's) Earth and Space Science course. At the time, she had 18 months remaining to finish her degree from a large mid-Atlantic University in teaching science and math in middle school classrooms (4–8th grade). Crawford was then chosen intentionally for this case study because of (1) her background experiences related to climate change impacts; (2) her preparation on reform based, responsive science teaching at middle schools; and (3) her dedication to learn and teach climate change in middle schools.

Crawford is a white female, who grew up in New Jersey, a state that was heavily impacted by "Superstorm Sandy" in 2012. During this time, Crawford volunteered to work at her hometown to tutor kids whose houses or schools were flooded. Since then, she gained interest in taking part in climate change solutions because she "doesn't want future generations to experience negative impacts of climate change."

Context and Data Collection Process

The primary data for this study came from approximately 50-minute-long pre-, mid-, and post-interviews, conducted at the beginning of the study, after participating in the climate change education project, and after Ms. Crawford had been teaching science at a public school for two years. The study also utilized secondary data sources such as written reflections, lesson plans, student artifacts, and impromptu ethnographic interviews. These data were collected throughout a period of four years and at different learning and teaching contexts (see Figure 6.1).

Once Crawford was recruited for the study, we participated in an approximately 50-minute-long pre-interview. During September 2016, Crawford attended the one-day-long CLW. She then worked with a scientist, science educator, and a public middle school teacher to develop a four-day-long mini-unit around an activity, "It's a Gassy World." This was designed to introduce middle school students to the relationship between carbon dioxide (CO_2) and the warming of the Earth's surface (global climate change). In this activity students work toward answering

184 *Asli Sezen-Barrie and Lucy Avraamidou*

the driving question: "Will warming oceans be better or worse at soaking up CO_2?" As students worked on this question, they gained experience engaging in scientific practices by designing an experiment to explore how temperature affects water's ability to retain CO_2. Students were challenged to analyze and interpret the results of their experiment, and connect their findings to global patterns of climate change. During the main exploration, students were guided to measure how much CO_2 will be released from cold vs. warm ocean water. Alka-Seltzer tablets were used to add CO_2 to ocean water and balloons were used to capture the releasing CO_2. Students designed three trials of the experiments and chose their own measurement methods for the volume of the balloons (such as using a string to compare the diameter).

Crawford was later mentored by an experienced middle school science teacher, Ms. Buck, for the implementation of the activity in a middle school classroom. For her preparation, Crawford had to observe students multiple times to make contextual adjustments. During her week-long implementation, she wrote daily reflections about her practice. She also collected students' artifacts, including investigation design protocols, findings from the investigations, and Know-Learn-Evidence-Wondering charts in relation to the driving scientific question.

After this experience, Crawford decided to be part of the climate change education project group as a research assistant. As a research assistant, she participated in studies with experienced teachers. She helped with the implementation of activities for professional learning sessions and took part in writing research studies. She provided reflections on her readings and research meetings.

When Crawford graduated, she was hired as a science and math teacher at a local public school. During this time, she did not teach a unit on climate change education, but she took responsibility to lead the Green Team at her school. This was charged with finding and acting on solutions to environmental problems. As a team, they worked on STEAM (Science, Technology, Engineering, Arts, and Mathematics) nights and presented a year-long project on reusing cafeteria cups to build bird feeders. They also won a grant to collect mascara pens for cleaning oil spill from birds' wings to send to a pro-environmental organization.

Data Analysis Approach

We started our data analysis by organizing our interviews into transcripts as sociolinguistic tools that will help us identify how Crawford expressed her sense of agency, what subjects she used (herself, family members, future teachers, future scientists, new teachers), and what reasons/factors shaped her agency (Gee, 2014). First, we scanned through the transcripts and secondary data sources for macro-analysis of what, or if there was a, change in Crawford's sense of agency. Once we noticed that the

"A Different Kind of Middleman" 185

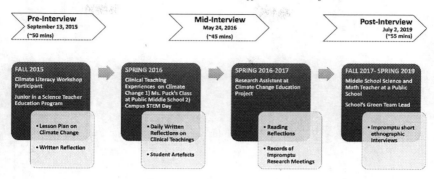

Figure 6.1 Primary and secondary data sources and related contexts.

change mostly occurred when she identified herself as a future teacher, we highlighted these excerpts in the transcript, as shown underlined in Table 6.1. We described the change in agency and identified a category for aboutness (e.g., scaffolding scientific practices). These categories have been iteratively revised by looking at intertextualities across secondary data sources and until two researchers reached 100% agreement.

Findings

Despite Crawford's strong agency to be part of the solution to climate change, she had a moderate sense of agency when she thought of herself as a future teacher. We witnessed changes in her sense of agency as a future teacher after her clinical teaching experiences in a middle school, and after participating in the climate change education project. We noticed that this change continued once she was hired as a science teacher and had her own classroom. In this section, we will first talk about the reasons behind her moderate sense of agency. We will then elaborate on the factors that led to change in her agency. Finally, we will talk about the constraints for her improved sense of agency.

Reasons for Initial Moderate Sense of PST Agency

At the beginning of this study, Crawford saw her role in the solution to climate change as "the middleman" who would learn the information about climate change and "give" this information to students. She was worried, however, that she would have challenges achieving this goal as a teacher. Below are the three reasons we identified across multiple data sources for the moderate sense of agency as a future educator.

Table 6.1 Sample representation from the data analysis process

Pre-interview transcript	Mid-interview transcript	Change in agency	Aboutness
I think I would be like especially in middle school it might be one of the first times that they're hearing about it. So I'll be the first person to provide solutions to them, which I think is a really cool role, also like educating them on what's happening. I like when students get to learn about real world events so having them – my role would be like having them current up-to-date with what information's really going out, going on out there right now. So being like <u>the middleman between what is happening and the students, I'll be like the information middleman because I'll be still educating myself just as much as the students will be getting educated, too.</u> Like I plan on staying current with it so …	I feel like even though maybe yes <u>as a middleman</u>, but I still was able to … like I might've been the middleman, but I was standing on the outside of the circle. Like I facilitated but the <u>students were the ones really learning for themselves, which I thought was cool</u>. So I set it all up for them, but then they got to dive in and <u>figure it out for themselves</u>. Like I asked the class at the end like so what do you guys think? I asked like the driving question. They were able to tell – like I didn't really tell them, but they were able to tell me that the warm water releases more CO_2 and I was like oh, thank God. <u>Did I see myself as the middleman? Yes but in a completely different way than I originally would've thought I would've felt.</u>	Ms. Crawford's agency as "the middleman" has changed from an information transmitter to "the middleman – in a completely different way" that is a guide helping middle school students figure out climate change evidence.	Experience teaching science as practice – Scaffolding scientific practices **Secondary Data Sources** Clinical Teaching Experience –Written reflections

Scale of the Population

During a reflection session following a climate change workshop, Crawford talked about the idea of becoming an environmental scientist instead of a teacher. Although she was successful at her teacher education program, she thought such a transition could help her to talk about climate change at "a larger scale":

> I think maybe talking to people on a larger scale or even, like I said before, like debating with the people who—like you know how like there's environmentalists against like the pipeline and stuff that's going on? Like I would be able to inform a larger public.

She thought that, in that context, she could have a higher impact and inform a larger portion of the public about issues of climate change.

Time Allocated

Crawford was also worried that there would be less time allocated for talking about climate change in her classroom:

> Oh, just like a bigger public or doing—so with teachers, right, like the climate change, like the days they're allowed to spend on climate change isn't that long. But if I have a job as an environmentalist and whatnot, I'll be doing that all year round, not just a few days out of the week or maybe just a week, so I'd be able to focus on it for a longer period of time.

Because of this limited time allocated to climate change in K-12 classrooms, Crawford didn't expect that she would be able to focus on climate change as much as she would have liked.

Type of Conversations

Another major reason for Crawford's moderate sense of agency as an educator was the difference in the type of conversations she could have as a scientist vs. as a teacher:

> And I enjoy having those intelligent conversations with someone like him [scientist] as to how he can help, like save the environment a little bit more but at the same time like still have a job, you know? With my students, I might not be able to, you know, have those dense conversations.

What becomes evident in this excerpt is that Crawford thinks that while she can have "intelligent conversations" with a scientist, these conversations would not be as "dense" with her students.

188 *Asli Sezen-Barrie and Lucy Avraamidou*

Factors Leading to an Improved Sense of Agency

After her involvement in the climate education project and clinical teaching experiences at Ms. Buck's middle school classroom, Crawford's sense of agency as a future educator was different in nature and much stronger. She said she still sees herself as the "middleman" but in a "completely different way." In her words, this completely different middleman felt a stronger agency in the classroom where she "facilitates" students "who really care." Below we will discuss two factors we identified that explain this difference in the feeling of agency.

Scaffolding of Scientific Practices

Teaching science as a practice has been a focus in the most recent science standards, Next Generation Science Standards (NGSS, 2013). However, science education scholars argue that enabling these standards requires creating opportunities for increased student epistemic agency (Miller, Manz, Russ, Stroupe, & Berland, 2018; Stroupe, 2014). This agency is the active participation of students during scientific knowledge (re)construction in classroom activities where their ideas are valuable in deciding on, for example, designing investigations and choosing their claims. Seeing what happens in a classroom when students had epistemic agency made Crawford rethink her sense of agency as an educator. In the following excerpt, right after a teaching clinic with Ms. Buck, Crawford talked about how she saw the excitement in the class when students were engaged in doing "the whole experiment," that is when they designed the experiment themselves:

> I felt like I was actually like doing something. Like sometimes I go to internship and I'm not like—I feel like I'm not always impacting them or getting like the aha! moments a lot because they don't like to do a lot of work. But like as soon as like the first group was like ahead of the other groups. And as soon as the one kid dropped in the Alka-Seltzer and did the whole experiment, they were like, "Whoa!" and instead of just being like all right, let's take notes and move on, they were like "Can we do it again?" And I was like if we have the seltzer tablets for it, yeah. So, I think seeing them so engaged and seeing them so like into it, you know, so I thought that was really cool. They were all really nice there.

When Crawford noticed students' engagement in the scientific practice in their decisions and ideas, she thought it was "really cool." After two years, when reminded of this observation, Crawford said:

> I think that while giving them [my students] epistemic agency, you know how I said how I feel like I am the middleman, I see them

"A Different Kind of Middleman" 189

becoming the middleman. Because we have like morning announcements ... We branch off into teams and at the end of the meeting as students are like, all right, let's write a script and try to get this on air. So, we can communicate to the school about the ones, and even like any initiative that we've done. We did the bird feeder one like collecting the bottles. We did like a tip of the week and so students would go on once a week, they would like during our meetings we had the TV crew film them and it would be their responsibility to look at tips.

After working with her own students on various pro-environmental projects, Crawford identified an intergenerational impact of her role. Each of her students cared about these issues like herself and are, themselves, becoming "middlemen" who will help communicate the climate change problem to other people.

Ethics of Care: Youth

Scholars have highlighted ethics of care as an important framework to look at people's decision-making processes (Gilligan, 1993; Noddings, 1992; Tronto, 2013). Studies highlighted that students who care about what they learn may better engage in school and show more academic success (Dance, 2002; Valenzuela, 1999). Noticing the care middle school students showed was significant in Crawford's decision to pursue a career as a teacher and feel that she can be an agent towards a solution to climate change. Following the completion of her clinical teaching experience on climate change, Crawford said:

I feel very optimistic about the country's youth because I feel my parents or my grandparents couldn't care less about it because they know that they can't—they're not gonna make enough of a difference in their lifetime for them to see the change, for it to reverse back or whatever. And, then my parents are kind of like: yeah, I mean it's there but I'm too small. I can't contribute.

After two years of having her own students, Crawford continues to feel that many family and friends around her show little concern about climate change. However, as a teacher, she is still "optimistic" about the youth, the middle school students who care to work on climate change projects. In the following, she explains what her impact will be by working with these students who care:

I probably had 170 students this year. So, I, in some way, impacted 170 students now, even if they just tell one person 170 times, that makes 340. And then after this year, I probably impacted 340 plus whatever students that I am going to get this upcoming year. So, I

190 *Asli Sezen-Barrie and Lucy Avraamidou*

feel, in terms of impact, if you look at it from like a graph standpoint, it should go up like from year to year, as people continue to maybe have me as their teacher or someone who is passionate about solving the climate change problem. Hopefully, those graphs will go up exponentially.

Challenges to Improved Sense of Agency

While Crawford's sense of agency as an educator is stronger, there remain some challenges which make her consider moving into a career as an educational researcher instead of a public school teacher.

The Isolated Nature of the Curriculum

One of the challenges is the current design of the curriculum at her school. Although Crawford feels that she has agency to revise her units to integrate climate change, particularly once she closes her classroom door, she thinks it is not usually practical to be able to do such integrations effectively because "there is such a push that I need to get through everything by the end of the year." She checks what she covered with her school regions' official website who recently revised their curriculum per the NGSS. She also checks her objectives with her department's chair. In the same interview, Crawford also highlighted that there might be more flexibility that she is not yet aware of because she feels like she is "such a rule follower." Due to these demands about covering all the scientific topics, she feels like she needs to follow the units described by her school region. This curriculum currently focuses on three scientific disciplines: physics, chemistry, and biology, and does not touch climate change until eighth grade (the last year of middle school). She explained this on a recent interview as:

> In our curriculum, in grade sixth, seventh, eight like we have a little bit of chemistry in all three. A little bit of physics in all three. A little bit of bio in all three. There is a unit in grade eight that's called "overstepping our resources" and that is when they are starting realize like how, what they are doing is impacting everywhere else. This is an issue! Why isn't it sprinkled throughout, even if it's just the words, climate change is introduced like weather vs. climate you know. We don't do any of that in sixth or seventh grade. Like sprinkling the topic starting at sixth grade so they won't be blindsided or not so ignorant once they do get to eight grade.

School Culture and the Lack of Administrative Support

Another challenge Crawford described was related to the lack of administrative support. Although other scholars speculated that the political controversy might lead to a lack of administrative support, in Crawford's case, the reason was different. The administrators at her school were focusing on language arts:

> Administration, because I feel as if when you don't have support from the administration, things can go south really quick and so if I like to have a specific climate initiative to happen in our school or if I get grant money to start some sort of initiative, if my administration is not on board, you know a program could go nowhere. My principal is more language arts based which means my head teacher is from a language arts classroom. So they are really focused on literacy right now. Now, it could be climate literacy, but if we are all about annotating like that's the kind of route they are going so I feel like as if I come from a strong science point of view. And if they don't really like see that as an importance.

Crawford, who comes with a strong scientific background, did not feel that administrators at her school gave importance to scientific issues.

Discussions and Further Implications

The study reported in this chapter is rooted within our own assumption and hope that teachers might serve as agents of change in relation to addressing issues connected to climate change in their classrooms. The analysis of ethnographic interviews, reflections, and other related artifacts showed a variance in Crawford's conceptualization of agency in her different roles such as a future teacher vs. a citizen of her community/town. Her sense of agency also evolved as she engaged in guided teaching practices of climate change in middle school classrooms. The findings explained how Crawford conceptualized agency in multiple contexts and across time. Driving from our intertextual analysis, we further elaborated on the reasons behind changes in her sense of agency.

Previous studies show that PSTs do not see themselves as capable of addressing climate change (e.g., Lee et al., 2012) which is seen as complex and (assumed to be) controversial (Sezen-Barrie, Shea, Borman, 2019). It is critical to prepare teachers for rigorous and equitable teaching of climate change for the next generations who will likely experience more of the already observed impacts of it. As Crawford noted, the middle school students will be the middlemen who will communicate climate change. Therefore, making climate change evidence and claims accessible to youth is necessary for intergenerational equity. This suggests that it is critical to have exposures to young students in preparation to teach climate change to help PSTs strengthen their sense of agency to feel powerful and to create impact in future classrooms. Other studies also highlighted the critical age of middle school youth in caring about climate change (Stevenson, Peterson, Bondell, Moore, & Carrier, 2014). While working with the middle school age group, we also observed that middle school students' care for the environment was an important factor for the PST, Ms. Crawford, to develop a high feeling of agency in positioning her role in climate change solutions. Although Schindel and Tolbert's (2017) study showed that teachers' carework led to more engaged students, our study indicated that the impacts can be bidirectional. In other words, students' carework can engage their teachers to feel themselves to be important agents in solving the climate change problem.

Even though working with future generations makes it easier to notice the unfair problems or impacts these young people will experience, the uncertain aspects of climate change impacts remains a concern. Teachers do not have much experience in working with uncertainties in science classrooms. A few recent studies have worked on how to integrate productive uncertainty into science classrooms (e.g., Manz & Suárez, 2018). We see this line of research as particularly important for teacher education programs. Even though teachers like Ms. Crawford will develop strong agencies about teaching climate change due to the impact they see in youth, this will only be more sustainable if they can work with uncertainties related to climate change impacts.

The findings of the study also show that promoting epistemic agency in scientific activity reshaped Crawford's sense of agency to feel that the students can be the population she can work with. Seeing students figure out their designs or explanations was inspiring to her. Previous studies explored how fostering students' epistemic agency can result in better engagement and better learning outcomes (Eriksson & Lindberg, 2016; Zimmerman & Weible, 2018). We see the potential for increased student epistemic agency impacting teachers' agency to act on reform-based ideas, which was integrating climate change in this study. Therefore, we suggest that further studies can explore the impacts of increased epistemic student agency on teachers. We do nevertheless acknowledge that this suggestion is more applicable in similar sociopolitical contexts similar to the one that defined this study, where students' families are from the middle or upper-middle class who share mostly liberal political views. Previous work showed that climate change denial is a more serious problem in low income, agricultural communities, despite living and working in areas that will be more vulnerable to anthropogenic climate change impacts (Stevenson et al., 2018). Other researchers found that the political affiliations of farmers are the most influential factor in their perceptions of risks and prioritizing broad scale climate policy (Smith et al., 2014). Therefore, we maintain that it will be more challenging for PSTs to promote epistemic agency in climate change learning if they are working in geographies where conservative political views spread doubt about climate change.

At the opening of this section, we highlighted how Ms. Crawford sees that her individual actions or individual concerns seem ineffective in

"A Different Kind of Middleman" 193

tackling the climate change problem. She gives many examples of individual efforts such as "not using straws," "driving a small car," or "small scale environmental projects with her students." Wynes and Nicholas's (2017) study regarding climate change mitigation cautions us that not every strategy is high impact. Indeed, they found that many textbook recommendations (e.g., recycling) are low to moderate impacts. The top three strategies they found in their study were: (1) have one fewer child, (2) live car free, and (3) avoid long flights. More importantly, many ideas Crawford mentioned focused on what Chawla and Cushing (2007) would call a "private sphere" (individual or household). This is unfortunately the case in our own previous work as well (Sezen-Barrie, Miller-Rushing, & Hufnagel, 2019). Therefore, we suggest that teacher preparation programs should also focus on collective action in solutions to climate change. Some scholars suggest the integration of principles from humanities into science learning so that, while learning about climate change, we can also be educated about tax reforms, policies, investigating different opinions, and arguing expert opinions based on scientific evidence (Ignell, Davies & Lundholm, 2018; Lundholm, 2011).

Education is a means to access larger populations and create an informed citizenry, and empower the public to act towards solutions to climate change. Educational settings such as schools have the potential to create equitable learning experiences where students can explore scientific evidence behind climatic change. An important role of teachers is to address the intergenerational dilemmas of climate change and bring about social change. In order to realize these goals, however, there is still work that needs to be done through a systemic approach that includes teacher education, professional development, as well as school systems.

References

Archer, D. (2005). Fate of fossil fuel CO2 in geologic time. *Journal of Geophysical Research: Oceans, 110*(C9), 1–6.

Avraamidou, L. (2014). Tracing a beginning elementary teacher's development of identity for science teaching. *Journal of Teacher Education, 65*, 223–240.

Avraamidou, L. (2019). Stories we live, identities we build: How are elementary teachers' science identities shaped by their lived experiences? *Cultural Studies of Science Education, 14*(1), 33–59.

Biesta, G.J.J., & Tedder, M. (2007). Agency and learning in the lifecourse: Towards an ecological perspective, *Studies in the Education of Adults, 39*, 132–149.

Boon, H.J. (2010). Climate change? Who knows? A comparison of secondary students and pre-service teachers. *Australian Journal of Teacher Education, 35*, 104–120.

Buber, M. (1965). *The knowledge of man: A philosophy of the interhuman.* New York: Harper.

Campbell, T., Schwarz, C., & Windschitl, M. (2016). What we call misconceptions may be necessary steppingstones toward making sense of the world. *Science and Children, 53*(7), 28.

194 *Asli Sezen-Barrie and Lucy Avraamidou*

Carter, L. (2012). *Investigating preservice science teachers' preferences in developing pro-environmental engagement. Paper presented at the XVth International Organisation for Science and Technology Education Symposium Hammamet,* Tunisia October 29 to November 3, 2012.

Chawla, L., & Cushing, D. F. (2007). Education for strategic environmental behavior. *Environmental Education Research, 13*(4), 437–452.

Cook, J., Oreskes, N., Doran, P.T., Anderegg, W.R., Verheggen, B., ... Nuccitelli, D. (2016). Consensus on consensus: A synthesis of consensus estimates on human-caused global warming. *Environmental Research Letters, 11*(4), 048002.

Creswell, J.W. (2007). *Qualitative inquiry and research design: Choosing among five approaches.* Thousand Oaks, CA: SAGE.

Damsa, C. I., Kirschner, P. A., Andriessen, J. E., Erkens, G., & Sins, P. H. (2010). Shared epistemic agency: An empirical study of an emergent construct. *The Journal of the Learning Sciences, 19*(2), 143–186.

Dance, L.J. (2002). *Tough fronts: The impact of street culture on schooling.* London: Falmer Press.

Donmoyer, R. (1990). Generalizability and the single-case study. In E. Eisner & A. Peshkin (Eds.), *Qualitative inquiry in education: The continuing debate* (pp. 175–200). New York, NY: Teachers College Press.

Engeström, Y., (1999). Activity theory and individual and social transformation. In Y. Engeström, R. Miettinen, and R-L. Punamaki-Gita (Eds.), *Perspectives on activity theory.* Cambridge, UK: Cambridge University.

Eriksson, I., & Lindberg, V. (2016). Enriching 'learning activity' with 'epistemic practices'–enhancing students' epistemic agency and authority. *Nordic Journal of Studies in Educational Policy, 2016*(1), 32432.

Gardiner, S.M. (2006). A perfect moral storm: Climate change, intergenerational ethics and the problem of moral corruption. *Environmental Values, 15*(3), 397–413.

Gardiner, S.M. (2010). Ethics and climate change: An introduction. *Wiley Interdisciplinary Reviews: Climate Change, 1*(1), 54–66.

Gee, J.P. (2014). *How to do discourse analysis: A toolkit.* New York, NY: Routledge.

Gilligan C. (1982). *In a different voice.* Cambridge, MA: Harvard University Press.

Gilligan, C. (1993). *In a different voice: Psychological theory and women's development* (revised ed.). Cambridge, MA: Harvard University Press.

Haggard, P., & Tsakiris, M. (2009). The experience of agency: Feelings, judgments, and responsibility. *Current Directions in Psychological Science, 18*(4), 242–246.

Held, V. (2006). *The ethics of care: Personal, political, and global.* Oxford: Oxford University Press.

Held, D. (2016). Climate change, migration and the cosmopolitan dilemma. *Global Policy, 7*(2), 237–246.

Hestness, E., Randy McGinnis, J., Riedinger, K., & Marbach-Ad, G. (2011). A study of teacher candidates' experiences investigating global climate change within an elementary science methods course. *Journal of Science Teacher Education, 22*(4), 351–369.

Ignell, C., Davies, P., & Lundholm, C. (2018). A longitudinal study of upper secondary school students' values and beliefs regarding policy responses to climate change. *Environmental Education Research,* 1–18. http://doi.org/10.1080/13504622.2018.1523369

Intergovernmental Panel on Climate Change. (2018) *Global warming of 1.5 C, an IPCC special report on the impacts of global warming of 1.5 C above pre-industrial levels and related global greenhouse gas emission pathways, in the context of strengthening the global response to the threat of climate change, sustainable development, and efforts to eradicate poverty.* Geneva, Switzerland.

Kenis, A., & Mathijs, E. (2012). Beyond individual behaviour change: The role of power, knowledge and strategy in tackling climate change. *Environmental Education Research, 18*(1), 45–65.

Læssøe, J., Schnack, K., Breiting, S., Rolls, S., Feinstein, N., & Goh, K.C. (2009). Climate change and sustainable development: The response from education. *A cross-national report from international alliance of leading education institutes. The Danish School of Education, Aarhus University.*

Lambert, J.L., & Bleicher, R.E. (2017). Argumentation as a strategy for increasing preservice teachers' understanding of climate change, a key global socioscientific issue. *International Journal of Education in Mathematics Science and Technology, 5*(2), 101–112.

Lawson, D.F., Stevenson, K.T., Peterson, M.N., Carrier, S.J., Strnad, R.L., & Seekamp, E. (2019). Children can foster climate change concern among their parents. *Nature Climate Change, 9*(6), 458.

Lee, H., Chang, H., Choi, K., Kim, S.W., & Zeidler, D.L. (2012). Developing character and values for global citizens: Analysis of pre-service science teachers' moral reasoning on socioscientific issues. *International Journal of Science Education, 34*(6), 925–953.

Lombardi, D., & Sinatra, G.M. (2013). Emotions about teaching about human-induced climate change. *International Journal of Science Education, 35*(1), 167–191.

Luehmann, A. (2008). Identity development as a lens to science teacher preparation. *Science Education, 91*, 822–839.

Lundholm, C. (2011). Society's response to environmental challenges: Citizenship and the role of knowledge. *Factis Pax, 5* (1), 80–96.

Manz, E., & Suárez, E. (2018). Supporting teachers to negotiate uncertainty for science, students, and teaching. *Science Education, 102*(4), 771–795.

Matkins, J.J., & Bell, R.L. (2007). Awakening the scientist inside: Global climate change and the nature of science in an elementary science methods course. *Journal of Science Teacher Education, 18*(2), 137–163.

McNeill, K.L., & Vaughn, M.H. (2010). Urban high school students' critical science agency: Conceptual understandings and environmental actions around climate change. *Research in Science Education, 42*, 373–399. http://doi.org/10.1007/s11165-010-9202-5

Miller, E., Manz, E., Russ, R., Stroupe, D., & Berland, L. (2018). Addressing the epistemic elephant in the room: Epistemic agency and the Next Generation Science Standards. *Journal of Research in Science Teaching*, 1–23. https://doi.org/10.1002/tea.21459

Moore, F.M. (2008). Agency, identity and social justice education: Preservice teachers' thoughts on becoming agents of change in urban elementary science classrooms. *Research in Science Education, 38*, 589–610.

NGSS Lead States. (2013). *Next generation science standards: For states, by states.* Washington, DC: The National Academies Press.

Noddings, N. (1992). *The challenge to care in schools: An alternative approach to education.* New York, NY: Teachers College Press.

Noddings, N. (2012). The caring relation in teaching. *Oxford Review of Education, 38*(6), 771–781.

Plutzer, E., & Hannah, A.L. (2018). Teaching climate change in middle schools and high schools: Investigating STEM education's deficit model. *Climatic change, 149*(3–4), 305–317.

Plutzer, E., McCaffrey, M., Hannah, A.L., Rosenau, J., Berbeco, M., & Reid, A.H. (2016). Climate confusion among US teachers. *Science, 351*(6274), 664–665.

Richmond, G. (2016). Making sense of the interplay of identity, agency, and context in the development of beginning science teachers in high-poverty schools. In L. Avraamidou (Ed), *Studying science teacher identity* (pp. 219–235). Rotterdam: Sense Publishers.

Rivera Maulucci, M.S., Brotman, J.S., & Fain, S.S. (2015). Fostering structurally transformative teacher agency through science professional development. *Journal of Research in Science Teaching, 52,* 545–559. http://doi.org/10.1002/tea.21222

Roth, W.-M., Tobin, K., Elmesky, R., Carambo, C., McKnight, Y.-M., & Beers, J. (2004). Re/making identities in the praxis of urban schooling: A cultural historical perspective. *Mind, Culture, & Activity, 11,* 48–69.

Schindel, A., & Tolbert, S. (2017). Critical caring for people and place. *The Journal of Environmental Education, 48*(1), 26–34.

Sezen-Barrie, A., Shea, N., & Borman, J. H. (2019). Probing into the sources of ignorance: science teachers' practices of constructing arguments or rebuttals to denialism of climate change. *Environmental Education Research, 25*(6), 846–866.

Sezen-Barrie, A., Miller-Rushing, A., & Hufnagel, E. (2020). 'It's a gassy world': starting with students' wondering questions to inform climate change education. *Environmental Education Research, 26*(4), 555–576.

Sezen-Barrie, A., Stapleton, M. K., & Marbach-Ad, G. (2020). Science teachers' sensemaking of the use of epistemic tools to scaffold students' knowledge (re) construction in classrooms. *Journal of Research in Science Teaching, 57*(7), 1058–1092.

Shanahan, M. C. (2009). Identity in science learning: Exploring the attention given to agency and structure in studies of identity. *Studies in Science Education, 45*(1), 43–64.

Smith Jr, W. J., Liu, Z., Safi, A. S., & Chief, K. (2014). Climate change perception, observation and policy support in rural Nevada: A comparative analysis of Native Americans, non-native ranchers and farmers and mainstream America. *Environmental Science & Policy, 42,* 101–122.

Spradley, J.P. (2016). *The ethnographic interview.* New York, NY: Routledge.

Stake, R. (2010). *Qualitative research: Studying how things work.* New York, NY: The Guilford Press.

Stevenson, K.T., Peterson, M.N., Bondell, H.D., Moore, S.E., & Carrier, S.J. (2014). Overcoming skepticism with education: Interacting influences of worldview and climate change knowledge on perceived climate change risk among adolescents. *Climatic change, 126*(3–4), 293–304.

"A Different Kind of Middleman" 197

Stevenson, K. T., King, T. L., Selm, K. R., Peterson, M. N., & Monroe, M. C. (2018). Framing climate change communication to prompt individual and collective action among adolescents from agricultural communities. *Environmental Education Research, 24*(3), 365–377.

Strauss, S., & Feiz, P. (2013). *Discourse analysis: Putting our worlds into words.* New York, NY: Routledge.

Stroupe, D. (2014). Examining classroom science practice communities: How teachers and students negotiate epistemic agency and learn science-as-practice. *Science Education, 98*(3), 487–516.

Tayne, K., Littrell, M.K., Okochi, C., Gold, A.U., & Leckey, E. (2021). Framing action in a youth climate change filmmaking program: Hope, agency, and action across scales. *Environmental Education Research, 27*(5), 702–726.

Tronto, J. (2013). *Caring democracy: Markets, equality, and justice.* New York: New York University Press.

Valenzuela, A. (1999) *Subtractive schooling: U.S.-Mexican youth and the politics of caring.* Albany: SUNY Press.

Walsh, E.M., & Cordero, E. (2019). Youth science expertise, environmental identity, and agency in climate action filmmaking. *Environmental Education Research, 25*(5), 656–677.

Weiss, E.B. (1983). The planetary trust: Conservation and intergenerational equity. *Ecology LQ, 11*, 495.

Weiss, E.B. (2008). Climate change, intergenerational equity, and international law. *Vermont Journal of Environmental Law, 9*, 615.

Wynes, S., & Nicholas, K.A. (2017). The climate mitigation gap: Education and government recommendations miss the most effective individual actions. *Environmental Research Letters, 12*(7), 074024.

Zimmerman, H.T., & Weible, J.L. (2018). Epistemic agency in an environmental sciences watershed investigation fostered by digital photography. *International Journal of Science Education, 40*(8), 894–918.

7 Leadership in Eco-Justice Environmental Educational Practice

A Case for Climate Change Curricula through Poetic Inquiry that Involves Storytelling and Walking the Land

Kelly Young and Andrejs Kulnieks

The impetus for this chapter comes from a need to bring forth an integrated framework for environmental educational leadership. Both authors are teacher educators of European descent who have been working with Indigenous Elders to engage in theoretical and practical approaches to curriculum development at Canadian universities. In this chapter we address exemplar curricula that foreground eco-justice educational practices that bring together theory and practice through an integrated approach to educational reform. We believe that educational reform is needed to help learners understand the volatility of the Earth and its ecosystems through climate-change-focused eco-justice curricula. The United Nations defines climate change as follows:

> Climate Change is the defining issue of our time and we are at a defining moment. From shifting weather patterns that threaten food production, to rising sea levels that increase the risk of catastrophic flooding, the impacts of climate change are global in scope and unprecedented in scale. Without drastic action today, adapting to these impacts in the future will be more difficult and costly.
> (https://libraryresources.unog.ch/climatechange/UN)

As a defining issue in our time, climate change education needs to include curricula that involves learners learning about their natural environments. We propose an integrated approach to climate change curricula followed by practical applications for pre-service teacher education learning environments that explore (a) the importance of the storytelling and imagination in ecological awareness and (b) the need for interpretive practices through poetic inquiry in the development of identity that focuses on human/nature relationships by walking the land.

DOI: 10.4324/9780429326011-10

Storytelling, Imagination, and Identity-Formation

The natural world and human engagement with/in it play an important role in the development of identity formation because we identify with natural patterns and organized symmetry in nature. Paul Shepard (1977) writes:

> The habitat is not merely a container but a structured surround in which the developing individual makes tenacious affiliations, that something extremely important to the individual is going on between the complex structure of those particular places and the emerging, maturing self, a process of macro-micro correlation, mostly unconscious, essential to the growth of personal identity.
>
> (p. 26)

The structured surround that Shepard describes is our ever-ongoing need for relationships with the natural world. Carl Leggo (2012) writes: "As educators, we need to communicate, respond to, evaluate, and transform our stories by infusing our pedagogy with heart, humility, health, and hope" (p. 14). Infusing pedagogy with heart, humility, health, and hope involves a consideration of Shepard's "structured surround" and the connections among storytelling, our imagination, and identity formation. For example, the immediacy of thought and place is organically connected to the child and development (Cobb, 1959) and if dominant culture and curricula nurtured that connection rather than denying its legitimacy then, in David Orr's (1992) words, "all education is environmental education" (p. 90). For example, children typically enter formal public schooling at the age of five. Their first three years of schooling spans the first two stages of development as outlined by Kieran Egan (1986). His stages of development occur circularly, beginning with a mythic stage in which children engage with the natural world as innocent, environmentally fearless children embracing the more-than-human world (Abrams, 1996). In this stage, story is as real as reality and vice versa. In Egan's (1986) second stage, children understand their environment as a cosmology that is subsequently diminished through the practice of education. In this stage, Egan suggests children develop a need for stories with heroes and heroines who represent real life achievement that is frequently superhuman.

Storytelling also fulfills one of the principles of environmental and sustainable education for naturalizing cultural identities within a biocultural context. Cajete (1994) writes: "stories have deep roots stemming not only from the physiology and contexting process of the brain, but also from the very heart of the human psyche" (pp. 138–139). Stories are like places, and just as places combine to make continents, stories are constituents in a larger body, misidentified as myth by the conventions of

200 *Kelly Young and Andrejs Kulnieks*

dominant culture, but identified as sacred teachings by Indigenous cultural authorities. Cajete (1994) writes: "stories mirror the way the human mind works, and they map the geography of the human soul. Yet, stories go beyond education and the recitation of words. Indigenous stories related the experience of life lived in time and place" (p. 139). Stories are always culturally embedded in the more-than-human life-world (Abrams, 1996) and are defined by Bringhurst (2002) as follows:

> Trees grow in and on the earth. Where do stories grow? They grow in and on storytelling creatures. Stories are epiphytes: organisms that grow on other organisms, the same way tree-dwelling lichens – Alectoria, Bryoria, Letharaia, and so on – grow on trees … the function of storytelling creatures – humans for example – is to provide a habitat for stories … stories tend to have branching, fractal structures, very much like trees … Those trees, the trees of meaning we call stories, grow in your brain and the rest of your body. And there seems to be a symbiotic relation between those trees of meaning and ourselves. What the stories get out of it is, they get to exist. What we get out of it is guidance. Stories are the fundamental way in which to understand the world. They are our best maps and models for the world – and we may yet come to learn that the reason for this is that stories are the constituents of the world.
>
> (p. 17)

Similarly, story and place in the development of habits of mind involve relationships with the natural world and spark the "creative imagination of childhood both as a form of learning and as a function of the organizing powers of the nervous system" (Cobb, 1959, p. 537). What we have found is that storytelling has formed a strong basis for learners to develop an ecologically minded way of being. This is an area that needs to be expanded as it is our belief that studying facts about climate change does not bring learners closer to nature and to see their own identities as part of the Earth. While learners need to know about the effects of climate change in scientific terms through statistical data and other means, we believe that they will benefit immensely by making connections between themselves and what they are studying. This can be fostered by spending time in nature that includes pedagogical practices through poetic inquiry. For us, poetic inquiry provides us with a space to consider what we write about poetically as it relates to ecological imperatives that our students will need to consider for the rest of their lives. The environment, then, is a natural habitat for storytelling that can be a way of becoming a lasting memory. Poetic inquiry can provide a place for learners to tell the story of their experiences with nature, their personal writing process, and to research about the interconnectedness of all life. We consider Bowers's (2016) understanding that:

Leadership in Eco-Justice 201

values guiding decisions about relationships can also be exploitive, such as valuing profits over concerns about the fate of the worker, valuing a consumer lifestyle over that of an ecologically sustainable future, valuing the experience of killing an animal even though its species is headed for extinction.

(p. 63)

Curricula that help learners value their own relationships with the natural world is a vital part of learning and can be related to issues about climate change in an intimate way. Poetic inquiry is one of the practices that we ask teacher candidates to engage with as they develop their ability to pay close attention to the places where they live. Poetic inquiry provides a space where they can merge scientific knowledge, place-based learning, and a deep analysis of language. Eco-poetic writing becomes a space that enables students to develop their stories in relation to the information that they choose to work with. This form of literacy learning is a way of gathering information in deep and meaningful ways.

Poetic inquiry can provide learners with the opportunity to choose what they wish to investigate and write about what they consider to be important. Asking learners to engage with poems about climate change can provide an opportunity to consider why learning about related topics is something that they want to learn more about. The following poem helps us consider why we should be asking our students to include climate change in our curriculum. It also serves as an example of how poetic inquiry that is focused on ecological change can inspire a deep analysis of our dependence on our local environments.

The World is Burning

Move between where you once were and
where you would like to be
consider which thoughts are essential
there are people still talking about whether or not world climates
are changing

every phone includes a compass
find where the four directions are
explore where you are
in relation with rocks, trees, lakes, and streams around you

breathe with the plants around you
you are in the web of life
peer into your relationship
with the Earth

202 *Kelly Young and Andrejs Kulnieks*

pick berries from forests ravaged and abandoned by loggers
consider how we can gather electrolytes
learn to talk with plants as they grow
collectively influence changes in the climate

evoke shifts in environmental thought
remember smells, colours, and shapes of flowers
sew seeds for pollinators
as you get ready for life cycle changes

walk along the countryside that you knew
wonder what are the plants that make you feel good
learn to identify medicine plants to move beyond short term
answers
find where sugarplums live and what is contained therein

is it really no longer important to know if potatoes are genetically
modified?
when did we give up control of what we are eating?
does it take an epidemic to find the farmers that feed you?
notice the importance of food before processing plants shut
down

how much time does it take to consider?
which is better for you?
a field of wild strawberries
or paving them over to make room to park?

(Kulnieks, 2020)

Poetic inquiry involves writing activities that provide choices for learners as they consider their own relationships with the Earth. This freedom becomes particularly important when students are overloaded with information. Making choices provides a space to take ownership of learning as well as to share information. As we read, write, and share poetry surrounded by natural landscapes, we realize that we are all connected to our ecosystems and each other.

Poetic inquiry allows us to reflect on more than memorization of information. The above poem asks the reader to consider where the food that they eat comes from. This is important in terms of climate change because growing certain plants and animals does have an impact on local environments. Wendell Berry (2002) writes:

A nation will destroy its land and therefore itself if it does not foster in every possible way the sort of thrifty, prosperous, permanent rural households and communities that have the desire, the skills, and the means to care properly for the land they are using.

(p. 196)

Understanding stories of place and the people who live there provides an opportunity to consider the world beyond the classroom. Poetic inquiry begins with learners reflecting upon their oldest memories of natural landscapes and their relationship with nature. Being in nature and walking the land is an important part of landscape learning. Paying attention to our surroundings that include trees, plants, and animals that live in our local environments is an essential way of learning about ourselves. Engaging stories in that natural world through poetic inquiry often involves walking the land in what we consider to be "healthy literacies."

Walking the Land: Toward Healthy Literacies

In *Wanderlust: A History of Walking*, Rebecca Solnit (2000) outlines the importance of walking. She describes the challenges that have faced groups of people who wished to make it possible for future generations to have access to public spaces. When we take walks with students in their communities, we try to inspire them to connect with local knowledge and understandings of place. Fostering an ethic of care involves a connection to the places where we live. Technologies have the power to disconnect us from our local surroundings. Taking time to move outdoors evokes the reality of our bodies and how climate has a deep impact on us. Martusewicz et al. (2011) write:

And while global climate change is suddenly on our radar screens as the primary challenge facing us in the twenty-first century, the use of fossil fuel-based energy and the economic system it encouraged has actually had enormous impacts on all aspects of the life-systems that we depend upon for our survival – from soil to water, to air, to plant and animal species.

(p. 3)

These are the key things that we need to foster as we encourage ecologically minded learners in their own development. Storytelling and poetic inquiry can inspire a consideration of where we are in the world as we walk the land. Deep thinking involves a consideration of what is out of control, and what are the bigger issues.

Solnit (2000) outlines work that has been taken up by numerous writers, organizations, ecologically minded thinkers, and walking enthusiasts to create opportunities to benefit from and become in tune with what Bowers (2016) refers to as "the commons." Public spaces that we have in common are essential for developing our relationship with the Earth.

204　*Kelly Young and Andrejs Kulnieks*

Writing about these spaces in the form of poetry allows the writer to create what Rebecca Luce-Kapler (1999) refers to as close writing: "I work with memoir, narrative, hypertext, poetry, and fiction, exploring the dimensions of genres as an interpretive practice" (p. 81). Poetic inquiry is the movement between different types of writing and includes a self-interrogation of one's own work. This type of self-interrogation is important because it allows the writer to ask questions: why is climate change important to me? Why is it important for me to think about what is being done about climate change? What can I do to make a small difference? It is through these small shifts that we can evoke positive changes with learners in the present, and in the future.

Michael Lannoo (2010) describes the importance of moving beyond urban centers to walk the land as he looks at the lives of Aldo Leopold, Ed Ricketts, John Steinbeck, and others. Poetic inquiry helps us to deepen our understandings about the world around us. Thinking about our climate and the changes that are taking place should be an integral aspect of learning about the Earth. Developing a deep relationship with the places where we live should include an eco-hermeneutic analysis of language as we wander through local spaces (Kulnieks, Longboat, & Young, 2010; 2016b). It is important to consider the work of ecologically minded writers of the past so that we can be aware of how the act of writing can make a difference, not only in how we see ourselves and others, but how we can make a difference in the relationships that we have with the local places where we live.

Knowing that the climate is changing and considering what this impact might be should be part of the critical thinking exercises that we ask students to engage with. It is important to provide learners with a great deal of time to consider what a variety of researchers are finding out about climate change. Opportunities to make a connection with land through researching a variety of perspectives is important if we are to inspire students to maintain healthy activities throughout their lives. Movement has always been an important part of a healthy lifestyle but as time is taken up by activities fostering a culture of consumerism, it becomes increasingly difficult to remain healthy as we become older. It is important to think about schooling as a place that makes us consider our long-term health in relation to the long-term health of intact ecosystems. Providing opportunities to theorize and look deeply into why particular classroom activities are important can help learners develop deeper connections with the places that give them life.

As mentioned earlier, it is important to recognize how language shapes our understandings with the world around us. As Fritjof Capra (1996) suggests:

> Most organisms are not only members of ecological communities but are also complex ecosystems themselves, containing a host of

Leadership in Eco-Justice 205

smaller organisms that have considerable autonomy and yet are integrated harmoniously into the functioning of the whole.

(p. 34)

Capra (1996) understands the world as a living planet as theorized by James Lovelock and Lynn Margulis in the 1970s (p. 33). The idea that the Earth is alive is difficult for some learners to imagine. We believe that in light of the way that the generation of wealth usually takes precedence over creating sustainable relationships with the Earth, one of our essential roles as educators is to inspire learners to explore and create stories that explore the life-giving properties that the Earth holds. Poetic inquiry provides a space for readers and writers to expand their thinking about what they already know about their own relationships to the land. It takes a good deal of time in nature to engage with these deep and meaningful learning practices. Similarly, it is helpful to outline the ways in which, historically, *anthropocentrism* has played a central role in climate change through an eco-justice pedagogical lens.

Eco-Justice Pedagogy, Climate Change, and Anthropocentrism

One of the many reasons why we are facing climate change as a society is anthropocentrism. We conceptualize anthropocentrism that through an Eco-Justice lens that is defined in the *EcoJustice Dictionary*:

The meaning of words used by educational reformers who have as their goals universal emancipation, a linear form of progress, and the continuation of an anthropocentric understanding of human/ Nature relationship is, from an ecojustice and revitalization of the commons perspective, part of the language that continues the tradition of Western colonization. An EcoJustice dictionary is intended to clarify how the words used by emancipatory educational theorists take on an entirely different meaning when used in a discourse that addresses the importance of conserving linguistic and biodiversity, the commons as sites of resistance to the further spread of the West's industrial culture, and the need to introduce reforms in the universities and public schools that contribute to achieving ecojustice for the world's diverse peoples.

(Bowers, 2004, p. 1)

Linking an understanding of anthropocentrism with climate change requires that we consider our human/nature relationship in deep ways. Rather than conceptualizing ourselves as humans over or versus nature, we consider what it means to dwell in nature as an important part of introducing climate change in educational settings. If we view ourselves as separate from nature, we are unable to see in which ways we are part

206   *Kelly Young and Andrejs Kulnieks*

of an ecosystem and reliant on biodiversity for life. While anthropocentrism is a term that is used in ecojustice education, it can be applied to all aspects of education, as we are not separate from our planet—indeed, we are very much part of the Earth. We draw upon Field et al.'s (2020) recent definition of climate change education in Canada:

> Climate change is the most complex and wide-reaching challenge facing humankind today. Reducing the impacts of climate change and moving Canada toward resilience and adaptability for climate impacts will require substantial changes at all levels of Canadian society. It is critical that Canadians understand climate change causes, impacts and risks. An educated public, including youth, is essential to driving the required transformation.
>
> (p. 1)

As climate change education is complex, it is important for researchers to respond to the needs of a curriculum that addresses the human/ nature relationship. Field et al. (2020) write:

> Climate change education demands a multi-pronged approach that directly addresses predominant misconceptions and also facilitates critical questioning of societal norms and cultural drivers, such as: the definition of progress; the idea of perpetual growth on a finite planet; the roles of science and technology; the viability of capitalism, consumerism, and the exploitation of nature; and values such as "freedom," "independence," "success," and "comfort." Climate change, therefore, requires an integrated and transdisciplinary approach that includes systems perspectives, spans from local to global, cultivates respectful ways of approaching contested positions (such as deliberative dialogue), and develops capacity and collective action – all approaches that are transferable to supporting students' development in other areas.
>
> (p. 1)

Identifying a multi-pronged approach to climate change education requires an integrated model that is transdisciplinary in nature. In 2009, we introduced our model in *Beyond Dualism: Toward a Transdisciplinary Indigenous Environmental Studies Model of Environmental Education Curricula* that was subsequently republished in *Contemporary Studies in Environmental and Indigenous Pedagogies: A Curricula of Stories and Place* (Kulnieks, Longboat, & Young, 2013a). We developed an integrated approach to infusing Indigenous Knowledge (IK) and Eco-Justice Education (EJE) in teacher education. We wrote: "we propose a transdisciplinary Indigenous environmental studies curriculum model enacted in an environmental studies program and in faculties of education through an eco-justice framework" (ibid., p. 9).

An ecojustice framework includes learning more about the places where learners live. It engages us in an exploration of our anthropocentrism and asks us to consider our relationship with the natural world. It is essential for educators to create opportunities for learners to consider their relationship with the places where they live because the Earth provides what is needed for life to continue. It is important for learners to engage with stories that are based within local places. Engaging with stories provides an opportunity to consider ways in which people can relate with the Earth around them. Thinking about how we relate with the Earth can help to evoke a healthy dialogue that includes activities that strengthen student understandings about how to become connected with the Earth. Reflecting upon activities like gardening, food collection, and cooking are also ways that learners can connect with intergenerational learning and relationship building. To engage in ecological activities is to engage with and to create stories about life.

In addition to disseminating our integrated framework (Kulnieks, Longboat, & Young, 2013a), we advanced an eco-hermeneutic approach to curricula (Kulnieks, Longboat, & Young, 2010): "An eco-hermeneutic curriculum includes moving beyond exclusively print-centered forms of learning in order to develop a deeper understanding of place" (p. 17). Many of the practices described in this chapter involve an eco-hermeneutic approach to curricula that engages learners to consider their identity through storytelling in relation with the natural world.

We consider the importance of activities that explore where words come from to help students to understand the immense power that language holds. Thinking about where words come from can help students understand that words come from somewhere and that language has a history. Thinking about where words come from and that they are used to achieve certain results is also a way of helping students to be critical of how ideas are communicated. Looking at the deeper meanings behind language is important in a time of ever-increasing information when students need to engage beyond their classroom experiences. An example of analyzing the history of language can involve an eco-hermeneutic inquiry to explore how to connect language with nature by tracing the etymology of words and revealing a mechanistic framework for language. Consider for example, the way we refer to trees and forests as lumber, timber, and wood lots. When we begin to examine the implications and associations of these words, we can see that an abstract view of trees as lumber impedes our relationship with the natural world (see Bowers, 2002; Martusewicz, Edmundson, & Lupinacci, 2011). This example of an inquiry into the abstract nature of language can help humans reveal how language hides and illuminates meanings at the same time and may help us see nature *as* nature and not as a resource.

To bring learners closer to the natural world, we explored Indigenizing environmental education curricula (Kulnieks, Longboat, & Young,

208   *Kelly Young and Andrejs Kulnieks*

2011), and in this chapter we consider how textual investigations can reveal the importance of investigation, both in oral and literary traditions, as a way of developing relationships with the places where we live. We examined a curriculum that fosters educational leadership (Kulnieks, Longboat, & Young, 2013b; 2013c). We believe that by bringing Indigenous perspectives into environmental education, all aspects of biodiversity and climate change dangers can be discovered by learners. Subsequently, we considered Canadian environmental curriculum studies (Kulnieks, Ng-A-Fook, Stanley, & Young, 2012), and explored educating teachers about IKs through an EJE framework that helps learners engage in nature (Kulnieks, Longboat, & Young, 2013d). For Bowers (2004), climate change is integral to all aspects of environmental education as life is dependent on all biodiversity. He defines EJE as:

> The aspects of ecojustice that should be the focus of educational reforms at both the university and public level are connected with the need to reduce the impact of the industrial/consumer dependent culture on everyday life while at the same time ensuring that people are not impoverished and limited in terms of equal opportunity.
>
> (p. 1)

Attending to Bowers's (2004) call to introduce educational reforms at all levels of schooling, we bring together theory and practice to address climate change education in the twenty-first century through the arts. Our arts-infused EJE-related publications include engaging in an arts-informed eco-justice pedagogy that we expand on in this chapter (Kulnieks & Young, 2014a), as well as fostering a curriculum of ecological awareness through poetic inquiry (Kulnieks & Young, 2014b). We have integrated indigenous curricula through an eco-justice-arts-informed pedagogy and eco-hermeneutical methods (Kulnieks, Longboat, & Young, 2016b). We have developed ecological literacy through an integrated model as a primer for EJE curricula (Kulnieks, Longboat, & Young, 2018) as we explored ecological literacy in teacher identity that involves the natural world. Most recently, we developed a pedagogy for reconciliation and eco-justice-oriented education in a Canadian context (Longboat, Kulnieks, & Young, 2020). Moving forward in our trajectory of research, we continually return to the importance of the arts in our relationship with the natural world in general and poetic inquiry specifically.

Thinking Forward: Implications for Climate Change Education

Living in the same place over a course of time in a sustainable way can help to foster a close relationship with the Earth. Being part of the process

Leadership in Eco-Justice 209

of helping learners to better understand how the climate is changing involves learning about the world beyond the classroom. Ancestral stories about different ways of understandings places can demonstrate how vital it is to consider ways of thinking about the impact that our behaviors will have on future generations. It is important to reflect about the gifts that plants give us, and to be part of the process of experiencing the interconnection of living in a close relationship with the Earth. The unfamiliarity of being in landscapes that we are keen to learn about is also an opportunity to see things that we know with a different attitude, which is one of not taking things for granted. The following poem illustrates how movement can inspire shifts in thinking about the places where we live.

Walk Places You Know

> catch a lift as your body moves
> take a bus, get on the subway, drive
> skateboard, roller blade, ride your bicycle
> slow down and listen to the sounds that surround you
>
> do you contribute to the well-being of the Earth
> breathe with trees
> know how deep breaths make you feel
> share air that racoons, groundhogs, cats, dogs, robins, squirrels, birds
>
> know the different types of trees
> move away from the work that you will complete
> before your head becomes one with your pillow
> acknowledge your place in photosynthesis
>
> remember you need to have fun
> beyond the screens that pull you to what may be forgotten by the end of the day
> did decades pass when you blinked as you moved
> beyond highly taxed beverages
>
> remember your grandparents
> your parents
> childhood friends
> actions that seemed so essential in the moment
>
> ask the oldest members of your family
> to remember stories
> generate a connection
> with places that you once were

210 *Kelly Young and Andrejs Kulnieks*

there are lessons in the stories
are you craving for time to walk
along the shore

plant something on your window sill
your deck, a garden
your backyard
watch it grow

pick fruits from the plant that you know
wave your hand over plants
that need the gift of elasticity
as you learn about what it likes

it will give you seeds to distribute
but the gift of relationship
extends beyond the plant
to share moments of the harvest

(Kulnieks, 2020)

Poetic inquiry involves considering your thoughts and feelings so that others can share what you have learned through the process of writing. Poetic inquiry involves a further step to writing poetry as the writer considers why their story is important and what they (and others) can learn from their experiences. It can provide learners with a reason to explore their thoughts as they deepen their communication abilities by changing forms of writing. It is a form of what Luce-Kapler (1999) refers to as the "liberating constraint." Writing poetry about the climate allows the learner to engage with their own stories as they consider why climate is important. This act of writing is liberating because it asks the writer to consider thoughts, feelings, actions, and experiences as they create their story. The constraint is that they then have to consider the facts about climate change and how their story fits with what researchers have to say as they mediate different forms of information.

As educators, we have to ask what the things are our students will need in the future. What are some of the lessons that could help convey teachings that will make a difference in the future? Wendell Berry (2002) writes: "We have an 'environmental crisis' because we have consented to an economy in which by eating, drinking, working, resting, travelling, and enjoying ourselves we are destroying the natural god-given world" (p. 251). It is important to provide opportunities for students to consider their place in the world. Educators can provoke students to consider how they engage with the Earth. Engaging with intact ecosystems through walking the land and learning which plants live there becomes a curriculum of place.

Ultimately, as part of an eco-justice pedagogical practice that includes an eco-hermeneutic approach to poetic inquiry, learners connect with what is important because this methodology asks the reader and writer to inquire about what they are writing about in relation to their natural surroundings and identities. It is our hope that this chapter has outlined some helpful suggestions about how poetic inquiry can provoke learners to consider their place in the world and to help students develop a deeper understanding about how language shapes our understandings. Poetic inquiry involves an exploration of language and identity formation with a hope that learners can be inspired to make healthier choices. We believe that becoming in tune with the world around us through ecologically motivated activities can provoke discussions and debates that can lead toward understanding the effects of climate change.

References

Abrams, D. (1996). *The spell of the sensuous: Perception and language in a more-than-human world*. Vintage.

Berry, W. (2002). *The art of the commonplace: The agrarian essays of Wendell Berry*. Counterpoint.

Bowers, C.A. (2002). Toward an eco-justice pedagogy. *Environmental Education Research, 8*(1), 21–34.

Bowers, C.A. (2004). *The EcoJustice dictionary*. https://cabowers.net/CAdictmain.php

Bowers, C.A. (2016). *Digital detachment: How computer culture undermines democracy*. Routledge.

Bringhurst, R. (2002). The tree of meaning and the work of ecological linguistics. *Canadian Journal of Environmental Education, 7*(2), 9–22.

Cajete, G. (1994). *Look to the mountain: An ecology of indigenous education*. Kivaki Press.

Capra, F. (1996). *A new scientific understanding of living systems: The web of life*. Double Day.

Cobb, E. (1959). The ecology of imagination in childhood. *Daedalus: Journal of the American Academy of Arts and Sciences, 88*(Summer), 537–548.

Egan, K. (1986). *Literacy, society, and schooling: A reader*. Cambridge University Press.

Field, E., Schwartzberg, P., Berger, P., & Gawron, S. (2020). Climate change education in the Canadian classroom: Perspectives, teaching practice, and possibilities. *EdCan Network*. https://www.edcan.ca/articles/climate-change-education-canada/?utm_source=EdCan+Network+Newsletters&utm_campaign=abfc426d41-Bulletin_ENGLISH_JULY_2019_COPY_01&utm_medium=email&utm_term=0_82bbb8cbfe-abfc426d41-447733521

Kulnieks, A. (2020). Excerpts. *Walking landscapes of stories*. Unpublished poetry manuscript.

Kulnieks, A., & Young, K. (2014a). Ekphrastic poetics: Fostering a curriculum of ecological awareness through poetic inquiry. *In Education, 20*(2), 79–89.

Kulnieks, A. & Young, K. (2014b). Literacies, leadership, and inclusive education: Socially justice arts-informed eco-justice pedagogy. *LEARNing Landscapes, 7*(2), 183–194.

212 Kelly Young and Andrejs Kulnieks

Kulnieks, A., Longboat, D., & Young, K. (2010). Re-indigenizing learning: An eco-hermeneutic approach to curriculum. *AlterNative: An International Journal of Indigenous Peoples, 6*(1),15–24.

Kulnieks, A., Longboat, D., & Young, K. (2011). Indigenizing curriculum: The transformation of environmental education. In D. Stanley & K. Young (Eds.), *Contemporary studies in Canadian curriculum: Principles, portraits & practices* (pp. 351–374). Brush Education.

Kulnieks, A., Ng-A-Fook, N., Stanley, S., & Young, K. (2012). Reconsidering Canadian environmental curriculum studies. In N. Ng-A-Fook, & J. Rottmann (Eds.), *Reconsidering Canadian curriculum studies* (pp. 107–136). Palgrave MacMillan.

Kulnieks, A., Longboat, D., & Young, K. (2013a). Beyond dualism: Toward a transdisciplinary indigenous environmental studies model of environmental education curricula. In A. Kulnieks, D. Longboat & K. Young (Eds.), *Contemporary studies in environmental and indigenous pedagogies: A curricula of stories and place* (pp. 9–18). Sense Publishers/Brill.

Kulnieks, A., Longboat, D., & Young, K. (2013b). Eco-literacy development through a framework for indigenous and environmental educational leadership. *Canadian Journal of Environmental Education, 18*, 112–126.

Kulnieks, A., Young, K., & Longboat, D. (2013c). Indigenizing environmental education: Conceptualizing curriculum that fosters educational leadership. *First Nations Perspectives – The Journal of the Manitoba First Nations Education Resource Centre, 5*(1), 65–81.

Kulnieks, A., Longboat, D., & Young, K. (2013d). Engaging literacies through ecologically minded curriculum: Educating teachers about indigenous knowledges through an ecojustice education framework. *In Education, 19*(2), 138–152.

Kulnieks, A., Longboat, D., Sheridan, J., & Young, K. (2016a). Oral history education through poetic inquiry: Developing ecologically sustainable language arts curriculum. *Our Schools/Our Selves. Canadian Centre for Policy Alternatives Quarterly Journal on Education, 25*(2), 127–134.

Kulnieks, A., Longboat, D., & Young, K. (2016b). Engaging eco-hermeneutical methods: Integrating indigenous curriculum through an eco-Justice-arts-informed pedagogy. *AlterNative: An International Journal of Indigenous Peoples, 12*(1), 43–56.

Kulnieks, A., Longboat, D., & Young, K. (2018). Developing eco-literacy through an integrated model: A primer for eco-justice education curricula. In C. Bowers (Ed.), *Eco-justice: Essays on theory and practice in 2017* (pp. 11–22). Eco-Justice Press.

Lannoo, J. (2010). *Leopold's shack and Ricketts's lab.* University of California Press.

Leggo, C. (2012). Challenging hierarchy: Narrative ruminations on leadership in education. *Education, 18*(1, 9–22.

Longboat, D., Kulnieks, A., & Young, K. (2020). Developing curriculum through Engaging oral histories: A pedagogy for reconciliation and eco-justice-oriented education. In K. Llewellyn & N. Ng-A-Fook (Eds.). *Storying historical consciousness in times of reconciliation: Oral history, public education, and cultures of redress* (pp. 183–196). Routledge.

Luce-Kapler, R. (1999, March) White chickens, wild swings, and winter nights. *Language Arts, 76*(4), 298–303.

Leadership in Eco-Justice 213

Martusewicz, R., Edmundson, J., & Lupinacci, J. (2011). *Ecojustice education: Toward diverse, democratic, and sustainable communities.* Routledge.

Orr, D. (1992). *Ecological Literacy: Education and the transition to a postmodern world.* Albany, NY: State University of New York Press.

Shepard, P. (1977). Place in American culture. *North American Review, Fall,* 22–32.

Solnit, R. (2000). *Wanderlust: A history of walking.* Penguin Books.

United Nations. (n.d.). *Climate Change.* https://libraryresources.unog.ch/climatechange/UN

8 Land-Based Environmental Education as a Climate Change Resilience

A Learning Experience from a Cross-Cultural Community Garden

Ranjan Datta, Jean Kayira, and Prarthona Datta

It is evident that climate change poses a major threat to humanity and the environment, particularly to the education of children in vulnerable communities. Each Intergovernmental Panel on Climate Change (IPCC) report confirms the increasing extent and impact of climate change (IPCC, 2001, 2007, 2014). It has been argued that climate change will impact poor communities the most (Limon, 2010; Muttarak & Lutz, 2014; UNESCO, 2015), hence the need to address justice issues (Tuck & McKenzie, 2015; Waldron et al., 2016). Climate justice is concerned with "the inequitable distribution of the adverse impacts of climate change on economically, politically, and socially marginalized communities around the world" (Mitchell & Chakraborty, 2014, p. 476) and focuses on protecting the rights of those who are least responsible for the current climate crisis, yet who remain most vulnerable to its impacts (Gibbons, 2014; Running, 2015).

Environmental education (EE) has a key role to play in addressing the impacts of climate change (UNESCO, 2015). Indeed, climate change education:

> Seeks to achieve profound, long-term changes in understanding, particularly among young people. It involves developing educational curricula, training of trainers and teachers and adequate pedagogies. The results of a successful programme would ultimately be a population whose deep-seated appreciation of the climate challenge leads to greater national action and commitment.
> (UNESCO & UNFCCC, 2016, p. 14)

Furthermore, climate change education can help increase the resilience of communities most adversely affected by climate change (UNESCO, 2015). Vulnerable communities (Indigenous, Black, immigrants, and refugees) globally have high exposure to effects caused by climate change and are often considered an "at-risk" population, although there is growing evidence of their resilience (Datta, 2020; Ford et al., 2020;

DOI: 10.4324/9780429326011-11

Rumbach & Foley, 2014; Vinyeta et al., 2015). Additionally, others have argued that resilience is not new; rather, it has been present in the everyday routines, practices, strategies, and policies of communities as they meet the social and economic challenges of a post-industrial world (Agyeman et al., 2003; Reich et al., 2010). In this chapter, we examine the common factors affecting this resilience. Acknowledging that many people will engage with climate change issues outside formal classrooms (Stephens & Graham, 2008) and that climate change education needs to take place in different informal and formal settings (Roussell & Cutter-Mackenzie-Knowles, 2020), this chapter uses land-based education framing and the setting of a cross-cultural, transnational, and intergenerational community garden.

We posit that land-based education is a possible solution to addressing the impacts of climate change, particularly on children and youth. It uses an Indigenized and environmentally focused approach to education by recognizing the physical, mental, cultural, social, and spiritual connections to the land (Bang, et al., 2014; Castellano, 2000; Champagne, 2015; Datta, 2018; Tuck et al., 2014). Essentially, Indigenous land-based education refers not only to learning about people, land, history, culture, and spirituality, but also taking responsibility to protect the land and people. It has also been argued that using land-based education as an intervention improves the lives of Indigenous youth by helping create connections to the land, and developing resilience and wellbeing (Ritchie et al., 2015). Children and youth can also learn Indigenous food practices, food sovereignty, and caring for the land through land-based pedagogies (Johnson & Ali, 2019; Thompson et al., 2018; Wesche et al., 2016). Since the goal of land-based education is to sustain Indigenous life and knowledge, it directly challenges settler colonialism (Wildcat et al., 2014).

We focus on land-based EE respecting and honoring Indigenous peoples, their cultures, and knowledge. Our learning in the cross-cultural garden was holistic and non-hierarchical as we learned from each other, spanning different cultures, nations, ages, and knowledge systems and practices. We believe that centering land-based EE in a cross-cultural, intergenerational, and transnational garden has potential positive implications for climate resilience. We begin by situating ourselves as researchers and discussing the challenges of climate change education. We then explain how we have overcome those challenges by situating our description of the community garden case study, and finally, we reflect on our critical learning and practice which focuses on climate change education.

Situating Researchers

Situating ourselves as researchers is a relational responsibility in Indigenous land-based EE (Datta, 2018; Datta et al., 2015; Wilson, 2008). For situating ourselves, in this section, we explain a couple of important

216 *Ranjan Datta et al.*

points: who we are as researchers, where we come from, for whom we are doing this research, and how we are responsible for the land we live in and the people we live with.

Ranjan

I am a colored settler on Indigenous land (i.e., Treaty 6 and 7 territories) known as Saskatchewan and Alberta in Canada. I am thankful to all Indigenous people for providing the opportunity to learn, live, and dream. Mycross-cultural socialization and interdisciplinary education made him well situated for this work.

Coming from a racialized immigrant family in an Indigenous land presents many challenges that have to be faced in everyday life, including invisible poverty (issues of poverty including hunger, food insecurity, housing instability, discrimination, injustice, shame, exclusion, racism, and health problems that have remained socially invisible (Johnson, 2020)), mental stress, racism, food insecurity, and a lack of opportunity to know about Indigenous people and their history. Despite all these challenges our cross-cultural community garden activities open many opportunities to learn how Indigenous land-based practice can play a critical role in building community-led resilience of both Indigenous people and non-Indigenous people because it can potentially contribute to building resilience to food crises. In the last ten years living in Canada, I have seen that many immigrants and refugee people carry a lot of misconceptions about Indigenous people and culture: limited knowledge about the treaties, the residential schools, the cultural genocide, and reconciliation. In our community garden, cross-cultural activities helped us to take responsibility for learning about Indigenous people and the land. These land-based learning opportunities are not only helping to create more opportunities for personal interactions between newcomers and Indigenous peoples, but also create many openings for belongingness, empowerment, and resilience. As a colored settler family (Ranjan and Prarthona Datta), if we do not protect our environment, we may not be able to take care of ourselves. Therefore, for us, it is high time to take our own responsibility, individually as a family and collectively as a community; otherwise, there will be many climate change challenges yet to come.

Prarthona

As a 14-year-old child studying in grade 9, I became a part of this chapter because learning is a celebration for me, and the community garden has always been a place full of informal learning with the land. I am the first daughter of Ranjan Datta (the first author). My father has been doing gardening with me for the last eight years and I have had many opportunities to learn the importance of gardening from him directly. In our community garden, I have learned how to connect with my learnings at school. We learned science, social science, and environmental education at school, but at the community garden, we learned how to practice all those learnings with the land and learn how to become more responsible for climate change. Our community garden activities with diverse community children inspired me to be a transnational performer. My transnational performances help me to understand the importance of learning about the climate change crisis and how to be resilient with my performances. For example, as a transnational performer, I do Indian classical dance and music to build a connection with my ancestors' culture. I am learning an Indigenous powwow dance to build relationships with Indigenous people in Canada, and I am also learning Western ballet, lyrical dance, and jazz to build relationships with non-Indigenous relatives. I am writing about my experiences because I have been involved with our cross-cultural community garden for the last eight years with many cross-cultural friends and families. Through situating me in this chapter, I hope my learning stories will inspire other children to become more responsible for climate change actions through community gardening.

Jean

I am a Malawian living and working on the traditional ancestral lands of the Abenaki Peoples of New Hampshire, USA. I have also had the opportunity to live and study on Treaty 6 territory in Saskatchewan, Canada. I am aware of my intersectionality—I have many privileges such as education, dance, learning, and gardening. At the same time, I am a woman and a visible minority. I am interested in Indigenous knowledge, land-based and cross-cultural environmental education, youth participatory action research, and decolonizing methodologies. I have done research and taught courses on these topics. My research and teaching is guided by the sub-Saharan concept of Ubuntu/uMunthu which is captured in the saying "I am because we are, and because we are, therefore, I am" (Mbiti, 1969, p. 108). Essentially, respectful relationships with participants and the environment are central in my work (Anderson et al., 2016; Kayira, 2013a, 2013b; McVittie et al., 2019). In my teaching I strive to create an inclusive environment for students to feel comfortable to have critical conversations. It was during my doctoral studies at the University of Saskatchewan that I met Ranjan and his daughter Prarthona, who was three years old at the time. Ranjan and I had the same advisor because we have similar research interests. We have co-authored two papers since we graduated. It is my part of our relational responsibility to continue our collective learning, and this chapter created an opportunity to continue our learning journey.

218 *Ranjan Datta et al.*

Climate Change Education Challenges

Current climate change education needs to address justice issues—paying attention to who benefits and to who is most impacted by our collective lack of action (Tuck & McKenzie, 2015). Waldron et al. (2016) argue that any engagement with climate change raises issues of justice, particularly with regard to the global distribution of responsibility for causation and the need to support climate change adaptation in areas most affected. Indeed, countries that have suffered the worst effects of climate change have contributed the least to the cumulative global load of greenhouse gas emissions (Gibbons, 2014; Limon, 2010; Rosen, 2015; Running, 2015). There is also the issue of intergenerational justice as the consequences of current actions and decisions will be felt most by future generations (Rosen, 2015). Many scholars have called for innovative and effective forms of climate change education for children and youth across the globe since they will deal with the uncertain effects of climate change brought by previous generations (Devine-Wright et al., 2004; Ekpoh & Ekpoh, 2011; Kagawa & Selby, 2012).

In a recent systematic review of climate change education literature, Roussell and Cutter-Mackenzie-Knowles (2020) found top-down approaches have dominated. Nonetheless, a few bottom-up, participatory approaches are starting to emerge. They cite examples of projects where learners designed their own climate change projects (Feierabend Jokmin, & Eilks, 2011; Figueiredo & Perkins, 2013). Additionally, they found a small number of studies that focused on approaches that provoke emotional responses to climate change issues and concerns through engagement with art, imagery, and narrative (Duxbury, 2010; Leiserowitz, 2006). Roussell and Cutter-Mackenzie-Knowles (2020) advocate for developing "new forms of climate change education that directly involve young people in responding to the scientific, social, ethical, and political complexities of climate change" (p. 191). They challenge "educational researchers to be daring enough to research beyond redundant investigations interrogating children and young people's knowledge of climate change science" (p. 203). Similarly, Hargis and McKenzie (2020) found that Canadian youth want more action than cognitive knowledge. The Canadian students want to see their school leaders take action—not only regarding teaching and curriculum, but also in domains of overall governance and decision making, and in the operations or footprints of schools. Others have identified the relevance of Indigenous knowledge for climate change education (Datta, 2020; Nam et al., 2013; Roehrig et al., 2012). It is also argued that climate change education could benefit from holistic approaches (Schreiner et al., 2005).

This chapter directly responds to many of the shortfalls highlighted above, focusing on children learning EE and climate change in a cross-cultural community garden. It showcases a variety of equity and justice

Land-Based Environmental Education 219

aspects. For instance, one of the children (Prarthona Datta) who participated in the community garden project for the eight-year duration is a co-author. She was four years old when the project started and was 12 at the time it ended. She gives an account of how and what she learned as well as *actions* she and her cross-cultural peers performed so as to be resilient and address the impacts of climate change. Intergenerational learning was key in this learning space—children learned from Elders, Knowledge-keepers, adults, and from each other. In a way, there was holistic learning encapsulating the non-hierarchical exchange of knowledge and skills among gardeners. Cross-cultural gardeners learned land-based epistemologies, including Indigenous knowledge and practice, and food sovereignty as a way to be resilient against the impacts of climate change. Their age, gender, ethnicity, sexual orientation, country of origin, or any additional socially constructed identity became less irrelevant; instead it was a community of gardeners working and learning together. The informal setting of a community garden provided a venue where the children took an active role in creating meaningful, cross, and interdisciplinary learning opportunities with Elders and adults from all over the world.

Case-Study Focusing on Land-based Environmental Education as Climate Change Resilience Actions

Following cross-cultural community-based participatory action research, we learned about climate change adaptation strategies created from our community garden that started in 2011 as a self-initiative by ten gardeners from three different countries with ten garden plots. By 2019 our community garden had extended to 120 plots from 28 different nationalities with more than 400 adults and 100 children. Most of our gardeners were inspired by other gardeners as our community garden space was located within the university residence for international students. Members of the community have seen many benefits of our community garden, particularly indirect community-led climate change adaptation strategies. We know community-led climate change initiatives can have many adaptation strategies; in our community garden, our gardeners discussed and explained community-led climate change adaptation strategies from and within cross-cultural garden activities, including food security, children's informal learning, land-based learning, recycling, children's art activities, networking, socializing, and informal learning activities in the playground for children. From 2015 to 2019 our community garden received support from various organizations including the city, university, and other local organizations for various intercultural activities. For instance, as a founder and coordinator (Ranjan and his family) for the last eight years, we had many opportunities to create intercultural activities, including building-bridge programs between

220 *Ranjan Datta et al.*

Indigenous people and newcomers, cross-cultural food story sharing programs, children's art activities, music and dance, informal climate change learning, and women sharing circles. All of these activities were developed with ongoing community discussions, engagement, and leadership. We met weekly for workshops and monthly for community decision making. Additionally, our community space became a celebratory place every sunny evening, and the community could use it for a variety of personal events and small cross-cultural events. All of these opportunities inspired us to keep growing as a community and to develop our community garden as an intercultural and intergenerational space.

This case study is based on our eight years of community garden activities. Our garden is situated in Saskatoon city in Saskatchewan, Canada. Given that the poverty around us includes a lack of affordable nutritious food and is compounded by community isolation and culture shock, we wanted to build a cross-cultural, environmentally sustainable garden community. With our desire to engage with food sovereignty and reconciliation, we hoped to engage Indigenous peoples, racialized minorities, and non-visible minorities to talk about community-led climate change adaptation strategies.

Our garden was not only a collective growing food space but also a cross-cultural, transnational, and intergenerational learning space. For example, we started our garden with gardeners from three different countries in 2011; by 2019 we had gardeners from 28 different countries. These gardeners included Indigenous people, settlers, new immigrants, and refugees. Gardeners were from all different backgrounds such as white, Black, visible and non-visible minorities, and LGBTQ2+ (i.e., lesbian, gay, bisexual, transgender, queer, and two-spirited. The plus-sign refers to a number of other identities and is included to keep the abbreviation brief when written out). While settlers, new immigrants, and refugees had many opportunities to learn from Indigenous Elders and knowledge-keepers' gardening stories, they (i.e., settlers, new immigrants, and refugees) had also many opportunities to share their cross-cultural stories with each other. In the story-sharing method, community gardeners learned the significance of stories and storytelling, including Indigenous worldviews, land, colonization, and resilience. For example, we used to invite Indigenous Elders into our garden to share their stories with cross-cultural communities. We all (children, youth, and adults from many different communities) had opportunities to learn and, at the same time, other Elders from immigrant communities used to share their land-based stories. This cross-cultural story-sharing space became a transnational land-based learning space. In this learning space, we not only learned the importance of Indigenous land-based stories, but also tried to connect our learning with our ancestors' stories.

Our garden space created an intergenerational learning opportunity for children, youth, parents, and grandparents. In this chapter, we focus

Land-Based Environmental Education 221

on the cross-cultural stories from Indigenous, transnational immigrants' Elders, knowledge-keepers, adults, and children, as well as music, children's arts, growing foods, and recycling.

By starting small and working steadily, we were able to grow our garden and, along with that, our knowledge and our cross-cultural community. Many children were in the garden daily, especially during weekends and in the summer, when schools were closed. In the last eight years, we have learned that a cross-cultural community garden creates many opportunities to enact climate change adaptation strategies, including cross-cultural children's informal learning activities for climate change, taking responsibility for climate change, learning challenges, and finding solutions with land-based stories.

In writing this chapter we gave a particular focus to children's voices: of their own land-based learning activities including learning stories from Indigenous Elders and knowledge-keepers, of learning how to build relationships with different species, and of taking children-led actions for climate change learning and actions. As such we *italicize* the child author's (i.e., Prarthona Datta) voice below.

Children's Learning Opportunities as a Climate Change Resilience Action

A cross-cultural community garden can inspire many children to learn about climate change. *We (i.e., cross-cultural children) learned from our parents, grandparents, Indigenous Elders, and knowledge-keepers about the many ways a community garden can help reduce climate change. We learned different stories about the land and how we can protect mother earth by collaborative gardening, learning stories, and taking responsibility to learn, unlearn, and relearn our relationships with Indigenous peoples, culture, and environment. The stories our parents, grandparents, Indigenous Elders and knowledge-keepers told us, helped us to understand as second-generation immigrant children who we are in this Indigenous land, what are our responsibilities in this, and what we need to do to create our belonging; all these learnings help reduce climate change. In addition to belonging stories, we also learned how gardening can help us to reduce our use of plastic, and use of driving. As children and youth in our community garden, now we know why we need to grow our own food in response to climate change. Our parents, grandparents, Indigenous Elders and knowledge-keepers inspired us to learn more about the ways we can help keep the earth healthy.*

Learning from Elders and knowledge-keepers is an essential piece of Indigenous land-based education. Elder Courchene (2019) has argued that the root cause of climate change is a lack of respect for the Earth. He calls for a change in how humanity treats the Earth. In his view, knowing that the Earth has a spirit and is alive is "fundamental to having a sacred relationship with the Earth." A respectful relationship calls for responsibility to protect the land (Bang et al., 2014; Castellano, 2000; Champagne, 2015; Datta, 2018; Hansen, 2009, 2018; Tuck et al., 2014).

222 *Ranjan Datta et al.*

As children in our cross-cultural community garden, *we also learned how to develop our friends' solidarity network for environmental activism. For instance, inspired by our community garden, we created a children-led environmental-activism community at our elementary school. We participated in a number of environmental protection movements, including Earth Day, a reducing climate change rally in the city, a garbage cleanup day, and many more. We urged our peers to help make a difference in climate change with community gardens. We as a children's group learned the meanings of climate change not only from Indigenous Elders, knowledge-keepers, parents, and adults, but also led our critical discussions about our responsibility for climate change activists. Our children-led group initiated the discussion among children regarding what we can do to help the climate change situation. We have seen that our last three years' initiatives helped us realize that what our parents, grandparents, Indigenous Elders, and knowledge-keepers said was correct. The activists and our parents, grandparents, Indigenous Elders, and knowledge-keepers helped us connect from two different perspectives on the matter, the scientific and spiritual points of view. We took this new knowledge to help us understand what we were learning at school, and many of our school friends were interested in it. Together we went to climate change strikes which helped us be more aware of the issue.*

The actions taken by children in our garden contributed to the burgeoning youth-led protests for climate action. Indeed, climate strikes, called various names such as StudentStrike4Climate (SS4C), Fridays For Future, or Youth Striker 4 Climate, have been on the rise (Sengupta, 2019; Taylor, Watts, & Bartlett, 2019; Zummo, Gargroetzi, & Garcia, 2020), although 2020 saw a decline due to the COVID-19 pandemic. On September 20, 2019, over six million people from 185 countries participated in a global strike (Taylor et al., 2019).

Learning Challenges as a Climate Change Resilience Action

In our community garden, we had many opportunities to critically discuss and learn about challenges in climate change among children, parents, and grandparents. For example, *we do not know any stories of the food that we are eating, including how the food is being grown, who is producing the food, where it is being made, what is being put into our food. While gardening, my parents would tell me all sorts of stories about our grandparents' stories and how my parents gardened. From these stories, we learnt how effective gardening is for the environment. There are many positive factors for community gardens. From our personal experience, we realized that a community garden can reduce the impact of climate change. It helps decrease the amount we are driving, which reduces the amount of emissions, as we do not have to drive to the grocery store to buy vegetables because we are growing all we need ourselves. Not buying vegetables is cheaper since we are able to use that money for other things. Adding on to this, gardening also helps reduce the number of plastics we use daily. We know this because when we are at the grocery store, many things are wrapped in plastic, and when we are at a community garden, we can pick it and take it home. These are some of the reasons the community garden is so beneficial.*

Activities and lessons highlighted by the children align with the benefits of community gardens addressed in the literature. Gardening plays a role in reducing climate change directly by mitigating greenhouse gases through carbon sequestration, carbon emissions reduction from food transportation, packaging, and refrigeration (Okvat & Zautra, 2011). Community gardens save money, provide increased access to healthy food options, promote physical activity, and improve mental and social well-being (Okvat & Zautra, 2011; Stein, 2008).

We as a community critically discussed the connection between climate change challenges and impacts on communities such as COVID-19. Although we do not have direct evidence that climate change is influencing the spread of COVID-19, climate change alters how we relate to other species on land and that matters to our health and our risk of infections. We learned from our discussion that as the land heats up, animals big and small, on land and in the water, are headed to the poles to get out of the heat. That means animals are coming into contact with other animals they normally wouldn't, and that creates an opportunity for pathogens to get into new hosts. Many of the root challenges of climate change also increase the risk of natural disasters such as pandemics. We have many reasons to take climate action to improve our health, and reducing the risk of infectious disease emergence is one of them.

Intergenerational Learning Space

We developed our garden as an intergenerational learning space for both children and adults. The space had multiple meanings to us, including within and from transnational and trans-cultural, trans-gender, trans-age, and Indigenous. For instance, our garden had more than 100 children with various nationalities and cultures. Our intergenerational learning activities helped us to overcome national, cultural, and gender boundaries, including learning opportunities for both children and adults: (1) from own grandparents and parents, regarding their own community garden cultural stories; (2) the importance of stories shared by other cross-cultural grandparents and adults; and (3) learning gardening stories from Indigenous people. Since many of the events were facilitated through Indigenous youths and knowledge-keepers, we followed Indigenous story sharing processes so that children/adults would have their own story—all stories are important, and all stories are relationally connected. In our Indigenous intergenerational story sharing circle, we also learned that every plant/insect/food has its own story. We need to respect and honor every child, adult, plant, and animal story. We are related to each other and have relational accountability to each other. Indigenous youths and knowledge-keepers helped to relate our

224 *Ranjan Datta et al.*

intergenerational stories in our everyday learning and practicing, through our gardening.

Parents also had many opportunities to learn from children. For instance, during artwork, children drew what they understood about their relationships with insects. Many children showed that they learnt about environment science education informally. They asked many critical questions that parents did not think about during gardening time, such as why people cultivate green grass in their yards when no animals, people, or insects use or eat them; why there are so many plastics in the food store; why people do not cultivate foods in their yard; why many do not have food to eat when market food stores waste so much every day.

Food Sovereignty as a Climate Change Resilience Action

In our community garden, we learned the importance of food sovereignty from Indigenous Elders and knowledge-keepers in response to climate change. As Elders and knowledge-keepers suggested, the meaning of food sovereignty in climate change is like food as a teacher, food as medicine, and food as a relative. They identified four guidelines that cross-cultural communities can reclaim in their everyday practice, such as (1) maintaining and developing relationships with plants, animals, and the land that provides food; (2) learning the importance of traditional knowledge on food culture and cultural harvesting activities; (3) the know-how of growing food can enrich independence and self-determination; and (4) the establishment of policies that support Indigenous and cross-cultural ways of knowing about food and relationships. Elders and knowledge-keepers also suggested that in order to achieve food sovereignty we need to learn land-based knowledge and practice, including all traditional, Western, and spiritual land-based ways of growing, harvesting, transportation, and consumption of food. As a community, we learned how food sovereignty can be a community-led action in response to climate change. Food sovereignty is a process of different ways to think about and work towards localizing food systems, valuing food producers, engaging with nature, transferring the food-producing knowledge to the next generation, and making decisions locally.

Children's Relationships with Insects and Plants as a Climate Change Resilience Action

Children can learn many things from plants and insects. For example, every day when we went to the garden, we would see insects like bees pollinating our crops, worms in the ground, ladybugs, caterpillars on the trees and butterflies flying around. All the children would play with the insects and interact with the plants and insects around us.

The community garden taught us a lot about the different insects and plants. The caterpillars and ladybugs would move around on our hands and on sticks, and we were learning why caterpillars and ladybugs were important for our garden. With our garden learning activity, we were learning how to connect with our school, parents, and internet learning. From our informal learning activities, we also learned that without bees and butterflies' pollination, our food would not grow, and without worms, we would not have compost. Being around the plants and insects was calming for many children.

Taking Responsibility as a Climate Change Resilience Action

Our cross-cultural community garden created new opportunities for children, youth, and adults to take responsibility through the learning and relearning of Indigenous meanings of gardening and belonging. As we learned from Indigenous Elders and knowledge-keepers, we need to know Indigenous meanings of the land as they bring all human and non-human elements (e.g., plants, insects, sun, and moon) together in a relationship. Indigenous meanings of the land are also important as they teach responsible ways of knowing about the natural world and its food systems.

Our community also helped us take responsibility for the community garden as not just about growing our foods but as also about relearning colonial history, people, traditional culture, and the Earth. For instance, in our community garden, Elders and knowledge-keepers' evening stories helped us to learn about the legacy of colonial stories: how colonization has and continues to negatively impact food security in Indigenous communities; how colonization continues as an ongoing challenge to Indigenous sovereignty. Taking responsibility to reconnect with the harvest and traditional knowledge helped us to create our belongingness with the land and people. Now we know that the land is our responsibility and which can strengthen us at individual and community levels.

Land-Based Practice as a Climate Change Resilience Action

Various cultures, particularly Indigenous peoples, have strong connections with the land and land-based learning. As Indigenous Elders and knowledge-keepers explained in our community garden, many Indigenous peoples in Canada share deep social, cultural, and spiritual ties to their "lands"—a term that captures Indigenous territories in general, including terrestrial, water, and associated spiritual environments—and their livelihoods, health, and well-being are closely linked to activities such as hunting, fishing, herding, foraging, small-scale farming, and land- and water-management practices that have developed over many generations. We, as cross-cultural gardeners, also relearned that living in

226   *Ranjan Datta et al.*

a health-sustaining relationship with the land is a fundamental respect of the connectedness between all living and non-living things and an appreciation for the essential balance of all creation (Bang et al., 2014; Berkes, 2008; Champagne, 2015; Datta, 2018; Hansen, 2009, 2018).

Recycling as a Climate Change Resilience Action

Picking up garbage around the neighborhood was an important way to reduce climate change through the community garden (Okvat & Zautra, 2011). For example, *we as children learned that picking up garbage helps the animals, plants, and the earth stay healthy. Therefore, we used to go around the community garden, picking up garbage and putting it into garbage cans. We were picking up garbage around the neighborhood, even though the garbage was not ours. We also learned how garbage can have negative impacts on our community garden and environment. For instance, if an animal eats a piece of plastic, it will die. Additionally, all the garbage everyone throws on the ground will pollute ponds, lakes, rivers, seas, and the land. If we don't pick up trash or put the recycling in the recycling, we are going to lose trees, and trees are our main source of oxygen, and if we have no oxygen, then there will be no humans or animals. Cleaning up garbage after others and ourselves means caring for the earth because if we don't take care of the earth then, we won't have food, freshwater to drink, and the planet would be full of garbage, and we would have nowhere to go. It would cause global issues such as climate change, global warming, and other problems that one day might make the earth unlivable.*

Therefore, through the cross-cultural activities in our community garden, we attempted to uncover the complex climate change entanglements among the communities of refugees, immigrants, and non-immigrants (Indigenous and non-Indigenous) and their children, youth, and adults. Our garden offered tangible EE strategies for immigrants, refugees and other vulnerable or marginalized populations to build community and community connections in order to explore community-led climate change adaptation strategies. Through our community garden activities, we learned that reducing climate change impact became not only necessary in EE, but was also one of our individual and collective responsibilities. As gardeners, we were inspired to engage in community-led critical conversations on climate change, climate crisis, or climate EE responsibility. We found our critical engagement and practice in our community garden to be the source of our empowerment, hopes, and happiness in EE. We not only see our collaborative learning as a cultural bridge within and from diverse cultures, but also as giving us hope that we can make change collectively. The process of gardening and the cultivation of community inspired all of us. Having cross-cultural activities in a garden, where we go to educate ourselves and others about how we can live together within different cultures, helps us to understand and respect each other.

Our Reflections on Climate Change Education

As we learn more about climate change in a cross-cultural community garden, traditional EE knowledge can be challenging, especially for children and youth populations who are contemplating life pathways. Our cross-cultural, transnational, and intergenerational community garden activities helped us to relearn, rethink, and retake not only our learning but also our resilience actions to environmental change among cross-cultural communities.

Indigenous Land-Based Learning and Practice

According to Indigenous land-based practice, we need to be as healthy as our environments (Hansen, 2018; Radu, House, & Pashagumskum, 2014). And so our research addresses cross-cultural community garden activities that feed the well-being of "all our relations": plants, animals (including human), water, land, spirit. Indigenous land-based learning offers an avenue for hope, embedded in action. This approach has been taken up in recent years by a number of post-secondary institutions in Canada and internationally (Datta, 2020, 2018; Hansen, 2018, 2013; Tuck et al., 2014; Wildcat et al., 2014).

Indeed, the cross-cultural, transnational, and intergenerational community garden provided an excellent venue where land-based environmental education occurred. Children and young people learned from Indigenous Elders and knowledge-keepers: the Indigenous meaning of land (as sacred, a gift that comes with responsibility to take care of); Native food systems and agricultural practices including how they were disrupted upon European settlement and the displacement of Native peoples from their lands; stories of Native plants; and the importance of growing one's own food for sustainable living. Before participating in the study, many cross-cultural families had substantially learned and replaced their traditional diets with new food that could be described as unhealthy. Through the years of community gardening, many families learned to grow healthy food and build a supportive community. Essentially, for gardeners who participated in the study, food sovereignty has become a resilient action in addressing the impacts of climate change, and children and youth are actively involved. With the increasing uptake of land-based education in EE, it is promising that we may change the way upcoming generations envision the environment and shape the future that unfolds on it. Strong connections to the "land" held by many Indigenous peoples bring unique considerations for understanding and responding to environmental change (Bang et al., 2014; Castellano, 2000; Champagne, 2015; Datta, 2018; Hansen, 2009, 2018; Tuck et al., 2014). Thus, the indirect effects of environmental change on interpersonal and environmental relationships, life experiences,

228 *Ranjan Datta et al.*

spiritual considerations, family, kinship, and oral history are often as important as, if not more so, the more direct impacts of change.

Environmental Challenges

Climate change poses a serious threat to the health and well-being of vulnerable peoples (Limon, 2010; Muttarak & Lutz, 2014; UNESCO, 2015). Despite living in diverse contexts, cross-cultural peoples face a number of common challenges due to a range of factors including unique relationships with the environment, socioeconomic deprivation, a greater existing burden of disease, poorer access to and quality of health care, and political marginalization. Our community garden provided an opportunity to rethink environmental challenges from our everyday practice. For instance, garbage became one of the important factors of environmental racism which can have a high impact on climate change. Poor and racialized communities most often live near to landfills and other waste management systems (for example, Amegah and Jaakkola, 2016; Furedy, 1993; Mothiba, Moja, & Loans, 2017; Parizeau, 2006) and bear a disproportionate burden of persistent exposure to the risks, hazards, and contamination of pollution (Hird, 2016). Similarly climate change affects poor communities the most (Limon, 2010; Muttarak & Lutz, 2014; UNESCO, 2015). In our case study, we have seen how children in a community garden not only took the learning initiative on recycling but also showed how they have been active in everyday practice to minimize both garbage and the climate change crisis. We surmise that by participating in the garden children developed a sense of agency that would not have occurred otherwise.

Intergenerational Learning

Intergenerational learning can build bridges between formal and informal learning activities. Our community garden helped us with different forms of intergenerational learning. Intergenerational stories have the capacity to change lives, in a small but very important way. We had the opportunity to learn about land, gardening, climate change, and culture from and within various generations. Our intergenerational learning helped us to be responsible for learning and practicing. It also helped us to respect and honor cultural knowledge in younger generations, especially in families that have immigrated from their countries or communities of origin. Communities from a variety of cultural backgrounds were able to transform knowledge about growing fruit and vegetables to their grandchildren through joint gardening activities.

Community gardens are ideal spaces for intergenerational learning. In these spaces different generations grow vegetables and fruit together and learn from each other (Allen, Alaimo, Elam, & Perry, 2008). As we have

Land-Based Environmental Education 229

mentioned earlier, for us, the intergenerational learning space had multiple meanings including within and from transnational and transcultural, trans-gender, trans-age, and Indigenous people.

Holistic Learning

Through engaging the cross-cultural community garden, we were able to generate a unique learning emerging from each setting and a more holistic picture of the learning potential grounded in climate change education (Datta, 2019; McVittie, Datta, Kayira, & Anderson, 2019). Our garden enriched holistic interconnectedness, collaboration, reciprocity, and spirituality; more importantly, it impacted positively on practice.

Therefore, we agree with those who are calling for the need for a different type of climate change education, one that centers on equity and justice, authentically engages children and youth, considers cross-cultural, transnational, and intergenerational issues, and is embedded in Indigenous land-based approaches. This chapter has demonstrated that while on the one hand, young gardeners learned from Elders, knowledge-keepers, and adults, on the other hand, all gardeners learned from each other—there was respect for the knowledge, practice, and skills brought by each gardener regardless of age, gender, ethnicity, country of origin, or any other socially constructed identity. The space provided a venue for land-based EE which enabled non-hierarchical learning among gardeners to thrive for eight years. Our work responds to calls to reimagine climate change education where youth take an active role (Roussell & Cutter-Mackenzie-Knowles, 2020), justice issues are addressed (Tuck & McKenzie, 2015; Waldron et al., 2016), Indigenous knowledge is considered (Datta, 2018; Datta, et al., 2015 Nam et al., 2013; Roehrig et al., 2012), and holistic approaches are employed (Schreiner, Henriksen, & Hansen, 2005). It was apparent that a cross-cultural, transnational, intergenerational, and land-based community garden was an excellent setting for climate change education. Children and youth led a number of climate resilience actions such as food sovereignty, relationships with insects and plants, land-based education, and recycling.

References

Agyeman, J., Evans, B., & Bullard, R.D., (2003). *Just sustainabilities: Development in an unequal world.* Earthscan.

Allen, J.O., Alaimo, K., Elam, D., & Perry, E. (2008). Growing vegetables and values: Benefits of neighborhood-based community gardens for youth development and nutrition. *Journal of Hunger and Environmental Nutrition, 3*(4), 418–439. http://dx.doi.org/10.1080/19320240802529169

Amegah, A.K., & Jaakkola, J.K. (2016). Household air pollution and the sustainable development goals. *Bull World Health Organ, 94,* 215–221. http://dx.doi.org/10.2471/BLT.15.155812

Anderson, V., Datta, R., Dyck, S., Kayira, J., & McVittie, J. (2016). Meanings and implications of culture in sustainability education research. *The Journal of Environmental Education, 47*(1), 1–18. http://dx.doi.org/10.1080/00958964.2 015.1056077

Bang, M., Curley, L., Kessel, A., Marin, A., Suzukovich III, E.S., & Strack, G. (2014). Muskrat theories, tobacco in the streets, and living Chicago as Indigenous land. *Environmental Education Research, 20* (1), 37–55. http://dx.doi.org/10.1080/13504622.2013.865113

Berkes, F. (2008). *Sacred ecology*. Routledge.

Castellano, M.B. (2000). Updating Aboriginal traditions of knowledge. In G.J.S. Dei, B.L. Hall, & D.G. Rosenberg (Eds.), *Indigenous knowledges in global contexts: Multiple readings of our world* (pp. 21–36). UBC Press.

Champagne, D. (2015). *Indigenous nations within modern nation states*. JCharlton.

Courchene, D. (2019, November 9). *Traditional indigenous knowledge on climate change*. Cultural Survival. https://www.culturalsurvival.org/news/traditional-indigenous-knowledge-climate-change

Datta, R. (2018). Traditional storytelling: An effective Indigenous research methodology and its implications for environmental research. *AlterNative: An International Journal of Indigenous Peoples, 14*(1), 35–44. http://dx.doi.org/10.1177/1177180117741351

Datta, R. (2019). Sustainability: through cross-cultural community garden activities, *Local Environment, 24*(8), 762–776. http://dx.doi.org/10.1080/13549839 .2019.1641073

Datta, R. (Ed.), (2020). *Reconciliation in practice: Cross-cultural perspectives.* Fernwood Publishing.

Datta, R., Khyang, U.N., Khyang, H.K.P., Kheyang, H.A.P., Khyang, M.C., & Chapola, J. (2015). Participatory action research and researcher's responsibilities: An experience with Indigenous community. *International Journal of Social Research Methodology, 18*(6), 581–599. http://dx.doi.org/10.1080/13645579.20 14.927492

Devine-Wright, P., Devine-Wright, H., & Fleming, P. (2004). Situational influences upon children's beliefs about global warming and energy. *Environmental Education Research, 10* (4), 493–506.

Duxbury, L. (2010). A change in the climate: New interpretations and perceptions of climate change through artistic interventions and representations. *Weather, Climate, and Society, 2*(4), 294–299.

Ekpoh, U.I., & Ekpoh, I.J. (2011). Assessing the level of climate change awareness among secondary school teachers in Calabar municipality, Nigeria: Implication for management effectiveness. *International Journal of Humanities and Social Science 1* (3), 106–110.

Feierabend, T., Jokmin, S., & Eilks, I. (2011). Chemistry teachers' views on teaching 'climate change'-an interview case study from research-oriented learning in teacher education. *Chemistry Education Research and Practice, 12*(1), 85–91.

Figueiredo, P., & Perkins, P. E. (2013). Women and water management in times of climate change: participatory and inclusive processes. *Journal of Cleaner Production, 60,* 188–194.

Ford, J.D., King, N., Galappaththi, E.K., Pearce, T., McDowell, G., & Harper, S.L. (2020). The resilience of Indigenous Peoples to environmental change. *One Earth, 2*(6), 532–543.

Land-Based Environmental Education   231

Furedy, C., (1993). Recovery of wastes for recycling in Beijing. *Environmental Conservation, 20,* 79–82.

Gibbons, E.D. (2014). Climate change, children's rights, and the pursuit of inter-generational climate justice. *Health and Human Rights, 16* (1): 19–31.

Hansen, J.G. (2013). *Swampy Cree justice: Researching the ways of the people* (2nd ed.). JCharlton.

Hansen, J.G. (2018). Cree Elders' perspectives on land-based education: A case study. *Brock Education Journal, 28*(1), 74–91.

Hargis, K., & McKenzie, M. (2020). *Responding to climate change: A primer for K-12 education.* Saskatoon, Canada: The Sustainability and Education Policy Network.

Hird, M.J. (2016). The phenomenon of waste world making. In K. Sellberg, & P. Hinton (Eds.), *Rhizomes: Cultural studies in emerging knowledge* (p. 30). https://doi.org/10.20415/rhiz/030.e15

IPCC (Intergovernmental Panel on Climate Change). (2001). *Climate change 2001: Synthesis report.* Retrieved October 25, 2020 from https://www.ipcc.ch/site/assets/uploads/2018/08/TAR_syrfull_en.pdf

IPCC (Intergovernmental Panel on Climate Change). (2007). *Climate change 2007: Synthesis report.* Retrieved October 25, 2020 from https://www.ipcc.ch/site/assets/uploads/2018/02/ar4_syr.pdf

IPCC (Intergovernmental Panel on Climate Change). (2014). *Climate change 2014: Synthesis report.* Retrieved October 25, 2020 from https://ar5-syr.ipcc.ch/ipcc/ipcc/resources/pdf/IPCC_SynthesisReport.pdf

Johnson, J.W. (2020). Invisible poverty: Awareness, attitudes, and action. https://digitalcommons.luthersem.edu/cgi/viewcontent.cgi?article=1060&context=dmin_theses

Johnson, J., & Ali, A.E. (2019). Paddling as resistance? Exploring an Indigenous approach to land-based education amongst Manitoba youth. *Studies of Migration, Integration, Equity, and Cultural Survival, 14* (4), 205–219. https://doi.org/10.1080/15595692.2019.1669015

Kagawa, F., & Selby, D. (2012). Ready for the storm: Education for disaster risk reduction and climate change adaptation and mitigation. *Journal of Education for Sustainable Development, 6* (2), 207–217.

Kayira, J. (2013a). (Re)creating spaces for uMunthu: Postcolonial theory and environmental education in southern Africa. *Environmental Education Research, 21,* 106–128.

Kayira, J. (2013b). Re-learning our roots: Youth participatory research, Indigenous knowledge, and sustainability through agriculture. (Unpublished PhD dissertation). University of Saskatchewan.

Leiserowitz, A. (2006). Climate change risk perception and policy preferences: The role of affect, imagery, and values. *Climatic Change, 77*(1), 45–72.

Limon, M. (2010). Human rights obligations and accountability in the face of climate change. *Georgia Journal of International & Comparative Law, 38*(3), 534–592.

Mbiti, J.S. (1969). *African religions and philosophy.* Praeger.

McVittie, J., Datta, R., Kayira, J., & Anderson, V. (2019). Relationality and decolonisation in children and youth garden spaces. *Australian Journal of Environmental Education.* Advance online publication. http://dx.doi.org/10.1017/aee.2019.7

Mitchell, B.C., & Chakraborty, J. (2014). Urban heat and climate justice: A land-scape of thermal inequity in Pinellas County, Florida. *Geographical Review, 104*(4), 459–480. http://dx.doi.org/10.1111/j.1931-0846.2014.12039.x

Mothiba, M., Moja, S., & Loans, C. (2017). A review of the working conditions and health status of waste pickers at some landfill sites in the city of Tshwane Metropolitan Municipality, South Africa. *Advances in Applied Science Research, 8*(3), 90–97. https://www.imedpub.com/articles/a-review-of-the-working-conditions-and-health-status-of-waste-pickers-at-some-landfill-sites-in-the-city-of-tshwane-metropolitan-m.pdf

Muttarak, R., & Lutz, W. (2014). Is education a key to reducing vulnerability to natural disasters and hence unavoidable climate change? *Ecology and Society, 19*(1), 42–49. http://dx.doi.org/10.5751/ES-06476-190142

Nam, Y., Roehrig, G., Kern, A.L., & Reynolds, B. (2013). Perceptions and practices of culturally relevant science teaching in American Indian classrooms. *International Journal of Science and Mathematics Education, 11*(1), 143–167.

Okvat, H.A., & Zautra, A.J. (2011). Community gardening: A parsimonious path to individual, community, and environmental resilience. *American Journal of Community Psychology, 47*(3–4), 374–387.

Parizeau, K. (2006). Theorizing environmental justice: Environment as a social determinant of health. In J.C. Cohen & L. Forman (Eds.), *Comparative program on health and society Lupina foundation working papers series, 2005–2006* (pp. 101–128). University of Toronto.

Radu, I., House, L., & Pashagumskum, P.E. (2014). Land, life, and knowledge in Chisasibi: Intergenerational healing in the bush. *Decolonization: Indigeneity, Education & Society, 3*(3), 86–105.

Reich, J., Zautra, A.J., & Hall, J.S. (Eds.). (2010). *Handbook of adult resilience.* Guildford Press.

Ritchie, S.D., Wabano, M.J., Corbiere, R.G., Restoule, B.M., Russell, K.C., & Young, N.L. (2015). Connecting to the good life through outdoor adventure leadership experiences designed for Indigenous youth. *Journal of Adventure Education and Outdoor Learning, 15*(4), 350–370. http://dx.doi.org/10.1080/14729679.2015.1036455

Roehrig, G., Campbell, K., Dalbotten, D., & Varma, K. (2012). CYCLES: A culturally-relevant approach to climate change education in native communities. *Journal of Curriculum and Instruction, 6*(1), 73–89. https://climate.nasa.gov/effects/

Rosen, A.M. (2015). The wrong solution at the right time: The failure of the Kyoto Protocol on climate change. *Politics & Policy, 43*(1), 30–58. http://dx.doi.org/10.1111/polp.12105

Roussell, D., & Cutter-Mackenzie-Knowles, A. (2020). A systematic review of climate change education: Giving children and young people a 'voice' and a 'hand' in redressing climate change. *Children's Geographies, 18*(2), 191–208. http://dx.doi.org/10.1080/14733285.2019.1614532

Rumbach, A., & Foley, D. (2014). Indigenous institutions and their role in disaster risk reduction and resilience: Evidence from the 2009 Tsunami in American Samoa. *Ecology and Society, 19*(1), 19. http://dx.doi.org/10.5751/ES-06189-190119

Running, K. (2015). Towards climate justice: How do the most vulnerable weigh environment-economy trade-offs? *Social Science Research, 50*, 217–228. http://dx.doi.org/10.1016/j.ssresearch.2014.11.018

Schreiner, C., Henriksen, E.K., & Kirkeby Hansen, P.J. (2005). Climate education: Empowering today's youth to meet tomorrow's challenges. *Studies in Science Education, 41*(1/2), 3–49.

Land-Based Environmental Education   233

Sengupta, S. (2019, September 20). Protesting climate change, young people take to streets in a global strike. *The New York Times.* https://www.nytimes.com/2019/09/20/climate/global-climate-strike.html

Stein, M.J. (2008). Community gardens for health promotion and disease prevention. *International Journal for Human Caring, 12*(3), 47–52.

Stephens, J.C., & Graham, A.C. (2008). Climate science to citizen action: Energizing nonformal climate science education. *EOS, Transactions American Geophysical Union, 89*(22), 204–205.

Taylor, M., Watts, J., & Bartlett, J. (2019, September 27). Climate crisis: 6 million people join in latest wave of global protests. *The Guardian.* https://www.theguardian.com/environment/2019/sep/27/climate-crisis-6-million-people-join-latest-wave-of-worldwide-protests

Thompson, H.A., Mason, C.W., & Robidoux, M.A. (2018). Hoop house gardening in the Wapekeka First Nation as an extension of land-based food practices. *ARCTIC, 71*(4), 407–421. http://dx.doi.org/10.14430/arctic4746

Tuck, E., & McKenzie, M. (2015). *Place in research: Theory, methodology, and methods.* Routledge.

Tuck, E., McKenzie, M., & McCoy, K. (2014). Land education: Indigenous, post-colonial, and decolonizing perspectives on place and environmental education research. *Environmental Education Research, 20*(1), 1–23. http://dx.doi.org/10.1080/13504622.2013.877708

UNESCO. (2015). *NOT JUST HOT AIR: Putting climate change education into practice.* United Nations Educational, Scientific and Cultural Organization (UNESCO). https://unesdoc.unesco.org/ark:/48223/pf0000233083

UNESCO & UNFCCC. (2016). Action for climate empowerment: Guidelines for accelerating solutions through education, training and public awareness. United Nations Educational, Scientific and Cultural Organization (UNESCO). https://unfccc.int/topics/education-and-outreach/resources/ace-guidelines

Vinyeta, K., Whyte, K.P., & Lynn, K. (2015). Climate change through an intersectional lens: Gendered vulnerability and resilience in indigenous communities in the United States. Gen. Tech. Rep. PNW-GTR-923. U.S. Department of Agriculture, Forest Service, Pacific Northwest.

Waldron, F., Ruane, B., Oberman, R., & Morris, S. (2016). Geographical process or global injustice? Contrasting educational perspectives on climate change. *Environmental Education Research, 25*(6), 895–911. http://dx.doi.org/10.1080/13504622.2016.1255876

Wesche, S.D., O'Hare-Gordon, M.A.F., Robidoux, M.A., & Mason, C.W. (2016). Land-based programs in the Northwest Territories: Building Indigenous food security and well-being from the ground up. *Canadian Food Studies/La Revue Canadienne Des Études Sur L'alimentation, 3*(2), 23–48. http://dx.doi.org/10.15353/cfs-rcea.v3i2.161

Wildcat, M., Simpson, M., Irlbacher-Fox, S., & Coulthard, G. (2014). Learning from the land: Indigenous land based pedagogy and decolonization. *Decolonization: Indigeneity, Education & Society, 3*(3), I–XV.

Wilson, S. (2008). *Research is ceremony: Indigenous research methods.* Fernwood Publishing.

Zummo, L., Gargroetzi, E., & Garcia, A. (2020). Youth voice on climate change: Using factor analysis to understand the intersection of science, politics, and emotion. *Environmental Education Research, 26*(8), 1207–1226, http://dx.doi.org/10.1080/13504622.2020.1771288

9 Children's Environmental Identity Development in a Changing Arctic Environment

Carie Green

Introduction

The Arctic is warming at a rate of almost twice the global average. Permafrost melt, loss of sea ice, and coastal flooding are among the changes documented by Arctic researchers (Thoman & Walsh, 2019). Such changes are having a profound impact on Alaska Native communities, who depend on the Land and sea for survival. Indeed, climate change and its related social, cultural, and economic implications exacerbate inequalities of already vulnerable rural northern Indigenous communities. Furthermore, the complexity of the climate crisis threatens the livelihood of both current and future Alaskan children. While education is recognized as essential to mitigating climate change impacts, it is important that such educational approaches be culturally relevant and responsive to the lived experiences of the children and youth in which they serve.

This chapter explores the social and cultural dimensions of climate change education by considering the environmental identity formation of four-year-old Alaska Native children from a northwest Alaska Native rural village. The Environmental Identity Development (EID) theory will be introduced as a framework for interpreting young children's agency in their environment and their developing relations with the natural world. Through highlighting the voices and perspectives of young Alaska Native children, this chapter seeks to expand the dialogue on equitable climate change education by legitimizing important attributes of children's environmental identity formation.

Climate Change and Inequity in the Arctic

Research from around the globe reveals that socially and economically disadvantaged and marginalized people are and will be the most impacted by global climate change (Olsson et al., 2014). Indigenous peoples, women, children, the elderly, and the disabled, who are already susceptible to uneven power structures and social inequality, are also the most susceptible in the climate crises (IPCC, 2012). The physical and biological changes associated

DOI: 10.4324/9780429326011-12

Children's Environmental Identity Development 235

with Arctic climate change are multi-faceted (Thoman & Walsh, 2019). Depletion of sea, river, and lake ice, changes in abundance and distribution of terrestrial and marine life, erosion related to thawing permafrost, and rising sea levels are among some of the ecological changes disproportionately affecting the livelihood of Alaska Native communities (Cordalis & Suagee, 2008; Crate, 2013). Alaska Native people still very much depend on subsistence from the Land and sea for survival. Changing and unpredictable environmental conditions have altered access to traditional hunting and gathering sites, limiting the availability of natural food sources and negatively impacting economies dependent on such sources (Brinkman et al., 2016). In some cases, entire Alaskan communities have been forced to relocate due to erosion; and in other cases, families whose income is dependent on fishing or other sources of sea harvest have been forced to leave the village for other sources of income (Moerlein & Carothers, 2012). Additionally, warmer waters have opened up international shipping and trade in previously impassable northern seas, bringing new sources of pollution and further environmental impact on an already vulnerable population and geographical region.

In considering social justice in climate change education, approaches must be responsive to the needs of communities marginalized the most by the climate crisis. What happens in one place, affects another. Namely, waste deposited in the ocean in California for instance, may wash up on the beach of the Alaskan Bering Sea. Furthermore, carbon emittance from anthropogenic and natural sources have contributed to the acidification of the ocean, which in turn implicates Land and sea subsistence resources. Warmer waters have already revealed the implications on spawning salmon populations, which provide a viable food source for a large majority of Alaskans (Thoman & Walsh, 2019). Similarly, as the planet warms and rivers fail to freeze, access to traditional hunting grounds are also changing—what once was a viable source of subsistence may no longer be accessible for families who rely on the flora and fauna of the Land.

Given the profound impacts of climate change in the Arctic coupled with the loss of access to natural resources, Alaska Native children are particularly vulnerable in the climate crisis. Indeed, the need to consider the livelihood of children was echoed by Gautam Narasimhan, UNICEF Senior Adviser on Climate Change, Energy, and the Environment:

> The consequences of the climate crisis are all around us, affecting children the most and threatening their health, education, protection and very survival. Children are essential actors in responding to the climate crisis. We owe it to them to put all our efforts behind solutions we know can make a difference.
>
> (UNICEF, 2019)

Children's "survival and development rights" are a foundational part of early childhood education for sustainability (Davis, 2014, p. 25): "These

236 Carie Green

comprise rights to the resources, skills and contributions necessary for survival including rights to adequate food, shelter, [and] clean water ... and cultural activities." Children's environmental rights not only include protections from environmental degradation, they should also include rights for children to share their views and perspectives. The United Nations Convention on the Rights of the Child (UNCRC) set a precedence for children's citizenship and rights of participation recognized under international law (UNCRC, 2005); children have also voiced their own views as to what their rights should entail. Common visions shared by children across the world suggest an inclusive citizenry entailing: (1) participation and liberty to "express opinions, be listened to, make choices," (2) protection and "to be treated fairly," and (3) provision, including care and a healthy environment (Taylor & Smith, 2009, p. 171). Children have the right for their views and perspectives to be heard; this chapter posits that in understanding how Alaskan children perceive and experience their environment will better inform the development of climate change education from an equitable and social justice lens.

Alaska Children's Environmental Identity Development

The findings presented in this chapter make up part of a longitudinal research project aimed at understanding children's environmental identity formation in an Alaskan rural and non-rural context, among Native and non-Native children. Environmental identity, an aspect of self-identity, focuses on an individual's self-concept in relation to the natural world and is generally concerned with the degree in which one is willing to act for the environment (Clayton, 2003). Environmental identity is defined as:

> A sense of connection to some part of the nonhuman natural environment, based on history, emotional attachment ... that affects the way in which we perceive and act toward the world; a belief that the environment is important to us and an important part of who we are.
>
> (Clayton, 2003, pp. 45–46)

EID theory is informed by psychosocial theories of child development and contemporary sociological understandings of childhood (Green, 2018). Psychodynamic theories of child development emphasize the significance of inner emotional conflicts as well as the outer social, cultural, and environmental influences of such conflicts. Emotions signal our human connection to place and to our environment (Morgan, 2010). Emotions also play a significant role in learning and behavior (Hinton, Miyamoto, & Della-Chiesa, 2008). Nature is often over-romanticized as a place of pure joy and wonder for children. Little is known about the early emotional experiences (both positive and negative) in nature that influence the

Children's Environmental Identity Development 237

development of children's developing environmental identity. The over-arching goal of this research is to add to the understanding of the affective dimensions of young children's interactions with nature and how emotions provide a foundation for shaping children's identity attributes, that is, their values, perspectives, beliefs, and behaviors towards their environments.

EID draws from sociological understandings of childhood, particularly children's agency and the significance of children's active contributions to culture and change (Corsaro, 2017). Children's agency, that is, their inherent interests, dispositions, and behaviors, informs how children develop their sense of self in nature (Heggen et al., 2019). Extending the first four stages of Erikson's psychosocial model (1980) to a natural world context, the EID framework includes four tensions/dilemmas that inform children's environmental identity formation:

- Trust in Nature vs. Mistrust in Nature;
- Spatial Autonomy vs. Environmental Shame;
- Environmental Competency vs. Environmental Disdain;
- Environmental Actions vs. Environmental Harm.

In the first progression, *Trust in Nature vs. Mistrust in Nature*, a child's sense of comfort and security in nature as opposed to feelings of anxiety and fear are essential to the development of a healthy environmental identity. In the second progression, *Spatial Autonomy vs. Environmental Shame*, feelings of trust with nature propel a child to explore and discover their sense of place, discovering who they are in nature. In opposition, a feeling of *Environmental Shame*, or inadequacy in nature, might emerge through anxious encounters or discouragement from exploration. A sense of *Spatial Autonomy vs. Environmental Shame* works hand in hand with the third progression of *Environmental Competency vs. Environmental Disdain*. Through exploration, experimentation, and creative innovations, children gain a sense of *Environmental Competency*, which enriches the way they relate with nature. With young children this may be achieved through exploration, play, and/or problem solving, leading to a heightened sense of ecological understanding. The opposite, a lack of opportunities to take initiative in nature, could lead to *Environmental Disdain*, or feelings of contempt or ignorance that separate children from the natural world. In the fourth progression, *Environmental Action vs. Environmental Harm*, a child's previously developed competencies are applied toward care and stewardship of nature or neglect or disregard toward the natural environment. Engagement in *Environmental Action* is an indicator of a strong and healthy environmental identity (Clayton, 2003). A child's agency as well as the socio-cultural contexts in which a child develops informs the progression of EID (Figure 9.1).

The progression of a child's EID is fluid, meaning that attributes may be revisited, refined, and/or reestablished with new encounters and new

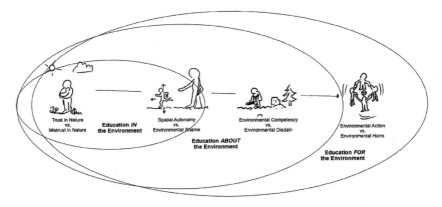

Figure 9.1 A model of Environmental Identity Development.
© Carie Green, 2015.

experiences throughout one's life (Green et al., 2016). In other words, there is not one ideal timeframe for progression, rather EID is represented by an interdependent system of ever-broadening circles building from one progression to the next. With each environmental encounter and/or experience, a child might move through one or more EID progressions. Movement can occur quite rapidly for some and rather slowly for others, depending on prior experiences. Certain dilemmas encountered in nature might take longer than others to overcome. Resolved or unresolved, all experiences are informative to a child's environmental identity formation. Adults and peers play a significant role in shaping children's EID, particularly in supporting them in negotiating their environmental experiences.

Research Questions

The following research questions inform this inquiry:

- What are the emotional and behavioral attributes of young Alaskan children's interactions with the natural world?
- How do such interactions demonstrate how these young children are developing their sense of self in nature?
- How can the attributes of young Alaska Native children's Environmental Identity Development inform climate change education from a social justice and equitable perspective?

Research Context

The study was conducted in a small rural northwestern Alaska Native village of approximately 708 people (U.S. Census Bureau, 2015). The village is located in a sound along the Bering Sea; the region is known for

Children's Environmental Identity Development 239

its salmon and king crab harvests. There is also a freshwater river that flows into the sound near the village and large hills of tundra and boreal forest above the village, away from the sea. Fifteen 4–5-year-old children participated in the project. All but two were identified by their families as Alaska Native, primarily of Iñupiat decent. The children, with their teachers, the researchers, and parent volunteers participated in the outdoor activities during a week-long visit in September (autumn) 2019.

Researcher Positioning

As a White non-Indigenous researcher/educator, and as an outsider to the culture and visitor to the Land, I recognize that my interpretation of children's lived interactions on the Land are limited. It is the intention of this research to honor the voices of young children who have been historically oppressed. Thus, by utilizing data collection and analysis approaches that honor children's voices and perspectives, I continuously called to question, bracketing to the extent possible, my own conceptions of children's place and environmental experiences, in order, to the extent possible, to see the world through the lens of a child.

Research Methods

The approach taken in this research was largely qualitative, focusing on the lived experiences of children as they interacted with each other in their environment. The study utilized sensory tours in which children were invited to put on small wearable cameras around the forehead as they played, explored, and engaged in subsistence activities during family and class visits to wilderness settings. Sensory tours provide a means to see the world through the lens of a child (Green, 2016). The wearable camera records what children say, what they do, and how they interact with their environment. It captures their self-talk and expressions, and their interactions and exchanges with other living and non-living beings in their environment. Families chose the settings, activities, and who participated in the family-led nature tours, whereas the class tours occurred in three different outdoor settings. These included play on a beach adjacent to their school, berry picking on open tundra near the village, and fishing at Pebble Creek, approximately 15 miles north of the village up the Bering Sea coastline. By exploring children's interactions with family members, peers, and teachers during culturally relevant outdoor activities in familiar settings, this study supports the importance of cross-setting research approaches in inclusive equitable climate change education.

Videos captured by wearable cameras were viewed in their entirety, transcribed on a Word document, and analyzed holistically. The researcher took notes on children's micro-interactions with their

240   *Carie Green*

environment, which refer to themes of children's behaviors in each particular setting and which were time stamped and critically analyzed to consider the variables in each setting, the persons involved, observed behaviors, emotional responses, children's verbal and non-verbal forms of communication, and their relational orientations towards other living and non-living beings. The study was framed around the understanding that micro-interactions form the basis of how these children come to relate with and see themselves as part of their environment. Such interactions are shaped by children's agency (emotions and behaviors), past and present experiences, the particular situation, as well as the environmental context. For the purposes of this chapter, particular micro-interactions will be presented in order to provide insight into the attributes of Alaska Native children's environmental identity formation and how these micro-interactions might inform climate change education from a social justice and equitable perspective.

Findings

Five vignettes of young Alaska children's micro-interactions are presented below to provide insight on important attributes of how these children are learning to relate with other living and non-living beings in their natural settings. Four of the micro-interactions (Grace's found treasure, Erin's blueberries, Jackson's trouble on the tundra, and Chloe's moose spotting) occurred during class visits to wilderness settings. One micro-interaction (Anne fishing) occurred during a family-led nature tour. I accompanied Anne and her mother fishing on the shores of North River, located in the boreal forest a 20-minute drive from the village. Each interaction reveals important attributes of how children from this rural Alaska Native village are developing their relations with the natural world. Additionally, some vignettes pose environmental tensions and how children navigate such challenges. Finally, the vignettes will be used as a springboard for posing critical questions for climate change education from an equitable and social justice perspective.

Grace's Found Treasure: Learning to be Resourceful in an Interconnected World

The following micro-interaction from Grace's sensory tour at the beach during the class field trip reveals how she is learning to be resourceful in an interconnected world:

> Grace runs down the hill of the sandy beach, the wearable camera around her forehead, shows from a distance a blue object in the sand. Grace moves towards the bright colored object, notably contrasted by the beige-colored sand. She circles her tall black

Children's Environmental Identity Development   241

rubber boots around what appeared to be a plastic bottle cap. Two of her peers run by and Grace quickly joins them giggling as she runs up the sandbank. She digs her hands into the sand and her laughter becomes louder as she nears the top.

"Cannon ball!" Grace exclaims, jumping on and over a driftwood log.

Landing in the sand, she notices another clear-colored bottle cap in the ground. She picks it up and carefully fills it with sand. She uses the cap as a scoop, tapping the bottom to ensure it is full. Giggling with excitement, she carries the cap to the driftwood log and dumps the sand into a small pile. She scoops the cap through the sand a second time, digging her hands into the sand to fill it. Still laughing she walks with the bottle cap and soon spots a bottle. She scoops the bottle up ensuring it is also full of sand and places the full lid on top. She tightens the lid and then takes it off, grabbing another scoop of sand with her hand and adding it into the bottle before tightening it again.

Overall, Grace's experience of the found rubbish in her environment was positive. Although it is not clear where the cap and bottle had come from, what is clear is that what is considered waste to one person becomes a treasure to another. While Grace's interaction with the bottle cap might be easily dismissed, a more critical reading of this interaction reveals insight into the attributes of her environmental identity formation. Grace appeared to have a strong sense of *Trust in Nature* and *Spatial Autonomy*; this was demonstrated in her laughter and her comfort in navigating through the environment (climbing up the sand dune and jumping over the logs). Her *Environmental Competency* was revealed, in part, through her interaction with the bottle cap: to Grace the bottle cap and bottle were seen as an opportunity and a tool to explore the sand of her environment. Her interaction appeared typical for her, particularly because it was repeated during this one visit to the beach; she was also observed interacting with found objects during visits to the other settings.

How is this interaction connected to climate equity education? As this interaction and other observations revealed, finding treasures on the beach seemed to be an acceptable norm to children from this rural Alaska Native village. Instead of being disgusted by discarded rubbish, the found objects became a source of excitement and fun. In fact, during a family boating tour, a father made extra effort to rescue and repurpose an orange buoy that had been caught up in the reeds near the shore. This becomes a powerful lesson on recycling and reusing accessible resources. The interaction might serve as a lesson to demonstrate how the world is interconnected. An educational inquiry might be framed around interrogating the origin and production of the plastic and perhaps a reading

242 *Carie Green*

of the bottle might indicate where it is from. A further link might be made to petroleum, its implications at a local and global level, and its relation to climate change. Perhaps a look at ocean currents and movement might reveal oceanic connections with other parts of the world.

Erin's Blueberries: Excitement and Skills for Subsisting on the Land

During the second outing, the children piled into three 4x4 pickup trucks and drove to the water tanks right outside the village to harvest berries on the tundra. Erin's interactions reveal her excitement and skills for subsisting on the land:

> "Five, six, seven, eight, we love blueberries!" Erin shouts as she and her classmates make their way down to the spongy tundra and begin picking the wild blueberries growing on the short stubby vines.

"I squeeze some blueberries, I squeeze blueberries," Erin giggles with excitement while telling her friends. She continues picking and tasting the wild berries and while doing so she comes across some wild mushrooms. "And we found some mushrooms," Erin tells her teacher.

> Stepping across the tundra, her boot slips into a low spot. She raises her hand in the air, momentarily losing her balance. However, she quickly regains her posture and continues to move assuredly across the uneven terrain. She continues to pick the wild berries until her cup is full and then she proudly holds it up.

Like Grace, Erin's interactions with her environment reveal a strong sense of *Trust in Nature*, which provides the foundation of her Environmental Identity Development. Without hesitation, she marched down across the boulders from the road to the tundra. She chanted happily about the blueberries growing abundantly on the short stubby bushes. Indeed, her emotional and behavioral interactions on the tundra were positive. She giggled and named the berries as "squishy," excitedly sharing her discovery with her peers. Although she momentarily slipped on the uneven terrain, she quickly regained her balance, demonstrating *Spatial Autonomy*, a sense of confidence and assurance in navigating her place. Not only did she reveal her *Environmental Competency* in locating the wild blueberries, she identified other flora, including wild mushrooms. Her sense of confidence, competence in identifying berries, and ability to move upon the spongy Land are necessary skills for participating in her traditional cultural practices.

What does this interaction reveal in regards to equitable climate change education? Erin's participation in gathering berries make up a significant

Children's Environmental Identity Development 243

part of her cultural and environmental identity development. Since time immemorial, her ancestors have harvested berries from the Land, preserved them, and subsisted on them throughout the winter months. Not only that, sharing berries is an important Alaska Native cultural tradition embedded within the communal value of caring for others. Children are taught to gather for those who cannot, including the sick, the elderly, and new mothers (personal communication, family nature tour, September 2019). Berry growth is temperamental: changes in weather patterns, warmer temperatures, lack of sunlight, or too much precipitation affect how much and to what extent berries are produced. Climate change threatens berry production and accessibility in rural isolated Alaska Native communities. By sharing Erin's interaction in her place, climate change education can be oriented towards social justice, recognizing that human-induced global warming threatens the livelihood of children growing up in rural isolated Arctic communities. Not only that, Erin's comfort, confidence, and competence in her environment is inspiring; it demonstrates how early experiences subsisting on the Land can instill positive connections with place and resilience for survival.

Jackson's Trouble on the Tundra: Mistrust and Uncertainty in a Novel Environment

Jackson's experience on the tundra was almost the complete opposite of Erin's. Jackson had recently moved to the village only a few days before his visit to the tundra. His sensory tour reveals his anxiety and uncertainty of being on the Land:

> While the other children venture down the hill to the tundra with excitement, four-year-old Jackson stands motionless. He looks towards the ground and his knees begin to wobble.
> "Uh guys, maybe …" Jackson calls out to his peers.
> "UH! I'm scared," Jackson states.
> "AHHHHHHH!" Jackson lets out a loud scream.
> His teacher comes up behind him.
> "Jackson, you can go that way," she states.
> "I can't, I don't know how." Jackson stands motionless.
> His teacher begins to coach him down the large rocks.
> "You are very brave," his teacher says.
> "Whoah!" Jackson gasps as he cautiously scales down the rocks to the tundra.
> "Just pick away!" says his teacher, putting a blueberry in Jackson's bucket.
> "I'll let you do them. K-sir," Jackson responds to his teacher.
> "This is how we learn," his teacher says, "just reach down and grab one."

244 *Carie Green*

> "I'll let you do them and put them in my bucket," Jackson repeats.
> "You can do it!" his teacher encourages, asking Jackson if he wants to taste one.
> "Nope," says Jackson, "I want to go back to the car. I don't want to pick any."
> Jackson circulates from one adult to the next, stating his desire to leave. His peers and teachers encourage him to pick and taste the blueberries. Jackson refuses.
> "I am pretty chilly," Jackson tells Carie.
> "Do you want to try a blueberry?" Carie asks.
> "No, I do not. No, I don't want to take any. I just want to go to the car ..." Jackson repeats, "I don't want to do it outside. I want to do it inside the class."

Jackson's anxiety walking onto the tundra demonstrates his *Mistrust in Nature*. Within minutes of his arrival, he let out a loud scream, and although his teachers coached and encouraged him, he was still very uncomfortable in his environment. On the tundra, his peers and teacher encourage him to pick and taste the wild berries, yet he refused. He demonstrated a sense of *Environmental Shame* by closing himself off from his environment. He refused to explore, taste, experiment, and, to this extent, fully experience berry picking on the tundra. He was bothered by the cold weather and circulated from adult to adult stating he was cold. He begins to demonstrate *Environmental Disdain*, stating he wanted to leave, that he would rather be in the car, and that he wants to go back to school.

The interaction reveals how Jackson's *Mistrust in Nature* influenced negative emotional and behavioral responses to the environment. Jackson was unfamiliar with the tundra. Perhaps this was his first experience of it. Noticing his hesitancy, his teachers and his peers coached and encouraged him to navigate the tundra and to pick and try the berries. Jackson, however, refused, stating he wanted to go back to the car and be inside the school.

Novel experiences in an unfamiliar setting might provoke feelings of *Mistrust in Nature*, *Environmental Shame*, and *Environmental Disdain* for children, and even adults. Through appropriate support, positive affirmation, and repeated exposure one can overcome feelings of discomfort. For some, such feelings might be easily overcome, and for others it may take more time. Establishing a sense of *Trust in Nature* will depend on a child's prior experiences, their dispositions, their learned cultural values, and the quality of support offered by peers, family, and other adults.

Jackson's interaction in the tundra provides a powerful example for considering equity and social justice in climate change education. Namely, no two children or two experiences are alike. It is important as

Children's Environmental Identity Development 245

educators that we pay attention to these differences; without a sense of comfort and positive feelings towards an environment, it is difficult, if not impossible, for a child to engage in any kind of climate change action. As Sobel (1996) puts it, "what's important is that children have an opportunity to bond with the natural world, to learn to love it and feel comfortable in it, before being asked to heal its wounds" (p. 10).

Chloe's Moose Spotting: Awareness and Readiness to Read the Landscape

This next interaction occurred during the class fishing trip at Pebble Creek. From the rocky beach, the wearable camera shows when four-year-old Chloe, unprompted, spotted a moose on the distant hillside.

> "I see a moose," Chloe shouts, pointing to a grassy ridgeline several kilometers away.
> "You see a moose, where do you see a moose?" the researcher asks.
> "Uh hugh," Chloe says, "Titto! Titto!"
> Lucas stands near to Chloe. "I see the moose," he says.
> "Show me," the researcher asks.
> "Titto!" Chloe calls, excitedly, "I see it walking."
> "Oh there is a moose. Right there – straight up that hill," Ms. Lizzie confirms.
> "See!" Chloe yells, "Titto!"
> Chloe intently watches the ridgeline. Her classmates, teachers, and the researcher gather over driftwood on the rocky beach, looking out across the tundra towards the hill to see if they could spot it. After several seconds, Chloe looks away.
> "I see a moose nowhere," she says.
> "Who ha!" her friends call for the moose.
> "I see nowhere," Chloe repeats.
> After a few minutes, Chloe joins her friends on a log to eat her lunch.
> A few minutes go by, and Chloe mutters to herself, "There's a moose."
> Ms. Lizzie asks her if the moose has antlers. Chloe says no.
> "Nope, it was a mama one?" Ms. Lizzie confirms.
> "Yeah," Chloe says.

This interaction demonstrates how Chloe, at four years old, is tuned in to the Land and other living beings that she shares it with. Her familiarity with her environment reveals her strong sense of *Trust in Nature* and *Spatial Autonomy*. Chloe observed movement on the hillside several kilometers away, recognizing a cow moose poised in the distance. Her ability to read the landscape and discern the cow demonstrated her *Environmental*

246   *Carie Green*

Competency. The moose spotting happened just seconds after the researcher had placed a wearable camera on her forehead. Although the non-Native researcher and teachers, who were not from the region, were unable to spot the moose, an Alaska Native parent volunteer, Ms. Lizzie, confirmed its location. It was moose season in this northwestern Alaska Native village, and Chloe's spotting was significant. It might result in families' packing away food for the winter. Indeed, minutes after the spotting, Ms. Lizzie texted her husband and Chloe's mom to notify them of the moose.

Climate change education from a social justice perspective must recognize the role in which colonization has and continues to implicate children's relations and experiences on the Land. Both historically and presently, education has been used as a primary vehicle to endorse settler colonialism (Berry, 1999). In Alaska and in other places, a whole generation of Alaska Native children were stolen from their families and communities and sent to boarding schools, which resulted in loss of language and learning of cultural skills and traditions necessary for survival (Darnell & Hoëm, 1996). A separation that resulted in loss of language, understandings of place, and acquired learning of skills and cultural traditions necessary for survival (Gone & Trimble, 2012). Equity in climate change education must include a discourse that decolonizes Western educational approaches that separate children from their environment. By sharing Chloe's deep awareness of place, this chapter aims to instill hope for climate change education that legitimizes Indigenous ways of knowing, and care and stewardship of the Land. At four years old, Chloe's awareness of her place and other living beings in her environment offers an inspiring lesson to teach us in our efforts to reconnect our children to the Land.

Anne Fishing: Developing Resiliency in Subsisting from the Land

The final vignette shows Anne and her mother fishing for salmon up the North River. The wearable camera reveals four-year-old Anne's confidence and competence in this important subsistence activity:

> Anne stands on the bluff above her mother next to the North River. In rhythm, each cast and reel their fishing lines. After only a few minutes, Anne's mother reels in a small 5 lb salmon. The fish jumps and squirms on the Land and her mother carefully picks it up to release the hook.
>
> Above, on the bluff, Anne continues to cast and reel her line while observing her mother with the fish.
>
> "It's got bumps on it," Anne's mother notes, looking closely at her catch.
>
> Anne's line gets tangled around her pole. Without hesitation, she quietly attempts to unravel it.

Children's Environmental Identity Development 247

> Next to the shore, her mother squeals as she releases the salmon from her hand and throws it back into the water.
>
> After several attempts to untangle the line, Anne indicates that she needs some help. Her mother takes the line, untwists it, and hands it back to Anne.
>
> "Scare you mama?" Anne asks.
>
> In silence, mother and daughter continue to cast and reel their lines. Although Anne's line does not always make it to the water, she persists to reel and cast while the cold drizzly rain patters against her jacket.

This interaction, of Anne and her mother fishing, reveals familial and cultural aspects of Anne's environmental identity development. First, Anne's sense of *Trust in Nature* is profound, demonstrated by her silent presence and comfort of being in the isolated wilderness setting, several miles from the village. Her mother also appeared quite comfortable fishing with her daughter alone, noting that they often frequented North Bridge together after school, on the weekends, and during the summer months. Through the rhythmic act of fishing, mother and daughter appeared to connect with their environment and each other. Anne confidently cast and reeled her line with ease, demonstrating a strong *Environmental Competency* in fishing. Without hesitation she practiced her skills while quietly observing what was happening around her. Although her cast from the bluff was more challenging than it would have been if she was near the shore like her mother, her mother did not tell her where to stand. Rather, by letting Anne choose where to cast her line, her mother supported her *Spatial Autonomy*. Even when she experienced difficulty (missing the water with her lure and a tangled line), Anne persisted without complaint. She quietly tried to unravel the line independently, only asking for help after several attempts. She demonstrated this same self-confidence in her interaction with peers during their class visit to Pebble Creek. She pointed out a peer's missing hook on her line and offered help to a peer who was just learning how to fish. When her peer cast the line successfully, Anne spoke encouragement: "You went way far. Way over there."

Anne's comfort and resilience in her environment offers educators an inspiring example of important attributes of young children's environmental identity formation. Through repeated family experiences, Anne was becoming deeply familiar with her environment and learning skills for survival.

In considering climate change education through a social justice and equity lens, the discovery of the salmon with unusual bumps is troubling. Even at four years old, Anne was aware of her mother's apprehension of the marred fish, stating "Scare you mama?" Indeed, the impact of a changing climate threatens the health, availability, and certainty of subsistence resources (Brinkman et al., 2016). Anne's mother stated that

248   *Carie Green*

this was her first time seeing a blemished fish of that sort. While it is impossible to be certain that the bumps on the fish were caused by global warming, it is likely that the mutation was related to some sort of environmental toxin. The interrelation between the health of our planet, the health of animals, and the health of people is palpable. Education should be aimed at revealing such interrelations as well as developing plans to mitigate and reduce carbon emissions and environmental pollutants.

Concluding Discussion

Change in the Arctic is occurring at a profound rate and without a doubt will have a direct impact on the lives of children both now and in the future. This research extends the discourse on climate change education from a social justice and equitable perspective by highlighting the promising attributes of Alaska Native children's interactions on the Land.

While research reveals that socially and economically disadvantaged and marginalized peoples will be the most impacted by climate change (IPCC, 2012; Olson et al., 2014), little is known about how climate change will affect the livelihoods of Alaska Native children. Research involving these children more often than not takes on a "damage-centered" approach, focusing on adverse childhood experiences (i.e., the effects of poverty, abuse, and poor health) (Tuck, 2009). Alternatively, this research takes a "desire-based" approach by documenting the promise of young Alaska Native children's interactions with the Land (Tuck, 2009). Specifically, the vignettes presented in this chapter were selected to show how many of these young Alaska Native children have a deep and profound connection with their place, a sense of strength and determination that offers lessons for all.

The vignettes presented point towards strong attributes of children's environmental identity formation (Green, 2018). Namely, the examples reveal a profound sense of *Trust in Nature*, indicated by expressions of joy and a keen sense of awareness in being on the Land. Additionally, from a young age these children are outside and emerged in their wilderness settings. This provides opportunities to exercise *Spatial Autonomy* through choosing where to stand, when to move, what to taste, and how to respond to environmental situations. Children's *Environmental Competency* is refined through persevering through challenges posed in nature, from untangling a fishing line to learning to navigate over unstable terrain. Such skills are necessary for developing resiliency to live on the Land. Additionally, examples reveal how children and families from this rural Alaska Native community learn to be resourceful through repurposing found objects (natural and manmade) for use. Furthermore, through learning how to read the landscape and identify plants and animals, children become intimately familiar with their places and develop the "necessary skills for survival" (Davis, 2014, p. 25).

Children's Environmental Identity Development 249

In this chapter, a counter-example was provided to show how limited exposure and experiences might cause children to respond with *Mistrust in Nature*, anxiety and discomfort, and even *Environmental Shame*, and so possibly choosing to avoid nature experiences altogether. This response was demonstrated by one child who had recently moved to the Alaska Native village from another region of Alaska. His unfamiliarity with the tundra instigated feelings of uncertainty, discomfort, and disdain at being on the Land. His teachers and peers tried to assist him, coaching him to navigate the difficult terrain and encouraging him to taste and pick the wild berries. Yet, he refused, choosing to close himself off from the experience. This detachment from nature is alarming, particularly in that a similar response might occur anywhere from any child across the globe. There is a growing concern that children are becoming disconnected from natural settings (Louv, 2005), and as such they are less likely to develop empathy for, and care and stewardship of, their place. It is important that we pay attention to children's early interactions with their environments at a very young age. Jackson's mistrust and anxiety on the tundra should not be viewed as a deficiency, rather as an opportunity for educators and caregivers to nurture a healthy connection. Through encouragement and recurrent exposure and experiences, educators can develop more equitable and inclusive approaches to, and meet with, children when they are in their environmental identity formation stage.

This chapter has expanded the dialogue on equitable climate change education through considering important attributes of Alaska Native children's Environmental Identity Development. Children's ways of being and ways of knowing the Land are under threat in the climate crisis. Specifically, changes in access, availability, and the health of subsistence resources are being reported alongside unpredictable ice conditions, rising sea levels, and the acidification of the ocean (Thoman & Walsh, 2019). We live in an interconnected world. Climate change education must focus on local and global interconnections, as well as cultural and geographical implications. This is a significant factor to consider in the design of climate change education informed by an equity and social justice lens. In other words, human interactions with the environment (good or bad) in one place influence human interactions with the environment in another. Anthropocentric climate change is the result of human ignorance and disregard for the environment and other living beings. Global warming is a social justice issue—its implications affect the most vulnerable, the poor, the elderly, and Indigenous populations who rely on the Land for a means of survival. Through highlighting the voices and perspectives of Indigenous children, this chapter has offered a counter-narrative for framing climate change education through an equitable and social justice lens. Children are the most vulnerable in a climate crisis and we owe it to them to not only ensure that they have a right to a safe and healthy planet, we also owe it to them to

250 *Carie Green*

ensure they have the right to share their experiences and perspectives. The way these Alaska Native children experience the world is inspiring and a powerful lesson that can encourage all children to come to know and reconnect with their place.

Acknowledgment

This research was supported by funding from the National Science Foundation under award #1753399.

References

Berry, J.W. (1999). Aboriginal cultural identity. *The Canadian Journal of Native Studies, 19*(1), 1–36.

Brinkman, T.J., Hansen, W.D., Chapin, F.S., Kofinas, G., Burnsilver, S., & Rupp, T.S. (2016). Arctic communities perceive climate impacts on access of subsistence resources. *Climate Change, 136*, 413–427.

Clayton, S. (2003). Environmental identity: A conceptual and an operational definition. In S. Clayton & S. Opotow (Eds.). *Identity and the natural environment* (pp. 45–65). MIT Press.

Cordalis, D., & Suagee, D.B. (2008). The effects of climate change on American Indian and Alaska native tribes. *Natural Resources & Environment, 22*(3), 45–49.

Corsaro, W.A. (2017). *The sociology of childhood.* Sage.

Crate, S.A. (2013). *Climate change and human mobility in Indigenous communities of the Russian north.* The Brookings Institution.

Darnell, F., & Hoëm, A. (1996). *Taken to extremes.* Scandinavian University Press.

Davis, J. (2014). Examining early childhood education through the lens of education for sustainability: Revisioning rights. In J. Davis & S. Elliot (Eds.), *Research in early childhood education for sustainability: International perspectives and provocations* (pp. 21–37). Routledge.

Erikson, E.H. (1980). *Identity and the life cycle.* New York, NY: Norton & Company.

Gone, J.P., & Trimble, J.E. (2012). American Indian and Alaska native mental health: Diverse perspectives on enduring disparities. *Annual Review of Clinical Psychology, 8*, 131–160.

Green, C. (2016). Sensory tours as a method for engaging children as active researchers: Exploring the use of wearable cameras in early childhood research. *International Journal of Early Childhood, 48*(3), 277–294.

Green, C. (2018). *Children's environmental identity development: Negotiating inner and outer tensions in natural world socialization.* Peter Lang.

Green, C., Kalvaitis, D., & Worster, A. (2016). Recontextualizing psychosocial development in young children: A model of environmental identity development. *Environmental Education Research, 22*(7), 1025–1048.

Heggen, M.P., Sageidet, B.M., Goga, N., Grindheim, L.T., Bergan, V., Krempig, I.W., … Lynngård, A. M. (2019). Children as eco-citizens? *NorDiNa, 15*(3), 387–402.

Hinton, C., Miyamoto, K., & Della-Chiesa, B. (2008). Brain research, learning and emotions: Implications for education research, policy and practice 1. *European Journal of Education, 43*(1), 87–103.

Children's Environmental Identity Development 251

IPCC. (2012). *Changes in climate extremes and their impacts on the natural physical environment.* Intergovernmental Panel on Climate Change, Cambridge University Press. http://www.fapesp.br/eventos/2012/08/IPCC/JMarengo.pdf

Louv, R. (2005). *Last child in the woods: Saving our children from nature-deficit disorder.* Algonquin Books.

Moerlein, K. J., & Carothers, C. (2012). Total environment of change: Impacts of climate change and social transitions on subsistence fisheries in northwest Alaska. *Ecology and Society, 17*(1), 1–10.

Morgan, P. (2010). Towards a developmental theory of place attachment. *Journal of Environmental Psychology, 30*(1), 11–22.

Olsson, L., Opondo, M., Tschakert, P., Agrawal, A., Eriksen, S. E., ... Zakieldeen, S.A. (2014). Livelihoods and poverty. In C.B. Field, V.R. Barros, D.J. Dokken, K.J. Mach, M.D. Mastrandrea, T.E. Bilir, ... L.L. White (Eds.) *Climate change 2014: Impacts, adaptation, and vulnerability* (pp. 793–832). Cambridge University Press.

Sobel, D. (1996). *Beyond ecophobia.* Great Barrington, MA: Orion Society.

Taylor, N. J., & Smith, A. B. (Eds.). (2009). *Children as citizens? International voices.* Otago University Press.

Thoman, R., & Walsh, J. E. (2019). *Alaska's changing environment: Documenting Alaska's physical and biological changes through observations.* International Arctic Research Center, University of Alaska Fairbanks.

Tuck, E. (2009). Suspending damage: A letter to communities. *Harvard Educational Review, 79*(3), 409–428.

UNCRC. (2005). *Convention on the rights of the child: General Comment No. 7. Implementing child rights in early childhood.* Geneva, Switzerland: UNCRC.

UNICEF. (2019). The climate crisis is a children's rights crises. https://www.unicef.org/press-releases/fact-sheet-climate-crisis-child-rights-crisis

U.S. Census Bureau. (2015). Alaska population estimate. https://www.census.gov/

10 Contested Agency and Authorship in Middle School Girls' Climate Science Digital Storytelling

Disentangling Individual and Collective Agency

Elizabeth Smullen and Elizabeth M. Walsh

Introduction

The agency of individual actors and communities in responding to climate change has consistently been indicated as a critical concern in the social transformation necessary to mitigate and respond to its inequities (Pelling, 2011). In education literature, interventions often foreground the designing of increased learner agency in transformative social work around climate change (e.g., McNeil & Vaughn, 2012; Walsh & Cordero, 2019; Trott, 2020), while in climate adaption research, community agency and institutional transformation often comes to the foreground (e.g., Seyfang & Smith, 2007; Pelling, 2011). When individual and community agencies are investigated in tandem, it is often through participatory strategies for supporting resonant connections between individual and community agency (Hall, Taplin & Goldstein, 2009; Trott 2019); however, the best ways to involve communities in these partnerships is still being debated (Few, Brown & Tompkins, 2011; Samaddar et al., 2021). Because under-resourced and higher poverty communities will suffer the most extreme consequences of climate change (Olsson et al., 2014) and impacts will likely be more severe and rapid than initially thought (Intergovernmental Panel on Climate Change, 2018), it is imperative to foreground the experiences, needs, and narratives of currently and historically marginalized communities to support agency in equitable adaption to climate change. However, there is a threat in considering communities as monolithic entities, as this may erase valuable perspectives and idiosyncratic, multifaceted, individual experiences. It follows, then, that we need to consider processes at the intersection of personal and community agency and the negotiated voices of individuals and collective groups.

In this chapter, we examine a group of sixth-grade girls as they engaged in a climate science curriculum that included a collaborative digital storytelling process and investigate their work as a microcosm of the mediation processes that occur between individuals and collectives

DOI: 10.4324/9780429326011-13

Contested Agency and Authorship 253

in the work of social transformation. We examine the relationship between the negotiation of identities, roles, and positionings within the group, the contestation over authorship of the story, and the ways in which individual learners took agency within the group and through the story. We consider the negotiation and development of a shared purpose and story to be a window into the practices that occur when individuals at a community level create a shared aim out of their individual experiences.

Voice and Agency in Science

Dorothy Holland and co-authors (2001) consider agency as improvisation, in which people "opportunistically use whatever is at hand to affect their position in the cultural game." They draw from Bakhtinian and Vygotskian theories in conceptualizing the *space for authoring* as a context for identity work. Holland et al. define human agency in relation to responding to the world through authoring:

> Authorship is a matter of orchestration: of arranging the identifiable social discourses/practices that are one's resources (which Bahktin glossed as "voices") in order to craft a response in a time and space defined by others' standpoints in activity, that is, in a social field conceived as the ground of responsiveness. Human agency comes through this art of improvisation.
>
> (p. 272)

In this space for authoring, identity is constructed through drawing on existing "voices"; thus, this authorship is necessarily social, rather than individual. In authoring, we use our agency to arrange discourses and practices to become or be recognized as particular kinds of people. Calabrese Barton and Tan (2010) similarly consider how agency plays an intersectional role with "context, position, knowledge, and identity" (p. 191), asserting that agency includes the ability to reimagine oneself (and assert that reimagining) as well as reimagining the world into a new context that may be transformative for one's identity (p. 192).

In considering the situated space of identity authorship, Holland et al. (2001) connect human agency and identity—and thus the ability to creatively conceptualize a possible self—back to culture and the "situating power of social position" where identities are "our way of figuring the interfaces among these dimensions of collective life" (p. 287). There exists, then, an inextricable link between agency and how one positions oneself within a context, how one is situated, and the landscape and historicity of power in the context itself. For our purposes, we conceptualize agency as the extent of an individual's authorship of their identity, the identity of others, and what power they can hold over a given context.

254 *Elizabeth Smullen and Elizabeth M. Walsh*

Beyond individual human agency, however, one can also consider community or group agency. In studies of community adaptation to climate change (often cast as "resilience" studies) or in studies of community transformation, individual and community agency are often considered separately. For example, researchers may argue that it takes both "individual" and "collective" action on climate change (a result of "individual" or "collective" agency) to respond to impacts. However, this divorce between the one and the many is artificial. If we consider community or group agency as existing in a *space for authoring* similar to an individual, the community's agency is similarly improvisational, drawing on similar resources but also, perhaps, on the identities and authored identities of the individuals in the collective. This improvisation would be collectively negotiated among group members, and in and of itself could limit the suite of available resources for individual authorship. These group and individual authorings, existing in the response to similar social fields, occur concurrently but remain distinct. The negotiation between collective and individual agency results in a heteroglossic collective voice that is neither the same as, nor totally distinct from, individual voices.

In group settings, it then becomes of interest to determine what voices are taken in group authorship and what the implications of this are for individual and group agency. Langer-Osuna (2011) examined how, throughout a year-long project-based mathematics course, the positioning of two students—and the import of their individual voices—diverged. In this work, student leader Brianna was repeatedly positioned as "bossy." Her voice was effectively silenced over time as a male student took over as the group leader. This and similar examinations of group work in collaborative projects emphasize that, despite best intentions to promote students' positioning as developing experts through student-driven or project-based curricula, students' voices may be differentially taken up in group practice. This becomes of concern to educators wishing to support more equitable learning structures, or to support collective agency for community transformation, because as a group, the collective may continue to perpetuate marginalization (e.g., an authoritative female figure being "bossy" leads to a trajectory of decreased participation and limited individual agency). Clearly, agency is then related also to the suite of identities available, the positioning of learners into particular roles and identity spaces, and the cultural meanings and consequences of those identities and roles.

Identity and Middle School Science

Many studies have demonstrated the crucial role that identity plays in dimensions of science learning (Bell et al., 2009). The success of similar types of people in science pathways can be understood in relation to the

Contested Agency and Authorship 255

current culture of power. As Banks et al. (2007) state, "every society has a culture of power, and students must learn the languages or codes of the culture of power to advance to higher education, to obtain good jobs, and to experience social-class mobility" (Delpit, 1988, p. 22). This is as true in the classroom as it is in the larger social structure outside of school. To participate competently, students—especially those not already encultured into the culture of power—need to be explicitly taught how to engage in a meaningful way. Researchers have demonstrated that explicit teaching of the rules of the culture of power makes acquiring power easier (Gibbons, 2014, p. 59). Many have argued that even well-intentioned progressive classrooms reinforce existing inequalities between those within the culture of power and those without, as not explicitly teaching what is expected of students shifts the blame from the classroom environment to the learner (Gibbons, 2014, p. 59).

This holds true in science classrooms. Although many students enjoy science and even excel at it in the classroom, they may not see themselves as scientists or do not identify with science. DeWitt & Archer (2015) argue that "identity, or sense of self, has a central role to play" in students' participation in science, as students construct their "horizons of choice"—a picture of their possible futures—within the confines of the structures in place, such as gender, ethnicity, and social class (pp. 2173–2174). Without the ability to conceptualize oneself as a scientist, that career path is shut, even if one excels in the science classroom. Further, identity must be *recognized*: "One cannot have an identity of any sort without some interpretive system underwriting the recognition of that identity" (Taylor, 1994, p. 107 in Gee (2001)). To associate (or disassociate) oneself with (or from) an identity, it must be defined by a set of characteristics or traits. Individuals can then display those characteristics (or avoid them) to "bid" for recognition as having that identity (or avoid acquiring that label in the eyes of others) in a given context. This positioning to be recognized as a certain kind of person (or avoid being recognized as such) is a useful lens for how students negotiate their identities over time. Positioning, like identity itself, is fluid, allowing students to redefine and renegotiate their bid.

Agency Through Narrative and Digital Storytelling

In this study, students engaged in a curriculum that leveraged digital storytelling and narrative with the aim of supporting student agency in climate change action. Avraamidou and Osborne (2009) theorize that narrative can be an effective tool in science education, as it leverages the narrative versus expository nature of common discourse, promotes understanding, may transform understandings of self, and can support meaningful communication. In their case they were interested not only in student-authored narrative, but also narratives by scientists, researchers, and educators. However, though acknowledging the power of personal storytelling, these authors mainly address the form and content of stories that may promote understandings of established scientific discourse. Bang and Marin (2015) address Indigenous storywork through the sharing and telling of stories by American Indian groups as a decolonizing design pedagogy, as stories are a key foundation of Indigenous epistemologies. This perspective aims to desettle normative expectations of science and promote valuable understandings and practices of Indigenous communities, support learners in negotiation between these epistemologies, and transform normative science.

The telling of narratives through digital media has developed as one mode of promoting the sharing of personal narratives, in part due to the rise in accessibility and ease of use of digital technological tools (Lambert, 2009). Digital storytelling has been lauded as engaging for students (Lambert, 2013), a way of making sense of one's place in sociohistorical events and challenging institutional structures (Rolón-Dow, 2011), and promoting self-reflection and consideration of possible futures (Staley & Freeman, 2017). Burgess (2006) notes that digital stories can draw on "vernacular creativity" to tell stories of "ordinary people," and that in contrast to commercial stories, they tend to be "deeply felt, poignant and gently humorous rather than archly self-aware, witty or formalist" (pp. 209–210). Learner and societal narratives can inform meaning making, ways of knowing, identity construction, and how learners position themselves in relation to societal institutions.

Further, Hull and Katz (2006) have demonstrated the possibility for digital storytelling to promote community participation and support learner voice and agency in community discourse. Through this easily sharable medium, more stories may be accessible to more groups of people, disrupting the dominant understandings of the experiences of minority groups. One potential benefit of this proliferation of individual stories is to negate the essentialization of group narratives through the telling of complex, multifaceted stories that can live in the intersectionality of lived experiences. Pinkard, Erete, Martin, and de Roystan (2017) demonstrated that creation of narratives through digital media incorporated in project-based learning experiences could promote the telling of counter-narratives and support learner agency. However, they found disparate levels of perceived and acted agency in two different school contexts, suggesting situated and perhaps group-specific or individual-specific affordances of these experiences.

In this analysis, we examine the negotiation of power and authorship that occurred as a group of five sixth-grade girls created a digital story of climate change action. We aim to understand how youths were positioned and positioned themselves as authors of their own and their shared stories, and the implications of this for how they took agency in the storytelling and filmmaking processes. We examine instances of successful and contested bids for positions of power and authorship, and consider the processes that informed whose story(ies) were ultimately reified on film.

Methodology

Context and Participants

Manzanita School (pseudonym) is a K-8 inclusive school with some Spanish immersion features in the western United States. When this study took place, many students reported as "Socioeconomically Disadvantaged" (69%). Most students (82%) reported as "Hispanic or Latino," with "Asian" being the next highest reported category (6%). The sixth-grade class consisted of 60 students, whose ethnicity broadly matched the overall school population. Here, we focus specifically on five out of the thirty students in Ms. C's (pseudonym) class who participated in a digital storytelling and science curriculum pilot implementation.

Curriculum Overview

The "Green Ninja" is a curriculum development effort to engage middle school students in climate change science and action through humorous educational films, a Next Generation Science Standards (NGSS)-aligned science curriculum, and digital storytelling. The Green Ninja curriculum, nicknamed GENIE, is divided into multiple sections, first introducing students to the science surrounding climate change. In this unit, students learn about the types of data that scientists use to understand climate patterns, how to interpret that data, how their own habits and patterns of energy usage impact the earth, and the causes and consequences of climate change. The second section is about the art of storytelling and how to create a compelling story arc, and introduces them to cinematography practices. The last section of the curriculum invites students to create their own story and film as a group that will help educate or inspire others to act on climate change. The students also created a written portfolio to contextualize the science and intentions of their film.

Data and Analysis

This study is contextualized in a larger iterative design-based research (DBIR) study (Barab, 2014), which focused on the iterative design of the GENIE curriculum and how it mediated student learning about climate science and/or empowered students to engage in climate action through multidisciplinary science filmmaking (Walsh & Cordero, 2019). Here, we use cross-case analysis to examine the experiences of each student who was part of the Sapphire Table Group and who collaborated to create a single story and film. Data were collected over five weeks in spring 2017, and included survey assessments, curricular artifacts, classroom observations, and interviews. The study was bracketed by two pre- and post-assessments, one focused on climate science content and practices, and one focused on identity and agency with respect to science and the environment. Classroom observations included video and audio recordings of 23 curricular days. Over 25 hours each, audio and video data were collected of the Sapphire Table Group. Observations also included qualitative field noting (c.65 pages). We collected the student-made videos and associated science portfolios and conducted semi-structured interviews with students and the teacher at the end of the unit. Student interviews focused on their experience with and perception of the curriculum, climate change, and storytelling. Interviews totaled about 3.5 hours of video and audio, and interview durations ranged from 22 minutes to 74 minutes.

We used a grounded analysis method in which inductive, emergent coding led to theory development through an iterative process; in this way, the theory was "grounded" in the data (Lofland, Snow, Anderson, & Lofland, 2007). After the curriculum enactment, the data corpus was reviewed for "codable moments," moments that stood out as salient (Saldana, 2008, p. 16). We began the coding process with initial codes to yield emergent categories, which we refined by reexamining codes and categories, yielding concepts and themes for theory development. The major emergent themes coded included: agency/sphere of control ("I don't have the right stuff"); positioning—self, other ("Alexis, you're making this so hard"); and role—expand, constrain, enforce/define ("you're the filming person, so yeah you technically are the director"). Throughout the analytical process, we used memos to record procedures, initial analytical thoughts, coding categories' interconnectedness, and emerging themes with examples, and to "exhaust" our thinking about the topic and make sense of a large data set (Lofland et al., 2007, pp. 209–210).

Researcher Positioning

As case studies are qualitative in nature and any interpretation of events is necessarily subjective, it is important to recognize that the researcher is the instrument of qualitative research analysis (Borman, Clarke, Cotner, & Lee, 2006, p. 130). First, we consider the importance of our positioning as white female researchers in a predominately Hispanic/Latinx classroom, and that the focal students are all female students of color. To a large extent, we were outsiders in this community, which shapes and potentially limits our perspective. Researcher Walsh (Elly) was the principal investigator on the project and attended about half of the class periods, while researcher Smullen (Liza) attended all class meetings and developed stronger relationships with the student participants. Initially, we were both more observers, seeking to understand the norms of the classroom. However, as we grew to know the students more fully, we were also seen as content experts and were sometimes positioned as resources for students; in the story-making section of the curriculum, we also became a sounding board for students to bounce ideas off. While we began observations with a very broad set of research questions, over time they narrowed as we made notes of salient features, and these evolved over time. Initial written observations were mostly about what was said but expanded into visible markings of engagement or disengagement (waving at teammates, putting head down on desk), eventually making bracketed notes of implied or expressed emotions.

Findings

Overview

In this analysis, we described how students negotiated their roles in the story and filmmaking processes. Across the student cases, we saw that a student's positioning enabled her to bid for certain roles and be seen as productive in certain ways. For example, the author role (which the students created, defined, and negotiated the responsibilities for) was a way for students to impose their own structures over the process and thus create their own spheres of control. Enacting specific roles enabled students to exercise their agency over both the story plot and process (Figure 10.1). Students positioned others and themselves in certain roles, which led to the empowerment or denial of agency. While the roles of author, actress, director, and set manager (costumes, cue cards, setting) were outlined by the group early on, the perceived value of participation in each of these roles shifted throughout the story development process. In the analysis below, we first present the story created by the group, and then examine the roles taken on by Eva, Lena, and Alexis. We specifically explore how group negotiations constrained and afforded empowerment, voice, and agency during filmmaking.

Story Overview

The Sapphire Table Group's story for their film focused on the implications of climate change for humans. Lena's interest in the personal ramifications of the effects of climate change were clear early in the curriculum, when she asked, "but what does that mean for *us*?" (Lena, day 3). Alexis revealed her interest in "how it affects other people [when a climate disaster] happens to their, to like their daily life" (Alexis, exit interview). The major plot points and characters for the group's final film were drawn from Lena's story about twins who were opposites of each other but had to work together to help the environment, and Naomi's story of an old lady who goes back in time. The final plot of the story involved Rhonda (an old lady who lives in a dystopian future) traveling in time to meet twins Laila (who cares about the environment) and

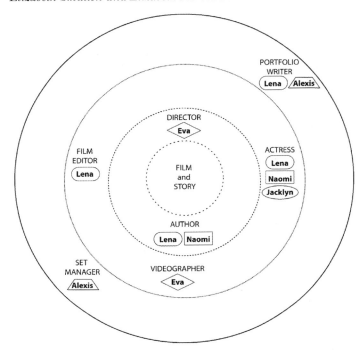

Figure 10.1 The roles each student took on in relation to the construction of the story and film. Roles are visualized in concentric circles, with the innermost circle being the positions of greatest agency to affect the story and film, and the outermost being least agency to affect the story and film. Negotiations could occur within a circle, as well as across circles, as indicated by the dashed boundaries. Each student is outlined by a distinct shape.

Mary (who likes robots). Rhonda switches the twins' minds, so the two sisters must learn to see each other's point of view. In the process, Rhonda loses her memory and recruits Laila (who now has the mind of Mary) to plant evil seeds that will emit carbon dioxide like factories do (instead of removing it from the atmosphere as plants normally do). The story resolves when Laila confesses to Mary and the sisters work together to confront Rhonda, who regains her memory and helps them pick up the evil seeds, preventing further harm to the environment.

Eva: Bidding to Be a Director

Eva identified as Mexican/Hispanic and was interested in a career as an emergency room doctor. She was present for 20.5 days of curriculum, and her presence had a significant influence on the group. In Ms. C's exit interview, she characterized Eva as a "second mother" to the group, and

Contested Agency and Authorship   261

someone who "tries to do the right thing" even if it's "not received very well" by her groupmates. Students positioned Eva as the director, reinforced that position, and allowed her to have a major influence on what made it on the camera. Even before the iPad came out for filming, Eva was allowed to direct her group into their roles of actor or author, tell specific students what to work on, and generally bid for and receive recognition as a leader in the group. As soon as roles were introduced, Naomi and Lena asked to act, and Eva stated she would be the one filming (in quotations double parentheticals indicate gestures and context, two slashes "//" indicate an interruption, and two or more colons "::" indicate an extended sound):

EVA: Are we going to be acting? ((holds up her drawing of the characters so far))
NAOMI: I wanna be the old lady! ((raises hand)) I wanna be the old lady. ((Alexis and Lena laugh))

[…]

EVA: Are we gonna be acting, or are we gonna be animating? I wanna be acting. ((uptone))
LENA: I wanna act, I wanna act.
ALEXIS: Can I be the one—
EVA: //I'll be the one who's filming everything.
ALEXIS: //Darn i:::t.
EVA: You ((to Alexis)) can help Naomi looking an old lady.
NAOMI: You can be Mary.
ALEXIS: ((pfft)) No.
LENA: I'll act Laila.
NAOMI: ((pointing at Alexis)) You'll be Mary.
ALEXIS: No::o. ((high pitched)) I don't wanna act.
LENA: ((points at self)) I'll act Laila and Mary.

Eva asserts herself as a director who is in charge of the group. She suggests that the story should be told with live actors, and Naomi physically raises her hand, the classroom normative way to attract a teacher's attention, when she makes her bid to play her character in the group's film. Lena also states her desire to act as her two characters (which is successful). Alexis, however, is not allowed to finish her request to be cinematographer before Eva asserts herself as the one behind the camera, in charge of the filming. Although Alexis voices her disappointment, Eva immediately tells Alexis what she could do instead and assigns her a supporting role.

Throughout that day, Eva continues to assert herself as in charge of filming, appearing to dance around the idea of being jokingly in charge and seriously in charge:

262 *Elizabeth Smullen and Elizabeth M. Walsh*

EVA: ((looking at Lena)) If you laugh, we're re-taping this whole thing. Just so you know. This director is bossy.
LENA: Okhhhhkay ((laughing. Alexis is also laughing and leaning over))
EVA: ((leans forward)) This director is bossy. ((Alexis and Lena laugh and lean over again))
LENA: I'm not the director, I'm the actor—
NAOMI: ((inaudible, in her narrator voice))
LENA: *You're* the director. ((holding hand toward Eva))

In this exchange, Eva is positioning herself as being in charge of the filming process. She is referring to herself by her role, claiming the title of "this director." She is also giving herself permission to be "bossy" about what is allowed on the film for the group's final project. The term "bossy" takes on more importance as the group continues to interact. Eva suggests that her opinion matters the most, because she is allowed to demand that the actors redo their scenes until she is satisfied. The other group members appear to laughingly acknowledge both her title ("director") and the associated description ("bossy"), although it appears that Lena may be misattributing the bossy term to herself. She appears confused, and finds it necessary to clarify that she is not the director. In so doing, she reinforces Eva's role as director and her own as actor. There is no contestation of Eva's ownership of the filming process, although there is continued negotiation over the leadership of the group in the classroom space.

While at the end of that day a struggle between Lena and Eva to assert themselves as in charge arose when Eva implied Lena was "bossy," in general, for taking the lead in introducing the group members to a visiting film mentor, Eva was allowed to exercise her role of director by redefining the roles of her other group members. For example, Eva reinforced both Lena's and Naomi's role as authors:

LENA: Naomi, you need to focus on the story. (inaudible)
EVA: No. No. No—*you and her* have to be working on the story. (inaudible)

In this exchange, Lena and Eva are both enforcing the role of author as being in charge of the storyline and positioning Naomi as an author. However, Lena's bid to take charge of other group members' roles was denied by Eva, who insisted that Lena was an author, too, and thus needed to focus on the story. Eva asserted her power over the responsibilities of other group members, expanding her role of director to include the definition of responsibilities for other roles and making sure they do not overlap. This positioning of Lena as a storyteller contributed to the cementation of Lena's identity as an author, not the leader, for the rest of the unit.

Contested Agency and Authorship 263

In this way, Eva declared herself as the group's director, established the responsibility of her role (initially as in charge of the film), and negotiated the expansion of her purview (to include the ability to redefine the roles and associated responsibilities of other group members). She enacted her role by asserting her agency over the future filming process ("if you laugh, we're re-taping this whole thing") and her group members' roles ("*you and her* have to be working on the story"). As the unit continued, she exercised more authority over group decisions.

Eva also used the agency afforded her by her director positionality to bid for a good school identity—directing her group members to do well on the assignment. Eva repeatedly drew her group's attention to the fact that if they did not do what was required, their grade would suffer: "Story story story. Story. Honestly, we're gonna get Fs if we don't do the story" (day 13), "hey, we're not getting an F just because we're not getting along" (day 15). By putting the group's efforts on a scale of school worth (the grading system), she emphasized the importance of doing well in school, and leveraged this importance to strengthen her position as leader.

Eva also deferred to the teacher's authority in a bid to be positioned as successful at school. When Ms. C noticed the group having difficulties resolving their storyline toward the close of a class period, she came over and tried to facilitate a brainstorm. After this was unsuccessful, she suggested a plot of her own (day 15):

MS. C: So what's this magical—maybe there's a fruit that's gonna start sucking up the carbon? Making the environment better. And then she's gonna realize that they need to stop producing it. There's your story. Let's go.

NAOMI: Ye:::ah. ((neutral face, sounds flat))

EVA: Wait, what. Can you repeat that? Let me write it on a post-it—where are the post-its?

ALEXIS: ((speaking quickly, hands Eva a post-it pad)) Here here here. Write write write.

EVA: Okay, what did you say Ms. C?

Eva immediately tried to implement the storyline that the teacher had suggested. On one hand, this may be interpreted as a way to resolve the disagreements about the group plot; however, the impact of this uptake was to effectively silence the voices of her group and magnify the voice of the teacher. Eva used her agency as the director to steer her group toward the plot that the teacher suggested rather than successfully inviting her groupmates to have their voices heard in the story. Eva's positionality as the director resulted in the expansion of the teacher's influence over the group's plot.

The storyline remained somewhat in flux, as each group member continued to negotiate for the plot they wanted to see, and Eva's bids for

264 *Elizabeth Smullen and Elizabeth M. Walsh*

control were not always successful. For example, Eva tried to write lines for the story she wanted to tell, and the authors/actresses pushed back against her version of the story (day 20). On this day, Naomi stood up to her in defense of Lena and the existing story, stating: "No. We're saying that we should just change our lines [that Eva had written]" (Naomi, day 20). This was a direct challenge to the story direction Eva was trying to implement and involved a long discussion among the actors and the director. Eventually Eva acquiesced to the authors: "Okay, so why don't you guys just make up the story and I'll just film it" (day 20). After more discussion, and as Naomi and Jacklyn continued to consider the order and content of the scenes for the original story, Eva loudly tore up the lines for the scenes she wrote as she stared at her two groupmates. This (only about ten minutes) incident showed Eva in an unsuccessful bid to steer the story in her own direction, and also illustrated the agency of the actors to stand up for their roles in the story.

However, generally Eva's authority was felt even when she wasn't there. In one instance, Eva was missing for the beginning of class while Lena and Naomi worked to revise their story because Alexis did not want to appear onscreen.

LENA: I came up with my story and it's being demolished. My story's being demolished.
NAOMI: Where's the other one?
LENA: We're rewriting it.
NAOMI: Why?
LENA: Eva's orders.

Even though the discussion above was taking place while Eva was absent from the group, it is clear that Eva was perceived to be in charge, and that if she had decided the story needed to be altered, it was up to the authors to change it. Again, Eva's agency as director and her identity as a good student led her to both assert the changes suggested by an outside adult were vital and also provided leverage to support her perceived importance of those changes. When the two authors tried to convince Alexis to act rather than have them rewrite the story, Lena and Naomi couldn't get Alexis to agree. Lena declared: "this is why we need Eva." The implication is that if Eva had been there, Alexis would have listened to her and done as she said because she was the group leader.

Lena: Bidding to Be an Author

Lena identified as Japanese and Mexican, was proud of being trilingual, and was very active in the school's STEM club. She was very excited about engineering, loved to take things apart and try to put them back together, and planned to become a mechanical engineer. In the climate change curriculum, she took on the roles of author and actor, and established a pattern of oscillating between interested engagement, when she would ask questions and listen to answers, and extended periods of isolation during which she would refuse to work with her group.

After having shared their own individual story idea with the group, the students were asked to choose one or create a new story for the group to tell. Lena, often an outsider in the group, positioned herself here as a uniter and a person who could productively combine aspects of each person's story to make an interesting story for the group, where everyone has ownership over a piece.

EVA: So, would you guys like to create a combined story? [...]

LENA: My idea here is, remember I noticed an old lady, right? What if that old lady was your character?

NAOMI: All right.

LENA: And then Eva, you know how I said Laila thought technology was bad.

NAOMI: //Yeah, cuz—

LENA: Right? ((Eva nods)) In your story you said electric cars were better than normal cars. What if Laila (invented) an electric car and (tested it) with a normal car and saw electric cars were better and decides to build more and more electric cars. ((Eva nods))

By literally combining their three stories, Lena laid out a plan for each of them to take over a section of the story, enabling each author to shape their plot into something cohesive and at the same time personally relevant.

During the videoconference with the film expert, Lena and Naomi dominated the conversation to tell her what their story was about. When Eva and Alexis added comments or details, Lena and Naomi did not hesitate to correct them. By the end of the class, both Lena and Naomi had successfully bid for the role of author in their group, as well as actor, with each planning to play her own character(s) in the film.

Lena strongly identified with her characters and explicitly stated so: "since I really love robots, that's where I put Mary" (interview). She displayed strong ownership over her characters, taking the lead when discussing them both in the group and to outside adults. Lena would correct her other group members, too; when Naomi and Eva tried to explain "Laila is, like, nice" (Naomi) and "Mary is, like, bad" (Eva), Lena interrupted them to say, "Wait wait, I'll explain since they're my characters." In her explanations, Lena added nuance to the characterization of Laila and Mary, explaining that Mary "is not like a *bad* bad person," and provided a clarifying example—she "gets detention" but "doesn't care" about it. Instead, Mary cares about "technology" and "building robots." Mary also doesn't care much about the environment, which is in contrast

266 Elizabeth Smullen and Elizabeth M. Walsh

to her sister Laila, who "cares about the earth" and "doesn't like technology." Lena's section of the story revolved around her two characters coming to learn something from the other's perspective:

LENA: You know how people say technology is *bad*, it's not good for the earth. That's not 100% true. Technology is also, can influence the earth in a very good way. Ecofriendly technology can (can do that). And Mary learn—Laila learns that. Because she always thought technology was bad. And then Mary learns that saving the earth is also important, as ecofriendly technology. So that's kind of the moral of the story, not both of them are bad. (day 13)

Lena's story brings out the nuances of characterization, along with her empathy with these two characters, and strived to show that there are things we can learn from each other as people. Each sister finds value in the perspective of the other, and fights against the simplified narrative that all technology is bad.

Lena's classroom identity involved an oscillation between enthusiastic engagement with the material and her peers and resolute detachment. For example, Lena started off one day with interested questions for the teacher, asking how some of the effects of climate change "affect *us*?" (day 3). She worked with her group to discuss some of the personal implications of climate change ("this is causing climate change right now"). However, as this group discussion continued, other group members made a comment that Lena interpreted as them not knowing very much about Japan. Lena became upset with her group, disengaging from the conversation by reading a book under the table. Later, she laid her head down at the table. When Liza asked her if she was going to answer any more questions she responded by saying "I am too mad right now" to continue working (day 3).

During this class period, Lena's cultural identity became a wedge between herself and her group. Throughout the curriculum, there were many instances when Lena would get frustrated and intentionally disengage from her group. Her pattern of participation aligned with a classroom identity of someone who is willing to work hard and well with others until there was conflict, at which point her strategy was to remove herself from the situation (often with overt physical positions, such as leaving the group to go pick out a book to read, reading with her book on her desk in a way that blocked other group members, reading under her desk to avoid looking at her group and detection by the teacher, and putting her head down on her desk). Even though Lena was physically present for all 23 days of the curriculum, she exercised her agency to detach herself from uncomfortable situations regularly.

This pattern of engagement and detachment mirrored how Lena authored her section of the group's story, as she participated enthusiastically when the group solicited and encouraged her creativity, and quietly

Contested Agency and Authorship 267

refused to discuss her story when the group challenged her ideas or demanded changes. Both Lena and the teacher discussed with us that Lena was "in counseling" for "anger management issues." Because of this, disengaging may have been a coping strategy to remove herself from a threatening situation before her anger intensified. However, more than that, Lena appeared to have difficulty interacting with her peers when her identification with a valued role was under attack. When "Eva's orders" were to rewrite the story by striking out one of Lena's characters, Lena despaired: "My story's being demolished" (day 15). Lena clearly gave up, telling Naomi to write Lena's story for her: "Just write whatever I don't care" (day 15). When her identity as an author was under fire, Lena chose to detach herself from the story and refused to help with the plot development for an extended period, not speaking to her group again until the teacher and Liza both prompted her.

Lena also found that her role within the group as an author did not have as much power over the classroom interactions as that of director. When her peers were distracted by the costume props they had brought in, Lena watched them with a neutral expression that changed with her mounting frustration. She finally burst out:

LENA: Okay can we pay attention to the story now?
NAOMI: ((high pitched, fast)) I am paying attention to the story! ((lower voice)) You're the one who wasn't paying attention to the story.
EVA: ((quiet voice)) And to our conversation earlier.
(six-second pause) ((Lena takes a deep breath and puts her hand over her face))
LENA: ((high pitched)) Fine then. ((emphatically)) if you think I'm *that* not paying attention to the story, maybe I *shouldn't.* ((turns away from group, pulls knees up and puts head on knees, puts hand over face))
NAOMI: ((low, quiet voice)) You weren't before, so—

Here, we see Lena made a bid to take charge of the classroom space, trying to get her group back on track. However, her group pointed out her previous lack of engagement (earlier this lesson, when she put her head down instead of engaging in plot discussions) and Lena responded, clearly upset, and put her head down again. In this exchange, her bid to take charge over the classroom space, and the actions of her group, was denied. Her group decided that her oscillations weren't worth dealing with and were upset that their earlier attempts to pull Lena into the storyline discussion were ineffective. So, when Lena decided to try and help the group get back on task, she was met with resentment and resistance.

The contested positionings and shifting value of the director and author roles were personified in the negotiation over who was "bossy" and "bossiness." Bossiness can be considered a negative framing of behavior that might otherwise be seen as leadership and was used by the group members to designate someone who was attempting to assert their control on the film or story. Initially, as described above, Eva claimed the right to be "bossy" as the leader, and this was seen as appropriate to her role. However, Lena's efforts to take control were positioned as "bossy" and inappropriate given her author role and perhaps her social positioning in the group. Lena told us in her interview that she was new to the school, having transferred at the end of fifth grade, whereas most of the rest of the class had been together since kindergarten. She told us that she didn't have a lot of friends and could be an outsider sometimes. She stated that she was not "charismatic," a trait often associated with leadership positions, and indeed her bids for authority were often much more fraught than Eva's. Eventually the "bossy" label was applied to Lena, in a negative way, subverting Lena's attempts to agentically lead the film process, and was applied so pointedly to Lena that in retrospect during analysis we considered that it might be considered an instance of bullying.

For example, at the end of the lesson on day 13, during the videoconference with the film expert, Lena reinforced each person's role by introducing them to the adult by their role:

LENA: ((pointing at Eva)): She's our director. She's our filmer.
((Lena and Naomi shout for Alexis to come on camera))
EVA: ((looking back and forth between the film expert and Lena)) (I thought) the director is supposed to be bossy, but the actors are bossy to:::o.

Toward the end of the unit, the group was tasked with creating a shared document on their Chromebooks. At the start, they first engaged in typing random words on the screen to make each other laugh. When Lena asked a serious question of the group, and chastised the group for being off task, the word "BOSSY" appeared on the screen in very large and bold font. Someone immediately typed over it "SO TRUE" in the same large font. Lena disengaged from her bid to take charge, but after a while tried again, trying to organize the group to work, and it appeared that two people wrote "bossy" on the screen at the same time. In response, Lena raised her hands in surrender and closed her laptop lid, saying: "I'm done. If this is how you guys get I'm not gonna work. I'm not gonna work if you guys don't work" (day 19). The negotiation over who got to be "bossy" and the appropriateness of bids for control constrained Lena's participation and ultimately her voice in the film process, while allowing Eva greater positions of power and greater agency in the shaping of the final product.

At other times, however, Lena's position as an author was considered a creative and productive position. Group members referred to their story as "your [Lena's] story" on multiple occasions throughout the storytelling portion of the unit. Even after they had combined their stories

Contested Agency and Authorship 269

into a group story, they would often reference the group story as belonging to Lena. When the group was divvying up the work for the portfolio, Eva acknowledged Lena's expertise: "Why doesn't Lena do the log line, because she knows more about the story" (Eva, day 19). Others consistently acknowledged Lena's leadership in the story, asking her advice for characterization and plot.

Alexis: Bidding Not to Act

Alexis identified as American and was interested in becoming a marine veterinarian. She was present for only 11 days of the curriculum; notably, she was absent for the last four days, and so did not have as much direct input into the final filming process. In her interview, Ms. C described Alexis as "kind of a survivor, going through lots of challenging living situations" which included homelessness that may have contributed to her high number of absences. Alexis's contributions to the story were framed by her desire not to appear on camera, which was initially accepted but later became a source of tension and eventually resulted in them recruiting Jacklyn into the group to take on an actress role.

The trajectory of Alexis's participation in the filmmaking was set in motion by her unsuccessful bid to become the director in the exchange presented earlier:

ALEXIS: Can I be the one—
EVA: //I'll be the one who's filming everything.
ALEXIS: //Darn i:::t.

This dialogue, first presented above, shows Eva's successful bid for director coming at Alexis's expense. Her bid to take on a specific role ("Can I be the one—") was dismissed by Eva, who cut her off before she could complete her thought and instead assigned Alexis a supporting role. The lack of challenge to this assignment by her other group members, who all were able to choose their own role, suggests that the group had already positioned Alexis as lower in agency than other group members. After her first abortive attempt to take on a valued, productive role, Alexis's participation became mainly characterized by seeking to not take roles on. Friction in the group was caused by her refusal to act on camera, a decision that necessitated Jacklyn's inclusion in the group.

After Eva became director, in the rest of the conversation about assigning group roles, Alexis was the only student to position herself as wanting the absence of something, saying, "I don't wanna act." Although Naomi tried to assign Alexis the role of actress, Alexis refused, and the group then decided how Alexis could be productive without filming or acting. Eva initially assigned Alexis to a role of supporting the actors, positioning her as someone who can help the group, but should not take charge

270 *Elizabeth Smullen and Elizabeth M. Walsh*

over the group's actions or the story itself. In further negotiations over who would take on what role, this positionality was not challenged by the other group members, including Alexis herself. Working together, the group decided that Alexis could oversee costumes and cue cards.

The next day, however, Alexis found herself at odds with Naomi and Lena over her refusal to act. In one exchange, Naomi convinced Lena that Alexis's choice to not act made it hard for the group to tell their story:

NAOMI: ((groans)) Alexi::::s. You're making this so hard.
LENA: She just doesn't want to act.
NAOMI: Which is making it hard.
LENA: Yeah, she's making it hard. Alexis, we want, we want you to participate.
ALEXIS: I'm just listening.
LENA: We just want you to participate, if you—
NAOMI: In the movie.
LENA: If you that badly *hate* being on camera then fine. Doing absolutely nothing. If you want that, then fine.

In this exchange, Naomi and Lena position Alexis as unproductive, and their use of pronouns underscores this positioning. At first Naomi suggests she is talking directly to Alexis ("Alexi::::s. You're"), but Lena shifts the conversation to being about Alexis, saying "she" doesn't want to act ("she" being an indirect address, which excludes the subject from interaction). Naomi and Lena, the two authors and actresses, then try to appeal directly to Alexis saying "we want you" to participate. The "we" signals the united front of the two authors, and the "you" positions the address directly at Alexis. This use of pronouns can be revealing, as Wortham and Reyes (2015) explain: "Distinguishing between 'we' and 'they,' for example, does more than refer to two groups. It also presupposes a boundary between one group that includes the speaker and another group that excludes him or her" (p. 5). These speech acts appear to indicate a united front of two authors against Alexis, whose role was under debate.

Lena took Naomi's initial view of Alexis being difficult to the extreme view that Alexis wants to do "absolutely nothing" for their film. This contrasts with the excitement of the previous day. In the previous session, Alexis's contribution was validated and valued by all group members, but today Alexis's refusal to act was cast as a refusal to participate productively. The possible paths to valued participation had been narrowed by the two group members who planned to act. This negative positioning of Alexis and her non-acting role continued throughout filming. Despite the negative pushback—such as when Alexis was positioned as someone who was unwilling to contribute to the group by Lena: "that's basically saying you don't want to put any effort in to this film" (Lena, day 15)—Alexis successfully avoided being on camera.

After this exchange, Alexis used her agency within the group to negotiate for fewer contributions to the storyline and less responsibility. When the idea was put forward of a narrator and holding the lines, Alexis claimed this role for herself, and even drew the group's attention to the fact that this role doesn't demand much of her, saying "it's kind of easy—I'm just holding up the lines" (day 13). In this supporting role, however, her agency to influence the story was minimal. From the beginning, Alexis tried to emphasize her support of her group members' story, and repeatedly told Naomi "I like *your* idea" for a story (day 13). Indeed, since she did not bring a story to the table (having been absent the previous two days), she may also have felt that she had less right to demand a specific role in the group story.

Later, Alexis stated very clearly that she felt no agency over what happened in the story: "yeah, you guys give me the lines of what you want to say and then I just write them and then I'll just show them to you" (Alexis, day 13). This positions the story as very clearly not belonging to Alexis as it is up to the authors to write the lines for what they want to happen in their story. There are similar instances of Alexis using her agency to shirk being in charge, and she also positioned herself as selectively available. For example, when she was charged with drawing one of Lena's characters, she would take a suggestion from Lena and then refuse to respond to further input until she was satisfied with the first idea (even when Lena tried to tell her multiple things at once).

Thus, Eva's act of assigning Alexis a supporting role positioned Alexis as someone who could help the group but should not take charge over the group's actions or the story itself. Alexis's language and actions within the group reinforced this position.

Discussion

Supporting Youth Voice Through Digital Media

This curriculum encouraged students to explore different ways of looking at science, storytelling, and their expertise in each. Students were given the freedom to try on different roles, which may have encouraged them to leverage their experiences to create spaces and stories with personal meaning. Lena's story, for example, mirrored her own negotiation between engagement and disengagement, her own valuing of nuance and multiple perspectives, and the need for resolution between two possible selves. The negotiation process to produce the final story was very fluid, with the sphere of control shifting, depending on who was present and the feelings of the group. We saw that through this process, students were able to "play" with their identities and draw on a variety of resources

272 *Elizabeth Smullen and Elizabeth M. Walsh*

to improvise their agency throughout the process. While their sense of ownership fluctuated, in the end, each student in the group was proud of the film they had created. Naomi summarized the group's efforts as "everyone got a little bit of their own story." No one's individual story was told in its entirety, but each member was able to contribute something to the final version. This aligns to prior work that suggests that youth construction of digital narratives can support identity work (e.g., Pinkard, Erete, Martin, and de Roystan, 2017).

Identity Work and Agency under Threat

While overall students reported that they found the digital storytelling experience engaging, we documented instances in which youth agency and identity work were contested. In their longitudinal study, Calabrese Barton et al. (2013) documented how youth identity work is dynamic and potentially contentious, and argue that transformations can best occur when identities are recognized over time. This resonates with Gee's (2001) assertion that identities must be recognized to be accepted. In this study, we saw that when roles and positions were valued by the group, such as Eva's position as a director, agency over the story generally increased. However, when a bid for a particular role or possible self (e.g., Alexis's bid to be director) was not recognized, that trajectory and possibility could become unavailable. We saw this oscillation particularly with Lena, who adjusted her participation greatly depending on the recognition of her bids for particular kinds of identities. Her role as author was valued, but her role of leader was rejected and she was accused of being "bossy."

In their examination of coproduction of identities through group position, Goodwin and Alim (2010) point out the influence of social aggressions within an all-girl peer group: "In sharp contrast to the paradigm that asserts that females are socialized to be nonconfrontational, ethnographic work and recent studies in psychology of adolescent girls have documented forms of social aggression (Underwood 2003) in girls' interactions" (p. 183). In their analysis, they discussed how girls reproduced characterizations that enforced race, class, and gender labels without necessarily stating them explicitly (Goodwin & Alim, 2010). Much like the situation characterized by Goodwin and Alim (2010), Lena's outsider position became more entrenched as the group interacted. Such repeated instances that are dangerous for thickening a student's identity, and the thickening of a student in a negative role can be detrimental not only in their current science class, but can lead to their disaffiliation with science or STEM completely, removing it from their range of possible future selves. These processes are illustrated in longterm case studies, such as Wortham's "Tyisha" (2004), Langer-Osuna's "Brianna" (2011), and Calabrese Barton et al.'s "Diane" (2013).

Contested Agency and Authorship 273

In addition to disparities and potential constraints on kinds of identity work, we also saw a differential ability for the girls to take agency in telling a personally consequential story. Within the group, not everyone's story was told, and notably Alexis had little or no input in the final plot. This was due in part to her absences, and while it makes sense that the student who missed the most classes would potentially have the least contribution to the story arc, it was clear that she felt her voice had not been heard in the telling of the story. While as a group, creating the film allowed for a group voice to be heard, some individuals felt that their own personal voice was limited by the dynamics of the process, problematizing the relationship between collective and individual agency.

In some climate change response literature, there is an assumption that community agency corresponds to increased perceptions of individual agency. This assumption presupposes that the coming together of individuals with limited agency can lead to a community with greater agency, and that the collective positively impacts the whole. This was demonstrated in Hall, Taplin and Goldstein's (2009) participatory action research project, in which participating in a legislative endeavor led individuals to experience an increased sense of agency as they grew in knowledge of the skills and steps needed to successfully affect change and were able to distribute tasks across individuals with time and expertise. This resonance is not always the case, however, as described by Otsuki, Jasaw, and Lolig (2017) who found a separation between the individual agency felt by four farmers and their ability to take collective action and bolster community agency. Further, Burgess (2006) warns that the proliferation of digital media, which in some ways has led to the democratization of media production, may act in counter-purpose to promote community agency. She argues that creativity does not equate to agency, and that, in taking on particular roles and presenting one's voice in digital discourse, one can constrain one's agentic self by referencing limited cultural roles. This perspective resonates with our findings and suggests that more attention should be paid to the relationships that mediate transformations of collective and individual agency. Though individual and community agency are often considered together as having a reciprocal relationship, it is clear that the relationship is more fraught and we need a more robust conceptualization of their interactions.

Whose Story Is Told?

For researchers interested in promoting community voice, either in social decision making around a wicked problem like climate change, or in scientific institutions, it is important to consider whose voice(s) ultimately are privileged in community discussions. Approaches for increasing community agency in science or socioscientific issues may focus specifically on individual or collective voices. Designers, for example, may target a specific community or population, perhaps bounded by a geographic area (e.g., a specific neighborhood in a city). However, it is important to consider that even in participatory design assessments of community needs, not all individuals' voices will be equally privileged. In this analysis, Eva's leadership guided the direction of the film, while Naomi and Lena's personally consequential narratives were heard in the story told. Lena, however, found it difficult to participate in the collective narrative when she felt that her own story was not being valued. Though Lena was willing to fight for her story to be included, Alexis, due to her absences, did not even share her own story. Alexis's voice was ultimately barely present in the final film. This mirrors concerns about who has the opportunity to participate in collective decision making and thus community agency for specific aims; school for Alexis was often inaccessible for reasons outside of her control. It is worth underscoring that Alexis was interested in a STEM career, wanting to be a marine veterinarian; however, because of absences and social dynamics her voice was effectively sidelined, perpetuating and perhaps exacerbating the marginalization she already experienced in her life. In a worst-case scenario, repeated instances of marginalization and devaluing of her voice in and out of science classes, like that experienced in the filmmaking, could dissuade her from pursuing her desired career. The loss of Alexis's voice cautions us to be mindful of how we may miss key perspectives in both science classrooms and community partnerships and thus perpetuate persistent inequities.

In addition to the negotiation between the group members, it is important to note that in this analysis the teacher also had a significant voice in the room, playing a pivotal role in shaping the ultimate story told. This has direct implications for conducting group digital storytelling in classrooms, and more indirect implications for community partnerships. In this study, though Ms. C. generally encouraged the creativity of her students, we noted episodes where the teacher's evaluation of situations could have served to limit the agency of students (e.g., "That's your story"). There were also moments when the teacher actively countered positioning by a student (e.g., when Lena chose to read rather than work with her group, Ms. C would often say "Lena, put the book away"). However, we also observed that some of these moments were transformed by the students into actionable items that led to powerful positionality within the group (such as Eva's use of Ms. C's story suggestion to reinforce her own authority).

The teacher's role here was clearly influential in the ultimate direction of the story. While it is difficult to say with certainty how her suggestions and directives were received by each group member, in multiple instances, the voice of educational authority was magnified by Eva. When Ms. C suggested the magical fruit plot, Eva immediately tried to implement that storyline, using her agency as director to encourage her group members to accept it. We saw a similar phenomenon in the videoconference with the film expert, who provided advice during a consultation when story ideas were still nascent, and thus may have served to constrain the voices of the students by passing judgment on potential plotlines before the students had a chance to test them for themselves. The film expert mentioned that the story seemed a little confusing, with too many main characters and two different plotlines. While she did not explicitly state they pare down the cast or the plot, she did cite points of confusion and suggested the Sapphire Table consult with other groups to make sure that others understood the story. Again, the suggestions made by the film expert were taken up by the group, and particularly by Eva, as necessary changes.

We are not suggesting that the influence of adults on youth stories is in all ways negative; indeed, the group may have continued to struggle internally to create their story without some guidance. However, it is worth noting that the final story told was not, in fact, purely constructed of youth voices, but rather, drawing on one of Holland et al.'s (2001) conceptualization of agency, the adult voice was used as an available resource in the space for authoring in which agency is improvised. Similarly, the threat of an overly authoritative outside voice is of concern in participatory projects and research-practice partnerships in cases where one group may be recognized as an authority. This underscores the importance of considering whose voice is privileged even in an environment meant to support and represent the needs and solutions of many. To better understand these, further research should examine more types of student or community groups in more diverse contexts.

Conclusion

Responding effectively to environmental changes and promoting students from a diversity of backgrounds in science requires challenging normative understandings of the what and who of science, as well as desettling persistent narratives of the characteristics of particular groups. Digital filmmaking experiences, like the one discussed here, foreground personally consequential narratives and thus have the potential to bring to social conversations and scientific enterprises ways of knowing, acting, and valuing that will promote a more equitable future. This analysis demonstrated the potential opportunity afforded by digital storytelling for youth to tell personally consequential stories, take agency in crafting the direction of their story, and play with possible future selves. However, we also found that agency and identity work was constrained by the ways in which the group negotiated positions, recognized the value of those positions, and promoted some voices over others. This finding has implications for the design of open-ended, creativity-focused projects that aim to promote a diversity of voices. It suggests that design of these curricula and learning experiences must critically attend to how each youth is positioned and who has agency to tell their story.

276 *Elizabeth Smullen and Elizabeth M. Walsh*

In many ways, these five girls were successful in telling a personally consequential climate action story that they took pride in and were eager to share with family and friends. This may support these youth to become agents of change within their communities in addressing environmental impacts. Ultimately, however, not all students had the same space for authorship, whether because of absences and thus lack of access to the creative space or due to interpersonal positioning. Similarly, not all individuals will be equally welcomed, empowered, or able to participate in community action around climate change, to the detriment of equitable social transformation and mitigation of climate impacts. Moving forward, it is important to further disentangle the processes that mediate relationships between individual and collective agency, with the aim of making sure all voices are represented.

Acknowledgment

This research was supported by funding from the National Science Foundation Directorate for Education and Human Resources award #151322.

References

Avraamidou, L., & Osborne, J. (2009). The role of narrative in communicating science. *International Journal of Science Education, 31*(12), 1683–1707.

Bang, M., & Marin, A. (2015). Nature-culture constructs in science learning: Human/non-human agency and intentionality. *Journal of Research in Science Teaching, 52*(4), 530–544.

Banks, J.A., Au, K.H., Ball, A.F., Bell, P., Gordon, E.W., Gutiérrez, K., … Zhou, M. (2007). Learning in in out of school in diverse environments: Life-long, life–wide, life-deep. The LIFE Center, Center for Multicultural Education, University of Washington.

Barab, S. (2014). Design-based research: A methodological toolkit for engineering change. In *The Cambridge handbook of the learning sciences, second edition.* Cambridge University Press.

Bell, P., Lewenstein, B., Shouse, A.W. & Feder, M.A. (Eds.). National Research Council. (2009). *Learning science in informal environments: People, places, and pursuits.* Board on Science Education, National Academy of Sciences. Washington, DC: The National Academies Press.

Borman, K., Clarke, C., Cotner, B., & Lee, R. (2006). Cross-case analysis. In J.L. Green, G. Camilli, & P.B. Elmore (Eds.), *Handbook of complementary methods in education research* (pp. 123–139). Mahwah, NJ: Lawrence Erlbaum Associates Publishers.

Burgess, J. (2006). Hearing ordinary voices: Cultural studies, vernacular creativity and digital storytelling. *Continuum, 20*(2), 201–214.

Calabrese Barton, A., & Tan, E. (2010). We be burnin'! Agency, identity, and science learning. *The Journal of the Learning Sciences, 19*(2), 187–229.

Calabrese Barton, A., Kang, H., Tan, E., O'Neill, T.B., Bautista-Guerra, J., & Brecklin, C. (2013). Crafting a future in science: Tracing middle school girls' identity work over time and space. *American Educational Research Journal, 50*(1), 37–75.

Carlone, H.B., Haun-Frank, J., & Webb, A. (2011). Assessing equity beyond knowledge- and skills-based outcomes: A comparative ethnography of two fourth-grade reform-based science classrooms. *Journal of Research in Science Teaching, 48*(5), 459–485.

Delpit, L.D. (1988). The silenced dialogue: Power and pedagogy in educating other people's children. *Harvard Educational Review, 58*(3), 280–298.

DeWitt, J., & Archer, L. (2015). Who aspires to a science career? A comparison of survey responses from primary and secondary school students. *International Journal of Science Education, 37*(13), 2170–2192.

Few, R., Brown, K., & Tompkins, E.L. (2011). Public participation and climate change adaptation: Avoiding the illusion of inclusion. *Climate Policy, 7*(1), 46–59.

Gee, J.P. (2001). Identity as an analytic lens for research in education. In W.G. Secada (Ed.), *Review of research in education* (pp. 99–126). Washington, DC: AERA.

Gibbons, P. (2014). *Scaffolding language, scaffolding learning: Teaching second language learners in the mainstream classroom* (pp. 57–60). Portsmouth, NH: Heinemann.

Goodwin, M.H., & Alim, H.S. (2010). "Whatever (neck roll, eye roll, teeth suck)": The situated coproduction of social categories and identities through stancetaking and transmodal stylization. *Journal of Linguistic Anthropology, 20*(1), 179–194.

Hall, N.L., Taplin, R., & Goldstein, W. (2009). Empowerment of individuals and realization of community agency. *Action Research, 8*(1), 71–91.

Holland, D., Skinner, D., Lachiotte, W., & Cain, C. (2001). *Identity and agency in cultural worlds.* Cambridge, MA: Harvard University Press.

Hull, G.A., & Katz, M. (2006). Crafting an agentive self: Case studies of digital storytelling. *Research in the Teaching of English, 41*(1), 43–81.

Intergovernmental Panel on Climate Change (IPCC). (2018). Summary for policymakers. *Global Warming of 1.5°C.*

Lambert, J. (2009). *Story circle: Digital storytelling around the world.* West Sussex, UK: Blackwell Publishing.

Lambert, J. (2013). *Digital storytelling: Capturing lives, creating community.* Routledge.

Langer-Osuna, J.M. (2011). How Brianna became bossy and Kofi came out smart: Understanding the trajectories of engagement for two group leaders in a project-based mathematics classroom. *Canadian Journal of Science, Mathematics and Technology Education, 11*(3), 207–225.

Lofland, J., Snow, D., Anderson, L., & Lofland, L. (2007). Developing analysis. In *Analyzing social settings a guide to qualitative observation and analysis* (pp. 195–219). US: Thomson Wadsworth.

McNeil, K.L., & Vaughn, M.H. (2012). Urban high school students' critical science agency: Conceptual understandings and environmental actions around climate change. *Research in Science Education, 42*, 373–399.

Olsson, L., Tschakert, P., Agrawal, A., & Eriksen, S.E. (2014). Livelihoods and poverty. In C.B. Field, V.R. Barros, D.J. Dokken, K.J. Mach, M.D. Mastrandrea, T.E. BIlir … L.L. White (Eds.), *Climate change 2014: Impacts, adaptation and* vulnerability. Part A: Global and sectoral aspects. Contribution of working group II to the fifth assessment report of the intergovernmental panel on climate change (pp. 793–832). Cambridge, UK and New York, NY: Cambridge University Press.

Otsuki, K., Jasaw, G.S., & Lolig, V. (2017). Linking individual and collective agency for enhancing community resilience in Northern Ghana. *Society and Natural Resources, 31*(2), 1–15.

Pelling, M. (2011). *Adaptation to climate change: From resilience to transformation.* Oxon UK and New York, NY: Routledge.

Pinkard, N., Erete, S., Martin, C.K., & de Roystan, M.M. (2017). Digital youth divas: Exploring narrative-driven curriculum to spark middle school girls' interest in computational activities. *Journal of the Learning Sciences, 26*(3), 477–516.

Rolón-Dow, R. (2011). Race(ing) stories: Digital storytelling as a tool for critical race scholarship. *Race Ethnicity and Education, 14*(2), 159–173.

Saldana, J. (2008). An introduction to codes and coding. In *The coding manual for qualitative researchers* (pp. 1–31). Sage.

Samaddar, S., Oteng-Ababio, M., Dayour, F., Ayaribila, A., Obeng, F.K., Ziem, R., & Yokomatsu, M. (2021). Successful community participation in climate change adaptation programs: On whose terms? *Environmental Management, 67,* 747–762.

Seyfang, G., & Smith, A. (2007). Grassroots innovations for sustainable development towards a new research and policy agenda. *Environmental Politics, 16*(4), 584–603.

Staley, B., & Freeman, L. (2017). Digital storytelling as student-centered pedagogy: Empowering high school students to frame their futures. *Research and Practice in Technology Enhanced Learning, 12*(21). http://dx.doi.org/10.1186/s41039-017-0061-9

Trott, C.D. (2019). Reshaping our world: Collaborating with children for community-based climate change action. *Action Research, 17*(1). http://dx.doi.org/10.1177/1476750319829209

Trott, C.D. (2020). Children's constructive climate change engagement: Empowering awareness, agency, and action. *Environmental Education Research, 26*(4), 532–554.

Underwood, M.K. (2003). *Social aggression in girls.* New York, NY: Guilford Press.

Walsh, E.M., & Cordero, E. (2019). Youth science expertise, environmental identity, and agency in climate action filmmaking. *Environmental Education Research, 25*(5), 656–677.

Wortham, S. (2004). From good student to outcast: The emergence of a classroom identity. *ethos, 32*(2), 164–187.

Wortham, S., & Reyes, A. (2015). *Discourse Analysis beyond the Speech Event.* Oxford, UK and New York, NY: Routledge.

Index

Abdulkarim, Zeena 44
abstract/concrete spectrum 83
abstraction 71, 83
acceptance 59
action 5–7, 12–15, 18, 20–21, 26–28, 35, 38, 42–52, 54–58, 60, 62, 64, 66–74, 76–78, 81–84, 86, 89–92, 97, 101–102, 117, 119–124, 126–128, 131–132, 134–139, 141, 143, 150, 155–156, 166, 174–176, 178, 180–182, 192–193, 195, 197–198, 206, 209–210, 214, 217–219, 221–227, 229–231, 233, 237, 245, 254–257, 267, 270–271, 273, 276–278; climate action 26, 28, 38, 43, 45, 47, 56, 64, 67, 123, 139, 197, 222–223, 257, 276, 278; collective action 51, 58, 90–91, 175, 181, 193, 197, 206, 273; cooperative action 71; environmental action 35, 51, 76–78, 81–82, 86, 89, 121, 138, 195, 237, 277; individual action 72, 81, 97, 180, 192, 197; resilience action 219, 221–222, 224–227, 229
action-oriented learning 28, 55, 57
active learning 126, 139, 143
activism 1, 43, 46, 50–55, 57–58, 60–62, 64–65, 67–71, 73, 98, 100, 102, 117, 133, 142, 222; *see also* youth activism
activist pedagogies 60
activity systems 176
actor 48, 70, 81, 85–86, 177, 180, 235, 252, 261–262, 264–265, 268–269
adaptation 2–5, 8–9, 11–18, 23–25, 29–34, 37, 83, 93, 142, 172–173, 181–182, 218–221, 226, 231, 251, 254, 277–278
adaptation planning 14

adaptation strategies 93, 219–221, 226
adaptive capacity 13, 33, 80
administrative support 190–191
advocacy 48, 117–118
affective 57, 86, 89–90, 176, 237
affective dimension 237
affective domain 176
African 10–11, 19, 31, 34–35, 69, 99, 123, 139, 148–149, 231; African communities 19; African ways of knowing 19
African American 10–11, 31, 35, 99, 123, 139; *see also* Black
agency 20, 22, 27–31, 33, 35, 37–38, 47–49, 51, 56, 58, 61, 70, 125–126, 133, 143, 146, 167, 171, 174–182, 184–188, 190–197, 228, 234, 237, 240, 252–261, 263–269, 271–278; children's agency 234, 237, 240; collective agency 20, 29, 252, 254, 276–277; community agency 252, 254, 273–274, 277; critical science agency 29, 35, 195, 277; epistemic agency 181, 188, 192, 194–195, 197; human agency 253–254, 276; individual agency 29, 48, 254, 273; learner agency 252; political agency 56; PST agency 185; relational agency 51; sense of agency 51, 61, 175, 177–178, 182, 184–185, 187–188, 190–192, 228, 273; teacher agency 176–178, 196; transformative agency 28, 30, 33, 37; youth agency 38, 47, 49, 272
agents of change 27–29, 119, 138, 176–177, 191, 195, 276
agriculture 19, 51, 125, 131–132, 139, 231, 233
aid 9–10, 108, 159, 164, 171

Index

AIR model 88–89, 93
air pollution 122, 128, 138, 144, 229
air quality 128
alarmists 101
Alaska 122, 234–236, 238–241, 243, 246, 248–251
Alaska Native 122, 234–235, 238–241, 243, 246, 248–250
Alaska Native children 234–235, 238, 240, 246, 248–250
algorithms 79
alt-right 100, 112
Amazon Rainforest 1, 43, 48
amplifying 23, 56
anger 54–55, 67, 78, 101, 152, 267
anthropocentrism 205–207
anthropogenic 12, 128, 172, 192, 235
antiracism 45, 98, 110
anxiety 54, 60–62, 64, 66, 71, 83, 237, 243–244, 249; eco-anxiety 54, 61
Appardurai, Anjali 46
Arctic 23, 32–33, 44, 233–235, 243, 248, 250–251
Argentina 47, 58
art 56, 70, 171, 184, 191, 208, 211–212, 218–221, 253, 257
Article 12, 47, 58
artifact 28–29, 176–177, 182–184, 191, 257
arts-informed 208, 212
Asian 1, 11, 17–18, 130, 138, 257
Asian American 1, 17–18
Asian Pacific Environmental Network 130, 138
assessment 32–34, 37, 93, 119, 124, 138, 142, 165–166, 168, 171–173, 257–258, 274, 277
assignment 152–153, 163–165, 177, 263, 269
asthma 122, 138
attitude change 27, 77
attitudes 27, 51, 74–78, 92, 94, 96, 159, 170, 172, 176, 231
Australia 1, 5, 44
Australian Youth Climate Coalition 44
authentic participation 20, 28
author 18, 20–25, 28, 48, 102–103, 145, 149, 152–154, 163, 177, 183, 198, 216, 221, 256, 259, 261–262, 264–265, 267–268, 270–272
authoring 253–254, 275
authority 49, 194, 200, 263–264, 268, 274–275

authorship 252–257, 259, 261, 263, 265, 267, 269, 271, 273, 275–277

Bahamas 71–72, 93, 146, 172
Bangladesh 26, 37, 44, 70
Bastida, Xiye 41, 49–50, 69
behavior 8, 16, 23, 27–28, 30, 33–34, 59, 64, 72–73, 75–81, 83, 85, 89, 92, 119–120, 122, 137, 140, 152, 156, 181, 194, 209, 236–237, 240, 267
behavior change 27–28, 30, 33, 119
behaviorally engaged 89
beliefs 7, 71, 73–75, 77–79, 82, 85, 92, 94, 96, 100, 176, 194, 230, 237
Bellamy, Joshua 136
bid 255, 257, 259, 261–265, 267–269, 272
Biden-Harris Administration 47
Bikini 9
Black 1, 6, 8, 10–11, 17–18, 32–33, 36, 41–42, 44, 49–55, 61, 68, 83, 102–103, 118, 122, 127–129, 133, 139–140, 143, 149, 151, 214, 220, 240; Black children 18; Black communities 128; Black neighborhoods 11, 103; Black populations 10, 128; Black women 53
Black Lives Matter 1
blame 23, 79, 180, 255
bossy 254, 262, 267–268, 272, 277
BP 102, 112
Brownhill, Leigh 110

California 66, 79–80, 90, 93–94, 139, 212, 235; Los Angeles 90; San Francisco Bay Area 10; wildfires 71, 93, 175
Callinicos, Alex 111
Cambodia 58
Canada 5, 54, 56, 58, 65–68, 206, 211, 216–217, 220, 225, 227, 231
Canadian 31–32, 35, 44, 53, 56, 60–61, 64, 66, 70, 198, 206, 208, 211–212, 218, 233, 250, 277
capacity 4, 12–13, 28, 30, 33, 35, 48, 51, 62, 80, 151, 168, 206, 228
capital 5–6, 71, 104, 111, 113
capitalism 7, 42, 44, 53, 55, 60, 67, 104–105, 108–113, 149, 206
capitalist democracy 108
carbon footprint 72–73, 174
carbon neutral 75

Index 281

carbon offsets 72
carbon pollution 101
career development 131
career path 125, 255
carework 179, 192
Caribbean 148–149, 151, 160, 165,
   168, 170–172
central planning 107–109
change-making 58–59
characterization 265–266, 269, 272
Charlottesville, VA 100
Chasing Coral 165
Chasinghorse, Quannah 44
Chesapeake Bay 18, 35
children 1, 4, 11, 18, 25, 31–32,
   36, 38, 46–49, 54–55, 62–70, 91,
   95–96, 108, 113, 122, 140, 143, 164,
   171, 178, 193, 195, 199, 214–215,
   217–232, 234–251, 277–278
Children's Environmental Rights 236
China 80
Cho, Ryan 56
cinematography 257
citizen 4, 15, 18, 21, 32, 34, 46, 60–61,
   64, 67, 69, 108, 121, 148, 151, 174,
   191, 195, 233, 251
citizenship 6, 60–61, 119–120, 122,
   195, 236
civil rights 1, 42–43, 127
Civil Rights Movement 42–43
classism 53
classroom 21, 32–33, 37–38, 55–57,
   59, 64–65, 69, 86, 90, 92, 129–130,
   141, 175, 177, 181–185, 187–188,
   190–192, 195–197, 203–204, 207,
   209, 211, 215, 232, 255, 257–258,
   261–262, 266–267, 274, 276–278
climate change education 1–3, 5, 7,
   9, 11, 13, 15–19, 21, 23–27, 29–37,
   39, 42, 55–58, 62–63, 65, 67–69, 96,
   115, 117–118, 125–127, 129–130,
   137, 141–143, 169, 174, 178–179,
   181–185, 196, 198, 206, 208, 211,
   214–215, 218, 227, 229, 232–236,
   238–240, 242–244, 246–249; *see also*
   climate education
climate change impact 1, 6, 8–9, 11,
   13, 24, 44, 50, 52, 56, 61, 128, 130,
   147, 163, 175, 179, 182–183, 192,
   226, 234
climate change policies 7, 130, 139
climate change solutions 117–118,
   129, 183, 192

climate crisis 25, 41, 46–47, 55–56,
   58–59, 70, 73, 75, 105, 112,
   117–118, 125, 143, 165, 214, 226,
   233–235, 249, 251
climate denial 30
climate denying 79
climate education 2, 16, 18, 25–27,
   30, 41, 56, 59, 63–64, 125–126, 140,
   188, 232
Climate Education Reform British
   Columbia 56, 59, 64
climate equity 71, 73–77, 79, 81,
   83–85, 87, 89–91, 93, 95, 97, 241
climate governance 54
climate hazard 4, 29–30
climate impact 4, 6, 9–11, 15–18, 23,
   25, 42, 49, 53, 129, 165, 179, 206,
   250, 276
climate injustice 25–26, 37, 41, 43, 45,
   47–49, 51, 53, 55, 57, 59, 61, 63, 65,
   67, 69–70
climate justice 18, 26, 34–37, 41–45,
   47, 50, 52–66, 68–70, 118, 126–130,
   133, 135, 137–139, 142–143, 214,
   231–232
climate justice curriculum reform 56
Climate Literacy Workshop (CLW)
   183
climate migrants 80
climate scientists 86, 174, 181
climate solution 16, 59, 130
climate strike 41, 43–50, 57–58, 64–65,
   137, 222
close writing 204
coding 258, 278
cognitive 53, 57, 73–75, 77, 80–81,
   87–90, 92–95, 97, 176, 218;
   cognitive barriers 73; cognitive
   disequilibrium 87; cognitive
   dissonance 75
collaboration 13, 124, 133, 148, 157,
   159, 168, 229
collaborative argumentation 88
collaborative project 254
collective conservatism 78, 80–81
college 17, 31, 98, 124, 133, 135–137,
   146, 151, 171–172, 175, 194, 196
colonial 4–6, 8–9, 14, 24, 31, 38, 41,
   50, 52, 56, 148, 225, 233; colonial
   history 41, 225; colonial stories
   225
colonialism 4–5, 8, 14, 19, 27, 36,
   38, 44, 52, 55, 149, 215, 246;

282 *Index*

exploitative colonialism 4–5, 111; settler colonialism 5, 8, 38, 215, 246
colonialist perspective 17
colonization 5, 19, 111, 205, 220, 225, 246
colonizers 4–5
common but differentiated responsibilities 12–13, 138
common good 106
communication 16, 23, 32–35, 38, 49, 57, 65, 68–69, 94, 96, 122, 133–134, 138, 150, 168, 173, 197, 210, 240, 243, 255
communities of color 42, 93, 122–123, 126–132, 136
community action planning 119, 122
community action project 119–122, 126, 131–132
community asset 132
community garden 25, 214–230, 233
community infrastructure 132
community needs 29, 119, 124, 126, 170–171, 274
community needs assessment 119, 124, 171
community participation 256, 278
community science expert 29
community-based 56, 121, 125, 127, 131–132, 138, 151, 219, 278
community-level growth 162
conceptual change 16, 23, 73, 78, 84, 87–88, 92–97
conceptual understanding 29, 35, 74, 84, 195, 277
confidence 54, 57, 93, 119, 121, 242–243, 246
Congo 5
Congressional Black Caucus 127, 139
consequences 3–4, 26, 72, 79, 81, 84, 90, 92, 109–110, 147, 218, 235, 252, 254, 257
consumerism 56, 204, 206
content 18, 22, 27, 29, 32, 48, 56, 68–70, 77, 79, 85, 92, 94, 130, 152, 165, 176, 256, 258, 264
context 8, 14, 16, 20, 26–28, 33, 36–37, 42, 44, 52, 67, 70, 76, 80, 84–86, 89, 99, 105, 125–129, 140–141, 146, 148, 150, 176–178, 181–183, 185, 187, 191–192, 195–196, 199, 208, 228, 230–231, 236–238, 240, 253, 255–257, 261, 275
contextual factors 177–178

COP 43, 46; COP24 54, 68; COP25 49
Corbyn, Jeremy 46, 67
Coronavirus 36, 113, 123, 143; *see also* COVID-19; pandemic
corporation 6–7, 10, 33, 37, 134
counter-narrative 249, 256
court 48–49, 53, 64, 66–67
COVID-19 36, 53, 64, 122, 128, 140, 144, 147, 166, 222–223
creativity 168, 256, 266, 273–276
critical environmental education 20, 37
critical justice education 55
critical race theory 61, 112
critical theory 20, 25
critical thinking 87, 124, 168, 204
cross-cultural 25, 214–230
culpability 26
cultural diversity 149
cultural processes 21, 31
cultural-historical activity theory 176
culturally competent 169
culturally relevant 118–119, 125, 232, 234, 239
culturally sustaining pedagogy 165, 172
culture 4, 10, 16, 18, 24, 33, 36–37, 61, 65, 70, 96, 98, 105–106, 110, 148, 150, 154, 170, 190, 194, 196, 199–200, 204–205, 208, 211–213, 215–217, 220–221, 223–226, 228, 230, 237, 239, 253, 255
culture of power 255; *see also* power
curricula 17, 19, 21, 24, 26, 38, 42, 56–57, 59, 61, 65, 70, 85, 117–118, 141–142, 152, 165, 190, 198–199, 201, 206–208, 210–212, 214, 218, 232, 252, 254–255, 257–260, 265–266, 269, 271, 275, 278
curriculum development 198, 257

Dakota Access Pipeline 8, 37
damage 5, 9–10, 13, 18, 50, 71, 80, 139, 146–148, 156–157, 160, 175, 248, 251
damage-centered approach 248
damage-centered focus 18
data 10, 16, 32, 79, 88–89, 132, 145, 166, 177–178, 182–186, 200, 239, 257–258
Davos 65, 68, 101–102, 112, 114
decision-making 15–16, 30, 45, 79, 89, 96, 106, 108–109, 117, 120, 127, 179, 189, 218, 220, 273–274

Index 283

decolonization 62, 65, 232–233
decolonizing 36, 38, 58, 217, 233, 256
decolonizing design pedagogy 256
default bias 81
deficit lens 18
deforestation 48, 71
Democrat 7, 47
democratic 79, 105–110, 127, 213
democratic ecological planning 105,
   107–108
democratic socialism 108
denial 30, 34, 69, 79, 154–155, 182,
   192, 259
Denmark 47
design principle 20–21; *see also*
   guiding principle
desire-based approach 248
despair 54, 69, 108
detachment 211, 249, 266
Detroit, Michigan 118, 133–134, 141
developing countries 12, 49; *see also*
   industrializing
development 3–4, 6, 11–12, 14, 20,
   22–23, 25, 28–29, 31–33, 35, 38, 42,
   57–59, 63, 66–67, 93–94, 107–108,
   110, 117–118, 122, 124, 127, 131,
   138–139, 141, 143, 161, 167–168,
   170–172, 175–176, 180, 182, 193–196,
   198–200, 203, 206, 212, 229, 231,
   234–239, 241–243, 245, 247,
   249–251, 253, 257–259, 267, 278
dialogue 130, 206–207, 234, 249, 269,
   277
differentiated responsibility 12–13,
   138
differentiated risk 14
digital discourse 273
digital storytelling 252, 255–257, 272,
   274–278
director 49, 65, 122, 137, 258–264,
   267–269, 272, 274
discourse 18–19, 22, 31, 42, 44, 52, 61,
   69, 72, 75, 94, 96, 98–99, 111, 117,
   129, 142, 194, 197, 205, 246, 248,
   253, 255–256, 273, 278
discrimination 10, 37, 52, 128, 216
discriminatory 10, 127
disengage 75, 266
disengagement 88, 259, 271
disinformation 79, 85–86
displacement 19, 84, 132, 227
disproportionate environmental
   degradation 42

disproportionate health effects 127
disproportionate impacts 127–128,
   130, 149
disproportionately impacting 122
diverse 14, 16–18, 23, 31, 55, 70, 75,
   119, 125, 137, 148–149, 164, 205,
   213, 217, 226, 228, 250, 275–276
dominant discourse 19, 61
dominant groups 82
dominant perspective 17
dominant understanding 256
double exposure 6, 36
double oppression 61
double stimulus 28
drought 71, 90, 94, 147, 175
dystopian 259

early childhood education 235, 250
Earth Guardians Youth Council 54
Earth Summit 12, 41, 54
Earth Tomorrow Program 16,
   119–120, 122–127, 137
Earth Tomorrow Summer Institute
   118–119, 124, 136–137
eco-hermeneutic approach 207,
   211–212
eco-poetic writing 201
eco-refugees 71; *see also* refugees
ecofeminism 98, 110–111, 113
ecojustice 20, 24, 34–36, 44, 199, 201,
   203, 205–209, 211–213
ecojustice framework 207
ecological awareness 110, 198, 208,
   212
ecological conceptualization of
   agency 177
economic 1, 3–7, 25, 27, 30–31, 33,
   36, 41, 57, 59, 62, 71, 73, 76, 80,
   84, 90, 101–103, 105–109, 111,
   114, 119, 123, 127–130, 142, 146,
   148–149, 170, 174, 203, 215, 234;
   economic disparities 25, 119;
   economic impact 130; economic
   structure 102–103; economic
   transformation 105
economy 3, 5, 12, 36, 42, 56, 101–102,
   105, 107–109, 150, 169, 210, 235
ecophobia 91, 95, 97, 251
ecosocialism 7, 98, 102–105, 107,
   110–113
ecosystem 9, 24, 33, 75, 121, 125, 131,
   151, 165, 167, 169, 175, 198, 202,
   204, 206, 210

284 *Index*

education 1–3, 5, 7, 9, 11, 13–39, 41–42, 48, 55–70, 84–86, 92, 94–98, 106, 112–115, 117–119, 122, 125–127, 129–131, 136–143, 150–151, 165–169, 171–172, 174–185, 187–188, 192–200, 206–208, 211–219, 221, 223–225, 227, 229–236, 238–244, 246–250, 252, 255, 276–278

education systems 19, 25, 30, 42, 55, 59, 62, 86

educational inquiry 20, 241

educational leadership 58, 198, 208, 212

educational reform 113, 198, 208

educator 16–17, 19–24, 29–30, 56–57, 60–61, 68, 91, 98, 140, 175, 177, 181, 183, 185, 187–188, 190, 198–199, 205, 207, 210, 239, 245, 247, 249, 254, 256

Elders 150, 198, 219–222, 224–225, 227, 229, 231

election 47, 66, 100, 109, 135, 140; 2020 election 135; general election 100, 135

emancipation 205

emancipatory education 20

emergency preparedness 165–166, 169

emissions 1, 3, 9, 11–12, 23, 32, 42, 44–45, 47–48, 58, 72, 78, 97, 102–103, 128, 130, 174–175, 218, 222–223, 248

emotion 52, 54–55, 74–75, 77–78, 86, 90–92, 94–97, 152, 159–162, 175–176, 179, 195, 233, 236–237, 240, 250, 259; epistemic emotions 78, 95; negative emotion 75, 91; positive emotion 86, 91; topic emotions 78, 86

emotional 16, 52, 54, 61, 73, 78, 80, 86, 88, 90–91, 108, 151, 159–161, 163, 218, 236, 238, 240, 242, 244

empathy 26, 71, 73, 83–84, 90–92, 94–95, 179, 249, 266; *see also* engaged empathy

empower 27, 47, 118–119, 168, 193

empowered 29, 59, 121, 257, 276

empowerment variables 121

energy efficiency 134

engaged empathy 26, 71, 84, 90–92

engagement 18, 24, 36, 38, 48, 55, 59–61, 68–69, 77, 88–92, 94–96, 117–118, 120, 126, 130–135, 137, 142–143, 151, 167, 169–170, 181, 188, 192, 194, 199, 218, 220, 226, 237, 259, 265–267, 271, 277–278; *see also* disengagement; agentic engagement 90; cognitive engagement 90; community engagement 151, 167, 170; engagement strategies 91; engagement with climate change 38, 69, 218; environmental engagement 69, 92, 194; student engagement 60, 96, 126, 142; teachers' engagement 181; voter engagement 135, 137

enthusiasm 125

entry level variables 120

environmental careers 119, 125

environmental changes 30, 78–79, 81, 83–84, 90, 275

environmental citizenship behavior model 119–120

environmental competency 237, 241–242, 247–248

environmental crisis 67, 71, 210

environmental degradation 13, 42, 236

environmental disdain 237, 244

environmental education (EE) 3, 16–17, 19–20, 22–24, 27, 29–38, 57, 61, 63–64, 66–70, 95–97, 118–119, 125, 131, 136, 138–140, 143, 194–197, 199, 206–208, 211–212, 214–215, 217–219, 221, 223, 225–227, 229–231, 233, 250, 278

environmental harm 127, 237

environmental health 125, 143

Environmental Identity Development (EID) 234, 236–238, 242–243, 247, 249

environmental injustice 68, 122, 172

environmental justice 25–26, 29, 31, 33, 35–37, 42, 44, 49, 56–57, 65–66, 68–70, 118–119, 122, 124–128, 130, 132–134, 136–139, 142–143, 232

environmental leadership 118, 124–125, 130, 135

environmental literacy 118–119, 124, 139

Environmental Protection Agency (EPA) 117, 126–127, 130, 143

environmental regulation 132

environmental sensitivity 120–121, 124

Index 285

environmental shame 237, 244, 249
environmental stewards 118
environmental tension 240
epistemic agents 182
epistemic beliefs 78, 92
epistemic cognition 73–74, 77, 88–89, 93–95, 97
epistemic ideals 88
epistemologies 21, 23–24, 31–32, 219, 256; *see also* ways of knowing
equitable 2, 13–16, 20–21, 29–31, 61, 74, 81, 117, 119, 121, 123, 125, 127, 129, 131, 133, 135, 137, 139, 141, 143, 191, 193, 234, 236, 238–240, 242, 248–249, 252, 254, 275–276
erasing 80
escape 128, 155
escaping 156
essay 31, 33–34, 151, 153–169, 211–212
essentialization 256
ethical 14, 16, 174, 178, 181–182, 218
ethics of care 179, 189, 194
ethnicity 10, 36, 127, 141, 219, 229, 255, 257, 278
ethnographic 182–183, 191, 196, 272
Eurocentricism 46
Europe 13, 16, 97, 114, 175
European Union 12
evacuate 152, 155–156
evidence 52, 59, 74–75, 87–88, 94, 148, 161, 163–165, 169, 172, 175, 180, 184, 186, 191, 193, 214, 223, 232
excitement 188, 241–243, 270
expectancy-value theory 97
experiential 27, 119, 126, 129, 131
exploitation 47, 110–111, 206
exposure 1, 6, 11, 14, 35–36, 38, 94, 118, 126–128, 130, 135, 137–138, 152, 191, 214, 228, 244, 249
Extinction Rebellion 46, 98, 102–103
extractive states 5
extreme weather 71, 83, 128, 148, 175

fair 12, 34, 76, 83, 126, 128, 131, 180
fairness 2, 31, 56
faith 103, 151, 164
family 1, 10, 47, 50, 61–62, 90, 112, 154–159, 162–163, 168, 171, 178–179, 182, 184, 189, 192, 209, 216–217, 219, 227–228, 235, 239–241, 243–244, 246–248, 276

fascism 98, 100, 112
Fauci, Anthony 122
fear 54–55, 61, 67, 69, 71, 83, 145, 159–160, 162, 164, 237
Federal Emergency Management Agency (FEMA) 146, 148, 158, 170–171
field study 120, 124, 131–132, 134–135, 138
fieldwork 29
filmmaking 197, 256–257, 259, 269, 274–275, 278
finance 12–13
financial interest 7
financial resources 14
financial stress 147
financing 13
First Nations 54, 212; *see also* Indigenous
Flint, Michigan 44, 134
flooding 6, 18, 71, 145, 147–148, 198, 234
food desert 72, 97
food insecurity 1, 117, 216
food sovereignty 215, 219–220, 224, 227, 229
formal education 19, 28, 42, 48, 55, 59, 62, 65
fossil fuel 9, 41, 43, 45, 71, 76, 79, 97, 101, 105, 108, 129, 193, 203
Fourth Industrial Revolution (4IR) 102, 104–108, 112–114
frame 5, 15, 19–20, 27–29, 36, 56, 65, 70, 154, 177, 278
Frederiksen, Mette 47
Fridays for Future (#FridaysForFuture) 43, 45, 47, 50–51, 63, 98, 100, 222
friend 23, 36, 61, 86, 89, 101, 154, 158–159, 189, 209, 217, 222, 242, 245, 268, 276
funding 10, 13, 17, 122, 149, 158, 250
fundraising 122
future generation 41, 48, 117, 125, 136, 179–180, 183, 192, 203, 209, 218
future selves 272, 275

gaps 6, 42, 56–57, 143, 151
garbage 222, 226, 228
garden 18, 25, 32, 133, 151, 167, 210, 214–231, 233; *see also* community garden

286 *Index*

gardening 207, 216–217, 220–228, 232–233
gender 29, 45, 61, 68, 99, 107, 111–112, 219, 223, 229, 255, 272
gender equity 29
generation 10, 24, 31, 41, 46, 48, 51, 62, 71, 84, 96, 102, 108, 113–114, 117, 125, 136, 178–180, 183, 188, 191–192, 195, 203, 205, 209, 218, 221, 224–225, 227–228, 246, 257
gentrification 123, 132, 149
geographic area 4, 6, 18, 274
Georgia 118, 123, 135–137, 140, 231; Atlanta 118, 122, 124, 130–133, 137, 140; Capitol 134–135; senate runoff election 135, 140
Germany 47–48, 97
Giroux, Henry 99
Global Alliance of Territorial Communities 50
global justice 25, 140
global temperature 12, 71, 103, 148, 175
global warming, 7 35–36, 38, 46, 66, 87, 101, 103, 109, 194–195, 226, 230, 243, 248–249, 277
God 97, 145, 164, 186, 210
good citizen 60–61, 67
government 5–7, 10, 17–19, 37, 44–45, 48–50, 54, 58, 64, 66, 69, 79, 97, 99–100, 109, 125, 132–133, 148–151, 158, 197
grassroots 98, 127, 130, 132–133, 150, 278
great transition 105, 110, 113
green economies 56
green gentrification 132
Green New Deal 47, 67, 69
Green Ninja 257
greenhouse gas (GHG) 47–48, 58, 223
grit mindset 22
grounded analysis 258
group psychology 79
Guardians of the Forest 43–44, 50
guiding principle 20

habitat 131, 133–134, 148, 199–200
Hallam, Roger 103
hands-on 60, 120, 131–132
health disparities 122–123
healthy literacies 203
heat exposure 11, 38
heat risk 11

heteroglossic 254
heuristics 74, 87, 97
high school 26, 32, 35, 45, 58–59, 85, 95, 118, 123–124, 136, 146–147, 153–154, 163, 195–196, 277–278
Hirsi, Isra 49
Hispanic 11, 122, 257–258, 260
historical inequities 3
historical injustice 15
Historically Black Colleges and Universities (HBCU) 133, 137, 151
holistic 21, 41, 215, 218–219, 229
Holland, Dorothy 253
Home Owners' Loan Corporation (HOLC) 10–11, 33
hope 3, 8, 20, 30–31, 54–55, 67, 69, 82, 90, 101, 160, 167, 191, 197, 199, 211, 217, 226–227, 246
horizons of choice 255
hospitality 148
human health 121, 123, 142
human rights 44, 48, 70, 109, 112, 114, 127, 141, 231
human-induced 71, 73, 83, 95, 195, 243; *see also* anthropogenic
human/nature relationships 198
humor 163
hurricane 13–14, 24, 50, 71, 82–83, 133, 145–173, 175; Category 5, 71, 145, 154–156, 159–160, 170; Hurricane Dorian 71, 93, 145–146, 172; Hurricane Harvey 148, 172; Hurricane Irma 145, 153, 155, 158–160, 163, 168; Hurricane Katrina 83, 133, 146, 160, 168; Hurricane Maria 145, 153, 160, 168; Hurricane Sandy 50
hurricane essay 151, 153, 155, 159, 161–165, 167, 169
hurricane preparedness 154, 157
hurricane season 146, 157

identity 9, 21, 24, 29, 31–32, 64, 74, 76, 78, 80, 94, 99, 103–104, 154, 161–163, 176–178, 180–181, 193, 195–200, 207–208, 211, 219–220, 229, 234–243, 245, 247–251, 253–256, 258, 262–264, 266–267, 271–273, 275–278; classroom identity 266, 278; cultural identity 199, 250, 266; environmental identity 197, 234–243, 245, 247–251, 278; group identity 80; positional identities 177;

professional identity 177–178, 181; social identity 74, 78; teacher identity 176–177, 196, 208
identity construction 256
identity formation 199, 211, 234, 236–238, 240–241, 247–249
Illinois 8
imagination 112, 198–200, 211
immigration 9, 17
impact 1–4, 6, 8–18, 20, 22–26, 28, 30, 34–37, 42–44, 46–50, 52–53, 55–56, 58, 61–62, 66, 70–76, 78–81, 83, 85, 91, 93–94, 101, 117–119, 121, 123–124, 126–131, 133–135, 137, 139, 142–149, 152, 154, 156–157, 159–161, 163, 165–173, 175, 178–183, 187, 189–195, 198, 202–204, 206, 208–209, 214–215, 219, 222–223, 225–228, 234–235, 247–248, 250–252, 254, 257, 263, 273, 276–277
impact-adaptation divide 4
imperialism 109
implementation 14, 26, 122, 124, 126–127, 172, 183–184, 257
improvisation 253–254
inclusion 14, 16, 21, 26, 28, 50, 108, 118, 125, 137, 269, 277
India 36, 84
Indigenous 5–6, 8, 10, 14, 17, 19, 22–25, 32, 35–36, 38, 41–44, 49–54, 61, 65, 67–68, 102–103, 111, 198, 200, 206, 208, 211–212, 214–227, 229–234, 246, 249–250, 256; *see also* Alaska Native; concentrations onto reservation lands 80; Indigenous epistemologies 24, 256; Indigenous knowledge 19, 35, 206, 212, 217–219, 229–231; Indigenous narratives 61; Indigenous people 6, 50, 102, 216–217, 220, 223, 229; Indigenous sovereignty 103, 225; Indigenous stories 24, 200
industrialization 3–4, 27, 53, 72
industrialized 3–4, 7, 12, 26, 73
industrialized countries 3, 7, 12
industrialized nations 3, 12, 26; *see also* industrialized countries
industrializing 8
industry 43, 76, 92, 133
inequity 1, 3–4, 8, 13–17, 19, 25, 28, 30, 35, 42, 44, 49, 53, 71–72, 75, 79, 128–129, 231, 234, 252, 274

informal learning 51, 216, 219, 221, 225, 228
infrastructure 11, 48, 102, 132–133, 146–148
injustice 3, 8, 10, 15–16, 19–22, 25–27, 30, 37, 41, 43, 45, 47–49, 51, 53–55, 57, 59, 61, 63, 65, 67–70, 72, 112, 122, 124, 128–129, 133–134, 172, 216, 233
innocence 18
innovation 83, 106, 237, 278
inoculation theory 85, 93
inquiry 20, 57, 60, 129, 141, 172, 182, 194, 198, 200–205, 207–208, 210–212, 238, 241
institutional structure 256
instrument 168, 258
integrative learning 84
interdisciplinary 55, 57–58, 85, 97, 129, 142, 177, 194, 216, 219
intergenerational equity 179, 191, 197
intergenerational justice 218
intergenerational learning 207, 219–220, 223, 228–229
Intergovernmental Panel on Climate Change (IPCC) 2, 4, 13–15, 30, 34, 43, 45–46, 66, 142, 169, 175, 195, 214, 231, 234, 248, 251–252, 277
intersectional 45, 129, 233, 253
intersectionality 53, 140, 217, 256
intervention 25, 30, 73, 76–77, 86–87, 93, 95, 215, 230, 252
invasive species 124, 132
IrMaria 145–147, 149, 159, 161, 163–164, 166–167, 169; *see also* Hurricane Irma; Hurricane Maria
Islamabad 58
isolation 150, 220, 265
Italy 58
iterative design-based research 257

Japan 266
Johnson, Boris 99
joy 41, 54, 236, 248
justice 1–3, 5, 8, 11, 16–23, 25–37, 39, 41–45, 47, 49–50, 52–66, 68–70, 72–73, 75, 94, 98–99, 102, 104, 108, 115, 118–119, 122–130, 132–143, 175, 177, 180, 195, 197–199, 201, 203, 205–209, 211–214, 218, 229, 231–232, 235–236, 238, 240, 243–244, 246–249
justice-centered education 20

288 *Index*

K-12 66, 84–85, 96, 178, 187, 231
Kenya 19
Kili 9
King, Jr., Martin Luther 104
knowledge 14–15, 18–19, 21, 24, 26, 28–29, 31, 35, 42, 48, 52, 56–57, 59–60, 62, 64, 73–79, 83–95, 113, 119, 121, 124, 126, 140, 149–150, 157, 166–167, 175–176, 181, 188, 193, 195–196, 201, 203, 206, 212, 215–225, 227–232, 253, 273, 276; cultural knowledge 19, 228; local knowledge 150, 181, 203; prior knowledge 24, 74, 93; scientific knowledge 85, 188, 201; traditional knowledge 14, 24, 224–225
knowledge acquisition 73
knowledge construction 15, 75, 77, 85, 90, 95, 181
knowledge funds 21, 28
knowledge reconstruction 73–74, 79, 86–87
knowledge set 78, 88
Kyoto Protocol 12, 15, 34, 232

land-based education 215, 221, 227, 229, 231; *see also* land-based environmental education
land-based environmental education 215, 217, 219, 221, 223, 225, 227, 229, 231, 233
land-based knowledge 224
land-extraction 56
language 4, 19, 32, 38, 56, 58, 148–149, 170, 191, 201, 204–205, 207, 211, 212, 246, 255, 271, 277
Latinx 11, 17, 52, 149, 258
lawmakers 134
leader 7, 14, 41–44, 48, 50, 53, 67, 75, 79, 105–106, 108–109, 111, 114, 118–119, 122, 124–125, 130–138, 140, 151, 158, 180, 218, 254, 261–264, 268, 272, 277
leadership 1, 26, 45, 50, 55, 58–60, 62, 118–119, 122–125, 130–131, 135–137, 139–140, 143–144, 151, 170–171, 198–199, 201, 203, 205, 207–209, 211–213, 220, 232, 262, 267–269, 274
Leghari, Ashgar 48
legislative 45, 134, 273
legislator 134–135
liberating constraint 210

lifestyle change 83
literacy 26, 37, 41, 65, 91, 118–119, 124, 126, 139, 141, 183, 191, 201, 203, 208, 211–213
Little Miss Flint 44
Liverpool 3
Logan, Jonathan 102
logic 80
London 31, 46, 103, 112–114, 194
Louisiana's Cancer Alley Corridor 133
low-income 4, 17, 30, 103, 123, 127–131
Löwy, Michael 105–111, 113

Malawi 19
Maldives 44, 72, 83
malinformation 85–86
Mandela, Nelson 136
manufacturing 4, 53
marginalized 4, 6, 17–18, 21–26, 30, 43–45, 49, 52–53, 55–56, 61, 137, 149–150, 170, 179, 214, 226, 234–235, 248, 252; marginalized communities 18, 44, 53, 56, 61, 149, 214, 252; marginalized learners 61; marginalized perspectives 26, 55
Margolin, Jamie 49, 53
Marshall Islands 9, 31, 47, 72, 83
Marx, Karl 113
Maryland 6, 11, 18, 31, 171
May, Theresa 99, 112
meaning making 256
means of production 106
media 7, 45–54, 62–65, 69, 79–80, 86, 92, 98–100, 102, 117, 124, 134–135, 138, 141–142, 144, 155, 166, 170, 256, 271, 273; Associated Press 52; digital media 256, 271, 273; fake news 93, 100; film 163, 170, 189, 257, 259–265, 268, 270–275; mainstream media 49, 53; social media 45, 48–49, 51, 53, 62–63, 65, 79, 86, 92, 98, 100, 117, 124, 135, 138, 155, 166
mediation processes 252
mental health 54, 61, 151, 161, 169–170, 172, 250
mental representation 73
mental stress 71, 216
mentor 124, 133, 136, 262
Mexico 43, 50, 58
micro-interaction 239–240
middle class 27

Index 289

middle school 17, 174–175, 183–186, 188–192, 196, 252, 254, 257, 276, 278

middleman 174–175, 177, 179, 181, 183, 185–189, 191, 193, 195, 197

migration 9, 84, 93, 194, 231

misconceptions 81, 87, 93–94, 97, 130, 175, 193, 206, 216

misinformation 76, 79–80, 84–87, 93, 97, 99

misogyny 99–100

mitigate 42, 58, 71–72, 118, 123, 128, 135, 137, 248, 252

mitigation 2, 7, 11–14, 25, 29, 59, 80, 97, 149, 182, 193, 197, 231, 276

model 5, 9, 13, 16, 22, 27–29, 33, 64, 74, 79, 85, 87–89, 92–93, 95–96, 107, 118–122, 139, 141, 145, 182, 196, 200, 206, 208, 212, 237–238, 250

model-evidence-link 88

moral 12–13, 37, 45, 49, 103, 174, 178–179, 181, 194–195, 266

moral responsibility 45, 179

Morehouse College 136–137

motivated reasoning 73–74, 94, 97

motivation 73–74, 79, 81–83, 94, 96–97, 134

motivational barriers 72–73, 92

motivators 77

multiplier effect 128

Nakate, Vanessa 49, 51–52, 65, 68–69

narrative 16–17, 22–24, 35, 52–53, 61–62, 66, 74, 91, 94–95, 153, 178, 204, 212, 218, 252, 255–256, 266, 272, 274–276, 278

National Wildlife Federation (NWF) 29, 117–119, 122, 124–127, 129, 131, 133, 135, 137, 139–142

natural disaster 128, 145–149, 151–155, 157, 159–161, 163–165, 167–171, 173, 223, 232

natural hazards 151, 163, 166–167

natural world 24, 91, 110, 124, 199–201, 203, 207–208, 225, 234, 236–238, 240, 245, 250

nature 18, 38, 48, 67–68, 75, 82–84, 86, 91, 93–94, 96, 107, 109–113, 123, 125, 131, 140, 144, 157, 172, 176–177, 179–180, 188, 190, 195, 198–200, 203, 205–208, 224, 236–245, 247–249, 251, 255, 258, 276

negotiation 50, 70, 253–254, 256, 259–260, 262, 267–268, 270–271, 274

neighbor 72, 150, 155–158, 162–164

neoliberal 6–8, 60, 109, 111

neoliberalism 33, 66, 99

net-zero emissions 103

Netherlands 48, 70

New Deal 10, 47, 67, 69

New Jersey 58, 69, 183

New York 32, 34, 37–38, 49–50, 64–65, 92, 95–96, 112–114, 142, 170–172, 193–194, 196–197, 213, 233, 250, 277–278

New Zealand 5, 58

Next Generation Science Standards 96, 188, 195, 257

non-humans 17, 24, 26, 107, 110, 225

non-profit 121, 125, 127, 131, 133, 137, 150

normative 60–61, 87, 256, 261, 275

North Dakota 8, 80, 96

novice teacher 176, 181

observation 130, 149, 166, 182, 188, 196, 241, 251, 257–259, 277

observer 258

Ocasio-Cortez, Alexandria 46

oligarchy 106

oppression 45, 52, 54, 61, 99, 108, 110

outdoor 27, 124–125, 136, 203, 232, 239

outreach 119, 131, 233

outsider 239, 258, 265, 268, 272

over-consumption 71–72

ownership 19, 120–121, 202, 262, 265, 272

ownership variables 121

Pacific 8–9, 29, 37–38, 130, 138, 233

Pacific Island 8–9, 37–38

pandemic 1, 38, 53–54, 70, 128, 141, 147, 166, 222–223; *see also* COVID-19

parents 50, 62, 67, 89, 140, 178, 189, 195, 209, 220–225

Paris Agreement 12–13, 15, 36, 43, 46, 58, 65, 94, 100–101, 114, 165, 172

Parkland, Florida 45

participation 15–16, 18, 20, 22, 24, 26, 28, 54, 107, 111, 125–126, 167, 181, 188, 236, 242–243, 254–256, 259, 266, 268–270, 272, 277–278

290 Index

participatory action research 217, 219, 230, 273
participatory approach 218
pedagogical framework 55, 60
pedagogical practice 21, 200, 211
pedagogy 21, 28, 32–33, 42, 55, 60, 67, 98–105, 107, 109, 111–114, 126, 129, 165, 172, 199, 205–206, 208, 211–212, 214–215, 233, 256, 277–278
pedagogy of transformation 129
Pelosi, Nancy 46
Peltier, Autumn 44, 49
people of colour 6, 8, 10, 53, 55, 64, 83, 99, 102–103, 111, 125, 128–130, 139, 149, 170
personal experience 95, 123, 130, 222
personally consequential 273–276
Peru 50
phenomenological 153, 171
physical health 130
pilot 257
place-based 24, 35–36, 68, 91, 96, 118, 137, 171, 201
place-based environmental education 24, 35, 68
plot 219, 259, 263, 265, 267, 269, 273–275
pluralism 148
Poland 54
policy 2–3, 6–8, 10–11, 13–18, 24, 26, 31–32, 35–36, 42, 44–47, 51, 56, 58, 63, 65–66, 71, 73–74, 82, 94, 99–100, 103, 105, 114, 118, 124–125, 127–128, 130–132, 134–135, 139, 170, 192–194, 196, 211, 215, 224, 231–232, 250, 277–278; educational policy 58, 63, 194; federal policy 118; global policy 11, 194; policy change 51, 58, 71; policymakers 34, 48, 58, 62, 277; racist policy 124
policy makers 18
political 1, 4, 6–8, 15–16, 25, 27, 30, 32, 37, 47–48, 56–59, 62, 66, 70–71, 76, 79, 84, 86, 100–104, 107–109, 113, 123, 127, 129, 134, 174–175, 190, 192, 194, 218, 228
political ideology 102
political polarization 76
political systems 25, 108
politics 16, 23–24, 30, 32–35, 45, 59, 65–66, 92, 102–103, 138, 140, 174, 197, 232–233, 278

poor 13, 71, 93, 102, 128, 131, 149–150, 214, 228, 248–249
Portland, Oregon 26–27, 37
position 8, 12, 14, 19, 21, 24, 26, 30, 45, 49, 70, 72, 85, 103, 135, 137, 155, 180–181, 206, 253, 256–257, 260–261, 263, 266, 268–272, 275
positionality 21, 263, 270, 274
post-capitalist 103, 111–112
post-colonialism 149
Post-Traumatic Growth (PTG) 152–154, 161–164, 166, 168
Post-Traumatic Stress Disorder (PTSD) 152, 159–161, 163–164, 169
poverty 1, 4, 11, 17–18, 28, 30, 32, 35, 38, 146, 149–150, 170, 175, 177, 181, 195, 216, 220, 231, 248, 251–252, 277
poverty rate 11, 146
power 4–5, 7–9, 15–16, 20–22, 26, 30, 32, 41, 48, 63, 92, 101–102, 106, 108–109, 134–135, 143, 146–148, 157–159, 165, 180, 195, 200, 203, 207, 234, 253, 255–257, 262, 267–268, 277
power dynamic 4, 9
power shift 135, 143
power structure 20, 234
practices 2–3, 7, 10, 19, 21–23, 30–31, 42, 51, 53, 58, 72–73, 83, 96, 127, 143, 171, 175–176, 178, 181, 184–186, 188, 191, 194, 196, 198, 200–201, 205, 207, 212, 215, 225, 227, 232–233, 242, 253, 256–258
pre-service 22, 60, 63–64, 174–175, 177–178, 180–183, 193–195, 198
preservice science teachers (PST) 174–175, 177–182, 185, 191–192, 194
president 79, 101, 112, 137
prevention 16, 233
pride 124, 153, 168, 276
principles 3, 20–21, 25–30, 34, 47, 61, 92, 104, 119, 130–131, 139, 141, 179, 193, 199, 212
Principles of Climate Justice 34, 130, 139
privilege 22, 41, 61, 83, 90, 106, 217
pro-environmental 34, 51, 72–73, 76, 184, 189, 194
profit 7, 86, 103, 106–107, 109, 111, 121, 125, 133, 137, 150, 201

Index 291

program 19–22, 25–31, 37, 54, 58–60, 85, 110, 117–120, 122–127, 129, 131, 136–137, 140–142, 166–167, 170, 173, 175, 178, 180, 187, 191–193, 197, 206, 219–220, 232–233, 278
project-based 167, 254, 256, 277
project-based learning 167, 256
protection 8–9, 126–127, 134, 143, 179, 222, 235–236
protest 44–45, 47, 51, 58, 63–64, 66–67, 71, 103, 117, 138, 222, 233
provision 13, 108, 236
provisioning 107–108
psychological 7, 20, 54, 61, 64, 71, 73, 75, 77–79, 81–85, 87, 89, 91–95, 97, 152, 168, 172, 194
psychological distance 82–83, 95, 97
public awareness 15, 58, 142, 233
public change 73
public health 36, 38, 128–129, 134, 140, 142, 170
public opinion 7
public pedagogy 60, 98–105, 107, 109, 111–114
public resource 132
public school 27, 37, 147, 175, 183–184, 190, 205
public sector 108
public space 203
Puerto Rico 146, 161, 168, 170–171

race 10–11, 16, 35–37, 41, 49, 61, 68, 71, 80, 99, 103, 112, 126–127, 141, 149, 171, 272, 278
racial equity 29, 118
racial injustice 45, 124, 128
racial justice 1, 68, 140
racial segregation 6, 10
racialized 18, 28, 42, 44, 49–54, 61, 131, 216, 220, 228; racialized minorities 220; racialized youth 44, 49–54, 61
racism 6, 10, 17, 21–22, 25, 44, 46, 49, 52–53, 55, 61–62, 68–69, 98–99, 112–113, 123, 127, 139, 216, 228; environmental racism 44, 127, 139, 228; government-sanctioned racism 10; institutional racism 6; systemic racism 123
reasoning 73–75, 77, 84–85, 87, 94, 96–97, 179, 195
recognition 42, 60, 111, 162, 255, 261, 272

reconstructed narrative 178
recovery 150–152, 163, 165–167, 169–171, 173, 231
recycling 27, 124, 175, 193, 219, 221, 226, 228–229, 231, 241
redlined 11, 72
redlining 10, 17, 32–33, 38, 131
reflection 22, 70, 74, 77, 118, 133, 157, 168, 171, 177, 183–184, 186–187, 191, 227
reform to transform 59, 64
reforms 59, 193, 205, 208
refugees 123, 214, 220, 226
refutation text 86–87, 93–97
reimagining 253
relational orientation 240
relationship 8, 10, 18, 24, 29, 35, 44, 51, 59–60, 62, 77, 87, 120, 138, 176, 178–179, 182–183, 198–210, 217, 221, 224–229, 253, 258, 273, 276
reparation 12–14
representation 7, 16, 18, 69, 73–74, 77, 123, 186, 230
representative democracy 108–109
reproductive labour 107
Republican 7, 79
resilience 29, 36, 69, 151, 163–165, 167–170, 173, 206, 214–216, 219–222, 224–227, 229–230, 232–233, 243, 247, 254, 277–278
resiliency 61, 168, 246, 248
resilient 44, 114, 135, 162, 169, 217, 219, 227
resistance 33, 42, 48, 58, 66, 109, 111, 205, 231, 267
resources 4–5, 8, 12, 14–15, 18–19, 21, 35, 62, 66, 71, 82–83, 106, 108, 119, 123, 125–126, 131–133, 139, 141–142, 149–150, 166, 169, 177, 179–180, 190, 231, 233, 235–236, 241, 247, 249–250, 253–254, 259, 271, 277
respectful relationship 217, 221
responsibility 4, 12–14, 33, 45, 51–52, 82, 93, 110, 117, 138, 141, 164, 179, 184, 189, 194, 215–218, 221–222, 225–227, 230, 259, 262–263, 271
restoration 131, 168
restorying 24
right-wing 99–100, 107–108
rights 1, 10, 42–44, 47–50, 52, 70, 103, 109, 112, 114, 127, 141, 214, 231, 235–236, 250–251

292 *Index*

Rio Summit 7, 12
Rise Up Movement 52
role 3, 7, 12–15, 19, 21–23, 27, 37–38, 50, 59–60, 62, 64–65, 67, 77, 79, 89, 92, 94–95, 97, 107, 111, 117, 124–126, 134, 137–138, 160, 175–176, 185–186, 189, 191–193, 195, 199, 205–206, 214, 216, 219, 223, 229, 231–232, 236, 238, 246, 253–255, 258–265, 267–274, 276
rural 19, 67, 76, 130, 164, 196, 203, 234, 236, 238, 240–241, 243, 248

Sanders, Bernie 109
Saskatchewan 216–217, 220, 231
scaffold 84, 87–88, 95, 196
scaffolded instructional tools 87
scene 262, 264
sceptics 53
schemas 75, 79, 86, 88
school 1, 17–18, 26–27, 32, 35, 37–38, 43–46, 48, 50, 53, 56–61, 64–65, 69–70, 75, 85, 94–95, 98, 100, 114, 117–119, 121–124, 126, 133–136, 138–139, 141–142, 146–148, 153–155, 161, 163, 166, 170–171, 174–175, 177, 179, 182–186, 188–196, 205, 211, 216–218, 221–222, 225, 230, 239, 244, 246–247, 252, 254–257, 263–264, 268, 274, 276–278
Schwab, Klaus 106
science classroom 37–38, 55, 177, 181, 192, 195, 255, 274, 276
science education 21, 24, 30–32, 34–35, 64, 67, 84, 92, 94–97, 139, 171, 175–177, 188, 193, 195–197, 224, 232–233, 255, 276–277
science pathway 254
scientific consensus 58, 70, 85, 87
scientific evidence 75, 94, 165, 193
scientific practices 175, 181, 184–185, 188
scientist 32, 36, 85–86, 89, 95, 174, 180–181, 183–184, 187, 195, 255, 257
sea level 9, 82, 148, 169, 171–172, 180, 198, 235, 249
secondary school 57, 70, 161, 194, 230, 277
self 38, 48, 76, 80, 82, 90, 93, 124, 127, 149, 160, 168, 199, 204, 211, 219, 224, 236–239, 247, 253, 255–256, 258, 261, 271–273, 275, 277

self-determination 127
self-esteem 124
self-interrogation 204
sense of place 120–121, 237
sensory tour 239–240, 243, 250
service learning 26, 119–120, 126, 131, 141, 152, 165, 167–169, 171, 173
Seventeen Principles of Environmental Justice 130
sexism 53, 99; *see also* gender equity; misogyny
share perspectives 91
shelter 150, 154, 156, 158, 236
skepticism 34, 84, 196
slavery 10, 14
social aggression 272, 278
social apathy 60
social change 65–66, 92, 98–99, 193
social class 99, 105, 112, 255
social conversation 1, 275
social dynamic 274
social field 253–254
social groups 59, 79
social inequities 16, 129
social injustice 20, 25, 124, 133
social interaction 37, 90, 176
social justice 20, 28–29, 43–44, 56, 59, 62, 70, 73, 75, 98–99, 102, 104, 108, 118, 123, 127, 129, 141, 175, 177, 180, 195, 235–236, 238, 240, 243–244, 246–249
social norms 59
social position 253
social structure 27, 180, 255
social systems 25, 30
social transformation 194, 252–253, 276
socialists 100–101, 104
societal narrative 256
society 33, 47, 51–52, 54, 56, 65, 74, 78, 81, 90, 97, 100, 106–110, 112, 117, 126, 142, 162, 169, 195, 205–206, 211, 230, 232–233, 251, 255, 277
socio-critical focus 25
socioeconomic status 4, 11
sociological 20, 35, 57, 59, 236–237
sociopolitical 78, 181, 192
socioscientific 73, 76, 84–85, 87, 195, 273
socioscientific issue 84, 195, 273
solastalgia 71

Index 293

solidarity 26, 56, 62, 222
solutions 9, 16, 27–28, 41, 59, 70, 74, 83, 91, 117–119, 123, 125–126, 129–130, 135, 137, 139–140, 162, 175, 178, 181, 183–184, 186, 192–193, 221, 233, 235, 275
South Africa 19, 232
space 3, 5, 11–12, 15, 17–18, 20–22, 24, 26, 30, 34, 36, 54, 56, 60–61, 64, 82, 98, 123, 130, 175, 183, 200–205, 219–220, 223, 228–229, 231, 253–254, 262, 267, 271, 275–276
space for authoring 253–254, 275
Spanish 149, 170, 257
spatial autonomy 237, 241–242, 245, 247–248
speech 41, 44–45, 47–48, 50, 54, 98–99, 101, 136, 270, 278
spheres of control 259
Standing Rock Sioux Tribe 8
standpoint theory 26
status quo bias 81–82, 96
steam 7, 106, 184
stem 17–18, 50, 74, 126, 129, 141–142, 168, 182, 196, 264, 272, 274
stereotype 17, 22, 36, 79
stereotyping 22, 52
story 23–26, 34–35, 38, 49, 56, 61–66, 68, 80, 91, 123–125, 132, 137, 139, 145, 153, 161–164, 169–170, 179, 193, 199–201, 203, 205–207, 209–212, 217, 220–225, 227–228, 253, 256–257, 259–278; *see also* restorying; storytelling; cross-cultural stories 220–221; digital story 256; hurricane story 161–162, 164; intergenerational story 223–224, 228; land-based stories 220–221
storytelling 91, 122, 198–200, 203, 207, 220, 230, 252, 255–258, 268, 271–272, 274–278; *see also* digital storytelling
strength 24, 37, 77–78, 87, 109, 133, 144, 153, 159, 161–164, 167–168, 248
structured surround 199
student 17–18, 21–22, 24–29, 31, 33–35, 43, 45, 47, 49–50, 54–64, 68, 70, 73–75, 78, 85–86, 88–89, 92–96, 100, 108, 118, 120–126, 129, 133–137, 139, 141–143, 145–146, 151–170, 172–173, 178–189,

191–197, 200–204, 206–207, 210–211, 217–219, 254–261, 264–265, 269, 271–278
student-directed 60
subsistence 235, 239, 246–247, 249–251
Sunrise Movement 43, 46, 70
survey 145–146, 165–167, 170, 177, 257, 277
survival 47, 71, 76, 91, 159, 161, 165, 170, 203, 230–231, 234–236, 243, 246–249
survivor 152–153, 160–161, 168, 170, 172, 269
sustainability 7, 16, 27, 31, 36, 38, 56, 58, 61, 63, 66–69, 102, 108, 119, 133, 137, 144, 151, 229–231, 235, 250
sustainable development 32, 57, 63, 67, 117, 141, 143, 180, 195, 229, 231, 278
system change 41, 103
systemic change 41, 72, 81
systemic injustice 22, 129
systems-based thinking 84

Teach the Future 56, 70
teacher candidate 60, 194, 201; *see also* preservice science teachers (PST)
teacher education 31, 63, 176, 180, 187, 192–195, 198, 206, 230
teachers 17, 22–23, 31, 35, 56–57, 60, 62–64, 69, 129, 140, 174–184, 187, 191–197, 208, 212, 214, 230, 239, 244–246, 249
technology 9, 11, 65, 106, 126, 141–143, 147, 165, 172, 184, 194–195, 203, 206, 265–266, 277–278
teen 44, 63, 66, 112, 119, 123–124, 139
teenage 123, 126
temperature 10–12, 32, 71–72, 100, 103, 147–148, 172, 175, 184, 243
Ten Principles for Just Climate Change Policies 130, 139
territorial status 148
territory 146–148, 151, 157, 159, 169, 216–217, 225, 233
third world 52; *see also* industrializing
Thunberg, Greta 41, 44–47, 49–50, 52, 58, 63–64, 68–71, 98, 100–103, 114, 138; #ClimateStrike 45; #FightFor1Point5 100; Thunberg Effect 45, 69

294 *Index*

totalitarianism 108
tourism 5, 9, 146
trade union 105, 111
Tragedy of the Commons 174, 180
training 15, 54, 58, 119, 122, 124, 131, 133, 143, 214, 233
trajectory 128, 137, 208, 254, 269, 272, 277
transdisciplinary 57–58, 206, 212
transformation 27–30, 59, 105–106, 110, 129, 134, 172, 194, 206, 212, 252–254, 272–273, 276, 278
transformative 28–30, 33, 37, 42, 55, 57, 61–62, 70, 94, 110, 113, 196, 252–253
transformative agency by double stimulation (TADS) 28, 33
transformative change 55
transgressive pedagogy 42, 55
transnational 64, 215, 217, 220–221, 223, 227, 229
trauma 152, 159–161, 163–164, 169–172
tribalism 79
Trump, Donald 80, 98–99
trust 48, 72, 75, 89, 94, 180, 197, 237, 241–242, 244–245, 247–248
trust in nature 237, 241–242, 244–245, 247–248
tundra 239–240, 242–245, 249
Turner, Terisa 110
Twitter 51–52, 99, 114

Ubuntu/uMunthu 217
Uganda 51, 65
UN Convention on the Rights of the Child (UNCRC) 47, 70, 236, 251
uncertainty 81, 96–97, 169, 181–182, 192, 195, 243, 249
undergraduate 94, 143, 168
underrepresented 22–24, 129, 143
UNESCO 3, 104, 118, 143, 214, 228, 233
United Kingdom (UK) 3, 7, 34, 102–104
United Nations 2, 12, 34, 38, 43, 47, 70, 97, 101, 117, 139, 143, 198, 213, 233, 236
United Nations Climate Change Conference 43
United Nations Environment Programme 97, 101
United Nations Framework Convention on Climate Change (UNFCCC) 2, 12–13, 15, 34, 36, 38, 43, 55, 57, 68, 143, 214, 233

United States (USA) 1, 5–10, 14, 17–18, 32, 34, 36–37, 42, 46–47, 69, 72, 78–80, 84, 96–102, 104–105, 108, 118, 123, 126, 128, 130, 139–146, 148–149, 151, 153, 157, 162, 168, 170, 173, 175, 177, 181, 217, 233, 257
university 17, 22, 31–32, 34–35, 37, 68, 98, 113–114, 133, 142, 147, 151, 162, 170–171, 183, 194–195, 197–198, 205, 208, 211–213, 217, 219, 231–232, 250–251, 276–277
University of the Virgin Islands (UVI) 147, 151, 153, 164, 168–172
urban 11, 18, 29, 32–33, 35–38, 50, 67–68, 94, 111, 119–121, 123, 125, 130–133, 138, 140, 148–149, 177, 195–196, 204, 231, 277
urban heat island 11, 29
US Virgin Islands (USVI) 14, 145–150, 161, 163, 167, 170–173; #VIStrong 149, 163; St. Croix 145–146, 148, 151, 153, 160–161; St. John 145, 148, 160–161; St. Thomas 145–146, 148, 151, 153, 160–161, 166, 170–171; St. Thomas Community Recovery Plan 151; St. Thomas Community Response Plan 151; St. Thomas Recovery Team (STRT) 151, 167; VI identity 162

value set 88
values 14, 18, 24, 27, 64, 74–77, 79, 81, 88, 90, 96, 179, 194–195, 201, 206, 229, 231, 237, 244
Vancouver, BC 59, 64
Vanuatu 29
vocational program 29
voice 15, 17, 23–25, 28, 41, 45, 52–54, 56, 59, 68, 119, 123, 134–135, 137, 151, 154, 157, 159, 164, 168, 170, 194, 221, 232–234, 239, 249, 251–254, 256, 259, 261–263, 267–268, 271, 273–276; youth voice 56, 123, 151, 154, 157, 159, 233, 271, 275
voter mobilization 135
voter registration 135
vulnerability 5–6, 9, 13–14, 32–34, 36, 38, 93, 142–143, 150, 164–165, 232–233, 251, 277
vulnerable 2, 4, 6, 9, 11, 13, 19, 29, 56, 71, 80, 83, 103, 128–130, 132, 146–147, 150–151, 164, 171, 181, 192, 214, 226, 228, 232, 234–235, 249

vulnerable population 128, 130, 147, 164, 235

walking the land 198, 203, 210
Warsaw International Mechanism for Loss and Damage 13
ways of knowing 17, 19, 21, 28, 224–225, 246, 249, 256, 275; *see also* African ways of knowing
wealthier countries 71
wealthy 6–7, 49, 72, 74, 76, 80, 82, 90
well-being 55, 60–61, 67, 69, 109, 157, 209, 223, 225, 227–228, 233
western countries 60
westernization 19
westernized 8, 17, 21, 24, 36
white savior complex 52
white supremacy 22, 100
will to improve 5, 35
women 21, 49, 52–53, 107–108, 110–111, 139, 142, 194, 220, 230, 234
workers 105–109, 111, 134, 158
working class 106, 109

Working Group II 14–15, 34, 142, 277
Working Group III 14–15, 34
World Economic Forum 101, 106
World Socialist Web Site 105, 114
worth 17, 52, 85, 105, 109–110, 263, 267, 274–275

Years of Living Dangerously 125, 141
youth activism 43, 55, 58, 61–62, 67, 142
Youth Climate Action Coalition 123
youth climate justice movement 41–42, 44–45, 53, 55–56, 63
youth climate litigation 48
youth climate summit 47
youth efficacy 55
Youth for Future Africa 52
youth leadership 119, 171
youth participation 54

Zero Hour 43–44, 49, 53
Zoo Atlanta 137

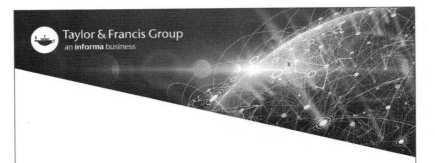